聞いて覚える英単語
キクタン
TOEIC® Test
Score 800

一杉武史 編著

英語は聞いて覚える！
アルク・キクタンシリーズ

「読む」だけでは、言葉は決して身につきません。私たちが日本語を習得できたのは、赤ちゃんのころから日本語を繰り返し「聞いて」きたから──『キクタン』シリーズは、この「当たり前のこと」にこだわり抜いた単語集・熟語集です。「読んでは忘れ、忘れては読む」──そんな悪循環とはもうサヨナラです。「聞いて覚える」、そして「読んで理解する」、さらに「使って磨く」──英語習得の「新しい1歩」が、この1冊から必ず始まります！

Preface
TOEIC800点突破に必要な単語と熟語がこの1冊で完ぺきに身につきます！

「適切な」から「十分な」コミュニケーションへ。この1冊が英語上級者へのトビラを開きます！

本書は、「どんな状況でも適切なコミュニケーションができる素地を備えている」と評価される730点を超え、さらに「Non-Nativeとして十分なコミュニケーションをとることができる」とされる860点が目前の「800点」を突破するための単語・熟語集です。では、「どんな状況でも」使われる単語・熟語はどのようなものでしょうか？

まずは、iron（〜にアイロンをかける）、water（〜に水をまく）、hail（〜を呼び止める）、microscope（顕微鏡）、sidewalk（歩道）といった、意外に知られていない日常表現が挙げられます。さらに、英語上級者に必須の5000語レベルを超える語、そしてderegulation（規制緩和）、revenue（総収益）、resign（辞職する）など、ビジネスシーンで多用される表現があります。それでは、こうした表現は何を基準として選ばれるべきなのでしょうか？

話題の「コーパス」を徹底分析！頻出単語・熟語を楽々マスターできます！

まず挙げられるのは、TOEICの公式問題です。また、TOEICに精通したネイティブライターによる模擬試験のデータも参考になります。しかし、いずれも量的には不十分です。本書では、上記2つに加え、膨大な数の話し言葉・書き言葉を集めたデータベース、「コーパス」をコンピューターで分析して見出し語・熟語を選定していますので、800点突破に必要な表現を、「頻度順」に身につけることができます。

「適切なコミュニケーション」から「十分なコミュニケーション」へ──。誰でもあこがれる夢の世界は目前です。さらにその先には、TOEIC満点（＝990点）が見えてきます。就職、海外勤務、そして昇進──TOEICを受験する理由は人それぞれでしょうが、いずれも通過点にすぎません。本書で身につけた英語力を基に、皆さんが世界を舞台に活躍することを心から祈っています！

Contents

1日16単語・熟語×10週間で
TOEIC800点突破の1120単語・熟語をマスター！

Chapter 1

名詞：超必修192

Page 13 ▶ 63

- Day 1 【名詞1】
- Day 2 【名詞2】
- Day 3 【名詞3】
- Day 4 【名詞4】
- Day 5 【名詞5】
- Day 6 【名詞6】
- Day 7 【名詞7】
- Day 8 【名詞8】
- Day 9 【名詞9】
- Day 10 【名詞10】
- Day 11 【名詞11】
- Day 12 【名詞12】

Chapter 2

動詞：超必修96

Page 65 ▶ 91

- Day 13 【動詞1】
- Day 14 【動詞2】
- Day 15 【動詞3】
- Day 16 【動詞4】
- Day 17 【動詞5】
- Day 18 【動詞6】

Chapter 3

形容詞：超必修96

Page 93 ▶ 119

- Day 19 【形容詞1】
- Day 20 【形容詞2】
- Day 21 【形容詞3】
- Day 22 【形容詞4】
- Day 23 【形容詞5】
- Day 24 【形容詞6】

Chapter 4
名詞:必修192
Page 121 ▶ 171

| Day 25 【名詞13】
| Day 26 【名詞14】
| Day 27 【名詞15】
| Day 28 【名詞16】
| Day 29 【名詞17】
| Day 30 【名詞18】
| Day 31 【名詞19】
| Day 32 【名詞20】
| Day 33 【名詞21】
| Day 34 【名詞22】
| Day 35 【名詞23】
| Day 36 【名詞24】

Chapter 5
動詞:必修96
Page 173 ▶ 199

| Day 37 【動詞7】
| Day 38 【動詞8】
| Day 39 【動詞9】
| Day 40 【動詞10】
| Day 41 【動詞11】
| Day 42 【動詞12】

Chapter 6
形容詞:必修96
Page 201 ▶ 227

| Day 43 【形容詞7】
| Day 44 【形容詞8】
| Day 45 【形容詞9】
| Day 46 【形容詞10】
| Day 47 【形容詞11】
| Day 48 【形容詞12】

Chapter 7
副詞:必修48
Page 229 ▶ 243

| Day 49 【副詞1】
| Day 50 【副詞2】
| Day 51 【副詞3】

Contents

Chapter 8
動詞句
Page 245 ▶ 307

Day 52 【動詞句1】「動詞＋副詞［前置詞］」型1
Day 53 【動詞句2】「動詞＋副詞［前置詞］」型2
Day 54 【動詞句3】「動詞＋副詞［前置詞］」型3
Day 55 【動詞句4】「動詞＋副詞［前置詞］」型4
Day 56 【動詞句5】「動詞＋副詞［前置詞］」型5
Day 57 【動詞句6】「動詞＋A＋前置詞＋B」型1
Day 58 【動詞句7】「動詞＋A＋前置詞＋B」型2
Day 59 【動詞句8】「動詞＋A＋前置詞＋B」型3
Day 60 【動詞句9】「動詞＋to do [doing]」型1
Day 61 【動詞句10】「動詞＋to do [doing]」型2
Day 62 【動詞句11】「動詞＋A＋to do [from doing]」型
Day 63 【動詞句12】「be動詞＋形容詞＋前置詞」型1
Day 64 【動詞句13】「be動詞＋形容詞＋前置詞」型2
Day 65 【動詞句14】「be動詞＋形容詞＋to do」型
Day 66 【動詞句15】その他

Chapter 9

形容詞句・副詞句
Page 309 ▶ 323

Day 67 【形容詞句・副詞句1】
Day 68 【形容詞句・副詞句2】
Day 69 【形容詞句・副詞句3】

Chapter 10

群前置詞
Page 325 ▶ 331

Day 70 【群前置詞】

Preface
Page 3

本書の4大特長
Page 8 ▶ 9

本書とCDの利用法
Page 10 ▶ 11

Index
Page 333 ▶ 355

【記号説明】
- CD-A1：「CD-Aのトラック1を呼び出してください」という意味です。
- 名 動 形 副 前 接 間：順に、名詞、動詞、形容詞、副詞、前置詞、接続詞、間投詞を表します。
- 見出し中の [ ]：言い換え可能を表します。
- 見出し中の ( )：省略可能を表します。
- 見出し中のA、B：語句（主に名詞・代名詞）が入ることを表します。
- 見出し中のbe：be動詞が入ることを表します。be動詞は主語の人称・時制によって変化します。
- 見出し中のdo：動詞が入ることを表します。
- 見出し中のdoing：動名詞が入ることを表します。
- 見出し中のoneself：再帰代名詞が入ることを表します。主語によって再帰代名詞は異なります。
- 見出し中のone's：名詞・代名詞の所有格が入ることを表します。
- 見出し中の「〜」：節（主語＋動詞）が入ることを表します。
- 見出し下の「Part 〜」「ビジネス問題」：該当するTOEICのPart、ビジネス関連問題で登場する可能性が高い単語・熟語を表します。
- 定義中の ( )：補足説明を表します。
- 定義中の [ ]：言い換えを表します。
- ❶：発音、アクセント、定義に注意すべき単語についています。
- ❷：補足説明を表します。
- ≒：同意・類義語［熟語］を表します。
- ⇔：反意・反対語［熟語］を表します。

だから「ゼッタイに覚えられる」！
本書の4大特長

1
公式問題・模擬試験 さらにコーパスデータを 徹底分析！

TOEICに出る！ 日常生活で使える！

TOEICのための単語・熟語集である限り、「TOEICに出る」のは当然──。本書の目標は、そこから「実用英語」に対応できる単語・熟語力をいかに身につけてもらうかにあります。見出し語・熟語の選定にあたっては、TOEICの公式問題・模擬試験のデータに加え、最新の語彙研究から生まれたコーパス*のデータを徹底的に分析。目標スコアに到達するだけでなく、将来英語を使って世界で活躍するための土台となる単語・熟語が選ばれています。

＊コーパス：実際に話されたり書かれたりした言葉を大量に収集した「言語テキスト・データベース」のこと。コーパスを分析すると、どんな単語・熟語がどのくらいの頻度で使われるのか、といったことを客観的に調べられるので、辞書の編さんの際などに活用されている。

2
「目」だけでなく 「耳」と「口」までも フル活用して覚える！

「聞く単（キクタン）」！ しっかり身につく！

「読む」だけでは、言葉は決して身につきません。私たちが日本語を習得できたのは、小さいころから日本語を繰り返し「聞いて・口に出して」きたから──この「当たり前のこと」を忘れてはいけません。本書では、音楽のリズムに乗りながら単語・熟語の学習ができる「チャンツCD」を2枚用意。「目」と「耳」から同時に単語・熟語をインプットし、さらに「口」に出していきますので、「覚えられない」不安を一発解消。読解・聴解力もダブルアップします。

『聞いて覚える英単語 キクタンTOEIC Test Score 800』では、TOEICの公式問題・模擬試験データと最新の語彙研究の成果であるコーパスを基に収録単語・熟語を厳選していますので、「TOEICに出る」「日常生活で使える」ものばかりです。その上で「いかに効率的に単語・熟語を定着させるか」──このことを本書は最も重視しました。ここでは、なぜ「出る・使える」のか、そしてなぜ「覚えられる」のかに関して、本書の特長をご紹介します。

3
1日16見出し×10週間、10のチャプターの「スケジュール学習」！

ムリなくマスターできる！

「継続は力なり」、とは分かっていても、続けるのは大変なことです。では、なぜ「大変」なのか？ それは、覚えきれないほどの量の単語や熟語をムリに詰め込もうとするからです。本書では、「ゼッタイに覚える」ことを前提に、1日の学習量をあえて16見出しに抑えています。さらに、単語は品詞ごとに「頻度順」に、熟語は「表現型別」に、計10のチャプターに分けていますので、効率的・効果的に学習単語・熟語をマスターできます。

4
1日最短2分、最長でも6分の3つの「モード学習」！

挫折することなく最後まで続けられる！

今まで単語集や熟語集を手にしたときに、「1日でどこからどこまでやればいいのだろう？」と思ったことはありませんか？ 見出し語・熟語、フレーズ、例文……1度に目を通すのは、忙しいときには難しいものです。本書は、Check 1（単語・熟語＋定義）→ Check 2（フレーズ）→ Check 3（センテンス）と、3つのポイントごとに学習できる「モード学習」を用意。生活スタイルやその日の忙しさに合わせて学習量を調整できます。

生活スタイルに合わせて選べる
Check 1▶2▶3の「モード学習」
本書とCDの利用法

Check 1

該当のCDトラックを呼び出して、「英語→日本語→英語」の順に収録されている「チャンツ音楽」で見出し語・熟語とその意味をチェック。時間に余裕がある人は、太字以外の定義も押さえておきましょう。

Check 2

Check 1で「見出し語・熟語→定義」を押さえたら、その単語・熟語が含まれているフレーズをチェック。フレーズレベルで使用例を確認することで、単語・熟語の定着度が高まります（センテンスが入っているDayもあります）。

Check 3

Check 2のフレーズレベルから、Check 3ではセンテンスレベルへとさらに実践的な例に触れていきます。ここまで学習すると、「音」と「文字」で最低6回は学習単語・熟語に触れるので、定着度は格段にアップします。

見出し語・熟語

1日の学習単語、熟語数は16です。見開きの左側に単語・熟語が掲載されています。チャンツでは上から順に単語・熟語が登場します。最初の8つが流れたら、ページをめくって次の8つに進みましょう。

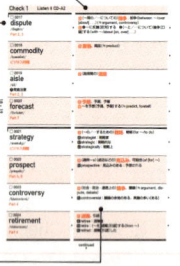

定義

見出し語・熟語の定義が掲載されています。単語・熟語によっては複数の意味があるので、第1義以外の定義もなるべく覚えるようにしましょう。

チェックシート

本書に付属のチェックシートは復習用に活用してください。Check 1では見出し語・熟語の定義が身についているか、Check 2と3では訳を参照しながらチェックシートで隠されている単語・熟語がすぐに浮かんでくるかを確認しましょう。

Quick Review

前日に学習した単語・熟語のチェックリストです。左ページに日本語、右ページに英語が掲載されています。時間に余裕があるときは、該当のCDトラックでチャンツも聞いておきましょう。

1日の学習量は4ページ、学習単語・熟語数は16となっています。1つの見出し語・熟語につき、定義を学ぶ「Check 1」、フレーズ中で単語・熟語を学ぶ「Check 2」、センテンス中で学ぶ「Check 3」の3つの「モード学習」が用意されています。まずは、該当のCDトラックを呼び出して、「チャンツ音楽」のリズムに乗りながら見出し語・熟語と定義を「耳」と「目」で押さえましょう。時間に余裕がある人は、Check 2とCheck 3にもトライ！

こんなアナタにオススメ！
3つの「学習モード」

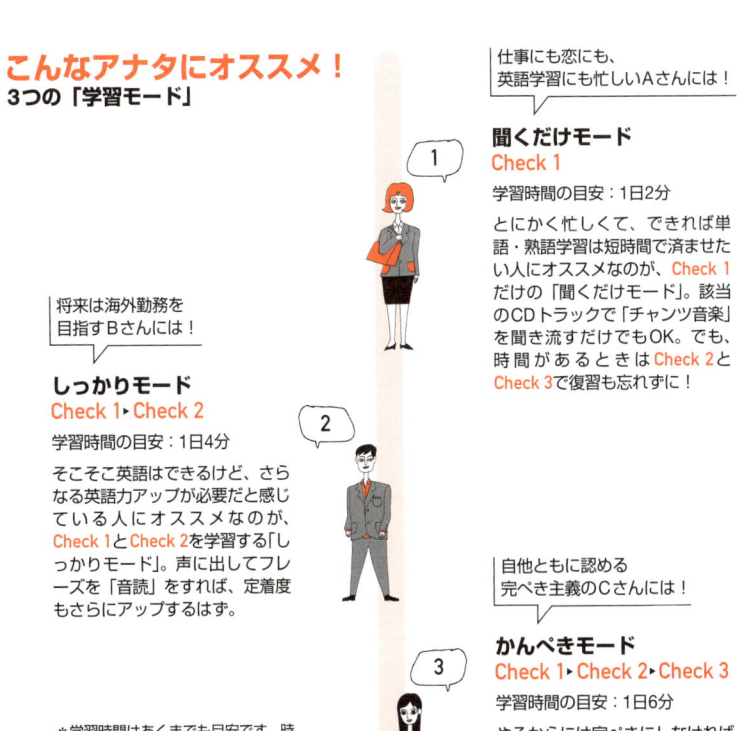

仕事にも恋にも、英語学習にも忙しいAさんには！

聞くだけモード
Check 1

学習時間の目安：1日2分

とにかく忙しくて、できれば単語・熟語学習は短時間で済ませたい人にオススメなのが、Check 1だけの「聞くだけモード」。該当のCDトラックで「チャンツ音楽」を聞き流すだけでもOK。でも、時間があるときはCheck 2とCheck 3で復習も忘れずに！

将来は海外勤務を目指すBさんには！

しっかりモード
Check 1 ▶ Check 2

学習時間の目安：1日4分

そこそこ英語はできるけど、さらなる英語力アップが必要だと感じている人にオススメなのが、Check 1とCheck 2を学習する「しっかりモード」。声に出してフレーズを「音読」をすれば、定着度もさらにアップするはず。

自他ともに認める完ぺき主義のCさんには！

かんぺきモード
Check 1 ▶ Check 2 ▶ Check 3

学習時間の目安：1日6分

やるからには完ぺきにしなければ気が済まない人には「かんぺきモード」がオススメ。ここまでやっても学習時間の目安はたったの6分。できればみんな「かんぺきモード」でパーフェクトを目指そう！

＊学習時間はあくまでも目安です。時間に余裕があるときは、チャンツ音楽を繰り返し聞いたり、フレーズやセンテンスの音読を重ねたりして、なるべく多く学習単語・熟語に触れるように心がけましょう。
＊CDには見出し語・熟語と定義のみが収録されています。

※CDに収録されていない例文音声は、ダウンロードコンテンツとして購入することができます。
　http://www.alc.co.jp/elearning/onsei-dl/
※コンテンツには「例文音声」「チャンツ+例文音声」の2種類があります。

〈CD取り扱いのご注意〉
●弊社制作の音声CDは、CDプレーヤーでの再生を保証する規格品です。
●パソコンでご使用になる場合、CD-ROMドライブとの相性により、ディスクを再生できない場合がございます。ご了承ください。
●パソコンでタイトル・トラック情報を表示させたい場合は、iTunesをご利用ください。iTunesでは、弊社がCDのタイトル・トラック情報を登録しているGracenote社のCDDB（データベース）からインターネットを介してトラック情報を取得することができます。
●CDとして正常に音声が再生できるディスクからパソコンやmp3プレーヤー等への取り込み時にトラブルが生じた際は、まず、そのアプリケーション（ソフト）、プレーヤーの製作元へご相談ください。

CHAPTER 1

名詞：超必修192

Chapter 1のスタートです！
このChapterでは、TOEIC「超必修」の名詞192をマスターしていきます。先はまだまだ長いけれど、焦らず急がず学習を進めていきましょう。

TOEIC的格言

One is never too old to learn.
学ぶのに遅すぎるということはない。

Day 1 【名詞1】
▶ 14
Day 2 【名詞2】
▶ 18
Day 3 【名詞3】
▶ 22
Day 4 【名詞4】
▶ 26
Day 5 【名詞5】
▶ 30
Day 6 【名詞6】
▶ 34
Day 7 【名詞7】
▶ 38
Day 8 【名詞8】
▶ 42
Day 9 【名詞9】
▶ 46
Day 10 【名詞10】
▶ 50
Day 11 【名詞11】
▶ 54
Day 12 【名詞12】
▶ 58
Chapter 1 Review
▶ 62

Day 1　名詞1

Check 1　Listen)) CD-A1

☐ 0001
revenue
/révənjùː/
ビジネス問題

名 ❶(会社の)**総収益**、総利益　❷(国などの)歳入(⇔expenditure：支出)；(個人などの)収入(≒income)

☐ 0002
award
/əwɔ́ːrd/
❶アクセント注意
Part 2, 3

名 (〜に対する)**賞**、賞品、賞金(for 〜)(≒prize)
動 (賞など)を(人に)授与する(to ...)

☐ 0003
candidate
/kǽndidèit/
Part 7

名 (〜への)**候補者**；志願者(for 〜)
名 candidacy：(〜への)立候補(for 〜)

☐ 0004
construction
/kənstrʌ́kʃən/
Part 1

名 ❶**建設**(⇔destruction：破壊)；建築工事　❷構造
動 construct：〜を(…で)建設する(of [from] ...)
形 constructive：(考えなどが)建設的な

☐ 0005
objection
/əbdʒékʃən/
Part 2, 3

名 (〜に対する)**反対**、異議(to [against] 〜)(≒disagreement)(⇔agreement)
動 object：(object toで)〜に反対[抗議]する

☐ 0006
prescription
/priskrípʃən/
Part 2, 3

名 **処方箋**
動 prescribe：(prescribe A for Bで)A(薬など)をB(病気)に対して処方する

☐ 0007
debt
/dét/
❶発音注意
ビジネス問題

名 **借金**、負債；借金状態
名 debtor：債務者、借り主

☐ 0008
résumé
/rézəmèi/
Part 2, 3

名 ❶**履歴書**(≒curriculum vitae)　❷要約、概要、レジュメ　➕resume(/rizúːm/)は「〜を再開する」

continued
▼

いよいよDay 1のスタート！ 今日から12日間は「超必修」の名詞192をチェック。まずは、CDでチャンツを聞いてみよう！

- ☐ 聞くだけモード　Check 1
- ☐ しっかりモード　Check 1 ▶ 2
- ☐ かんぺきモード　Check 1 ▶ 2 ▶ 3

Check 2　Phrase

- ☐ generate revenue（収益を上げる）
- ☐ revenue and expenditure（収支）

- ☐ awards ceremony（授賞式）
- ☐ receive an award of $10,000（1万ドルの賞金をもらう）

- ☐ a candidate for mayor（市長候補者）
- ☐ the prime candidate（最有力候補者）

- ☐ under construction（建設中で）
- ☐ a building of lightweight construction（軽量構造の建物）

- ☐ raise [voice] an objection（異議を唱える）
- ☐ have no objection to the plan（その計画に異存はない）

- ☐ get a prescription filled（処方箋を調合してもらう）

- ☐ repay [clear] a debt（借金を返済する）

- ☐ a 10-page résumé（10ページの履歴書）
- ☐ a résumé of the project（そのプロジェクトの概要）

Check 3　Sentence

- ☐ The company's estimated revenue totals $300 million worldwide.（その会社の概算の総収益は世界中で総計3億ドルになる）

- ☐ He is another possible for the award.（彼はその賞のもう1人の有力候補者だ）

- ☐ There are five candidates standing in the election.（その選挙には5人の候補者が出馬している）

- ☐ They are working at the construction site.（彼らは建設現場で働いている）

- ☐ There are strong objections to the construction of the building.（そのビルの建設には激しい反対がある）

- ☐ This drug is only available by prescription.（この薬は処方箋によってのみ入手できる）

- ☐ She is $2,000 in debt.（彼女には2000ドルの借金がある）

- ☐ He sent his résumé to 20 companies.（彼は履歴書を20社に送った）

continued ▼

Day 1

Check 1　Listen 》CD-A1

□ 0009
compliment
/kámpləmənt/
Part 5, 6

名 (〜についての)**褒め言葉**、賛辞；お世辞(on 〜)
動 (/kámpləmènt/)〜に賛辞を述べる　⊕complement(〜を補完する)と混同しないように注意
形complimentary：❶無料の　❷称賛の；お世辞の

□ 0010
representative
/rèprizéntətiv/
ビジネス問題

名❶**代理人**、代表者　❷代議士；(R〜)米国下院議員　⊕「上院議員」はsenator
名representation：❶代表　❷表現、描写
動represent：❶(団体など)を代表する、〜の代理をする　❷〜を表す、象徴する

□ 0011
negotiation
/nigòuʃiéiʃən/
ビジネス問題

名 (〜に関する)**交渉**、話し合い(on [over] 〜)
動negotiate：❶(〜と)交渉する(with 〜)　❷(契約など)を(…と)取り決める(with …)
形negotiable：交渉の余地がある

□ 0012
admission
/ædmíʃən/
Part 2, 3

名❶(〜への)**入場**[入学、入社]**許可**(to [into] 〜)　❷入場料　❸(罪などの)自白、告白(of 〜)
動admit：❶〜を認める　❷(admit doingで)〜したことを認める　❸(admit A to [into] Bで)AにBへの入場[入会、入学]を認める

□ 0013
workshop
/wə́:rkʃɑ̀p/
Part 2, 3

名❶**研修**[研究、講習]**会**、セミナー　❷作業場

□ 0014
personnel
/pə̀:rsənél/
❶発音注意
ビジネス問題

名❶**人事部**[課] (≒human resources)；(形容詞的に)人事[職員]の　❷(集合的に)(会社などの)人員(≒staff)
⊕personal(個人的な /pə́:rsənl/)と混同しないように注意

□ 0015
assignment
/əsáinmənt/
ビジネス問題

名❶**任務**；(仕事などの)割り当て　❷宿題、研究課題
動assign：❶(assign A to Bで)AをB(地位など)に任命する　❷(assign A to doで)Aを〜するように選任する

□ 0016
approval
/əprú:vəl/
Part 2, 3

名**承認**、認可(⇔disapproval)
動approve：❶〜を承認[是認]する　❷(approve ofで)〜に賛成する

Check 2 Phrase

- pay her a compliment（彼女を褒める）
- return the compliment（褒め返す；返礼する）

- a sales representative（販売代理人）
- the House of Representatives（[日本の]衆議院；[米国の]下院）

- enter into negotiations（交渉を始める）
- diplomatic negotiations（外交交渉）

- gain admission to ～（～に入る許可を得る）
- Admission Free.（[掲示で]入場無料）

- a management workshop（経営管理セミナー）

- a personnel manager（人事部長）
- cut in personnel（人員削減）

- assignment of the tasks（仕事の割り当て）
- a math assignment（数学の宿題）

- receive [win] approval（承認を得る）

Check 3 Sentence

- She got lots of compliments on her coat.（たくさんの人が彼女のコートを褒めた）

- Our company has 10 representatives in Europe.（当社にはヨーロッパ駐在の代理人が10人いる）

- Contract negotiations proceeded smoothly.（契約交渉は順調に進んだ）

- Admission to the party was by invitation only.（そのパーティーへの入場は招待によるものだけだった）

- There will be a workshop for students interested in graduate schools tomorrow.（明日、大学院に興味がある学生向けの講習会が開かれる予定だ）

- Susie works in the personnel division of the company.（スージーはその会社の人事部に勤務している）

- I was given a tough assignment by my boss.（私は上司から難しい任務を与えられた）

- The loan approval process is very complicated.（その融資の承認プロセスは非常に複雑だ）

Day 2 名詞2

Check 1 Listen)) CD-A2

☐ 0017
dispute
/dispjúːt/
Part 2, 3

名（～間の／…についての）**論争**；紛争(between ～/over [about] ...)(≒ argument, controversy)
動❶～に反論[反対]する ❷（～と／…について）論争[口論]する(with ～/about [on, over] ...)

☐ 0018
commodity
/kəmάdəti/
ビジネス問題

名 **産物**、商品(≒ product)

☐ 0019
aisle
/áil/
❶発音注意
Part 2, 3

名（座席間の）**通路**

☐ 0020
forecast
/fɔ́ːrkæst/
Part 7

名 **予想**、予測、予報
動 ～を予想[予測、予報]する(≒ predict, foretell)

☐ 0021
strategy
/strǽtədʒi/
ビジネス問題

名（～の／…するための）**戦略**、戦術(for ～/to do)
名 strategist：戦略家
形 strategic：戦略的な
副 strategically：戦略上

☐ 0022
prospect
/prάspekt/
Part 5, 6

名（通例～s）（成功などの）**見込み**、可能性(of [for] ～)
形 prospective：見込みのある；予想される

☐ 0023
controversy
/kάntrəvəːrsi/
Part 4

名（社会・政治・道徳上の）**論争**、議論(≒ argument, dispute, debate)
形 controversial：議論の余地のある、異論の多い[ある]

☐ 0024
retirement
/ritáiərmənt/
Part 4

名 **退職**、引退
名 retiree：退職者
動 retire：(～を)退職[引退]する(from ～)
形 retired：退職[引退]した

continued
▼

チャンツを聞く際には、「英語→日本語→英語」の2回目の「英語」の部分で声に出して読んでみよう。定着度が倍増するはず！

☐ 聞くだけモード　Check 1
☐ しっかりモード　Check 1 ▶ 2
☐ かんぺきモード　Check 1 ▶ 2 ▶ 3

Check 2　Phrase

☐ a dispute over working conditions（労働条件に関する論争）
☐ a border dispute（国境紛争）

☐ agricultural commodities（農産物）
☐ commodity price（物価）

☐ the middle aisle of the church（教会の中央通路）

☐ a sales forecast（販売予想）

☐ a marketing strategy（販売戦略）

☐ prospects of promotion（昇進の見込み）
☐ in prospect（予想されて）

☐ a fierce [heated] controversy（激しい論争）

☐ take early retirement（早期退職する）

Check 3　Sentence

☐ They will go on strike tomorrow if there is no resolution to the labor dispute.（労働争議が解決しない場合、彼らは明日ストライキに突入するつもりだ）

☐ Nickel is the country's most valuable export commodity.（ニッケルはその国の最も高価な輸出品だ）

☐ Would you like an aisle or a window seat?（通路側と窓側のどちらの席がよろしいですか？）

☐ According to the weather forecast, it is going to rain later today.（天気予報によると、今日はこれから雨が降るということだ）

☐ The CEO refused to give specifics of the company's strategy.（そのCEOは会社の戦略を詳細に述べることを拒んだ）

☐ Is there any prospect of economic recovery next year?（来年、景気が回復する見込みはありますか？）

☐ There is a religious controversy over evolution.（進化をめぐる宗教的な論争がある）

☐ Mr. Suzuki has five years to go before retirement.（スズキさんは退職まであと5年ある）

continued
▼

Day 2

Check 1　Listen))) CD-A2

☐ 0025
legislation
/lèdʒisléiʃən/
Part 5, 6

- 名 ❶(集合的に)**法律**(≒law)　❷法律制定
- 名 legislator：❶立法者　❷立法府の議員
- 名 legislature：議会；立法府
- 形 legislative：❶立法上の　❷立法府の

☐ 0026
procedure
/prəsíːdʒər/
ビジネス問題

- 名 ❶(〜の)**手順**、順序、方法(for 〜)　❷(法律などの)(正式な)手続き
- 名 proceeds：(〜s)収益、売上高
- 動 proceed：❶(proceed toで)〜へ進む、向かう　❷(proceed withで)〜を続ける

☐ 0027
transaction
/trænzǽkʃən/
ビジネス問題

- 名 ❶**取引**　❷(業務の)処理
- 動 transact：❶(〜と)取引[業務]を行う(with 〜)　❷(取引・業務など)を行う

☐ 0028
initiative
/iníʃiətiv/
Part 7

- 名 ❶**主導権**、イニシアチブ　❷自発性、独創力
- 名 initiation：❶(〜への)加入(into 〜)　❷開始
- 動 initiate：(計画など)を始める
- 動 initial：〜に頭文字を書く
- 形 initial：最初の

☐ 0029
grocery
/gróusəri/
Part 1

- 名 (〜ies)**食料雑貨類**

☐ 0030
survey
/sə́ːrvei/
Part 4

- 名 **調査**
- 動 (/sərvéi/)〜を調査する
- 名 surveillance：監視；査察

☐ 0031
colleague
/káliːg/
Part 2, 3

- 名 **同僚**(≒coworker, associate)

☐ 0032
departure
/dipáːrtʃər/
Part 4

- 名 (〜からの／…へ向けての)**出発**(from 〜/for …)(⇔arrival)
- 動 depart：(〜から／…へ向けて)出発する(from 〜/for …)

Day 1))) CD-A1
Quick Review
答えは右ページ下

☐ 総収益　☐ 反対　☐ 褒め言葉　☐ 研修会
☐ 賞　☐ 処方箋　☐ 代理人　☐ 人事部
☐ 候補者　☐ 借金　☐ 交渉　☐ 任務
☐ 建設　☐ 履歴書　☐ 入場許可　☐ 承認

Check 2 Phrase

- civil rights legislation（公民権法）
- the power of legislation（立法権）

- follow correct procedure（正しい手順に従う）
- legal procedure（法的手続き）

- real estate transactions（不動産取引）
- the transaction of business（業務の処理）

- seize [gain] the initiative（主導権を握る）
- show initiative（自発性を発揮する）

- a grocery store（食料雑貨店）

- conduct [carry out] a survey（調査を行う）

- colleagues at the office（職場の同僚）

- the departure lounge（[空港の]出発待合室）

Check 3 Sentence

- Japan has gun control legislation.（日本には銃規制法がある）

- What's the regular procedure for screening applicants?（求職者を選別する通常の方法は何ですか？）

- The bank offers secure transactions over the Internet.（その銀行はインターネット上での安全な取引を提供している）

- Mr. Brown took the initiative in carrying out the project.（ブラウン氏は率先してそのプロジェクトを実行した）

- The woman is carrying groceries.（女性は食料雑貨類を運んでいる）

- A recent survey showed that 55 percent of Americans are overweight.（最近の調査では、アメリカ人の55パーセントは肥満であることが明らかになった）

- He gets along with his colleagues.（彼は同僚たちと仲よくやっている）

- Our departure was delayed because of a snowstorm.（私たちの出発は吹雪のため遅れた）

Day 1))) CD-A1
Quick Review
答えは左ページ下

- revenue
- award
- candidate
- construction
- objection
- prescription
- debt
- résumé
- compliment
- representative
- negotiation
- admission
- workshop
- personnel
- assignment
- approval

Day 3 名詞3

Check 1　Listen ») CD-A3

☐ 0033
compensation
/kàmpənséiʃən/
Part 7

名❶(~に対する)**補償**[賠償](金)(for ~)　❷報酬
動compensate：❶(compensate for で)(損失など)の埋め合わせをする、~を償う、補う　❷(compensate A for B で)AにB(損害など)の賠償[補償]をする

☐ 0034
promotion
/prəmóuʃən/
ビジネス問題

名❶(~への)**昇進**(to ~)(⇔demotion：降格)　❷販売促進
動promote：❶を(…に)昇進させる(to . . .)　❷~の販売を促進する、~の宣伝活動をする
形promotional：宣伝[プロモーション]用の

☐ 0035
proceed
/próusi:d/
Part 5, 6

名(~s)**収益**、売上高
動(/prəsi:d/)❶(proceed to で)~へ進む、向かう　❷(proceed with で)~を続ける
名proceeding：❶(~s)議事録　❷(~s)手続き
名procedure：❶手順、順序　❷(正式な)手続き

☐ 0036
transition
/trænzíʃən/
Part 5, 6

名(~から／…への)**移行**、変遷；過渡期(from ~/to . . .)(≒change)
名transit：❶通過、通行　❷輸送、運送
形transitional：過渡期の

☐ 0037
qualification
/kwàləfikéiʃən/
Part 2, 3

名❶(~する)**資格**(to do)　❷(~の)適性、資質(for ~)
動qualify：❶(qualify as [for] で)~の資格を得る、~として適任である　❷(be qualified for で)~の資格[免許]がある

☐ 0038
resource
/rí:sɔːrs/
ビジネス問題

名(通例~s)**資源**；資産
形resourceful：❶臨機の才のある、機知に富んだ　❷資源に富んだ

☐ 0039
division
/divíʒən/
ビジネス問題

名❶(会社などの)**部局**、部門　❷(~への)分割(into ~)　❸割り算
動divide：❶~を(…に)分ける(into [in] . . .)　❷~を(…の間で)分配する(between [among] . . .)　❸(divide A by B で)A(数)をB(数)で割る

☐ 0040
accountant
/əkáuntənt/
Part 2, 3

名**会計士**
名account：❶(銀行)口座　❷(金銭の)計算書
動account：(account for で)❶(ある割合)を占める　❷~(の原因・理由)を説明する
名accounting：会計(学)、経理

continued
▼

「3日坊主」にならないためにも、今日・明日の学習がとっても大切！ CDを聞き流すだけでもOKなので、「継続」を心がけよう。

☐ 聞くだけモード　Check 1
☐ しっかりモード　Check 1 ▶ 2
☐ かんぺきモード　Check 1 ▶ 2 ▶ 3

Check 2　　Phrase

☐ compensation for the damage（損害に対する補償）
☐ pay compensation（補償金を支払う）

☐ get [gain] (a) promotion（昇進する）
☐ a promotion campaign（販売促進運動）

☐ the proceeds from the deal（その取引の売上高）

☐ make the transition from a dictatorship to a democracy（独裁制から民主制へと移行する）
☐ in transition（過渡期にある）

☐ a qualification to teach English（英語を教える資格）
☐ a necessary qualification for the job（その仕事に必要な適性）

☐ natural [human] resources（天然[人的]資源）➕human resourcesは「人事部[課]」という意味でも用いられる

☐ the sales division（販売部門）
☐ the division of powers（権限の分割）

☐ certified public accountant（公認会計士）➕略はCPA

Check 3　　Sentence

☐ He received $2,000 in compensation for the injury.（彼はそのけがの補償金として2000ドルを受け取った）

☐ The company announced the promotion of Mr. Baker to vice president.（その会社はベーカー氏の副社長への昇進を発表した）

☐ All the proceeds from the concert will be donated to local charities.（そのコンサートの全収益は地元の慈善団体に寄付される予定だ）

☐ China is in transition to market socialism.（中国は市場社会主義への過渡期にある）

☐ You need qualifications to get a good job.（いい仕事を得るには資格が必要だ）

☐ Mineral resources include coal, gold, copper, and other heavy metals.（鉱物資源には、石炭、金、銅や、そのほかの重金属が含まれる）

☐ She works in the advertising division of the company.（彼女はその会社の宣伝部に勤務している）

☐ My dream is to be an accountant.（私の夢は会計士になることだ）

continued ▼

Day 3

Check 1　Listen)) CD-A3

0041
stain
/stéin/
Part 2, 3

名 ❶**染み**、汚れ(≒blot)　❷(〜の)汚点(on [upon] 〜)
動 〜を(…で)汚す(with ...)、〜に染みをつける
形 stainless：ステンレス製の

0042
deposit
/dipázit/
Part 2, 3

名 ❶**預金**　❷(〜の)手付金、頭金(on 〜)　❸(石油などの)鉱床
動 (金)を(銀行・口座に)預金する(in ...)(⇔withdraw：[預金]を引き出す)

0043
banquet
/bǽŋkwit/
Part 2, 3

名 (公式の)**宴会**、祝宴(≒feast)

0044
maintenance
/méintənəns/
Part 4

名 (〜の)**管理**、維持、整備(of 〜)
動 maintain：❶〜を維持[保持]する　❷〜だと主張する

0045
destination
/dèstənéiʃən/
Part 2, 3

名 **目的地**、行き先
形 destined：❶(be destined to doで)〜する運命にある　❷(be destined forで)〜を受ける運命にある

0046
equivalent
/ikwívələnt/
❶アクセント注意
Part 7

名 **相当するもの**(≒counterpart)；同等[同量]のもの
形 (be equivalent toで)〜に相当する；〜と同等である

0047
solution
/səlúːʃən/
Part 4

名 (〜の)**解決策**；解答(to 〜)
動 solve：❶(困難など)を解決する　❷(問題など)を解く

0048
refreshment
/rifréʃmənt/
Part 1

名 (通例〜s)(会合などで出される)**軽食**
動 refresh：❶〜の気分をさわやかにする、〜を元気づける　❷(記憶)を新たにする

| Day 2)) CD-A2
Quick Review
答えは右ページ下 | □ 論争
□ 産物
□ 通路
□ 予想 | □ 戦略
□ 見込み
□ 論争
□ 退職 | □ 法律
□ 手順
□ 取引
□ 主導権 | □ 食料雑貨類
□ 調査
□ 同僚
□ 出発 |

Check 2 Phrase

- a coffee [an ink] stain(コーヒー[インク]の染み)
- a stain on one's reputation(評判についた汚点)

- make a deposit in ~(~に預金する)
- put a deposit on ~(~の手付金を支払う)

- give [hold] a banquet(宴会を催す)

- building [car] maintenance(建物の管理[車の整備])
- a maintenance worker([ビルなどの]用務員;[機械の]補修員)

- a popular tourist destination(人気の観光地)

- an English equivalent for the Japanese *motokare*(「元彼」に相当する英語) ➕ 「元彼」は英語ではex-boyfriend

- solutions to the problem of unemployment(失業問題の解決策)
- the solution to the crossword puzzle(そのクロスワードパズルの答え)

- light refreshments(茶菓子)

Check 3 Sentence

- Do you know how to remove a wine stain from carpet?(じゅうたんからワインの染みをどうやって取るか知っていますか?)

- You must make a minimum deposit of $100 to open an account.(口座を開くには最低100ドルを預金しなければならない)

- He was asked to make a speech at the banquet.(彼はその宴会でスピーチをするよう依頼された)

- Our primary concern is the maintenance of law and order.(私たちの一番の関心事は治安の維持だ)

- We arrived at our destination two hours late.(私たちは目的地に2時間遅れで到着した)

- A typhoon is the East Asian equivalent of a hurricane.(台風は東アジアにおける、ハリケーンに相当するものだ)

- The government has been seeking solutions to the financial crisis.(政府は金融危機の解決策を探し求めている)

- The guests are having refreshments.(来客たちは軽食を取っている)

Day 2))) CD-A2
Quick Review
答えは左ページ下

- dispute
- commodity
- aisle
- forecast
- strategy
- prospect
- controversy
- retirement
- legislation
- procedure
- transaction
- initiative
- grocery
- survey
- colleague
- departure

CHAPTER 1
CHAPTER 2
CHAPTER 3
CHAPTER 4
CHAPTER 5
CHAPTER 6
CHAPTER 7
CHAPTER 8
CHAPTER 9
CHAPTER 10

Day 4　名詞4

Check 1　Listen 》CD-A4

□ 0049
defect
/díːfekt/
ビジネス問題

名（〜の）**欠陥**、欠点(in 〜)(≒ fault)
形 defective：欠陥[欠点]のある

□ 0050
enthusiasm
/inθúːziæzm/
❶アクセント注意
Part 5, 6

名（〜に対する）**熱意**、熱狂、強い興味(for 〜)
形 enthusiastic：❶熱心[熱狂的]な　❷(be enthusiastic aboutで)〜に熱中している、夢中になっている

□ 0051
executive
/igzékjutiv/
❶発音注意
ビジネス問題

名**重役**、経営幹部
形 ❶実施[事務]の　❷重役の
名 execution：❶死刑執行　❷実行、実施
動 execute：❶(計画など)を実行する　❷〜を死刑にする

□ 0052
transportation
/trænspərtéiʃən/
Part 2, 3

名**輸送**、運送；交通[輸送]機関
動 transport：〜を(…へ)輸送[運送]する(to …)

□ 0053
courtesy
/kə́ːrtəsi/
Part 7

名 ❶**好意**；優遇　❷礼儀正しいこと、丁寧
形 courteous：(〜に対して)礼儀正しい、親切[丁寧]な(to [with] 〜)

□ 0054
site
/sáit/
Part 1

名 ❶(建物などの)**場所**、位置；(〜の)用地(for 〜)　❷(事件などの)現場　❸(インターネットの)サイト
動 (be sited inで)(建物などが)〜に位置する(≒ be located in)

□ 0055
code
/kóud/
Part 2, 3

名 ❶**規則**　❷記号、番号
動 〜を暗号にする(≒ encode)

□ 0056
substitute
/sʌ́bstətjùːt/
Part 7

名**代理人**；代用品
動 ❶(substitute A for Bで)AをBの代わりに用いる　❷(substitute forで)〜の代用[代理]になる
形 代理[代用]の
名 substitution：❶代理、代用　❷代理人、代用品

continued
▼

「細切れ時間」を有効活用してる?『キクタン』は2分でも学習可能。いつでもどこでもテキストとCDを持ち歩いて単語・熟語に触れよう!

☐ 聞くだけモード　Check 1
☐ しっかりモード　Check 1 ▶ 2
☐ かんぺきモード　Check 1 ▶ 2 ▶ 3

Check 2　Phrase

☐ a defect in the engine(エンジンの欠陥)

☐ enthusiasm for music(音楽に対する熱意)
☐ with enthusiasm(熱心に)

☐ a senior executive(上級管理職)

☐ a means of transportation(交通[輸送]手段)
☐ public transportation(公共交通機関)

☐ by courtesy of ~(~の好意によって)
☐ have the courtesy to do ~(~する礼儀をわきまえている)

☐ the site for the new mall(新しいショッピングセンターの用地)
☐ the site of the accident(その事故の現場)

☐ a code of ethics(倫理規範)
☐ an area code([電話の]市外局番)

☐ use A as a substitute for B(Bの代わりにAを使う)
☐ There is no substitute for ~.(~に代わる[勝る]ものはない)

Check 3　Sentence

☐ All the products are tested for defects before they are shipped.(すべての製品は出荷される前に欠陥がないか検査される)

☐ My colleagues showed little enthusiasm for my plan.(同僚たちは私の計画にほとんど興味を示さなかった)

☐ Mr. Smith earned over $100,000 last year as a sales executive.(スミス氏は販売担当重役として昨年10万ドル以上を得た)

☐ The city's transportation system is inefficient.(その都市の交通システムは非効率的だ)

☐ Twenty Chinese students were invited to Japan by courtesy of the airline.(その航空会社の好意により、20人の中国人学生が日本へ招かれた)

☐ The men are working at the building site.(男たちは建設現場で働いている)

☐ The high school's dress code is very strict.(その高校の服装規則はとても厳しい)

☐ Today, we had a substitute in English class.(今日、私たちの英語の授業に代理教員が来た)

continued
▼

Day 4

Check 1　Listen 》CD-A4

□ 0057
precaution
/prikɔ́:ʃən/
Part 7

名（～に対する）**予防策**[措置]；警戒、用心（against ～）

□ 0058
budget
/bʌ́dʒit/
ビジネス問題

名❶**予算**（案）❷経費
動（～の）予算を立てる（for ～）

□ 0059
objective
/əbdʒéktiv/
Part 5, 6

名（達すべき）**目標**、目的
形客観的な（⇔subjective：主観的な）
名object：❶物体 ❷対象 ❸目的
動object：（object toで）～に反対する
名objection：（～に対する）反対（to [against] ～）

□ 0060
estimate
/éstəmət/
❶アクセント注意
ビジネス問題

名❶**見積もり**、概算
動（/éstəmèit/）❶～を見積もる ❷～を評価する
名estimation：❶評価、判断 ❷見積もり
形estimated：見積もりの、概算の

□ 0061
facility
/fəsíləti/
Part 4

名（しばしば～ies）**施設**、設備
動facilitate：～を促進[助成]する；～を容易にする

□ 0062
asset
/ǽset/
ビジネス問題

名（通例～s）**資産**、財産（≒property, estate）（⇔liability：負債）

□ 0063
circumstance
/sə́:rkəmstæns/
Part 2, 3

名（通例～s）**状況**、事情

□ 0064
symptom
/símptəm/
Part 2, 3

名❶（～の）**兆候**、しるし（of ～）（≒sign）❷症状

Day 3 》CD-A3
Quick Review
答えは右ページ下

□ 補償　　□ 資格　　□ 染み　　□ 目的地
□ 昇進　　□ 資源　　□ 預金　　□ 相当するもの
□ 収益　　□ 部局　　□ 宴会　　□ 解決策
□ 移行　　□ 会計士　□ 管理　　□ 軽食

Check 2　Phrase

- ☐ take the precaution of doing (～〔～するという予防策を取る〕)
- ☐ as a precaution (用心のため)

- ☐ be over [under] budget (予算を上回って[下回って]いる)
- ☐ budget deficit (予算の赤字、財政赤字)

- ☐ the main [primary] objective (主要な目標)
- ☐ achieve [meet] an objective (目標を達成する)

- ☐ a rough estimate (大ざっぱな見積もり)

- ☐ research facilities (研究施設)

- ☐ liquid [fixed] assets (流動[固定]資産)

- ☐ under the circumstances (こういう状況[事情]では)
- ☐ under any circumstances (どのような事情でも)

- ☐ symptoms of recession (景気後退の兆候)
- ☐ symptoms of flu (インフルエンザの症状)

Check 3　Sentence

- ☐ All the workers must follow safety precautions. (全作業員は安全対策に従わなければならない)

- ☐ The company has drawn up a budget for the next fiscal year. (その会社は次期会計年度の予算案を作成した)

- ☐ Our objective is to increase productivity. (私たちの目標は生産性を上げることだ)

- ☐ According to a government estimate, the unemployment figure is about 10 million. (政府の概算によると、失業者数は約1000万人だ)

- ☐ The money will be used to build a new sports facility. (その金は新しいスポーツ施設を建設するために使われる予定だ)

- ☐ The company has $2.5 billion in assets. (その会社は25億ドルの資産を持っている)

- ☐ He could cope with the problem under exceptional circumstances. (異例の事態の下でも彼はその問題に対処することができた)

- ☐ The weak dollar is a symptom of the US trade deficit problem. (ドル安はアメリカの貿易赤字問題の表れだ)

Day 3　))CD-A3
Quick Review
答えは左ページ下

- ☐ compensation
- ☐ promotion
- ☐ proceed
- ☐ transition
- ☐ qualification
- ☐ resource
- ☐ division
- ☐ accountant
- ☐ stain
- ☐ deposit
- ☐ banquet
- ☐ maintenance
- ☐ destination
- ☐ equivalent
- ☐ solution
- ☐ refreshment

CHAPTER 1
CHAPTER 2
CHAPTER 3
CHAPTER 4
CHAPTER 5
CHAPTER 6
CHAPTER 7
CHAPTER 8
CHAPTER 9
CHAPTER 10

Day 5　名詞5

Check 1　Listen)) CD-A5

☐ 0065
exhibit
/iɡzíbit/
❶発音注意
Part 1

名 展示[陳列]品
動 ❶〜を展示する　❷〜を(感情などに)表す
名 exhibition：❶(〜の)展覧[展示]会(of 〜)　❷(〜の)展示(of 〜)

☐ 0066
coverage
/kʌ́vərɪdʒ/
Part 4

名 ❶**保険保護[担保]**；補償範囲　❷報道
名 cover：❶カバー　❷保険
動 cover：❶(費用など)を賄う、相殺する　❷〜に保険をかける　❸〜を取材する　❹〜に(…を)かぶせる(with ...)

☐ 0067
atmosphere
/ǽtməsfìər/
❶アクセント注意
Part 7

名 ❶**雰囲気**　❷大気
形 atmospheric：❶大気の　❷雰囲気を感じさせる

☐ 0068
currency
/kə́ːrənsi/
ビジネス問題

名 通貨、貨幣
名 current：❶(川などの)流れ　❷電流
形 current：現在の、今の
副 currently：現在は、現在のところ

☐ 0069
recession
/riséʃən/
ビジネス問題

名 景気後退、一時的不景気　❶depressionは「(長期の)不景気」
名 recess：休み；休憩、休会、休廷
動 recess：〜を休憩[休会]にする
動 recede：退く；遠ざかる

☐ 0070
certificate
/sərtífikət/
Part 7

名 ❶**証明書**　❷(課程の)修了証；免許状
動 (/sərtífikèit/)〜に証明書[免状]を与える
動 certify：❶〜を証明[保証]する　❷〜に証明書[免許状]を与える

☐ 0071
conference
/kánfərəns/
Part 2, 3

名 (通例年1回開催の)**会議**(≒convention)
動 confer：(〜と／…について)話し合う、協議する(with 〜/about [on] ...)

☐ 0072
administration
/ædmìnəstréiʃən/
ビジネス問題

名 ❶**管理**、経営　❷行政；(しばしばthe A〜)政府、内閣
動 administer：❶〜を管理[運営]する　❷〜を治める　❸(処罰など)を執行する
形 administrative：❶管理の、経営上の　❷行政上の

continued
▼

Quick Reviewは使ってる？ 昨日覚えた単語でも、記憶に残っているとは限らない。学習の合間に軽くチェックするだけでも効果は抜群！

- □ 聞くだけモード　Check 1
- □ しっかりモード　Check 1 ▶ 2
- □ かんぺきモード　Check 1 ▶ 2 ▶ 3

Check 2　　Phrase

- □ a sculpture exhibit(彫刻の展示品)

- □ insurance coverage(保険の補償範囲)
- □ election coverage(選挙報道)

- □ a relaxing atmosphere(くつろいだ雰囲気)
- □ the atmosphere on Mars(火星の大気)

- □ paper currency(紙幣)
- □ foreign currency(外貨)

- □ the recession of the 1990s(1990年代の景気後退)
- □ in recession(不況で)

- □ a birth [marriage] certificate(出生[結婚]証明書)
- □ a teaching certificate(教員免許状)

- □ have [hold] a conference(会議を開く)
- □ an international conference(国際会議)

- □ business administration(企業経営)
- □ the Obama administration(オバマ政権)

Check 3　　Sentence

- □ The exhibits are arranged on the table.(展示品が机に並べられている)

- □ Millions of people have no health-care coverage in the US.(アメリカでは数百万人の人々が医療保険に入っていない)

- □ Indirect lighting creates a romantic atmosphere.(間接照明はロマンチックな雰囲気を生み出す)

- □ The local currency in Thailand is the baht.(タイの国内通貨はバーツだ)

- □ The world economy is going into a recession.(世界経済は景気後退へと向かっている)

- □ You need to submit a medical certificate to your supervisor to take long sick leave.(長期の病気休暇を取るには、診断書を上司に提出する必要がある)

- □ Who will attend the conference next week?(来週の会議には誰が出席するのですか?)

- □ He has 30 years' extensive experience in administration.(彼には30年にわたる幅広い管理の経験がある)

continued ▼

Day 5

Check 1 Listen))) CD-A5

0073 machinery /məʃíːnəri/ ❶発音注意 Part 7
名 (集合的に) **機械** (類) ➕個々の「機械」はmachine

0074 emergency /imə́ːrdʒənsi/ Part 4
名 **緊急**[非常]**事態**、緊急[非常]の場合
動emerge: ❶(〜から)現れる(from 〜) ❷(事実などが)明らかになる

0075 delivery /dilívəri/ Part 2, 3
名 **配達**
動deliver: ❶〜を(…に)配達する(to . . .) ❷(意見など)を述べる、(講演など)をする

0076 reputation /rèpjutéiʃən/ Part 7
名 ❶(〜という／…としての)**評判** (for 〜/as . . .) ❷名声(≒fame)
形reputable: 評判のよい、尊敬すべき

0077 comparison /kəmpǽrisn/ Part 2, 3
名 (〜との)**比較** (with [to] 〜)
動compare: (compare A to [with] Bで)❶AをBと比較する ❷AをBに例える
形comparable: ❶(〜と)類似[同種]の(with [to] 〜) ❷(〜と)比較に値する、同等の(with [to] 〜)

0078 session /séʃən/ Part 7
名 ❶**会合**、会議 ❷(議会の)会期 ❸学期(≒term)

0079 recognition /rèkəgníʃən/ Part 5, 6
名 ❶(〜という)**認識**、評価(that節 〜) ❷承認、認可
動recognize: ❶〜を見分ける、識別する ❷(recognize A as Bで)AをBだと認める

0080 convention /kənvénʃən/ Part 2, 3
名 ❶**代表者会議**[大会](≒conference) ❷慣習、慣例
形conventional: ❶従来の、慣例[慣習]の ❷月並みな、平凡な

Day 4))) CD-A4
Quick Review
答えは右ページ下

- ☐ 欠陥
- ☐ 熱意
- ☐ 重役
- ☐ 輸送
- ☐ 好意
- ☐ 場所
- ☐ 規則
- ☐ 代理人
- ☐ 予防策
- ☐ 予算
- ☐ 目標
- ☐ 見積もり
- ☐ 施設
- ☐ 資産
- ☐ 状況
- ☐ 兆候

Check 2　Phrase

- a piece of machinery(1台の機械)
- agricultural machinery(農業機械)

- emergency surgery(緊急手術)
- an emergency exit(非常口)

- mail deliveries(郵便配達)
- cash on delivery(代金着払い) ⊕略はCOD

- a good [bad] reputation(好評[悪評])
- earn [gain, win] a reputation(名声を得る)

- in comparison to [with] 〜(〜と比べると)
- by [for] comparison(比べると[比較のために])

- a morning session(朝会)
- in [out of] session([会議などが]開会[閉会]中で)

- beyond [out of] recognition(見分けがつかないほど)
- give [pay] recognition to 〜(〜を認める)

- an annual convention(年次大会)
- by convention(慣例に従って)

Check 3　Sentence

- New machinery will improve the company's productivity.(新しい機器はその会社の生産性を向上させるだろう)

- Dial 911 for emergency cases only.(緊急の場合のみ、911に電話してください) ⊕911は警察・救急車・消防署を呼び出すためのアメリカの緊急電話番号

- The department store offers free delivery.(そのデパートでは無料配達を行っている)

- He has a reputation for being strict.(彼は厳しいという評判だ)

- In comparison to his other novels, this one is not so interesting.(彼のほかの小説と比べると、この小説はそれほど面白くない)

- We will have a planning session tomorrow.(私たちは明日、企画会議を開く予定だ)

- He gained recognition as an artist after his death.(彼は死後に芸術家として認められた)

- The Democratic Party convention will be held in Chicago next month.(来月、民主党の党大会がシカゴで開催される)

Day 4))CD-A4
Quick Review
答えは左ページ下

- defect
- enthusiasm
- executive
- transportation
- courtesy
- site
- code
- substitute
- precaution
- budget
- objective
- estimate
- facility
- asset
- circumstance
- symptom

Day 6 名詞6

Check 1 Listen 》CD-A6

0081 household
/háushòuld/
Part 7

名 **世帯**、家庭；(集合的に)家族
形 家庭用の；家族[家庭]の

0082 quantity
/kwάntəti/
ビジネス問題

名 ❶**数量**、分量(⇔quality：質) ❷多量、多数
形 quantitative：量的な、量の

0083 replacement
/ripléismənt/
Part 5, 6

名 (〜の)**後任**[後継]**者**；取り換え品(for 〜)
動 replace：❶〜を(…と)取り換える(with …) ❷(…として)〜に取って代わる、〜の後任になる(as …)

0084 associate
/əsóuʃiət/
ビジネス問題

名 **同僚**、仲間(≒colleague, coworker)
動 (/əsóuʃièit/)(associate A with Bで)❶AをBに関連づける ❷AをBと結びつけて考える
名 association：❶(共通の目的のための)協会、団体 ❷(〜との)提携、つき合い(with 〜)

0085 remark
/rimάːrk/
Part 5, 6

名 (〜についての)**見解**、発言、所見、感想(about [on] 〜)
動 〜と述べる、言う
形 remarkable：(〜で)注目すべき、顕著な(for 〜)

0086 conclusion
/kənklúːʒən/
Part 5, 6

名 ❶(〜という)**結論**(that節 〜) ❷結末(≒end)(⇔beginning)
動 conclude：❶〜と結論する ❷〜を(…で)終了させる(with …)
形 conclusive：(証拠などが)決定的な

0087 resident
/rézədənt/
Part 2, 3

名 **居住者**、在住者(≒inhabitant)(⇔visitor)
形 居住[在住]している
名 residence：❶居住、滞在 ❷邸宅、住宅
形 residential：住宅[居住]の

0088 dependent
/dipéndənt/
❶定義注意
Part 7

名 **扶養家族**、被扶養者
形 (be dependent onで)❶〜に頼っている(⇔be independent of) ❷〜によって決まる、〜次第である
名 dependence：(〜への)依存(状態)(on [upon] 〜)

continued
▼

名詞と前置詞の結びつきを確認してる？ a replacement for ～(～の後任者)のように名詞の後ろにつく前置詞にも注意していこう。

☐ 聞くだけモード　Check 1
☐ しっかりモード　Check 1 ▶ 2
☐ かんぺきモード　Check 1 ▶ 2 ▶ 3

Check 2　Phrase

☐ a general household (一般世帯)
☐ the head of household (世帯主)

☐ quantity of purchase (購買数)
☐ in quantity (大量[多量]に)

☐ a replacement for the secretary (その秘書の後任者)
☐ ship a replacement (取り換え品を送る)

☐ a business associate (仕事仲間)

☐ remarks on global warming (地球温暖化についての所見)
☐ make a remark about ～(～について見解を述べる)

☐ come to the conclusion that ～(～という結論に達する)
☐ in conclusion (結論として、終わりに臨んで)

☐ a resident of Australia (オーストラリア在住者)

☐ provide for one's dependents (扶養家族を養う)

Check 3　Sentence

☐ Most households have at least one computer. (ほとんどの世帯には少なくとも1台コンピューターがある)

☐ The price varies depending on the quantity you order. (価格は注文する数によって変わる)

☐ The company has to find Mr. White's replacement as CEO. (その会社はホワイト氏の後継者のCEOを見つけなければならない)

☐ I know Mr. Harrison as an associate, but not a close friend. (私はハリソン氏を同僚として知ってはいるが、親友ではない)

☐ The foreign minister apologized for his remarks about race. (その外務大臣は人種に関する発言を謝罪した)

☐ They couldn't come to any conclusion at the meeting. (彼らは会議で何も結論に達することができなかった)

☐ The residents of the city protested the closure of the city hospital. (その市の住民は市立病院の閉鎖に抗議した)

☐ How many dependents do you have? (扶養家族は何人いますか?)

continued
▼

Day 6

Check 1　Listen)) CD-A6

0089 luxury /lʌ́kʃəri/
❶発音注意
Part 5, 6
- 名❶**ぜいたくさ**、豪華さ、快適さ；(形容詞的に)ぜいたく[豪華]な　❷ぜいたく品(⇔essential：必需品)
- 形luxurious：豪華な、ぜいたくな

0090 welfare /wélfèər/
Part 2, 3
- 名❶**福祉**、福利(≒well-being)　❷生活保護(≒social security)

0091 anniversary /ænəvə́ːrsəri/
Part 4
- 名(〜の)**記念日**(of 〜)

0092 landscape /lǽndskèip/
Part 1
- 名❶**風景**、景色(≒view, outlook, scenery, sight)　❷風景画
- 動〜を造園する

0093 sacrifice /sǽkrəfàis/
Part 7
- 名❶(〜のための)**犠牲**(for 〜)　❷いけにえ
- 動〜を(…のために)犠牲にする(for …)

0094 component /kəmpóunənt/
Part 4
- 名(車などの)**部品**；構成要素

0095 physician /fizíʃən/
Part 5, 6
- 名**医者**(≒doctor)；内科医　➕「外科医」はsurgeon
- 名physical：身体[健康]検査
- 形physical：❶身体[肉体]の　❷物質[物理]的な

0096 commission /kəmíʃən/
❶定義注意
ビジネス問題
- 名❶(代理業務に対する)**手数料**、歩合(on 〜)　❷(任務の)委任、委託　❸(集合的に)委員会
- 動〜を依頼する
- 名commitment：❶約束、誓約　❷(〜への)献身(to 〜)
- 動commit：(commit A to Bで)AをBに委託する

Day 5)) CD-A5
Quick Review
答えは右ページ下

- ☐ 展示品
- ☐ 保険保護
- ☐ 雰囲気
- ☐ 通貨
- ☐ 景気後退
- ☐ 証明書
- ☐ 会議
- ☐ 管理
- ☐ 機械
- ☐ 緊急事態
- ☐ 配達
- ☐ 評判
- ☐ 比較
- ☐ 会合
- ☐ 認識
- ☐ 代表者会議

Check 2　Phrase

- □ live in luxury（ぜいたくに暮らす）
- □ a luxury like a large wide-screen TV（大型ワイドスクリーン・テレビのようなぜいたく品）

- □ welfare reform（福祉改革）
- □ live on welfare（生活保護を受けて暮らす）

- □ the 100th anniversary of the revolution（革命100周年記念日）

- □ a rural landscape（田舎の風景）

- □ at the sacrifice of ~（~を犠牲にして）
- □ human sacrifice（人身御供）⊕人間を神へのいけにえとすること

- □ computer components（コンピューターの部品）
- □ an essential component of a healthy lifestyle（健康的な生活に不可欠の要素）

- □ consult a physician（医者に診てもらう）

- □ sell cars on commission（歩合で車を売る）
- □ get a commission to do ~（~する委託を受ける）

Check 3　Sentence

- □ In that country, a few enjoy luxury while many others suffer poverty.（その国では少数の人々がぜいたくを享受する一方、ほかの多くの人々は貧困にあえいでいる）

- □ Many people are concerned about the welfare of their country.（多くの人々が自国の福祉を心配している）

- □ We celebrated our 10th wedding anniversary yesterday.（私たちは昨日、私たちの結婚10周年の記念日を祝った）

- □ The man is taking a picture of the landscape.（男性は景色の写真を撮っている）

- □ She made many sacrifices to send her son to college.（彼女は息子を大学に行かせるために多くを犠牲にした）

- □ The factory manufactures electrical components for cars.（その工場は車用の電気部品を製造している）

- □ She is a physician by profession.（彼女の職業は医者だ）

- □ He gets a 25 percent commission on his sales.（彼は売り上げの25パーセントを手数料としてもらっている）

Day 5　)) CD-A5
Quick Review
答えは左ページ下

- □ exhibit
- □ coverage
- □ atmosphere
- □ currency
- □ recession
- □ certificate
- □ conference
- □ administration
- □ machinery
- □ emergency
- □ delivery
- □ reputation
- □ comparison
- □ session
- □ recognition
- □ convention

Day 7　名詞7

Check 1　Listen 》CD-A7

□ 0097
burden
/bə́ːrdn/
Part 4

名 ❶(精神的な)**重荷**、負担　❷荷物(≒load)
動 (burden A with Bで)AにB(重荷など)を負わせる

□ 0098
reduction
/ridʌ́kʃən/
Part 4

名 **削減**；減少(≒decrease)
動 reduce：~を減らす、減少させる

□ 0099
source
/sɔ́ːrs/
Part 5, 6

名 ❶**源**　❷原因(≒cause)

□ 0100
estate
/istéit/
ビジネス問題

名 ❶**財産**(≒property, asset)　❷地所

□ 0101
contribution
/kɑ̀ntrəbjúːʃən/
Part 5, 6

名 ❶(~への)**貢献**、寄与(to [toward] ~)　❷(~への)寄付(金)(to [toward] ~)(≒donation)
動 contribute：❶(contribute A to [toward] Bで)AをBに寄付する　❷(contribute toで)~に貢献[寄与]する

□ 0102
achievement
/ətʃíːvmənt/
Part 7

名 ❶**業績**(≒accomplishment)　❷達成
動 achieve：(目的など)を達成する、成し遂げる

□ 0103
competitor
/kəmpétətər/
ビジネス問題

名 **競争相手**、競合他社
名 competition：(~を目指す/…同士の)競争、争い(for ~/between [among] …)
動 compete：(~と)競争する、張り合う(with ~)
形 competitive：❶競争力のある　❷競争の

□ 0104
occupation
/ɑ̀kjupéiʃən/
Part 2, 3

名 ❶**職業**、仕事(≒job, profession, employment)　❷(土地・家屋などの)占有；占拠(of ~)
動 occupy：❶(場所など)を占める、占有する　❷(be occupied withで)~に従事している、~で忙しい

continued
▼

今日で『キクタンTOEIC Test Score 800』は1週間が終了！ 残りはまだまだ長いけど、急がず焦らず学習を進めていこう。

- ☐ 聞くだけモード　Check 1
- ☐ しっかりモード　Check 1 ▶ 2
- ☐ かんぺきモード　Check 1 ▶ 2 ▶ 3

Check 2　Phrase

☐ the burden of responsibility（責任の重荷）
☐ a heavy burden（重い荷物）

☐ tax reduction（減税）
☐ a reduction in gasoline prices（ガソリン価格の引き下げ）

☐ a source of energy [information]（エネルギー[情報]源）
☐ the source of the problem（その問題の原因）

☐ real estate（不動産）
☐ a housing estate（住宅団地）

☐ make a contribution to ~（~に貢献する）
☐ contributions to charities（慈善団体への寄付金）

☐ a remarkable achievement（注目すべき業績）
☐ a sense of achievement（達成感）

☐ a business competitor（商売敵）

☐ a dangerous occupation（危険な仕事）
☐ the US occupation of Iraq（アメリカのイラク占領）

Check 3　Sentence

☐ The mortgage is a heavy financial burden on the family.（住宅ローンはその家族の大きな金銭的重荷になっている）

☐ The staff reductions will save over $2 million.（人員削減によって200万ドル以上が節約されるだろう）

☐ Fruit is a very good source of vitamin C.（果物は非常に優れたビタミンC源だ）

☐ He left his entire estate to his only daughter.（彼は全財産を一人娘に残した）

☐ She made a major contribution to the project.（彼女はそのプロジェクトに大きく貢献した）

☐ You should highlight your achievements and skills in your résumé.（あなたは自分の業績と技能を履歴書の中で強調したほうがいい）

☐ The company is trying to gain more market share from its competitors.（その会社は競合会社からより多くの市場占有率を取ろうと努力している）

☐ What is your current occupation?（あなたの現在の職業は何ですか？）

continued ▼

Day 7

Check 1　Listen)) CD-A7

0105
region
/ríːdʒən/
Part 4

名 **地域**、地方 (≒ area, district)
形 regional：地域の、地方の

0106
exhibition
/èksəbíʃən/
❶発音注意
Part 4

名 ❶(～の) **展覧[展示]会** (of ～)　❷(～の)展示 (of ～)
名 exhibit：展示[陳列]品
動 exhibit：❶～を展示する　❷～を(感情などに)表す

0107
advertisement
/ædvərtáizmənt/
❶発音注意
ビジネス問題

名 **広告**、宣伝　❶略語のadもよく用いられる
名 advertising：❶(集合的に)広告　❷広告業
形 advertising：広告の
動 advertise：❶～を宣伝[広告]する　❷(～を求める)広告を出す (for ～)

0108
portion
/pɔ́ːrʃən/
Part 5, 6

名 ❶(～の) **一部**、部分 (of ～) (≒ part)　❷(食べ物の)1人前 (of ～) (≒ share)

0109
status
/stéitəs/
Part 2, 3

名 ❶ **状態**、状況 (≒ state, condition, situation)　❷地位、身分 (≒ position)

0110
aspect
/æspekt/
Part 7

名 (問題・事態などの) **側面**、局面、状況

0111
compromise
/kámprəmàiz/
❶アクセント注意
ビジネス問題

名 **妥協**、歩み寄り
動 (～のことで／…と)妥協する (on ～/with ...)

0112
deadline
/dédlàin/
Part 2, 3

名 (～の) **締め切り** (時間)、最終期限 (for ～)

Day 6)) CD-A6
Quick Review
答えは右ページ下

- □ 世帯
- □ 数量
- □ 後任者
- □ 同僚
- □ 見解
- □ 結論
- □ 居住者
- □ 扶養家族
- □ ぜいたくさ
- □ 福祉
- □ 記念日
- □ 風景
- □ 犠牲
- □ 部品
- □ 医者
- □ 手数料

Check 2　Phrase

- desert [mountain] regions（砂漠［山岳］地域）

- an exhibition of Picasso's paintings（ピカソの絵画の展覧会）
- on exhibition（展示［公開］されて）

- put an advertisement in ~（~に広告を出す）
- a television advertisement for a new car（新車のテレビ宣伝）

- the first portion of the movie（その映画の最初の部分）
- four portions of chips（4人前のチップス）

- the future status of the world（将来の世界情勢）
- social status（社会的地位）

- various aspects of the problem（その問題のさまざまな側面）

- reach a compromise with ~（~と妥協に至る）
- a compromise between management and a union（経営陣と組合間の歩み寄り）

- meet [miss] the deadline（締め切りに間に合う［遅れる］）

Check 3　Sentence

- Emergency supplies were sent to the disaster-stricken region.（緊急物資がその被災地域に送られた）

- There will be an exhibition of medieval art at the city gallery next month.（来月、中世芸術の展覧会が市立美術館で開催される）

- I regularly check job advertisements in newspapers.（私は定期的に新聞の求人広告を調べている）

- A large portion of the workforce in the country is made up of immigrants.（その国の労働力の大部分は移民で構成されている）

- He didn't comment on the status of negotiations.（彼は交渉状況についてコメントしなかった）

- You need to study all aspects of business to get an MBA.（MBA［経営管理学修士号］を取得するためには、ビジネスのあらゆる側面を学ぶ必要がある）

- There will be no compromise with terrorism.（テロとの妥協はあり得ない）

- What is the deadline for submission of application forms?（申込用紙の提出期限はいつですか？）

Day 6　)) CD-A6
Quick Review
答えは左ページ下

- household
- quantity
- replacement
- associate
- remark
- conclusion
- resident
- dependent
- luxury
- welfare
- anniversary
- landscape
- sacrifice
- component
- physician
- commission

CHAPTER 1
CHAPTER 2
CHAPTER 3
CHAPTER 4
CHAPTER 5
CHAPTER 6
CHAPTER 7
CHAPTER 8
CHAPTER 9
CHAPTER 10

Day 8　名詞8

Check 1　Listen 》CD-A8

□ 0113
overhead
/óuvərhèd/
❶定義注意
ビジネス問題

名**諸経費**、間接費　●光熱費・賃貸料・税金・一般管理費などの経費をまとめたもの。overhead costs [expenses]とも言う
形❶諸経費の、包括的な　❷頭上の

□ 0114
spectator
/spékteitər/
Part 1

名(スポーツなどの)**観客**、見物人　●映画・コンサートなどの「観客」はaudience

□ 0115
expansion
/ikspǽnʃən/
Part 5, 6

名**拡大**、拡張
動expand：❶～を拡大[拡張]する　❷拡大[拡張]する

□ 0116
clue
/klúː/
Part 2, 3

名(難問などの)**手がかり**、糸口(to [about, as to] ～)

□ 0117
allowance
/əláuəns/
❶発音注意
Part 2, 3

名❶**手当**、支給額；お小遣い　❷割当量
動allow：❶～を許す　❷(allow A to doで)Aに～することを許す

□ 0118
reservation
/rèzərvéiʃən/
Part 2, 3

名❶(ホテルなどの)**予約**(≒booking)　❷(野生動物の)保護区
名reserve：❶(～の)蓄え(of ～)　❷遠慮
動reserve：❶～を予約する　❷(reserve A for Bで)AをBのために取っておく

□ 0119
headquarters
/hédkwɔ̀ːrtərz/
ビジネス問題

名**本社**(≒head office)(⇔branch：支店)；本部、本署　●略語はHQ

□ 0120
flu
/flúː/
Part 7

名**インフルエンザ**　●influenzaの短縮形

continued

同意語・類義語(≒)や反意語・反対語(⇔)もチェックしてる？ 余裕があれば確認して、語彙の数を積極的に増やしていこう

- ☐ 聞くだけモード　Check 1
- ☐ しっかりモード　Check 1 ▶ 2
- ☐ かんぺきモード　Check 1 ▶ 2 ▶ 3

Check 2　Phrase

☐ lower overhead and increase yields(諸費を抑えて収益を上げる)

☐ cheering spectators(声援を送っている観客たち)

☐ the expansion of the Internet(インターネットの拡大)
☐ the expansion of the freeway(高速道路の拡張)

☐ look for [find] clues(手がかりを探す[見つける])
☐ clues to the crime(その犯罪の手がかり)

☐ housing allowance(住宅手当)
☐ provide an allowance of time for ～(～に時間を充てる)

☐ make a hotel reservation(ホテルの予約をする)
☐ a wildlife reservation(野生生物保護区)

☐ the headquarters of Toyota(トヨタ社の本社)

☐ catch [get] (the) flu(インフルエンザにかかる)
☐ a flu shot(インフルエンザの予防接種)

Check 3　Sentence

☐ We should reduce our overhead.(私たちは諸経費を減らしたほうがいい)

☐ There are a lot of spectators in the stadium.(スタジアムには多くの観客がいる)

☐ Our boss is always talking about business expansion.(私たちの上司はいつも事業の拡大のことを話している)

☐ Police are searching for clues in the search for the missing boy.(警察は行方不明の少年の捜査における手がかりを探している)

☐ Does the salary include a family allowance?(その給料には家族手当は含まれていますか？)

☐ Have you confirmed your flight reservation?(飛行機の予約の確認はしましたか？)

☐ The company's headquarters is located in Osaka.(その会社の本社は大阪にある)

☐ She is at home with the flu.(彼女はインフルエンザにかかって家にいる)

CHAPTER 2
CHAPTER 3
CHAPTER 4
CHAPTER 5
CHAPTER 6
CHAPTER 7
CHAPTER 8
CHAPTER 9
CHAPTER 10

continued
▼

Day 8

Check 1 Listen 》CD-A8

0121 accommodation
/əkɑ̀mədéiʃən/
Part 5, 6

名 (通例～s) **宿泊設備**
動 accommodate: ❶(建物などが)(人)を収容できる ❷(要求など)を受け入れる

0122 critic
/krítik/
Part 5, 6

名 **評論**[批評]**家**(≒reviewer)
名 criticism: 批評、評論
動 criticize: ❶～のあら探しをする ❷～を批評[評論]する
形 critical: ❶重大な ❷批判[批評]的な

0123 remedy
/rémədi/
Part 7

名 ❶(～の)**改善法**、救済策(for ～) ❷(病気の)治療(法)(for ～)(≒cure)

0124 attendant
/əténdənt/
Part 4

名 ❶**店員**、接客[案内]係(≒clerk) ❷従者
形 ❶(～に)付随する(on ～) ❷つき添いの
名 attendance: ❶出席 ❷出席者数
動 attend: ❶～に出席する ❷(attend toで)～を処理する;～の世話をする;～に注意を払う

0125 endeavor
/indévər/
Part 7

名 (～しようとする)**努力**、試み(to do)(≒effort, attempt)
動 (endeavor to doで)～しようと努力する(≒try to do, attempt to do)

0126 identification
/aidèntifəkéiʃən/
Part 2, 3

名 **身分証明書**;身元確認 ⊕略語はID
名 identity: ❶身元、正体 ❷同一性、アイデンティティー
動 identify: ❶～が誰[何]であるか分かる ❷(identify A as Bで)AをBであると確認[認定、特定]する

0127 patent
/pǽtnt/
ビジネス問題

名 (～の)**特許**(権)(on [for] ～)
動 ～の特許権を取る
形 ❶特許の、特許を受けた ❷明白な(≒obvious)

0128 inquiry
/inkwáiəri/
Part 4

名 ❶(～についての)**問い合わせ**、質問(about ～)(≒question) ❷(事件などの)調査(into ～)(≒investigation)
動 inquire: (inquire aboutで)～について尋ねる、問い合わせる

| Day 7 》CD-A7
Quick Review
答えは右ページ下 | ☐ 重荷
☐ 削減
☐ 源
☐ 財産 | ☐ 貢献
☐ 業績
☐ 競争相手
☐ 職業 | ☐ 地域
☐ 展覧会
☐ 広告
☐ 一部 | ☐ 状態
☐ 側面
☐ 妥協
☐ 締め切り |

Check 2 Phrase

- cheap accommodation(安い宿泊施設)

- a food [film] critic(料理[映画]評論家)

- a remedy for the recession(景気後退の改善策)
- a home remedy(家庭治療法)

- a flight [gas station] attendant(客室乗務員[ガソリンスタンドの店員])
- a king's attendant(王の従者)

- in spite of one's best endeavors(最大限の努力にもかかわらず)

- carry identification at all times(常に身分証明書を携行する)
- the identification of the suspect(容疑者の身元確認)

- take out [file] a patent on the invention(その発明の特許を取る[申請する])

- make inquiries about flights(飛行機の便について問い合わせる)
- an inquiry into the fraud(その詐欺事件の調査)

Check 3 Sentence

- The hotel has accommodations for 500 guests.(そのホテルは500人の客が宿泊できる)

- The movie was favorably received by the critics.(その映画は評論家たちに好意的に受け止められた)

- The best remedy for unemployment would be big public works.(失業の最高の改善策は大規模な公共事業かもしれない)

- There is a guided tour of the gallery by our attendant.(当館の案内係による美術館のガイドつき見学がある)

- We have to make our best endeavor to preserve the environment.(私たちは自然環境を守るために最善の努力をしなければならない)

- You will be asked to show some identification to enter the building.(そのビルに入るには、何か身分証明書を見せるよう求められるだろう)

- The patent on the drug will run out in 2015.(その薬の特許は2015年に無効になる)

- For further inquiries, please contact us at 03-3323-12XX.(ほかにご質問がありましたら、03-3323-12XXまでご連絡ください)

Day 7)) CD-A7
Quick Review
答えは左ページ下

- burden
- reduction
- source
- estate
- contribution
- achievement
- competitor
- occupation
- region
- exhibition
- advertisement
- portion
- status
- aspect
- compromise
- deadline

CHAPTER 1
CHAPTER 2
CHAPTER 3
CHAPTER 4
CHAPTER 5
CHAPTER 6
CHAPTER 7
CHAPTER 8
CHAPTER 9
CHAPTER 10

Day 9　名詞9

Check 1　Listen ») CD-A9

☐ 0129
accounting
/əkáuntiŋ/
ビジネス問題

名**会計**(学)、経理
名account：❶(銀行)口座　❷(金銭の)計算書
動account：(account forで)❶(ある割合)を占める　❷～(の原因・理由)を説明する
名accountant：会計士

☐ 0130
inspection
/inspékʃən/
Part 5, 6

名**視察**、調査、監査(≒examination, scrutiny)
名inspector：調査[検査]官
動inspect：～を検査[調査]する

☐ 0131
deficit
/défəsit/
ビジネス問題

名**赤字**、不足額(⇔surplus)

☐ 0132
statistics
/stətístiks/
Part 2, 3

名**統計**；統計学
名statistician：統計学者
形statistical：統計(上)の

☐ 0133
innovation
/ìnəvéiʃən/
Part 5, 6

名**革新**、刷新；斬新な考え
動innovate：刷新[革新]する
形innovative：革新的な；創意に富んだ

☐ 0134
skyscraper
/skáiskrèipər/
Part 1

名**超高層ビル**、摩天楼

☐ 0135
excursion
/ikskə́ːrʒən/
❶発音注意
Part 7

名(～への)**遠足**、小旅行(to ～)(≒trip)

☐ 0136
participant
/pɑːrtísəpənt/
Part 4

名(～の)**参加者**、当事者(in ～)
名participation：(～への)参加、加入(in ～)
動participate：(participate inで)～に参加する

continued
▼

単語上のチェックボックスを使ってる？ 確実に押さえた単語にはチェックマーク、自信のないものには？マークなどをつけて復習に役立てよう。

☐ 聞くだけモード　Check 1
☐ しっかりモード　Check 1 ▶ 2
☐ かんぺきモード　Check 1 ▶ 2 ▶ 3

Check 2　Phrase

☐ major in accounting（会計学を専攻する）

☐ an inspection of the nuclear plant（原子力発電所の視察）

☐ a trade deficit of $750 million（7億5000万ドルの貿易赤字）

☐ crime [demographic] statistics（犯罪[人口]統計）

☐ technological innovation（技術革新）

☐ a 100-story skyscraper（100階建ての超高層ビル）

☐ go on an excursion（遠足に行く）

☐ participants in the marathon（そのマラソンの参加者）

Check 3　Sentence

☐ She has a good working knowledge of accounting.（彼女は実用的な会計知識を十分に身につけている）

☐ The officials made a safety inspection of the building.（当局はそのビルの安全調査を行った）

☐ The company went bankrupt with a deficit of approximately $2 million.（その会社は約200万ドルの赤字を抱えて倒産した）

☐ Statistics show that unemployment rates increased significantly over the past two months.（統計では、この2カ月で失業率が著しく上昇したことが明らかになっている）

☐ Creativity and innovation are key to business success.（創造性と革新が事業の成功にとって重要だ）

☐ Two skyscrapers are being built side by side.（2つの超高層ビルが並んで建設されている）

☐ There will be a whole school excursion on April 8.（4月8日に全校遠足が行われる予定だ）

☐ There were over 100 participants in the speech contest.（そのスピーチコンテストには100名以上の参加者がいた）

continued ▼

Day 9

Check 1　Listen 》CD-A9

□ 0137
ingredient
/ingríːdiənt/
Part 5, 6

名 (料理などの)**材料**；成分、要素

□ 0138
pension
/pénʃən/
❶定義注意
ビジネス問題

名**年金**
名 pensioner：年金受給者

□ 0139
consequence
/kánsəkwèns/
❶アクセント注意
Part 5, 6

名 (通例〜s)(〜の)**結果**、影響(of 〜)(≒result, outcome, effect)
形 consequent：(〜の)結果として起こる(on [upon, to] 〜)
副 consequently：その結果、従って

□ 0140
yield
/jíːld/
ビジネス問題

名 ❶**収益**、利回り(≒profit)　❷産出[収穫]高
動 ❶(結果など)をもたらす　❷〜を産出する　❸(yield toで)〜に屈する、負ける

□ 0141
reference
/réfərəns/
Part 4

名 ❶(〜への)**言及**(to 〜)(≒mention)　❷参照　❸(履歴書などの)推薦状
動 refer：❶(refer toで)〜を参照する；〜に言及する　❷(refer to A as Bで)AをBと呼ぶ、言う

□ 0142
extension
/iksténʃən/
Part 2, 3

名 ❶(電話の)**内線**　❷延期、延長　❸拡張、拡大
動 extend：❶〜を延長する　❷〜を拡張する
形 extensive：❶(調査などが)広範囲にわたる　❷(損害などが)大規模な、甚だしい
副 extensively：広範囲に、広く

□ 0143
era
/íərə/
Part 5, 6

名**時代**、年代(≒age, epoch)

□ 0144
strain
/stréin/
Part 5, 6

名**重圧**、負担、緊張
動 ❶(体)を無理をして痛める　❷〜を引っ張る

Day 8 》CD-A8
Quick Review
答えは右ページ下

□ 諸経費　□ 手当　□ 宿泊設備　□ 努力
□ 観客　□ 予約　□ 評論家　□ 身分証明書
□ 拡大　□ 本社　□ 改善法　□ 特許
□ 手がかり　□ インフルエンザ　□ 店員　□ 問い合わせ

Check 2　Phrase

- ☐ a list of ingredients（[食品などの]成分リスト）
- ☐ a vital ingredient of success（成功に不可欠な要素）

- ☐ live on a pension（年金で生活する）
- ☐ receive a pension（年金を受け取る）

- ☐ the consequences of the mismanagement（経営ミスの結果）
- ☐ as a consequence of ~（~の結果として）

- ☐ yields on preferred stocks（優先株の利回り）
- ☐ crop yields（作物の収穫高）

- ☐ with [in] reference to ~（~に関して）
- ☐ for future reference（今後の参考のために）

- ☐ an extension number（内線番号）
- ☐ the extension of the airport（空港の拡張）

- ☐ the Victorian [Meiji] era（ビクトリア[明治]時代）

- ☐ put a strain on ~（~に重圧[負担]をかける）

Check 3　Sentence

- ☐ The chef always uses the best and freshest ingredients.（そのシェフは最高品質で最も新鮮な材料を常に使っている）

- ☐ Mr. Yoshida draws a yearly pension of 3 million yen.（ヨシダさんは年間300万円の年金を受けている）

- ☐ You should take responsibility for the consequences of your actions.（あなたは自分が取った行動の結果の責任を取るべきだ）

- ☐ Investments with high yields are difficult to find.（収益[利回り]の高い投資は見つけるのが難しい）

- ☐ He made no reference to the project.（彼はそのプロジェクトに関して何も言及しなかった）

- ☐ I'd like extension 2426, please.（内線2426をお願いします）

- ☐ The world is entering a new era of globalization.（世界は国際化の新しい時代に入ろうとしている）

- ☐ She's been under a lot of strain recently.（彼女は最近、大きなストレスを感じている）

Day 8　CD-A8　Quick Review　答えは左ページ下

- ☐ overhead
- ☐ spectator
- ☐ expansion
- ☐ clue
- ☐ allowance
- ☐ reservation
- ☐ headquarters
- ☐ flu
- ☐ accommodation
- ☐ critic
- ☐ remedy
- ☐ attendant
- ☐ endeavor
- ☐ identification
- ☐ patent
- ☐ inquiry

CHAPTER 1
CHAPTER 2
CHAPTER 3
CHAPTER 4
CHAPTER 5
CHAPTER 6
CHAPTER 7
CHAPTER 8
CHAPTER 9
CHAPTER 10

Day 10　名詞10

Check 1　Listen 》CD-A10

□ 0145
association
/əsòusiéiʃən/
Part 4

名❶(共通の目的のための)**協会**、団体(≒organization)　❷(〜との)提携、つき合い(with 〜)
名associate：同僚、仲間
動associate：(associate A with Bで)❶AをBと関連づける　❷AをBと結びつけて考える

□ 0146
conflict
/kánflikt/
Part 5, 6

名❶(〜との／…の間の)**対立**、葛藤(with 〜/between . . .)(≒disagreement)　❷(〜との／…の間の)争い(with 〜/between . . .)
動(/kənflíkt/)(〜と)対立[矛盾]する(with 〜)(≒disagree)

□ 0147
identity
/aidéntəti/
Part 5, 6

名❶**身元**、正体　❷同一性、アイデンティティー
名identification：身分証明書；身元確認
動identify：❶〜が誰[何]であるか分かる　❷(identify A as Bで)AをBであると確認[認定、特定]する

□ 0148
pollution
/pəlúːʃən/
ビジネス問題

名**汚染**(≒contamination)；公害
動pollute：〜を(…で)汚染する(with . . .)

□ 0149
discipline
/dísəplin/
❶アクセント注意
Part 5, 6

名❶**規律**、しつけ　❷訓練
動❶〜を罰する(≒punish)　❷〜を訓練する(≒train)

□ 0150
satisfaction
/sætisfǽkʃən/
Part 5, 6

名**満足**、充足(⇔dissatisfaction：不満)
動satisfy：❶〜を満足させる　❷(必要など)を満たす　❸(be satisfied withで)〜に満足している
形satisfactory：(〜にとって)満足な；納得のいく(to [for] 〜)

□ 0151
reception
/risépʃən/
Part 2, 3

名❶**歓迎会**、宴会　❷受け入れること　❸(会社などの)受付、フロント
名receptionist：(会社・ホテルなどの)受付係
動receive：❶〜を(…から)受け取る(from . . .)　❷(意見など)を受け入れる

□ 0152
engagement
/ingéidʒmənt/
Part 7

名❶(〜との)**婚約**(to 〜)　❷(〜との)(面会などの)約束(with 〜)(≒appointment)
動engage：❶(be engaged inで)〜に従事[没頭]している　❷(be engaged toで)〜と婚約している

continued
▼

音と意味がつながるまでは「使える」ようになったとは言えない。チャンツの最初の「英語」部分で意味がすぐに浮かぶか試してみよう。

- □ 聞くだけモード　Check 1
- □ しっかりモード　Check 1 ▶ 2
- □ かんぺきモード　Check 1 ▶ 2 ▶ 3

Check 2　Phrase

- □ the National Education Association（[米国の]教育協会）
- □ in association with ~（~と提携して、~と共同で）

- □ conflict between labor and management（労使間の対立）
- □ bring A into conflict with B（AをBと対立させる）

- □ mistaken identity（人違い）
- □ identity crisis（同一性危機）➕青年期などに起こる精神的な苦悩の時期

- □ air pollution（大気汚染）
- □ noise pollution（騒音公害）

- □ school discipline（学校の規律）
- □ military discipline（軍隊の訓練；軍紀）

- □ get [obtain, derive] satisfaction from ~（~から満足を得る）
- □ job satisfaction（仕事のやりがい、仕事に対する満足）

- □ a wedding reception（結婚披露宴）
- □ receive a warm [cool] reception（温かく[冷たく]迎えられる）

- □ announce one's engagement（婚約を発表する）
- □ a previous [prior] engagement（先約）

Check 3　Sentence

- □ Myanmar is a member of ASEAN, the Association of Southeast Asian Nations.（ミャンマーはASEAN[東南アジア諸国連合]の加盟国だ）

- □ There was a lot of conflict between her and her mother.（彼女と彼女の母親との間には多くの葛藤があった）

- □ Police still don't know the identity of the victim.（警察はいまだに被害者の身元が分かっていない）

- □ The government is committed to tackling environmental pollution.（政府は環境汚染に対処することに力を注いでいる）

- □ Our school is very strict in discipline.（私たちの学校は規律に非常に厳しい）

- □ Our company aims at achieving customer satisfaction.（当社は顧客満足を得ることを目指している）

- □ There will be a reception for new students from 4 to 6 p.m. today in the gymnasium.（今日の午後4時から6時まで、体育館で新入生の歓迎会がある）

- □ Steve and Mary have broken off their engagement.（スティーブとメアリーは婚約を解消した）

continued
▼

Day 10

Check 1　Listen 》CD-A10

0153 athlete /ǽθliːt/
❶アクセント注意
Part 1

- 名 **運動選手**
- 名 athletics：運動競技
- 形 athletic：❶運動競技の　❷運動選手らしい

0154 resolution /rèzəlúːʃən/
Part 7

- 名 ❶**決議**(案)　❷(問題などの)解決(of [to] ～)　❸(～しようという)決意、決心(to do)(≒decision, determination)
- 動 resolve：❶(問題など)を解決する　❷(resolve to doで)～しようと決心[決意]する

0155 draft /drǽft/
Part 2, 3

- 名 ❶**草稿**、下書き　❷為替手形、小切手　❸すきま風

0156 decade /dékeid/
Part 5, 6

- 名 **10年間**

0157 acquaintance /əkwéintəns/
Part 2, 3

- 名 **知人**、知り合い　❶friendほど親密な関係ではない人に用いる
- 動 acquaint：❶(acquaint A with Bで)AにBを知らせる、熟知させる　❷(acquaint oneself withで)～に精通する、慣れる

0158 collapse /kəlǽps/
Part 5, 6

- 名 **崩壊**、倒壊
- 動 ❶(建物などが)崩壊する　❷(事業などが)つぶれる

0159 investigation /invèstəgéiʃən/
Part 2, 3

- 名 (～の)**調査**；捜査(into [of] ～)
- 名 investigator：調査員；(犯罪の)調査官
- 動 investigate：～を(詳細に)調査する、取り調べる

0160 suburb /sʌ́bəːrb/
Part 7

- 名 **郊外**；(the ～s)(集合的に)(大都市の)郊外(全体)、近郊(of ～)
- 形 suburban：郊外の

Day 9　》CD-A9　Quick Review
答えは右ページ下

☐ 会計　☐ 革新　☐ 材料　☐ 言及
☐ 視察　☐ 超高層ビル　☐ 年金　☐ 内線
☐ 赤字　☐ 遠足　☐ 結果　☐ 時代
☐ 統計　☐ 参加者　☐ 収益　☐ 重圧

Check 2 Phrase

- a professional athlete(プロの運動選手)

- approve [adopt] a resolution(決議案を承認[採択]する)
- a resolution of the conflict(紛争の解決)

- the first draft(第一草稿、最初の下書き)
- a bank draft(銀行為替手形)

- for two [three] decades(20[30]年間)

- a business acquaintance(仕事上の知人)
- make someone's acquaintance(〜と知り合いになる)

- the collapse of the building(そのビルの崩壊)
- the collapse of the Soviet Union(ソ連の崩壊)

- a thorough investigation(徹底的な調査)
- under investigation(調査中で)

- a suburb of London(ロンドン郊外)
- move to the suburbs(郊外に引っ越す)

Check 3 Sentence

- Some athletes are training on the track.(何人かの運動選手が陸上トラックで練習をしている)

- The UN passed a resolution to approve the use of force against Iraq.(国連はイラクに対する軍事力の行使を認める決議案を可決した)

- I asked my teacher to check the draft of my speech.(私はスピーチの草稿をチェックしてくれるよう先生に頼んだ)

- The world economy has dramatically changed over the past few decades.(ここ数十年の間に世界経済は劇的に変化した)

- David was introduced to his new girlfriend by a mutual acquaintance.(デビッドは彼の新しいガールフレンドを共通の知人に紹介された)

- Recent years have witnessed the collapse of many small businesses.(ここ数年、多くの中小企業の倒産が見られた)

- An investigation into the incident is under way.(その事件の捜査は進行中だ)

- They live in Long Island, a suburb of New York City.(彼らはニューヨーク市郊外のロングアイランドに住んでいる)

Day 9 CD-A9
Quick Review
答えは左ページ下

- accounting
- inspection
- deficit
- statistics
- innovation
- skyscraper
- excursion
- participant
- ingredient
- pension
- consequence
- yield
- reference
- extension
- era
- strain

Day 11　名詞11

Check 1　Listen 》CD-A11

☐ 0161
appetite
/ǽpətàit/
Part 2, 3

名❶**食欲**　❷(〜への)欲求(for 〜)(≒desire)

☐ 0162
output
/áutpùt/
ビジネス問題

名❶**生産高**(≒production)　❷(コンピューターの)出力(⇔input)
動〜を出力する

☐ 0163
excess
/iksés/
Part 7

名(〜の)**超過**(量)(of 〜)
形超過した、余分の(≒extra)
動exceed：❶〜を上回る、超える　❷〜の限界を超える
形excessive：過度の、極端な、法外な

☐ 0164
species
/spíːʃiːz/
Part 5, 6

名(生物の)**種**　+単複同形

☐ 0165
consideration
/kənsìdəréiʃən/
Part 2, 3

名❶**考慮**、考察　❷(〜に対する)思いやり(for 〜)
動consider：❶〜をよく考える、熟慮[熟考]する　❷(consider doingで)〜することをよく考える
形considerable：(数量などが)かなりの、相当な
形considerate：思いやりがある、理解がある

☐ 0166
characteristic
/kæ̀riktərístik/
Part 4

名(通例〜s)**特徴**、特性、特質
形❶典型[特徴]的な(≒typical)　❷(be characteristic ofで)〜に特有[特徴的]である(≒be typical of, be unique to, be peculiar to, be proper to)
名character：❶性格、個性　❷登場人物　❸文字

☐ 0167
sector
/séktər/
ビジネス問題

名(産業などの)**部門**、分野

☐ 0168
privilege
/prívəlidʒ/
Part 4

名**特権**、特典、名誉
動〜に(…する)特権を与える(to do)
形privileged：(〜する)特権[特典]を持つ(to do)；特権階級に属する

---

continued
▼

余裕があるときは、派生語・関連語も覚えておこう。そうすれば、1つの語彙から、2倍、3倍と語彙が増えていくよ！

- ☐ 聞くだけモード　Check 1
- ☐ しっかりモード　Check 1 ▶ 2
- ☐ かんぺきモード　Check 1 ▶ 2 ▶ 3

Check 2　Phrase

- ☐ lose one's appetite（食欲をなくす）
- ☐ an appetite for learning（学習欲）

- ☐ agricultural output（農業生産高）
- ☐ an output unit（出力装置）

- ☐ excess of debt（債務超過）
- ☐ to excess（過度に）

- ☐ *On the Origin of Species*（『種の起源』）⊕チャールズ・ダーウィン（1809-1882）の著書

- ☐ give serious [full] consideration to ~（~を真剣[十分]に考える）
- ☐ take ~ into consideration（~を考慮に入れる）

- ☐ physical characteristics（身体的特徴）

- ☐ the private [public] sector（民間[公共]部門）

- ☐ diplomatic privileges（外交特権）
- ☐ have the privilege of doing ~（~する特権[名誉]を与えられる）

Check 3　Sentence

- ☐ Some drugs cause a decrease in appetite.（食欲の低下を引き起こす薬もある）

- ☐ Most car companies plan to decrease their car output next year.（ほとんどの自動車会社は来年の自動車生産を減らすことを計画している）

- ☐ Deficit is defined as excess of expenditure over income.（赤字は収入に対する支出の超過と定義される）

- ☐ The giant panda is an endangered species.（ジャイアントパンダは絶滅危惧種だ）

- ☐ Her proposal is worthy of consideration.（彼女の提案は検討に値する）

- ☐ An important characteristic of good teachers is that they care about their students.（よい教師の重要な特徴は、彼らが生徒たちを気遣うということだ）

- ☐ The situation has become desperate in both the financial sector and the real economy.（状況は金融部門と実体経済の両方において絶望的になっている）

- ☐ Education should be a right, not a privilege.（教育は特権ではなく、権利であるべきだ）

continued
▼

Day 11

Check 1　Listen))) CD-A11

□ 0169
caution
/kɔ́:ʃən/
Part 5, 6

名 ❶**用心**、注意、警戒　❷警告(≒warning)
動 ❶(caution A about [against] B で)A に B を警告する　❷(caution A to do で)A に〜するよう忠告する
形 cautious：(be cautious about [of] で)〜に注意[用心]深い、慎重である

□ 0170
bond
/bάnd/
ビジネス問題

名 ❶**債券**、公債　❷(〜との／…との間の)きずな(with 〜/between . . .)
動 ❶(〜と)心のきずなを結ぶ(with [to] 〜)　❷結合する
名 bondage：奴隷の境遇

□ 0171
emphasis
/émfəsis/
❶アクセント注意
Part 5, 6

名 (〜の)**強調**、力説、重要視(on [upon] 〜)
動 emphasize：〜を強調[力説]する

□ 0172
investment
/invéstmənt/
ビジネス問題

名 (〜への)**投資**、出資(in 〜)
名 investor：投資家、投資者
動 invest：(invest A in B で)A(金など)を B に投資する

□ 0173
requirement
/rikwáiərmənt/
Part 4

名 (〜の)**必要条件**、資格(for 〜)
動 require：❶〜を必要とする　❷〜を要求する　❸(require A to do で)A に〜するよう要求する、命ずる

□ 0174
affection
/əfékʃən/
Part 5, 6

名 (〜に対する)**愛情**、愛着(for 〜)(≒love, attachment)
動 affect：〜に影響を及ぼす

□ 0175
alert
/ələ́:rt/
Part 5, 6

名 (警戒)**警報**(≒warning)；警戒態勢
動 〜に警報を出す
形 ❶(〜に)油断のない、用心深い(to 〜)　❷機敏な

□ 0176
depression
/dipréʃən/
ビジネス問題

名 ❶(長期の)**不景気**、不況　❶recession は「景気後退、一時的不景気」　❷うつ病
動 depress：❶〜を憂うつにさせる、意気消沈させる　❷(be depressed about [over] で)〜で憂うつになっている、意気消沈している　❸(市場など)を不景気にする

| Day 10))) CD-A10 **Quick Review** 答えは右ページ下 | □ 協会 □ 対立 □ 身元 □ 汚染 | □ 規律 □ 満足 □ 歓迎会 □ 婚約 | □ 運動選手 □ 決議 □ 草稿 □ 10年間 | □ 知人 □ 崩壊 □ 調査 □ 郊外 |

Check 2　Phrase

- ☐ exercise [use] caution（用心する）
- ☐ a word [note] of caution（注意書き；警告の言葉）

- ☐ government bonds（国債）
- ☐ a close bond between them（彼らの間の親密なきずな）

- ☐ put [place, lay] emphasis on ~（~を強調[重要視]する）

- ☐ a long-term [short-term] investment（長期[短期]投資）
- ☐ capital investment（資本投資）

- ☐ requirements for the job（その職の採用条件）
- ☐ college entry requirements（大学入学資格）

- ☐ have [feel] (an) affection for ~（~に愛情を抱く[感じる]）
- ☐ a mother's affection for her child（子どもに対する母親の愛情）

- ☐ a smog alert（スモッグ警報）
- ☐ put ~ on alert（~に警戒態勢を取らせる）

- ☐ a severe depression（深刻な不景気）
- ☐ suffer from depression（うつ病を患う）

Check 3　Sentence

- ☐ Climbers of the mountain should use extreme caution.（その山の登山者は細心の注意を払わなければならない）

- ☐ The bonds mature in 10 years.（その債券は10年で満期になる）

- ☐ The school puts special emphasis on English learning.（その学校は英語学習を特に重要視している）

- ☐ My financial adviser warned me against such a risky investment.（私の財務顧問はそのような危険な投資には注意するよう私に言った）

- ☐ If you fail to meet the requirements for the course, you won't be interviewed.（その課程の必要条件を満たさなければ、あなたは面接を受けられないだろう）

- ☐ Since the age of five, she has had a deep affection for literature.（5歳の時から、彼女は文学に深い愛着を抱いてきた）

- ☐ A tsunami alert was issued after the earthquake.（地震の後に津波警報が出された）

- ☐ The world economy could face a massive depression.（世界経済は大規模な不景気に直面するかもしれない）

Day 10))) CD-A10
Quick Review
答えは左ページ下

- ☐ association
- ☐ conflict
- ☐ identity
- ☐ pollution
- ☐ discipline
- ☐ satisfaction
- ☐ reception
- ☐ engagement
- ☐ athlete
- ☐ resolution
- ☐ draft
- ☐ decade
- ☐ acquaintance
- ☐ collapse
- ☐ investigation
- ☐ suburb

CHAPTER 1
CHAPTER 2
CHAPTER 3
CHAPTER 4
CHAPTER 5
CHAPTER 6
CHAPTER 7
CHAPTER 8
CHAPTER 9
CHAPTER 10

Day 12　名詞12

Check 1　Listen 》CD-A12

☐ 0177
infection
/infékʃən/
Part 7

名❶**伝染病**、感染症　➕接触による「伝染病」はcontagion　❷伝染、感染
動infect：(be infected withで)〜に感染している
形infectious：伝染性の、伝染病の

☐ 0178
exposure
/ikspóuʒər/
Part 2, 3

名(危険などに)**身をさらすこと**(to 〜)
動expose：❶〜を(…に)暴露する、ばらす(to …)　❷(expose A to Bで)AをB(危険など)にさらす；AをBに触れさせる

☐ 0179
sculpture
/skʌ́lptʃər/
Part 1

名**彫刻**(作品)　➕「像」はstatue
名sculptor：彫刻家

☐ 0180
belonging
/bilɔ́ːŋiŋ/
Part 7

名(〜s)(運ぶことのできる)**所持品**、所有物　➕家・土地・金銭などは含まない
動belong：(belong toで)❶〜に所属する、属する　❷〜のものである

☐ 0181
consumer
/kənsúːmər/
ビジネス問題

名**消費者**(⇔producer)
名consumption：消費；消費量[高]
動consume：❶〜を消費する　❷〜を摂取する

☐ 0182
gaze
/géiz/
Part 5, 6

名**凝視**、注視
動(gaze at [into]で)〜をじっと見つめる

☐ 0183
manufacturer
/mænjufǽktʃərər/
ビジネス問題

名**製造会社**、メーカー
名manufacture：❶製造、生産　❷(通例〜s)製品
動manufacture：(機械で大規模に)〜を製造[生産]する

☐ 0184
sentiment
/séntəmənt/
Part 5, 6

名❶(〜についての)**意見**、感想(on [about] 〜)(≒opinion)　❷感情、情緒(≒feeling, emotion)
形sentimental：感情[感傷]的な

continued
▼

今日でChapter 1は最後！ 時間に余裕があったら、章末のReviewにも挑戦しておこう。忘れてしまった単語も結構あるのでは?!

☐ 聞くだけモード　Check 1
☐ しっかりモード　Check 1 ▶ 2
☐ かんぺきモード　Check 1 ▶ 2 ▶ 3

Check 2　Phrase

☐ prevent infection（伝染病を防ぐ）
☐ a bacterial infection（細菌感染）

☐ radiation exposure（放射線被ばく）

☐ a life-sized sculpture（等身大の彫刻）

☐ personal belongings（私物）

☐ consumer demand [spending]（消費者需要[支出]）

☐ fix one's gaze on ～（～をじっと見つめる）
☐ meet someone's gaze（～と目が合う）

☐ a computer manufacturer（コンピューター製造会社）

☐ anti-war sentiment（反戦感情）
☐ be overwhelmed by sentiment（感情に圧倒される）

Check 3　Sentence

☐ This infection can be cured by penicillin.（この伝染病はペニシリンで治すことができる）

☐ Skin cancer can be caused by excessive exposure to the sun.（皮膚がんは太陽に長時間身をさらすことで起きることがある）

☐ The sculptures are lined up along the road.（彫刻が道に沿って並んでいる）

☐ Always keep your belongings in sight.（常に所持品を目に見える所に置いてください）

☐ The new law is meant to protect consumers.（その新しい法律は消費者を守るためにある）

☐ The actor is in the constant gaze of the media.（その俳優は常にメディアの注目を集めている）

☐ The car manufacturer announced its sales figures for the third quarter.（その自動車メーカーは第3四半期の売上高を発表した）

☐ Public sentiment against genetically modified crops is growing.（遺伝子組み換え作物に反対する世論が高まっている）

continued
▼

Day 12

Check 1   Listen)) CD-A12

□ 0185
awareness
/əwéərnis/
Part 7

名(〜の)**認識**、自覚(of 〜)
形aware：(be aware ofで)〜に気づいている、〜を承知している

□ 0186
evolution
/èvəlúːʃən/
Part 5, 6

名❶**進化**、進化論 ❷発展、進展(≒ development)
⊕revolution(革命)と混同しないように注意
動evolve：❶(〜から／…へ)進化[発展]する(from 〜/into …) ❷〜を進化[発展]させる

□ 0187
productivity
/pròudʌktívəti/
ビジネス問題

名**生産力**[性]；生産量
名product：製品
名production：製造、生産；生産高
動produce：〜を生産[製造]する
形productive：❶生産力のある ❷生産的な

□ 0188
acquisition
/ækwəzíʃən/
ビジネス問題

名❶(会社などの)**買収**；獲得、入手 ❷(言語運用能力の)習得
動acquire：❶〜を獲得[入手]する；〜を買収する ❷(知識など)を習得する

□ 0189
comprehension
/kàmprihénʃən/
Part 5, 6

名**理解**(力)(≒ understanding)
動comprehend：〜を(十分に)理解する
形comprehensive：包括的な；広範囲な

□ 0190
consent
/kənsént/
Part 7

名(〜に対する)**同意**(≒ agreement)、許可(≒ permission)(to 〜)
動(consent toで)〜に同意する、〜を承諾[許可]する
名consensus：❶合意 ❷(意見などの)一致、コンセンサス

□ 0191
laboratory
/lǽbərətɔ̀ːri/
Part 2, 3

名**実験室**[所]、研究室[所] ⊕短縮形はlab

□ 0192
evaluation
/ivæljuéiʃən/
Part 5, 6

名**評価**、査定(≒ assessment, appraisal)
動evaluate：〜を評価する

| Day 11)) CD-A11
Quick Review
答えは右ページ下 | □ 食欲
□ 生産高
□ 超過
□ 種 | □ 考慮
□ 特徴
□ 部門
□ 特権 | □ 用心
□ 債券
□ 強調
□ 投資 | □ 必要条件
□ 愛情
□ 警報
□ 不景気 |

Check 2 Phrase

- awareness of the problem (問題の認識)
- raise awareness about ~ (~に関する認識を高める)

- the theory of evolution (進化論)
- the evolution of the Internet (インターネットの発達)

- increase productivity (生産力を上げる)

- the acquisition of the steelmaker (その鉄鋼メーカーの買収)
- the acquisition of a second language (第2言語の習得)

- listening [reading] comprehension (聴解[読解]力)
- be beyond one's comprehension (理解できない)

- give one's consent to ~ (~に同意する)
- without parental consent (親の許可なしに)

- a sterile laboratory (無菌実験室)
- a language laboratory (語学ラボ)

- job evaluation (勤務評価)

Check 3 Sentence

- Young people tend to lack political awareness. (若者は政治意識が欠如しがちだ)

- Some people in the US want to ban the teaching of evolution. (アメリカには進化論の授業を禁止したいと思っている人もいる)

- Pleasant working conditions will improve employee productivity. (快適な職場環境は従業員の生産力を向上させるだろう)

- We spent $30 million for the acquisition of the company. (私たちはその会社の買収に3000万ドルを使った)

- He seems to have no comprehension of what is going on. (彼は何が起きているのか理解していないようだ)

- By common consent, Mr. Foster was chosen as chairman. (全会一致でフォスター氏は議長に選ばれた)

- You need permission to enter the laboratory. (その実験室に入るには許可が必要だ)

- He received positive evaluations by his supervisor. (彼は上司からよい評価を受けた)

Day 11))CD-A11
Quick Review
答えは左ページ下

- appetite
- output
- excess
- species
- consideration
- characteristic
- sector
- privilege
- caution
- bond
- emphasis
- investment
- requirement
- affection
- alert
- depression

CHAPTER 1
CHAPTER 2
CHAPTER 3
CHAPTER 4
CHAPTER 5
CHAPTER 6
CHAPTER 7
CHAPTER 8
CHAPTER 9
CHAPTER 10

Chapter 1 Review

左ページの(1)〜(20)の名詞の同意・類義語（≒）、反意・反対語（⇔）を右ページのA〜Tから選び、カッコの中に答えを書き込もう。意味が分からないときは、見出し番号を参照して復習しておこう（答えは右ページ下）。

- [ ] (1) objection (0005) ≒は? (　　)
- [ ] (2) commodity (0018) ≒は? (　　)
- [ ] (3) stain (0041) ≒は? (　　)
- [ ] (4) defect (0049) ≒は? (　　)
- [ ] (5) asset (0062) ⇔は? (　　)
- [ ] (6) conference (0071) ≒は? (　　)
- [ ] (7) associate (0084) ≒は? (　　)
- [ ] (8) resident (0087) ≒は? (　　)
- [ ] (9) achievement (0102) ≒は? (　　)
- [ ] (10) headquarters (0119) ⇔は? (　　)
- [ ] (11) inquiry (0128) ≒は? (　　)
- [ ] (12) deficit (0131) ⇔は? (　　)
- [ ] (13) reference (0141) ≒は? (　　)
- [ ] (14) pollution (0148) ≒は? (　　)
- [ ] (15) affection (0174) ≒は? (　　)
- [ ] (16) alert (0175) ≒は? (　　)
- [ ] (17) sentiment (0184) ≒は? (　　)
- [ ] (18) comprehension (0189) ≒は? (　　)
- [ ] (19) consent (0190) ≒は? (　　)
- [ ] (20) evaluation (0192) ≒は? (　　)

A. question
B. opinion
C. convention
D. disagreement
E. understanding
F. accomplishment
G. mention
H. fault
I. branch
J. assessment
K. blot
L. attachment
M. coworker
N. surplus
O. warning
P. product
Q. inhabitant
R. agreement
S. contamination
T. liability

【解答】(1) D (2) P (3) K (4) H (5) T (6) C (7) M (8) Q (9) F (10) I
(11) A (12) N (13) G (14) S (15) L (16) O (17) B (18) E (19) R (20) J

CHAPTER 2
動詞:超必修96

Chapter 2では、TOEIC「超必修」の動詞96を身につけていきます。Chapter 1を終え、学習のペースもだいぶつかめてきたのでは？「800点突破」を目指して、このペースをキープしていきましょう。

Day 13【動詞1】
▶ 66
Day 14【動詞2】
▶ 70
Day 15【動詞3】
▶ 74
Day 16【動詞4】
▶ 78
Day 17【動詞5】
▶ 82
Day 18【動詞6】
▶ 86
Chapter 2 Review
▶ 90

TOEIC的格言

Failure teaches success.

失敗は成功の元。
[直訳] 失敗が成功を教える。

Day 13　動詞1

Check 1　Listen)) CD-A13

□ 0193
guarantee
/gæ̀rəntí:/
❶アクセント注意
Part 5, 6

動 **～を保証する**
名 (～の)保証(書)(on [for] ～)(≒ warranty)

□ 0194
indicate
/índikèit/
Part 5, 6

動 **～を示す**、表す
名 indication：(～の／…という)兆候、しるし(of ～/that 節 …)

□ 0195
fold
/fóuld/
Part 1

動 ❶ **～を折り畳む**(⇔ unfold：[折り畳んだ物など]を開く、広げる)　❷(腕など)を組む

□ 0196
manufacture
/mæ̀njufǽktʃər/
ビジネス問題

動 (機械で大規模に)**～を製造[生産]する**(≒ produce)
名 ❶製造、生産　❷(通例～s)製品
名 manufacturer：製造会社、メーカー

□ 0197
decline
/dikláin/
Part 5, 6

動 ❶ **減少[低下]する**(≒ decrease)　❷～を断る(≒ refuse, turn down)(⇔ accept)　❸(decline to do で)～することを断る
名 減少、低下

□ 0198
enclose
/inklóuz/
Part 7

動 ❶ **～を(…に)同封する**(with [in] …)　❷～を取り囲む
名 enclosure：❶同封物；同封　❷囲われた土地、構内

□ 0199
postpone
/poustpóun/
Part 4

動 ❶ **～を(…まで)延期する**(until …)(≒ put off, delay, defer)　❷(postpone doing で)～するのを延期する

□ 0200
organize
/ɔ́:rgənàiz/
Part 2, 3

動 ❶ (催しなど)**を計画[準備]する**　❷(団体など)を組織する
名 organization：組織(体)、団体

continued
▼

Chapter 2では、6日をかけて「超必修」の動詞96をチェック。まずはCDでチャンツを聞いて、単語を「耳」からインプット！

☐ 聞くだけモード　Check 1
☐ しっかりモード　Check 1 ▶ 2
☐ かんぺきモード　Check 1 ▶ 2 ▶ 3

Check 2　Phrase

☐ guarantee health care to all citizens（医療を全国民に保証する）
☐ guarantee him a job（彼に職を保証する）

☐ indicate a connection between crime and poverty（[調査などが]犯罪と貧困の関係を示す）

☐ fold a handkerchief（ハンカチを折り畳む）
☐ fold one's arms（腕を組む）

☐ manufacture televisions（テレビを製造する）
☐ manufactured goods（製品）

☐ decline in value（価値が下がる）
☐ decline his invitation to dinner（夕食への彼の招待を断る）

☐ Enclosed please find ～.（[商用文で]～を同封しました）
☐ be enclosed by a wall（壁で囲まれている）

☐ postpone the game until tomorrow（その試合を明日まで延期する）
☐ postpone replying to the question（その質問への回答を先延ばしする）

☐ organize a farewell party（送別会を計画する）
☐ organize a labor union（労働組合を組織する）

Check 3　Sentence

☐ The product is guaranteed for five years.（その製品は5年間保証されている）

☐ These statistics indicate that the US economy is in a recession.（これらの統計はアメリカ経済が景気後退にあることを示している）

☐ The woman is folding a sheet of paper.（女性は紙を折り畳んでいる）

☐ The first typewriter was manufactured in 1874.（最初のタイプライターは1874年に製造された）

☐ Car sales declined nearly 10 percent this year.（自動車販売は今年10パーセント近く減少した）

☐ Please enclose your résumé with your application.（履歴書を願書に同封してください）

☐ We postponed the next meeting until next week.（私たちは次の会議を来週まで延期した）

☐ Who is in charge of organizing the company picnic this year?（今年、会社のピクニックの計画を担当するのは誰ですか?）

continued ▼

Day 13

Check 1　Listen))) CD-A13

□ 0201
affect
/əfékt/
Part 5, 6

動 **〜に影響を及ぼす**（≒ influence）　⊕effect（結果）と混同しないように注意
名 affection：（〜に対する）愛情、愛着（for 〜）

□ 0202
promote
/prəmóut/
ビジネス問題

動 ❶**〜を（…に）昇進させる**（to ...）（⇔demote：〜を降格する）　❷〜の販売を促進する、〜の宣伝活動をする
名 promotion：❶（〜への）昇進（to 〜）　❷販売促進
形 promotional：宣伝［プロモーション］用の

□ 0203
reveal
/rivíːl/
Part 7

動 （秘密など）**を明らかにする**、暴露する（≒ disclose, expose, uncover）（⇔conceal：〜を秘密にする）
名 revelation：❶暴露　❷意外な新事実、新発見

□ 0204
expand
/ikspǽnd/
Part 5, 6

動 ❶**〜を拡大［拡張］する**　❷拡大［拡張］する
名 expansion：拡大、拡張

□ 0205
launch
/lɔ́ːntʃ/
ビジネス問題

動 ❶（事業など）**に着手する**　❷（新製品）を売り出す　❸（ロケットなど）を打ち上げる
名 ❶（事業などの）開始　❷（新製品などの）発売　❸（ロケットなどの）発射

□ 0206
assume
/əsúːm/
Part 5, 6

動 ❶**〜だと想定［仮定］する**　❷（役目・責任など）を引き受ける（≒ undertake）
名 assumption：想定、仮定

□ 0207
fasten
/fǽsn/
❶発音注意
Part 4

動 **〜をしっかり固定する**、〜を結びつける（⇔unfasten：〜を外す、ほどく）

□ 0208
restore
/ristɔ́ːr/
Part 5, 6

動 ❶**〜を修復［復元］する**（≒ repair, fix, mend）　❷（信頼など）を取り戻す
名 restoration：❶回復　❷修復　❸返還

Day 12))) CD-A12
Quick Review
答えは右ページ下

- □ 伝染病
- □ 身をさらすこと
- □ 彫刻
- □ 所持品
- □ 消費者
- □ 凝視
- □ 製造会社
- □ 意見
- □ 認識
- □ 進化
- □ 生産力
- □ 買収
- □ 理解
- □ 同意
- □ 実験室
- □ 評価

Check 2 Phrase

- ☐ affect someone's health（健康に影響を及ぼす）
- ☐ directly [deeply] affect ～（～に直接的に［深く］影響を及ぼす）

- ☐ promote him to vice president（彼を副社長に昇進させる）
- ☐ promote new products（新製品の販売促進をする）

- ☐ reveal secrets（秘密を明らかにする）

- ☐ expand business（事業を拡張する）
- ☐ expand rapidly（［人口などが］急速に増加する）

- ☐ launch a new business（新事業に着手する）
- ☐ launch new cars（新車を発売する）

- ☐ Let's assume that ～.（～だと想定してみよう）
- ☐ assume responsibility for it（その責任を取る）

- ☐ fasten a string to a balloon（風船にひもを結びつける）

- ☐ restore an old church（古い教会を修復する）
- ☐ restore public confidence（国民の信頼を取り戻す）

Check 3 Sentence

- ☐ The coastal area was severely affected by the hurricane.（沿岸地域はハリケーンにより深刻な影響を受けた）

- ☐ She was promoted to sales manager last year.（彼女は昨年、営業部長に昇進した）

- ☐ Prosecutors revealed new evidence in court.（検察側は法廷で新しい証拠を明らかにした）

- ☐ The company plans to expand operations in Japan.（その会社は日本での事業を拡大することを計画している）

- ☐ Police have launched a search for a missing girl.（警察は行方不明の少女の捜索に乗り出した）

- ☐ It is assumed that the CEO will resign soon.（そのCEOは近いうちに辞任すると考えられている）

- ☐ Please make sure your seat belt is properly fastened.（シートベルトが正しく締められているかお確かめください）✚機内アナウンス

- ☐ The medieval painting was restored to its original state.（その中世の絵画は元の状態に修復された）

Day 12))) CD-A12
Quick Review
答えは左ページ下

- ☐ infection
- ☐ exposure
- ☐ sculpture
- ☐ belonging
- ☐ consumer
- ☐ gaze
- ☐ manufacturer
- ☐ sentiment
- ☐ awareness
- ☐ evolution
- ☐ productivity
- ☐ acquisition
- ☐ comprehension
- ☐ consent
- ☐ laboratory
- ☐ evaluation

CHAPTER 1
CHAPTER 2
CHAPTER 3
CHAPTER 4
CHAPTER 5
CHAPTER 6
CHAPTER 7
CHAPTER 8
CHAPTER 9
CHAPTER 10

Day 14 動詞2

Check 1　Listen)) CD-A14

□ 0209
ban
/bǽn/
Part 5, 6

動 ❶ ~を(法的に)禁止する(≒forbid, prohibit)　❷(ban A from doingで)Aが~するのを禁止する(≒forbid A to do, prohibit A from doing)
名(法による)(~の)禁止(on ~)

□ 0210
locate
/lóukeit/
Part 4

動 ❶(場所・原因など)**を突き止める**、探し出す　❷(be located in [at]で)(建物などが)~に位置する、ある
名 location：場所、位置

□ 0211
resolve
/rizálv/
Part 2, 3

動 ❶(問題など)**を解決する**(≒solve, settle)　❷(resolve to doで)~しようと決心[決意]する(≒decide to do, determine to do)
名 resolution：❶決議(案)　❷(問題などの)解決(of [to] ~)　❸(~しようという)決意、決心(to do)

□ 0212
appreciate
/əprí:ʃieit/
Part 2, 3

動 ❶ ~を感謝する　❷~を正当に評価する　❸価格[相場]が上がる(⇔depreciate)
名 appreciation：❶感謝　❷(~の)正しい理解(of ~)　❸(資産などの)値上がり、騰貴

□ 0213
quit
/kwít/
Part 2, 3

動 ❶(仕事など)**を辞める**　❷辞職[退職]する(≒retire, resign)　❸(quit doingで)~することをやめる(≒stop doing)

□ 0214
obtain
/əbtéin/
Part 5, 6

動 ~を獲得する、手に入れる(≒get, gain, acquire)

□ 0215
pursue
/pərsú:/
Part 5, 6

動 ❶(目的など)**を追求する**；(仕事など)を続行する　❷~を追う(≒chase)
名 pursuit：(~の)追求(of ~)；追跡

□ 0216
submit
/səbmít/
Part 2, 3

動 ❶ ~を(…に)提出する(to ...)　❷(submit toで)~に従う
名 submission：❶(報告書などの)提出　❷(~への)服従、屈服(to ~)

continued
▼

今日で『キクタンTOEIC Test Score 800』はようやく5分の1が終了。先はまだまだ長いけど、このペースで頑張っていこう！

☐ 聞くだけモード　Check 1
☐ しっかりモード　Check 1 ▶ 2
☐ かんぺきモード　Check 1 ▶ 2 ▶ 3

Check 2　Phrase

☐ **ban** smoking in public places（公共の場所での喫煙を禁止する）
☐ **ban** citizens from owning firearms（国民に小火器の所持を禁止する）

☐ **locate** the cause of ～（～の原因を突き止める）
☐ be **located** in the city center（街の中心部にある）

☐ **resolve** the dispute（紛争を解決する）
☐ **resolve** to do one's best（最善を尽くそうと決心する）

☐ **appreciate** his cooperation（彼の協力に感謝する）
☐ **appreciate** her abilities（彼女の才能を正当に評価する）

☐ **quit** one's job（仕事を辞める）
☐ **quit** drinking alcohol（禁酒する）

☐ **obtain** permission（許可を得る）

☐ **pursue** one's goal（目標を追い求める）
☐ **pursue** the suspect（容疑者を追跡する）

☐ **submit** an annual budget to the board of directors（年間予算案を取締役会に提出する）
☐ **submit** to the rules（規則に従う）

Check 3　Sentence

☐ The import of elephant ivory is **banned**.（象牙の輸入は禁止されている）

☐ Police are trying to **locate** the murderer.（警察はその殺人犯の居場所を突き止めようとしている）

☐ They should **resolve** their differences through dialogue.（彼らは対話によって意見の相違を解決すべきだ）

☐ I'd **appreciate** it if you could help me.（手伝っていただけるとありがたいです）

☐ Why did you **quit** college?（なぜ大学を辞めたのですか?）

☐ You must **obtain** a visa to enter the country.（その国に入国するにはビザを取らなくてはならない）

☐ She decided to **pursue** a career in journalism.（彼女はジャーナリズムの道に進むことを決心した）

☐ Have you **submitted** that report to your boss?（あの報告書を上司に提出しましたか?）

continued
▼

Day 14

Check 1　Listen))) CD-A14

□ 0217
harvest
/hάːrvist/
Part 1

動 〜を収穫する
名 ❶収穫　❷収穫物　❸収穫期

□ 0218
distribute
/distríbjuːt/
❶アクセント注意
ビジネス問題

動 〜を(…に)**配給[分配]する**(to ...)
名 distribution：❶分配、配給；(商品の)流通　❷(動植物などの)分布
名 distributor：配給[流通]業者、販売店

□ 0219
purchase
/pə́ːrtʃəs/
ビジネス問題

動 〜を購入する、買う(≒ buy)
名 ❶購入　❷購入品

□ 0220
attain
/ətéin/
Part 4

動 (目標など)**を達成する**、成し遂げる(≒ achieve, accomplish)
名 attainment：❶達成　❷(獲得した)技能

□ 0221
anticipate
/æntísəpèit/
Part 5, 6

動 ❶**〜を予想[予期、期待]する**(≒ expect)　❷(要求など)に事前に応じる
名 anticipation：予想、予測、期待

□ 0222
predict
/pridíkt/
Part 5, 6

動 〜を予測[予言、予想]する(≒ foretell)
名 prediction：(〜についての)予測、予報、予言、予想(about [of] 〜)

□ 0223
renew
/rinjúː/
Part 2, 3

動 ❶(契約など)**を更新する**　❷〜を再開する(≒ resume)
名 renewal：❶更新　❷再開

□ 0224
undergo
/ʌ̀ndərgóu/
Part 5, 6

動 ❶(苦難など)**を経験する**(≒ experience)　❷(治療など)を受ける

Day 13))) CD-A13
Quick Review
答えは右ページ下

- □ 〜を保証する
- □ 〜を示す
- □ 〜を折り畳む
- □ 〜を製造する
- □ 減少する
- □ 〜を同封する
- □ 〜を延期する
- □ 〜を計画する
- □ 〜に影響を及ぼす
- □ 〜を昇進させる
- □ 〜を明らかにする
- □ 〜を拡大する
- □ 〜に着手する
- □ 〜だと想定する
- □ 〜をしっかり固定する
- □ 〜を修復する

Check 2 Phrase

- ☐ harvest rice [wheat]（米[小麦]を収穫する）

- ☐ distribute food and clothing to the refugees（難民たちに食料と衣服を配給する）

- ☐ purchase a new car（新車を買う）

- ☐ attain one's objective（目標を達成する）

- ☐ anticipate what will happen（何が起きるか予想する）
- ☐ anticipate someone's question（質問を見越して答える）

- ☐ predict an increase in temperature（気温の上昇を予測する）

- ☐ renew one's contract（契約を更新する）
- ☐ renew peace talks（和平交渉を再開する）

- ☐ undergo hardship（苦難を経験する）
- ☐ undergo surgery（手術を受ける）

Check 3 Sentence

- ☐ The farmer is harvesting crops.（農夫が作物を収穫している）

- ☐ The agenda was distributed to each participant prior to the meeting.（会議の前に議事項目が各出席者に配られた）

- ☐ Compare prices before purchasing anything.（何かを買う前には価格を比較しなさい）

- ☐ Singapore attained independence in 1965.（シンガポールは1965年に独立を果たした）

- ☐ The company is anticipating an increase in revenue this year.（その会社は今年度の収益の増加を予想している）

- ☐ It is difficult to predict when an earthquake will occur.（地震がいつ起きるか予測するのは難しい）

- ☐ I forgot to renew my driver's license.（私は運転免許証を更新するのを忘れた）

- ☐ The world economy is undergoing a serious recession.（世界経済は深刻な景気後退を経験している）

Day 13 ») CD-A13
Quick Review
答えは左ページ下

- ☐ guarantee
- ☐ indicate
- ☐ fold
- ☐ manufacture
- ☐ decline
- ☐ enclose
- ☐ postpone
- ☐ organize
- ☐ affect
- ☐ promote
- ☐ reveal
- ☐ expand
- ☐ launch
- ☐ assume
- ☐ fasten
- ☐ restore

Day 15　動詞3

Check 1　Listen 》CD-A15

☐ 0225
stimulate
/stímjulèit/
ビジネス問題

動 ～を刺激する、活気づける
名 stimulation：刺激、興奮
名 stimulus：刺激（するもの）

☐ 0226
exceed
/iksíːd/
Part 2, 3

動 ❶～を上回る、超える　**❷**～の限界を超える
名 excess：（～の）超過（量）(of ～)
形 excess：超過した、余分の
形 excessive：過度の、極端な、法外な

☐ 0227
modify
/mάdəfài/
Part 5, 6

動 ～を修正する、変更する（≒ change）
名 modification：❶修正、変更　❷緩和

☐ 0228
register
/rédʒistər/
Part 2, 3

動 ❶～を（…として）**登録[記録]する**(as ...)（≒ record）　**❷**（郵便物）を書留にする　**❸**(register for で)～の入学[受講]手続きをする
名 登録[記録]（簿）
名 registration：登録、登記、記録

☐ 0229
annoy
/ənɔ́i/
Part 5, 6

動 ❶～をいらいらさせる、悩ます　**❷**(be annoyed at [with] で)～にいらいらしている
名 annoyance：いら立たしさ、困惑；迷惑なこと[物]
形 annoying：迷惑な、うるさい

☐ 0230
inspect
/inspékt/
Part 1

動 ～を検査[調査]する（≒ examine）
名 inspection：視察、調査、監査
名 inspector：調査[検査]官

☐ 0231
grab
/gráeb/
Part 2, 3

動 ❶～を素早く食べる　**❷**～をひっつかむ
名 ひっつかむこと、ひったくり

☐ 0232
withdraw
/wiðdrɔ́ː/
Part 2, 3

動 ❶（預金など）**を**（…から）**引き出す** (from ...)（⇔ deposit：～を預金する）　**❷**～を撤回する（≒ take back）　**❸**（～から）撤退する (from ～)
名 withdrawal：❶預金の引き出し　❷撤退、撤兵　❸（約束などの）撤回

continued
▼

1つの単語には1つの品詞の用法しかないとは限らない。複数の品詞の用法がある場合には、その意味もなるべく確認しておこう。

□ 聞くだけモード　Check 1
□ しっかりモード　Check 1 ▶ 2
□ かんぺきモード　Check 1 ▶ 2 ▶ 3

Check 2　Phrase

□ stimulate individual consumption(個人消費を刺激する)

□ exceed the speed limit(制限速度を超える)
□ exceed one's expectations(予想[期待]を上回る)

□ modify the schedule(予定を変更する)
□ genetically modified food(遺伝子組み換え食品)

□ register the house in joint names(その家を共同名義で登記する)
□ have the letter registered(その手紙を書留にしてもらう)

□ annoy her with questions(いろいろと質問をして彼女をいらいらさせる)
□ be annoyed at his behavior(彼の態度にいらいらしている)

□ inspect a car for damage(損傷がないか車を検査する)

□ grab a hot dog(ホットドッグを素早く食べる)
□ grab her hand(彼女の手をつかむ)

□ withdraw some money from an account(口座からお金を引き出す)
□ withdraw one's previous statement(前言を撤回する)

Check 3　Sentence

□ The opening of the amusement park will stimulate the local economy.(その遊園地の開園は地域経済を活性化するだろう)

□ Construction costs of the building exceeded $20 million.(そのビルの建設費は2000万ドルを上回った)

□ The architect modified the design according to the client's wishes.(その建築士は顧客の要望に従って設計図を修正した)

□ Owners of dogs must register their dogs with the city.(イヌの飼い主はイヌを市に登録しなければならない)

□ Noise from the airport annoys nearby residents.(空港の騒音は近隣の住民を悩ませている)

□ The man is inspecting the machine.(男性は機械を検査している)

□ Why don't we grab a bite before the movie?(映画の前に軽く食事をしませんか?)●grab a bite (to eat)で「軽く食事をする」という意味

□ I withdrew $2,000 to buy a new PC.(新しいパソコンを買うために私は2000ドルを引き出した)

continued
▼

Day 15

Check 1　Listen)) CD-A15

0233 install
/instɔ́:l/
Part 1

動 ❶〜を取りつける、設置する(≒put in)　❷〜を(…に)任命する(as . . .)(≒appoint)　❸〜をインストールする
名 installation：❶(機械などの)取りつけ、設置　❷任命　❸インストール

0234 detect
/ditékt/
Part 5, 6

動 〜を感知[探知]する；〜を見つける
名 detection：探知；発見
名 detective：刑事；探偵

0235 quote
/kwóut/
❶定義注意
ビジネス問題

動 ❶(値段など)を見積もる　❷(語句など)を(…から)引用する(from . . .)
名 ❶見積額(≒estimate)　❷引用文[句]
名 quotation：❶(〜からの)引用(文、句、語)(from 〜)　❷(〜の)見積額(for 〜)

0236 resume
/rizú:m/
Part 5, 6

動 ❶〜を再開する　❷再開する
名 resumption：再開

0237 accommodate
/əkάmədèit/
Part 7

動 ❶(建物などが)(人)を収容できる　❷(要求など)を受け入れる(≒accept)
名 accommodation：(通例〜s)宿泊設備

0238 stack
/stǽk/
Part 1

動 〜を積み重ねる(≒pile)
名 きちんとした積み重ね；(a stack of 〜で)〜の山；多数[多量]の〜

0239 revise
/riváiz/
Part 2, 3

動 〜を修正[改訂]する
名 revision：修正、改訂

0240 generate
/dʒénərèit/
Part 5, 6

動 〜を生み出す、発生させる(≒produce)
名 generation：❶(集合的に)同世代の人々　❷一世代　❸発生
名 generator：発電機

Day 14)) CD-A14
Quick Review
答えは右ページ下

- □ 〜を禁止する
- □ 〜を突き止める
- □ 〜を解決する
- □ 〜を感謝する
- □ 〜を辞める
- □ 〜を獲得する
- □ 〜を追求する
- □ 〜を提出する
- □ 〜を収穫する
- □ 〜を配給する
- □ 〜を購入する
- □ 〜を達成する
- □ 〜を予想する
- □ 〜を予測する
- □ 〜を更新する
- □ 〜を経験する

Check 2 Phrase

- □ install a washing machine（洗濯機を取りつける）
- □ install him as ambassador to the UN（彼を国連大使に任命する）

- □ detect poisonous gas（有毒ガスを感知する）
- □ detect a tumor（腫瘍を見つける）

- □ quote a price（見積額を言う）
- □ quote a saying from the Bible（聖書から格言を引用する）

- □ resume the meeting after a break（休憩の後に会議を再開する）

- □ accommodate 500 people（[ホテルなどが]500人を収容できる）
- □ accommodate his request（彼の要望を受け入れる）

- □ stack the books [chairs]（本[いす]を積み重ねる）

- □ revise a policy（政策を修正する）
- □ revise the estimate upward [downward]（見積もりを上方[下方]修正する）

- □ generate revenue（収益を生み出す）
- □ generate electricity（電気を発生させる）

Check 3 Sentence

- □ The man is installing lighting.（男性は照明を取りつけている）

- □ Ultraviolet light cannot be detected by the human eye.（紫外線は人間の目では感知できない）

- □ The architect quoted $150,000 to rebuild my house.（その建築家は私の家の改築を15万ドルと見積もった）

- □ The six-party talks were resumed after almost a year.（ほぼ1年の中断の後、6カ国協議が再開された）

- □ The bus accommodates up to 30 passengers.（そのバスは30人まで乗客を乗せることができる）

- □ The plates are stacked on the table.（テーブルの上に皿が積み重ねられている）

- □ Your report needs to be revised.（あなたの報告書は修正が必要だ）

- □ The project will generate 2,000 new jobs in the area.（そのプロジェクトは地域に2000人分の新しい仕事を生み出すだろう）

Day 14 ♪CD-A14
Quick Review
答えは左ページ下

- □ ban
- □ locate
- □ resolve
- □ appreciate
- □ quit
- □ obtain
- □ pursue
- □ submit
- □ harvest
- □ distribute
- □ purchase
- □ attain
- □ anticipate
- □ predict
- □ renew
- □ undergo

Day 16 動詞4

Check 1　Listen)) CD-A16

☐ 0241
boost
/búːst/
ビジネス問題

動 ❶(生産など)**を増加させる**　❷(士気など)を高める　❸〜を押し上げる
名 ❶(物価などの)上昇　❷景気づけ

☐ 0242
overlook
/òuvərlúk/
Part 1

動 ❶(場所が)**〜を見渡せる**、見下ろせる　❷〜を見落とす(≒miss)；〜を大目に見る(≒ignore)

☐ 0243
conclude
/kənklúːd/
Part 4

動 ❶**〜と結論する**　❷〜を(…で)終了させる(with ...)(≒finish, end)
名conclusion：❶(〜という)結論(that節 〜)　❷結末
形conclusive：(証拠などが)決定的な

☐ 0244
emerge
/imə́ːrdʒ/
Part 5, 6

動 ❶(〜から)**現れる**(from 〜)(≒appear)　❷(事実などが)明らかになる(≒come out)
名emergency：緊急[非常]事態、緊急[非常]の場合

☐ 0245
involve
/inválv/
Part 7

動 ❶**〜を**(議論などに)**巻き込む**(in ...)　❷(be involved inで)〜に参加している；〜と関係している
名involvement：(〜への)関与、参加(in 〜)

☐ 0246
scatter
/skǽtər/
Part 1

動 ❶**〜を**(…に)**まき散らす**、ばらまく(on [over] ...)
❷(群衆などが)四散する(≒disperse)

☐ 0247
adjust
/ədʒʌ́st/
Part 1

動 ❶(機械など)**を調節[整備]する**　❷〜を(…に)適合させる(to ...)　❸(adjust toで)(環境など)に適応[順応]する
名adjustment：❶調整、調節　❷適応
形adjustable：調節[調整]できる

☐ 0248
inherit
/inhérit/
Part 5, 6

動 (財産など)**を**(…から)**相続する**、受け継ぐ(from ...)
名inheritance：❶遺産、相続財産　❷(前代などから)受け継いだもの；(無形の)遺産

continued
▼

「声を出しながら」CDを聞いてる？ えっ、恥ずかしい?! 恥ずかしがっていては「話せる」ようにはならないよ！ ガンバって！

☐ 聞くだけモード　Check 1
☐ しっかりモード　Check 1 ▶ 2
☐ かんぺきモード　Check 1 ▶ 2 ▶ 3

Check 2　Phrase

☐ **boost** productivity（生産力を増加させる）
☐ **boost** morale（士気を高める）

☐ **overlook** mountains（山々が見渡せる）
☐ **overlook** his mistakes（彼の間違いを見落とす[大目に見る]）

☐ **conclude** that the defendant is innocent（被告は無罪だと結論を下す）
☐ **conclude** one's work（仕事を終える）

☐ **emerge** from the clouds（[太陽が]雲間から現れる）
☐ It **emerges** that ~.（~ということが明らかになる）

☐ **involve** him in the discussion（彼をその議論に巻き込む）
☐ be **involved** in political activities（政治活動に参加している）

☐ **scatter** seed on the ground（地面に種をまく）
☐ **scatter** in all directions（四方八方に散る）

☐ **adjust** the temperature（温度を調節する）
☐ **adjust** the chair to knee height（いすをひざの高さに合わせる）

☐ **inherit** $100,000 from one's parents（両親から10万ドルを相続する）

Check 3　Sentence

☐ Low mortgage rates will help **boost** home sales.（住宅ローンの低利率は住宅販売の増加に役立つだろう）

☐ The building **overlooks** the beach.（そのビルからは海岸が見下ろせる）

☐ It is too early to **conclude** that the domestic economy has moved into recovery.（国内経済が回復しだしたと結論するのは時期尚早だ）

☐ He **emerged** from the crowd.（彼は人込みの中から姿を現した）

☐ I don't want to get **involved** in an argument with him.（私は彼との論争に巻き込まれたくない）

☐ Fallen leaves are **scattered** on the sidewalk.（落ち葉が歩道に散っている）

☐ The man is **adjusting** the machine.（男性は機械を調節している）

☐ He **inherited** the land from his father.（彼はその土地を父親から相続した）

continued
▼

Day 16

Check 1　Listen 》CD-A16

☐ 0249
resign
/rizáin/
ビジネス問題

動 ❶(地位などを)**辞任**[辞職]**する**(from ～)(≒ retire)　❷(地位など)を辞める
名 resignation：❶辞職、辞任　❷辞表

☐ 0250
depart
/dipá:rt/
Part 2, 3

動 (～から/…へ向けて)**出発する**(from ～/for …)(≒ leave)(⇔arrive)
名 departure：(～からの/…へ向けての)出発(from ～/for …)

☐ 0251
extend
/iksténd/
Part 5, 6

動 ❶**～を延長する**　❷～を拡張する
名 extension：❶(電話の)内線　❷延期　❸拡張
形 extensive：❶(調査などが)広範囲にわたる　❷(損害などが)大規模な、甚だしい
副 extensively：広範囲に、広く

☐ 0252
overcome
/òuvərkʌ́m/
Part 5, 6

動 (困難など)**を克服する**；～に打ち勝つ(≒defeat)

☐ 0253
acquire
/əkwáiər/
Part 5, 6

動 ❶**～を獲得[入手]する**(≒get, gain, obtain)；～を買収する　❷(知識など)を習得する
名 acquisition：❶(会社などの)買収；獲得、入手　❷(言語運用能力の)習得

☐ 0254
declare
/diklέər/
Part 4

動 ❶**～を宣言[公表、布告]する**　❷(税関で)(課税品など)を申告する
名 declaration：❶宣言、公表、布告　❷申告(書)

☐ 0255
fulfill
/fulfíl/
Part 4

動 ❶(計画・約束など)**を果たす**、実行する(≒carry out)　❷(要求など)を満たす(≒meet, satisfy)
名 fulfillment：実現、成就；実行、遂行

☐ 0256
assemble
/əsémbl/
Part 1

動 ❶(機械など)**を組み立てる**(≒put together)　❷集まる　❸～を集める(≒gather)
名 assembly：❶(機械の)組み立て(作業)　❷集会、会合

Day 15 》CD-A15
Quick Review
答えは右ページ下

☐ ～を刺激する　☐ ～をいらいらさせる　☐ ～を取りつける　☐ ～を収容できる
☐ ～を上回る　☐ ～を検査する　☐ ～を感知する　☐ ～を積み重ねる
☐ ～を修正する　☐ ～を素早く食べる　☐ ～を見積もる　☐ ～を修正する
☐ ～を登録する　☐ ～を引き出す　☐ ～を再開する　☐ ～を生み出す

Check 2　Phrase

- ☐ **resign** from the company(その会社を辞める)
- ☐ **resign** one's position as sales manager(販売部長の職を辞する)

- ☐ **depart** from New York to Paris(ニューヨークからパリへ出発する)

- ☐ **extend** one's stay in Sydney(シドニーでの滞在を延長する)
- ☐ **extend** one's house(自宅の建て増しをする)

- ☐ **overcome** difficulties(難局を克服する)
- ☐ **overcome** one's fear(恐怖に打ち勝つ)

- ☐ **acquire** a reputation(名声を得る)
- ☐ **acquire** language skills(語学力を習得する)

- ☐ **declare** a state of emergency(非常事態を宣言する)
- ☐ Anything to **declare**?([税関で]課税品をお持ちですか?)

- ☐ **fulfill** one's promise [dream](約束[夢]を果たす)
- ☐ **fulfill** the requirements for ～(～のための必要条件を満たす)

- ☐ **assemble** a radio(ラジオを組み立てる)
- ☐ **assemble** in the meeting room(会議室に集まる)

Check 3　Sentence

- ☐ Did you know Mr. Tanaka **resigned** yesterday?(タナカさんが昨日辞職したことを知っていますか?)

- ☐ All passengers **departing** for London on flight BA182 should go to Gate 17.(BA182便でロンドンへ出発されるお客さまは17番ゲートへお進みください)❶空港のアナウンス

- ☐ You need to **extend** your visa to continue your studies here.(ここでの学業を続けるためには、あなたはビザを延長する必要がある)

- ☐ The two countries managed to **overcome** their differences.(両国はどうにか意見の相違を克服できた)

- ☐ She **acquired** US citizenship last year.(彼女は昨年、アメリカ国籍を得た)

- ☐ The brokerage **declared** itself bankrupt yesterday.(その証券会社は昨日、破産を宣言した)

- ☐ He has failed to **fulfill** his role as a father.(彼は父親としての役割を果たしてこなかった)

- ☐ The man is **assembling** the bookcase.(男性は本箱を組み立てている)

Day 15　CD-A15　Quick Review　答えは左ページ下

- ☐ stimulate
- ☐ exceed
- ☐ modify
- ☐ register
- ☐ annoy
- ☐ inspect
- ☐ grab
- ☐ withdraw
- ☐ install
- ☐ detect
- ☐ quote
- ☐ resume
- ☐ accommodate
- ☐ stack
- ☐ revise
- ☐ generate

Day 17　動詞5

Check 1　Listen 》CD-A17

☐ 0257
ensure
/inʃúər/
Part 5, 6

動 **〜を保証する**、確実にする　⊕insure(〜に保険をかける)と混同しないように注意

☐ 0258
imply
/implái/
Part 4

動 **〜をほのめかす**、暗示する(≒infer)
名implication：❶言外の意味、含み　❷(通例〜s)(予想される)(〜の)影響、結果(of 〜)

☐ 0259
drain
/dréin/
❶定義注意
Part 7

動 ❶(資産など)**を枯渇[消耗]させる**　❷(液体)を(…から)排出させる(from …)　❸流れ出る
名排水管[路]
名drainage：❶排水　❷排水設備

☐ 0260
abandon
/əbǽndən/
Part 5, 6

動 ❶**〜を断念する**、あきらめる(≒give up)　❷(人・家など)を見捨てる　❸(abandon oneself toで)(感情など)に身を任せる

☐ 0261
halt
/hɔ́ːlt/
Part 7

動 ❶**〜を停止[中止]させる**　❷停止[中止]する(≒stop)
名停止；中断

☐ 0262
confront
/kənfrʌ́nt/
Part 4

動 ❶(困難など)**に直面する**、立ち向かう(≒face)　❷(困難などが)(人)に立ちはだかる
名confrontation：(〜との)対面、直面(with 〜)

☐ 0263
recruit
/rikrúːt/
❶定義注意
ビジネス問題

動 (新入社員・新兵など)**を募集[採用]する**
名 ❶新入社員　❷新兵

☐ 0264
consume
/kənsúːm/
ビジネス問題

動 ❶**〜を消費する**　❷〜を摂取する
名consumer：消費者
名consumption：消費；消費量[高]

continued
▼

Quick Reviewは使ってる？ 昨日覚えた単語でも、記憶に残っているとは限らない。学習の合間に軽くチェックするだけでも効果は抜群！

- ☐ 聞くだけモード　Check 1
- ☐ しっかりモード　Check 1 ▶ 2
- ☐ かんぺきモード　Check 1 ▶ 2 ▶ 3

Check 2　Phrase

- ☐ **ensure** safety（安全性を保証する）
- ☐ **ensure** that ～（～ということを保証する）

- ☐ **imply** one's resignation（辞職をほのめかす）
- ☐ Are you **implying** (that) ～?（～とでも言いたいのですか？）

- ☐ **drain** the fund（資金を枯渇させる）
- ☐ **drain** the oil from the engine（エンジンからオイルを排出させる）

- ☐ **abandon** the climb because of the bad weather（悪天候のため登頂を断念する）
- ☐ an **abandoned** car（乗り捨てられた車）

- ☐ **halt** traffic（[悪天候などが]車の流れを止める）
- ☐ **Halt**!（止まれ！）

- ☐ **confront** danger（危険に立ち向かう）
- ☐ be **confronted** with ～（～に直面している）

- ☐ **recruit** volunteers（ボランティアを募集する）

- ☐ **consume** energy（エネルギーを消費する）
- ☐ **consume** a healthy diet（健康的な食事を取る）

Check 3　Sentence

- ☐ The government has a responsibility for **ensuring** law and order.（政府は治安を保証する責任がある）

- ☐ The prime minister **implied** that a general election would be held soon.（近いうちに総選挙が行われることを首相は示唆した）

- ☐ The country's resources had been **drained** by the war.（戦争によってその国の資源は枯渇した）

- ☐ We **abandoned** the plan due to lack of funds.（資金不足のため私たちはその計画を断念した）

- ☐ The electronics manufacturer has temporarily **halted** production lines for semiconductors.（その電気メーカーは半導体の生産ラインを一時的に停止させている）

- ☐ The country is **confronting** a financial crisis.（その国は金融危機に直面している）

- ☐ The company will **recruit** 100 new employees next year.（その会社は来年、100人の新入社員の採用を予定している）

- ☐ The US **consumes** 25 percent of the world's oil.（アメリカは世界の石油の25パーセントを消費している）

continued ▼

Day 17

Check 1 Listen))) CD-A17

0265 implement
/ímpləmènt/
❶アクセント注意
Part 4

動 (計画・約束など)**を実行**[履行]**する**(≒ carry out)
名 (/ímpləmənt/) 道具、用具(≒ tool, instrument, utensil)

0266 prohibit
/prouhíbit/
Part 7

動 ❶ **~を禁止する**(≒ forbid, ban) ❷(prohibit A from doingで)Aが~するのを禁止する(≒ ban A from doing, forbid A to do);Aが~するのを妨げる(≒ stop A from doing, keep A from doing, prevent A from doing)
名 prohibition:(~の)禁止(against [on, of] ~)

0267 exhaust
/igzɔ́ːst/
❶発音注意
Part 5, 6

動 ❶ **~を**(ひどく)**疲れさせる** ❷~を使い尽くす
名 排気ガス
名 exhaustion:❶極度の疲労 ❷使い尽くすこと
形 exhausted:❶(~で)疲れ切った、力尽きた(from [with] ~) ❷使い尽くされた

0268 disturb
/distə́ːrb/
Part 5, 6

動 ❶(平静など)**を乱す**、妨げる(≒ interrupt) ❷~に迷惑をかける
名 disturbance:❶妨害[邪魔](物) ❷(社会の)騒動、混乱
形 disturbing:平静を乱す、不安にさせる

0269 iron
/áiərn/
❶定義注意
Part 1

動 **~にアイロンをかける**(≒ press)
名 ❶鉄 ❷アイロン
形 鉄の

0270 initiate
/iníʃièit/
Part 7

動 (計画など)**を始める**(≒ begin, start)
名 initiative:❶主導権、イニシアチブ ❷自発性
名 initiation:❶(~への)加入(into ~) ❷開始
名 initial:頭文字
形 initial:最初の

0271 authorize
/ɔ́ːθəràiz/
Part 4

動 ❶ **~を認可**[認定、公認]**する**(≒ approve) ❷(authorize A to doで)Aに~する権限を与える
名 authority:❶(~に対する)権威、権力(over ~) ❷(~する)権限(to do) ❸(the ~ies)当局
名 author:❶著者 ❷立案者

0272 eliminate
/ilímənèit/
Part 7

動 **~を**(…から)**除去**[削除、排除]**する**(from ...)(≒ exclude)
名 elimination:(~からの)除去、削除、排除(from ~)

Day 16))) CD-A16
Quick Review
答えは右ページ下

- □ ~を増加させる
- □ ~を見渡せる
- □ ~と結論する
- □ 現れる
- □ ~を巻き込む
- □ ~をまき散らす
- □ ~を調節する
- □ ~を相続する
- □ 辞任する
- □ 出発する
- □ ~を延長する
- □ ~を克服する
- □ ~を獲得する
- □ ~を宣言する
- □ ~を果たす
- □ ~を組み立てる

Check 2 Phrase

☐ implement a contract [plan]（契約[計画]を実行する）

☐ prohibit the selling of pirated CDs（海賊版CDの販売を禁止する）
☐ prohibit him from driving a car（彼に車の運転を禁止する）

☐ It exhausts me to do ～.（～するのは疲れる）
☐ exhaust the world's oil supply（世界の石油供給を使い果たす）

☐ disturb the peace（治安を乱す）
☐ Don't disturb yourself.（どうぞお構いなく）

☐ iron trousers（ズボンにアイロンをかける）

☐ initiate a new business（新事業を始める）

☐ authorize the plan（その計画を認可する）
☐ authorize police officers to carry weapons（警官に武器を携帯する権限を与える）

☐ eliminate poverty from the world（世界から貧困をなくす）
☐ eliminate the possibility that ～（～という可能性を排除する）

Check 3 Sentence

☐ Safety measures have been implemented in most airports.（安全対策がほとんどの空港で実施されている）

☐ Parking in this area is strictly prohibited.（この地域での駐車は厳しく禁止されている）

☐ World Wars I and II exhausted Europe.（第1次・第2次世界大戦はヨーロッパを疲弊させた）

☐ The bark of a dog disturbed the silence of the night.（イヌの鳴き声が夜の静寂を破った）

☐ The woman is ironing the shirt.（女性はシャツにアイロンをかけている）

☐ Many companies have initiated environmental protection programs.（多くの企業は環境保護計画を始めている）

☐ His proposal was authorized by the board of directors.（彼の提案は取締役会で承認された）

☐ The car maker will eliminate 10,000 jobs over the next two years.（その自動車メーカーは今後2年で1万人の社員の削減を予定している）

Day 16 》CD-A16
Quick Review
答えは左ページ下

☐ boost ☐ involve ☐ resign ☐ acquire
☐ overlook ☐ scatter ☐ depart ☐ declare
☐ conclude ☐ adjust ☐ extend ☐ fulfill
☐ emerge ☐ inherit ☐ overcome ☐ assemble

Day 18　動詞6

Check 1　Listen)) CD-A18

0273
transmit
/trænzmít/
Part 5, 6

動❶(ニュースなど)**を放送する**、伝える　❷(病気など)を伝染させる、うつす
名transmission：❶(自動車の)変速装置、トランスミッション　❷伝達　❸送信、放送

0274
acknowledge
/æknάlidʒ/
Part 5, 6

動❶(過失など)**を認める**(≒admit, accept)(⇔deny)　❷(手紙など)を受け取ったことを知らせる
名acknowledgement：❶承認　❷感謝；(～s)謝辞

0275
disclose
/disklóuz/
Part 5, 6

動(秘密など)**を明らかにする**、暴露する、暴く(≒reveal, expose, uncover)(⇔conceal：～を秘密にする)
名disclosure：公表、発表；暴露、発覚

0276
specify
/spésəfài/
Part 5, 6

動**～を明確に述べる**、明記する、指定する
名specification：(通例～s)仕様書、設計明細者
名specific：(～s)詳細
形specific：❶特定の　❷明確な　❸(～に)特有[固有]の(to ～)

0277
preserve
/prizə́ːrv/
Part 5, 6

動**～を(…から)保護[保存]する**(from ...)(≒conserve)　⊕reserve(～を予約する)と混同しないように注意
名preservation：保存、保護、維持
名preservative：保存料、防腐剤

0278
reach
/ríːtʃ/
❶定義注意
Part 4

動❶(電話などで)**～と連絡を取る**(≒contact)　❷～に着く、到着する(≒arrive at)　❸～に達する　❹(reach forで)～を取ろうと手を伸ばす　⊕この意味ではPart 1で頻出
名届く範囲[距離]

0279
assert
/əsə́ːrt/
Part 5, 6

動**～だと断言[主張]する**(≒claim, maintain, affirm, allege)
名assertion：(～という)主張(that節 ～)
形assertive：自己主張の強い

0280
monitor
/mάnətər/
❶定義注意
Part 5, 6

動**～を監視する**
名❶(コンピューターの)モニター、ディスプレー　❷監視装置

continued
▼

今日でChapter 2は最後！ 時間に余裕があったら、章末のReviewにも挑戦しておこう。忘れてしまった単語も結構あるのでは?!

☐ 聞くだけモード　Check 1
☐ しっかりモード　Check 1 ▶ 2
☐ かんぺきモード　Check 1 ▶ 2 ▶ 3

Check 2　Phrase

☐ transmit news（ニュースを放送する）
☐ be transmitted to humans by mosquitoes（[伝染病などが]蚊によって人にうつされる）

☐ acknowledge one's shortcomings（欠点を認める）
☐ acknowledge receipt of ~（~を受け取ったことを知らせる）

☐ disclose details of the contract（契約の詳細を明らかにする）

☐ specify the date of delivery（配達日を明記する）

☐ preserve the environment（自然環境を保護する）

☐ reach her on the phone（電話で彼女と連絡を取る）
☐ reach Tokyo（東京に到着する）

☐ assert that he is innocent（彼は無罪だと断言する）

☐ monitor the patient's condition（患者の状態を監視する）

Check 3　Sentence

☐ The game was transmitted live via satellite.（その試合は衛星中継で生放送された）

☐ He acknowledged having lied.（彼はうそをついたことを認めた）

☐ The suspect disclosed the names of his accomplices.（その容疑者は共犯者の名前を明かした）

☐ He didn't specify when he would retire.（彼はいつ退職するかはっきりと述べなかった）

☐ It is important to preserve our natural resources.（私たちの天然資源を守ることが大切だ）

☐ You can reach us by phone, by fax, or by e-mail.（当社へは電話、ファクス、または電子メールでご連絡いただけます）

☐ She asserts that he stole money from her.（彼が彼女からお金を盗んだと彼女は主張している）

☐ Security cameras monitor the whole of the office.（防犯カメラはオフィス全体を監視している）

continued
▼

Day 18

Check 1　Listen)) CD-A18

□ 0281
chop
/tʃάp/
Part 1

動 ～を切り刻む、細かく切る
名 ❶厚切りの肉片　❷チョップ

□ 0282
compete
/kəmpíːt/
ビジネス問題

動 (～と／…を得るために)競争する、張り合う(with [against] ～/for . . .)
名 competition：競争、争い
名 competitor：競争相手、競合他社
形 competitive：❶競争力のある　❷競争の

□ 0283
stall
/stɔ́ːl/
❶定義注意
Part 4

動 ❶(車)をエンストさせる；～を立ち往生させる　❷エンストする；立ち往生する
名 ❶売店、屋台、露店　➡この意味ではPart 1で頻出　❷エンスト

□ 0284
retain
/ritéin/
Part 5, 6

動 ❶～を保持[維持]する；～を持ち続ける　❷～を記憶しておく
名 retention：保持、保有

□ 0285
fix
/fíks/
Part 1

動 ❶～を修理する(≒repair, mend)　❷(会合などの)(日時など)を決める(for . . .)(≒set, determine)

□ 0286
demonstrate
/démənstrèit/
❶アクセント注意
Part 5, 6

動 ❶～を証明[実証]する(≒prove)　❷(商品)を実演する　❸(～に反対の)デモをする(against ～)
名 demonstration：❶(～に反対の)デモ(against ～)　❷(商品の)実演
名 demonstrator：❶デモ参加者　❷実演する人

□ 0287
ache
/éik/
Part 4

動 (～で)痛む、うずく(from [with] ～)
名 痛み

□ 0288
calculate
/kǽlkjulèit/
Part 4

動 ❶～を計算する、算出する(≒count)　❷～を推定[判断]する
名 calculation：❶計算　❷見積もり、予測
名 calculator：計算器

Day 17)) CD-A17
Quick Review
答えは右ページ下

- □ ～を保証する
- □ ～をほのめかす
- □ ～を枯渇させる
- □ ～を断念する
- □ ～を停止させる
- □ ～に直面する
- □ ～を募集する
- □ ～を消費する
- □ ～を実行する
- □ ～を禁止する
- □ ～を疲れさせる
- □ ～を乱す
- □ ～にアイロンをかける
- □ ～を始める
- □ ～を認可する
- □ ～を除去する

Check 2 Phrase | ## Check 3 Sentence

Check 2 Phrase	Check 3 Sentence
☐ chop a carrot into pieces(ニンジンをみじん切りにする)	☐ The woman is chopping vegetables.(女性は野菜を切り刻んでいる)
☐ compete with foreign companies(外国企業と競合する)	☐ It's difficult for small stores to compete with big national chains.(小規模商店が大規模な全国チェーン店と競争するのは難しい)
☐ stall a bike(オートバイをエンストさせる) ☐ stall due to lack of gas(ガス欠でエンストする)	☐ Traffic is stalled on Highway 520 in both directions.(520号線は両方向とも渋滞している)
☐ retain ownership of ~(~の所有権を保持している) ☐ retain information(情報を記憶しておく)	☐ He will retain rights to the property.(彼はその財産の所有権を維持する予定だ)
☐ fix a car(車を修理する) ☐ fix a date for the next meeting(次の会議の日を決める)	☐ The man is fixing a computer.(男性はコンピューターを修理している)
☐ demonstrate one's ability(能力を証明する) ☐ demonstrate a new product(新製品の実演をする)	☐ The study demonstrates the link between poverty and violence.(その研究は貧困と暴力の関連を証明している)
☐ have an aching back(背中が痛む)	☐ I ache [I'm aching] all over.(体中が痛い)
☐ calculate the damages(損害額を算出する) ☐ calculate when the project will finish(プロジェクトがいつ終わるか推定する)	☐ Computers can calculate incredibly complex calculations in a second.(コンピューターは信じられないほど複雑な計算をすぐにすることができる)

Day 17))CD-A17
Quick Review
答えは左ページ下

☐ ensure ☐ halt ☐ implement ☐ iron
☐ imply ☐ confront ☐ prohibit ☐ initiate
☐ drain ☐ recruit ☐ exhaust ☐ authorize
☐ abandon ☐ consume ☐ disturb ☐ eliminate

CHAPTER 1
CHAPTER 2
CHAPTER 3
CHAPTER 4
CHAPTER 5
CHAPTER 6
CHAPTER 7
CHAPTER 8
CHAPTER 9
CHAPTER 10

Chapter 2 Review

左ページの(1)〜(20)の動詞の同意・類義語［熟語］（≒）、反意・反対語（⇔）を右ページのA〜Tから選び、カッコの中に答えを書き込もう。意味が分からないときは、見出し番号を参照して復習しておこう（答えは右ページ下）。

- (1) manufacture (0196) ≒は? (　　)
- (2) decline (0197) ≒は? (　　)
- (3) postpone (0199) ≒は? (　　)
- (4) reveal (0203) ⇔は? (　　)
- (5) ban (0209) ≒は? (　　)
- (6) obtain (0214) ≒は? (　　)
- (7) attain (0220) ≒は? (　　)
- (8) modify (0227) ≒は? (　　)
- (9) inspect (0230) ≒は? (　　)
- (10) withdraw (0232) ⇔は? (　　)
- (11) emerge (0244) ≒は? (　　)
- (12) resign (0249) ≒は? (　　)
- (13) depart (0250) ⇔は? (　　)
- (14) fulfill (0255) ≒は? (　　)
- (15) imply (0258) ≒は? (　　)
- (16) confront (0262) ≒は? (　　)
- (17) iron (0269) ≒は? (　　)
- (18) acknowledge (0274) ⇔は? (　　)
- (19) preserve (0277) ≒は? (　　)
- (20) assert (0279) ≒は? (　　)

A. deposit
B. prohibit
C. claim
D. produce
E. retire
F. examine
G. deny
H. gain
I. carry out
J. put off
K. face
L. accomplish
M. press
N. appear
O. decrease
P. arrive
Q. infer
R. change
S. conserve
T. conceal

【解答】(1) D (2) O (3) J (4) T (5) B (6) H (7) L (8) R (9) F (10) A (11) N (12) E (13) P (14) I (15) Q (16) K (17) M (18) G (19) S (20) C

CHAPTER 3

形容詞：超必修96

Chapter 3では、TOEIC「超必修」の形容詞96を押さえていきます。このChapterが終われば、本書も3分の1が終了。そして、「超必修」の名詞・動詞・形容詞384が身についたことになります。

Day 19【形容詞1】
▶ 94
Day 20【形容詞2】
▶ 98
Day 21【形容詞3】
▶ 102
Day 22【形容詞4】
▶ 106
Day 23【形容詞5】
▶ 110
Day 24【形容詞6】
▶ 114
Chapter 3 Review
▶ 118

TOEIC的格言

Constant dripping wears away a stone.
雨垂れ石を穿つ。
[直訳] 絶え間のない滴りは石を擦り減らす。

Day 19　形容詞1

Check 1　Listen))) CD-A19

☐ 0289
significant
/signífikənt/
❶アクセント注意
Part 5, 6

形 ❶(〜にとって)**重要な**、重大な(for [to] 〜)(≒important, vital, crucial)　❷かなりの　❸意味のある
名 significance：❶重要性、重大性　❷意味、意義
副 significantly：❶著しく　❷(more [most] 〜で)さらに[最も]重要なことに(は)

☐ 0290
annual
/ǽnjuəl/
Part 4

形 **年1回の**、毎年の、年次の；1年間の
副 annually：毎年、年1度

☐ 0291
outstanding
/àutstǽndiŋ/
Part 4

形 ❶**優れた**、傑出した；顕著な　❷未払いの　⊕この意味ではビジネス関連問題で頻出

☐ 0292
generous
/dʒénərəs/
Part 5, 6

形 ❶(金などに)**気前のよい**(with 〜)(⇔stingy：けちな)；(〜に対して)寛大な(to 〜)　❷たくさんの
名 generosity：気前のよさ；寛大
副 generously：❶気前よく　❷寛大にも　❸たっぷり

☐ 0293
appropriate
/əpróupriət/
Part 2, 3

形 ❶**適切な**(≒suitable, proper)　❷(be appropriate forで)〜に適している、ふさわしい(≒be suitable for, be fit for, be proper for)
動 (/əpróuprièit/)❶〜を着服[横領]する　❷(appropriate A for Bで)A(金など)をBのために充てる、使用する

☐ 0294
initial
/iníʃəl/
❶アクセント注意
Part 5, 6

形 **最初の**(≒first)
名 頭文字
名 initiative：❶主導権、イニシアチブ　❷自発性
名 initiation：❶(〜への)加入(into 〜)　❷開始
動 initiate：(計画など)を始める

☐ 0295
accurate
/ǽkjurət/
Part 5, 6

形 ❶**正確な**(≒right, correct, exact, precise)(⇔inaccurate)　❷精密な
名 accuracy：正確さ、精密さ
副 accurately：正確[精密]に

☐ 0296
thorough
/θə́ːrou/
❶発音注意
Part 5, 6

形 **徹底的な**、完全な、周到な　⊕through(〜を通り抜けて)と混同しないように注意
副 thoroughly：徹底的に、完全に

continued
▼

Chapter 3では、6日をかけて「超必修」の形容詞96をチェック。まずはCDでチャンツを聞いて、単語を「耳」からインプット！

- ☐ 聞くだけモード　Check 1
- ☐ しっかりモード　Check 1 ▶ 2
- ☐ かんぺきモード　Check 1 ▶ 2 ▶ 3

Check 2　Phrase

☐ a significant change (重要な変化)
☐ a significant amount of money (かなりの額の金)

☐ an annual conference (年次会議)
☐ an annual income (年収)

☐ an outstanding scientist (優れた科学者)
☐ an outstanding debt (未払いの借金)

☐ be generous with one's money (惜しみなく金を使う)
☐ a generous pay increase (大幅な賃上げ)

☐ take appropriate action (適切な行動を取る)
☐ be appropriate for children under five (5歳未満の子どもに適している)

☐ an initial plan (当初の計画)
☐ an initial phase (初期段階)

☐ an accurate calculation (正確な計算)
☐ an accurate machine (精密な機械)

☐ a thorough investigation (徹底的な調査)
☐ a thorough man (完全主義者)

Check 3　Sentence

☐ Opera is one of the most significant art forms in Western history. (オペラは西洋史で最も重要な芸術形式の1つだ)

☐ The company had to cut $2 million from its annual budget. (その会社は年間予算を200万ドル削減しなければならなかった)

☐ Her performance at the concert was outstanding. (そのコンサートでの彼女の演奏は傑出していた)

☐ Jenny is a very open-minded, generous person. (ジェニーは全く偏見がなく、寛大な人だ)

☐ The teacher's comments on my essay were appropriate. (私の小論文に関する先生のコメントは適切だった)

☐ The construction costs exceeded our initial estimates. (建設費は私たちの当初の見積もりを上回った)

☐ The information from him was quite accurate. (彼から得た情報はかなり正確だった)

☐ You should have thorough knowledge about the product that you sell. (あなたは自分が売る製品について完全に知っておくべきだ)

continued ▼

Day 19

Check 1　Listen))) CD-A19

□ 0297
current
/kə́:rənt/
❶アクセント注意
Part 2, 3

形 **現在の**、今の(≒present)
名 (川などの)流れ；電流
名 currency：通貨、貨幣
副 currently：現在は、現在のところ

□ 0298
alternative
/ɔ:ltə́:rnətiv/
❶アクセント注意
Part 5, 6

形 **代わりの**、二者択一の
名 (〜の)代替案[手段]、選択肢(to 〜)
名 alternate：代替物
動 alternate：❶交互に起こる　❷〜を交互にする
形 alternate：❶交互の　❷代わりの

□ 0299
precise
/prisáis/
❶アクセント注意
Part 5, 6

形 **正確な**(≒right, correct, exact, accurate)　❶concise (簡潔な)と混同しないように注意
名 precision：正確さ
副 precisely：正確に

□ 0300
moderate
/mάdərət/
Part 5, 6

形 ❶(程度などが)**適度の**(⇔excessive：過度の)　❷節度のある、穏健な(⇔extreme：過激な)
名 穏健な人
動 (/mάdərèit/)❶〜を和らげる　❷〜の司会をする
副 moderately：❶適度に　❷節度を守って

□ 0301
competitive
/kəmpétətiv/
ビジネス問題

形 ❶(価格などが)**競争力のある**　❷競争の
名 competition：(〜を目指す/…同士の)競争、争い(for 〜/between [among] …)
名 competitor：競争相手、競合他社
動 compete：(〜と)競争する、張り合う(with 〜)

□ 0302
numerous
/njú:mərəs/
❶発音注意
Part 7

形 **数多くの**、たくさんの(≒many)

□ 0303
adequate
/ǽdikwət/
Part 5, 6

形 ❶(〜のために)**十分な**(量の)(for 〜)(≒enough, sufficient, ample)(⇔inadequate)　❷(〜に)適した(for [to] 〜)(≒suitable, appropriate, fit, proper)
副 adequately：十分に、適切に

□ 0304
relevant
/réləvənt/
Part 7

形 (当面の問題と)**関係のある**(to 〜)；実際的な重要性を持つ(⇔Irrelevant：無関係の)

Day 18))) CD-A18
Quick Review
答えは右ページ下

□ 〜を放送する
□ 〜を認める
□ 〜を明らかにする
□ 〜を明確に述べる

□ 〜を保護する
□ 〜と連絡を取る
□ 〜だと断言する
□ 〜を監視する

□ 〜を切り刻む
□ 競争する
□ 〜をエンストさせる
□ 〜を保持する

□ 〜を修理する
□ 〜を証明する
□ 痛む
□ 〜を計算する

Check 2 Phrase

- the current price(時価)
- the current trend(現在の傾向)

- an alternative plan(代案)
- an alternative means(別の手段)

- precise measurements(正確な寸法)
- at the precise moment(まさにその時に)

- a moderate temperature(適温)
- a moderate demand(穏当な要求)

- competitive prices(競争力のある価格、安い価格)
- competitive sports(競技スポーツ)

- numerous mistakes(多くの間違い)
- on numerous occasions(何度も)

- adequate food for five guests(5人の客に十分な量の食べ物)
- be adequate to one's needs(〜の要望に合っている)

- relevant information(関連情報)

Check 3 Sentence

- My current income is about $50,000 per year.(私の現在の収入は年間5万ドルほどだ)

- They are looking for alternative sources of energy to oil.(彼らは石油に代わるエネルギー源を探している)

- The precise location of the sunken ship is still unknown.(その沈没船の正確な位置はいまだに分かっていない)

- A moderate amount of exercise is necessary for your health.(適量な運動は健康に欠かせない)

- The mobile company offers very competitive rates.(その携帯電話会社は非常に競争力のある料金を提供している)

- There were numerous witnesses to the incident.(その事件には多くの目撃者がいた)

- We don't have adequate funds to carry out the project.(私たちはそのプロジェクトを実行するのに十分な資金を持っていない)

- Applicants must have relevant experience in the hotel industry.(応募者はホテル産業に関係のある経験を有していなければならない)●求人広告の表現

Day 18 》CD-A18
Quick Review
答えは左ページ下

- transmit
- acknowledge
- disclose
- specify
- preserve
- reach
- assert
- monitor
- chop
- compete
- stall
- retain
- fix
- demonstrate
- ache
- calculate

Day 20 形容詞2

Check 1　Listen))) CD-A20

☐ 0305
diverse
/divə́ːrs/
Part 5, 6

形 **多様な**、さまざまの(≒various)
名 diversity：多様性；相違
動 diversify：❶～を多様化する　❷(投資)を多角的にする　❸事業を広げる

☐ 0306
valid
/vǽlid/
Part 4

形 ❶(契約などが)(法的に)**有効な**(≒effective)(⇔invalid, void)　❷(理由などが)妥当な(≒reasonable)
名 validation：実証、確証
動 validate：❶～を法的に有効にする　❷～を実証[確証]する

☐ 0307
reliable
/riláiəbl/
Part 4

形 **信頼できる**、頼りになる(≒dependable)(⇔unreliable)
名 reliability：信頼性
名 reliance：❶依存　❷信用、信頼
動 rely：(rely onで)～に頼る；～を信頼する

☐ 0308
bankrupt
/bǽŋkrʌpt/
ビジネス問題

形 **破産[倒産]した**(≒broke)
名 破産者
名 bankruptcy：破産、倒産

☐ 0309
urgent
/ə́ːrdʒənt/
Part 2, 3

形 **緊急の**、急を要する
名 urgency：緊急
名 urge：(～したいという)衝動(to do)
動 urge：(urge A to doで)Aに～するよう催促[説得]する、強く迫る

☐ 0310
intense
/inténs/
Part 5, 6

形 **激しい**、強烈[猛烈]な
名 intensity：激しさ、強烈さ
動 intensify：❶強まる、激しくなる　❷～を強める、激しくする

☐ 0311
remote
/rimóut/
Part 7

形 ❶(～から)**遠く離れた**、遠い(from ～)(≒far away)　❷(可能性などが)わずかな、非常に少ない
名 (テレビなどの)リモコン

☐ 0312
enormous
/inɔ́ːrməs/
Part 5, 6

形 **巨大な**、莫大な(≒huge, immense, massive)
副 enormously：非常に；莫大に

continued
▼

形容詞の役割は、名詞を修飾する「限定用法」と、文中で補語になる「叙述用法」の2つ。それぞれの使われ方をCheck 2, 3で押さえよう。

- ☐ 聞くだけモード　Check 1
- ☐ しっかりモード　Check 1 ▶ 2
- ☐ かんぺきモード　Check 1 ▶ 2 ▶ 3

Check 2　Phrase

☐ diverse opinions（さまざまな意見）

☐ a valid driver's license（有効な運転免許証）
☐ a valid reason（妥当な理由）

☐ a reliable source of information（信頼できる情報源）

☐ go bankrupt（破産［倒産］する）

☐ an urgent meeting（緊急の会議）
☐ be in urgent need of ～（～を緊急に必要としている）

☐ intense heat（激しい暑さ）
☐ an intense smell（強烈なにおい）

☐ a remote galaxy（遠く離れた銀河）
☐ a remote possibility（わずかな可能性）

☐ an enormous house（巨大な家）
☐ an enormous amount of money（莫大な額の金）

Check 3　Sentence

☐ London is a culturally diverse city.（ロンドンは文化的に多様な都市だ）

☐ Normally, the student visa is valid for one year.（通常、学生ビザは1年間有効だ）

☐ I don't think he is reliable.（彼を信頼できるとは私は思わない）

☐ The country's economy is virtually bankrupt.（その国の経済は実質的に破綻している）

☐ He has flown to New York on urgent business.（彼は緊急の仕事でニューヨークへ飛んだ）

☐ There has been an intense debate over the issue.（その問題をめぐっては激しい議論がなされている）

☐ She lives in a remote mountain village.（彼女は人里離れた山村に住んでいる）

☐ The company has an enormous debt.（その会社は巨額の負債を抱えている）

continued ▼

Day 20

Check 1　Listen 》CD-A20

□ 0313
profitable
/práfitəbl/
ビジネス問題

形 ❶**収益**[もうけ]**の多い**(≒lucrative)　❷有益な
名 profitability：収益性
名 profit：利益、もうけ
動 profit：(〜から)利益を得る(from [by] 〜)

□ 0314
rural
/rúərəl/
Part 7

形 **田舎**[田園、農村]**の**(≒rustic)(⇔urban)

□ 0315
efficient
/ifíʃənt/
❶アクセント注意
ビジネス問題

形 ❶**効率**[能率]**的な**　❷有能な
名 efficiency：効率、能率
副 efficiently：能率[効果]的に

□ 0316
fatal
/féitl/
Part 2, 3

形 **致命的な**(≒deadly, mortal)
名 fate：❶運命、運　❷運命の力

□ 0317
critical
/krítikəl/
Part 4

形 ❶(〜にとって)**重大な**(to 〜)(≒important, crucial)
❷批判[批評]的な
名 crisis：危機、重大局面
名 criticism：批評、評論
動 criticize：❶〜のあら探しをする　❷〜を批判する

□ 0318
reverse
/rivə́ːrs/
Part 7

形 ❶**逆**[反対]**の**(≒opposite)　❷裏の(⇔obverse)
名 (通例 the 〜)❶逆、反対　❷裏(面)
動 ❶〜(の位置など)を逆[反対]にする　❷(判決など)を破棄する

□ 0319
modest
/mádist/
Part 5, 6

形 ❶(〜に関して)**控えめな**、謙虚な(about 〜)(≒humble)(⇔proud)　❷あまり大きく[多く]ない
名 modesty：控えめ、謙遜
副 modestly：控えめに、謙遜して

□ 0320
urban
/ə́ːrbən/
Part 5, 6

形 **都市**[都会]**の**(⇔rural, rustic)
動 urbanize：〜を都市[都会]化する

Day 19 》CD-A19
Quick Review
答えは右ページ下

□ 重要な　　□ 適切な　　□ 現在の　　□ 競争力のある
□ 年1回の　□ 最初の　　□ 代わりの　□ 数多くの
□ 優れた　　□ 正確な　　□ 正確な　　□ 十分な
□ 気前のよい　□ 徹底的な　□ 適度の　　□ 関係のある

Check 2 Phrase

- a highly profitable business（収益性が非常に高い事業）
- a profitable experience（有益な経験）

- rural life（田舎暮らし）
- rural communities（農村社会）

- an efficient transport system（効率的な輸送システム）
- an efficient employee（有能な従業員）

- a fatal mistake（致命的なミス）
- a fatal illness（致死性の病気）

- a critical decision（重大な決定）
- a critical report（批判的な報告書）

- in reverse order（逆の順序で）
- the reverse side of a check（小切手の裏面）

- be modest about one's achievements（自分の業績を誇らない）
- a modest house（あまり大きくない家）

- urban development（都市開発）

Check 3 Sentence

- The cut in costs made the company profitable.（経費削減によってその会社は収益を上げた）

- Unemployment is a problem in rural areas.（失業が農村地域で問題になっている）

- The service at the hotel was efficient and friendly.（そのホテルでのサービスは効率的で親切なものだった）

- There is a fatal flaw in his argument.（彼の論点には致命的な欠点がある）

- Your support is critical to the success of the project.（あなたの支援はプロジェクトの成功にとって重要だ）

- The number of AIDS cases is in reverse proportion to age.（エイズの症例数は年齢と反比例している）

- Jack is a modest and kind young man.（ジャックは謙虚で親切な若者だ）

- Air pollution is a serious urban problem.（大気汚染は深刻な都市問題だ）

Day 19 » CD-A19
Quick Review
答えは左ページ下

- significant
- annual
- outstanding
- generous
- appropriate
- initial
- accurate
- thorough
- current
- alternative
- precise
- moderate
- competitive
- numerous
- adequate
- relevant

CHAPTER 1
CHAPTER 2
CHAPTER 3
CHAPTER 4
CHAPTER 5
CHAPTER 6
CHAPTER 7
CHAPTER 8
CHAPTER 9
CHAPTER 10

Day 21　形容詞3

Check 1　Listen 》CD-A21

☐ 0321
diligent
/dílədʒənt/
Part 5, 6

形 (〜に)**勤勉な**(in [about] 〜)(≒hardworking, industrious)(⇔idle, lazy)
名diligence：(〜での)勤勉、不断の努力(in 〜)
副diligently：勤勉に、こつこつと

☐ 0322
consistent
/kənsístənt/
Part 5, 6

形 ❶(言行などが)**首尾一貫した**(in 〜)(≒coherent)(⇔inconsistent)　❷(成長などが)堅実な、安定した(≒steady)　❸(be consistent withで)(言行などが)〜と一致[調和、両立]している
名consistency：❶一貫性　❷(液体などの)濃度

☐ 0323
flexible
/fléksəbl/
Part 2, 3

形 ❶(考えなどが)**柔軟な**；(予定が)融通の利く(≒adaptable)(⇔rigid, inflexible)　❷曲げやすい(≒pliable)
名flexibility：柔軟[融通]性

☐ 0324
regional
/ríːdʒənl/
Part 5, 6

形 **地域の**、地方の
名region：地域、地方

☐ 0325
distinguished
/distíŋgwiʃt/
Part 4

形 (〜で)**有名な**(for 〜)(≒famous)；優れた
名distinction：(〜の間の)区別(between 〜)
動distinguish：(distinguish A from Bで)AをBと区別する
形distinct：(〜と)異なった(from 〜)

☐ 0326
abundant
/əbʌ́ndənt/
Part 4

形 **豊富な**(≒plentiful, ample, affluent)
名abundance：豊富、多数、多量

☐ 0327
acute
/əkjúːt/
Part 2, 3

形 ❶(痛みなどが)**激しい**(≒sharp)；(病気が)急性の(⇔chronic：慢性の)　❷(状況などが)深刻な(≒severe, serious)　❸(感覚が)鋭い(≒keen)

☐ 0328
substantial
/səbstǽnʃəl/
Part 5, 6

形 ❶**かなりの**、相当な(≒considerable)　❷本質[実質]的な
名substance：❶物質　❷本質、内容
副substantially：かなり、大いに

continued
▼

今日で本書は3割の学習が終了。先を見ると道のりは長いけれど、1日1日着実に進めていこう。ゴールは確実に近づいている！

□ 聞くだけモード　Check 1
□ しっかりモード　Check 1 ▶ 2
□ かんぺきモード　Check 1 ▶ 2 ▶ 3

Check 2　Phrase

□ a diligent student（勤勉な学生）

□ a consistent policy（首尾一貫した政策）
□ consistent growth（安定した成長）

□ flexible thinking（柔軟な発想）
□ a flexible plastic（曲げやすいプラスチック）

□ a regional dialect（方言）

□ a distinguished politician（有名な政治家）

□ an abundant supply of food（豊富な食糧の供給）

□ acute tuberculosis（急性結核）
□ acute shortages of food（深刻な食糧不足）

□ a substantial salary（かなりの賃金）
□ substantial agreement（実質的な合意）

Check 3　Sentence

□ Sarah is very diligent in her work.（サラは非常に仕事に熱心だ）

□ He is consistent in his views.（彼は意見が首尾一貫している）

□ I'm retired, so my schedule is flexible.（私は退職したので、予定は融通が利く）

□ The purpose of the meeting was to stimulate the regional economy.（その会議の目的は地域経済を活性化することだった）

□ He was awarded a prize for his distinguished achievements in the field of journalism.（彼は報道分野での優れた業績により賞を与えられた）

□ There is abundant evidence for the past presence of water on Mars.（火星にかつて水があったことの豊富な証拠がある）

□ Radiation therapy can cause acute pain.（放射線治療は激しい痛みをもたらすことがある）

□ A substantial number of houses were damaged by the earthquake.（かなり多くの家がその地震で損傷を受けた）

continued
▼

Day 21

Check 1　Listen ♪ CD-A21

☐ 0329
productive
/prədʌ́ktiv/
ビジネス問題

形 ❶**生産力のある**(⇔unproductive)　❷生産的な
名 productivity：生産力[性]；生産量
名 product：製品
名 production：製造、生産；生産高
動 produce：〜を生産[製造]する

☐ 0330
conservative
/kənsə́ːrvətiv/
❶定義注意
Part 4

形 ❶(評価などが)**控えめな**　❷保守的な
名 保守的な人
名 conservation：(自然環境などの)保護、保存
動 conserve：〜を保護[保存]する；(エネルギーなど)を節約して使う

☐ 0331
beneficial
/bènəfíʃəl/
Part 2, 3

形 (〜にとって)**有益な**、(〜の)ためになる(to 〜)
名 benefit：❶(通例〜s)給付金、手当　❷利益
動 benefit：❶〜のためになる　❷(benefit from [by]で)〜によって利益を得る

☐ 0332
subtle
/sʌ́tl/
❶発音注意
Part 7

形 ❶**微妙な**、とらえがたい　❷(香りなどが)かすかな、ほのかな(≒faint)　❸(感覚などが)鋭い
名 subtlety：微妙、とらえがたいこと
副 subtly：微妙に

☐ 0333
ample
/ǽmpl/
Part 7

形 **十分な**、豊富な(≒enough, adequate, sufficient)
副 amply：十分に

☐ 0334
cozy
/kóuzi/
Part 5, 6

形 **居心地のよい**、気持ちのいい(≒comfortable)

☐ 0335
exclusive
/iksklúːsiv/
Part 5, 6

形 ❶**独占的な**　❷排他的な　❸(店などが)高級な
名 exclusion：(〜からの)除外、排除(from 〜)
動 exclude：(exclude A from Bで)AをBから締め出す、排除する
副 exclusively：独占的に、排他的に

☐ 0336
vacant
/véikənt/
Part 2, 3

形 ❶(家・座席などが)**空いている**(≒empty)(⇔occupied)　❷(職などが)欠員[空位]の
名 vacancy：❶空室、空き家　❷(職などの)欠員、空位

Day 20 ♪ CD-A20
Quick Review
答えは右ページ下

☐ 多様な
☐ 有効な
☐ 信頼できる
☐ 破産した

☐ 緊急の
☐ 激しい
☐ 遠く離れた
☐ 巨大な

☐ 収益の多い
☐ 田舎の
☐ 効率的な
☐ 致命的な

☐ 重大な
☐ 逆の
☐ 控えめな
☐ 都市の

Check 2 Phrase

- ☐ productive machinery(生産力のある機械設備)
- ☐ a productive meeting(実りのある会議)

- ☐ a conservative guess(控えめな推測)
- ☐ a conservative society(保守的な社会)

- ☐ a beneficial effect(有益な効果[影響])

- ☐ a subtle change(微妙な変化)
- ☐ a subtle smell(ほのかなにおい)

- ☐ ample opportunity(十分な機会)
- ☐ ample room(十分なスペース)

- ☐ a cozy room(居心地のいい部屋)

- ☐ an exclusive interview(独占インタビュー)
- ☐ an exclusive club(会員制の高級クラブ)

- ☐ a vacant lot(空き地)
- ☐ a vacant position(欠員になっている職)

Check 3 Sentence

- ☐ In order to be competitive, our company needs to be more productive.(競争力をつけるために、私たちの会社は生産力を高める必要がある)

- ☐ Conservative estimates indicate that there are two million unemployed.(控えめな概算では、200万人の失業者がいることが示されている)

- ☐ The volunteer activity is beneficial to our community.(そのボランティア活動は私たちの地域社会にとって有益だ)

- ☐ There is a subtle difference in meaning between the two words.(その2つの言葉には微妙な意味の違いがある)

- ☐ There is ample evidence that the climate is changing due to global warming.(地球温暖化によって気候が変化していることの十分な根拠がある)

- ☐ The hotel was cozy and the staff were friendly.(そのホテルは居心地がよく、従業員は親切だった)

- ☐ The lounge is for the exclusive use of hotel guests and members.(そのラウンジはホテル宿泊客と会員専用になっている)

- ☐ The school has no vacant classrooms.(その学校には空き教室がない)

Day 20 ») CD-A20
Quick Review
答えは左ページ下

- ☐ diverse
- ☐ valid
- ☐ reliable
- ☐ bankrupt
- ☐ urgent
- ☐ intense
- ☐ remote
- ☐ enormous
- ☐ profitable
- ☐ rural
- ☐ efficient
- ☐ fatal
- ☐ critical
- ☐ reverse
- ☐ modest
- ☐ urban

Day 22 形容詞4

Check 1　Listen 》CD-A22

☐ 0337
controversial
/kὰntrəvə́ːrʃəl/
Part 7

形 **議論の余地のある**、異論の多い[ある] (≒debatable)
名controversy：(社会・政治・道徳上の)論争、議論

☐ 0338
compulsory
/kəmpʌ́lsəri/
Part 7

形 **義務的な**、強制的な (≒obligatory, mandatory) (⇔voluntary：自発的な)
動compel：(compel A to doで)Aに無理やり[強いて]～させる

☐ 0339
internal
/intə́ːrnl/
Part 5, 6

形 ❶**内部の** (≒inner) (⇔external)　❷国内の (≒domestic) (⇔foreign)

☐ 0340
stable
/stéibl/
Part 5, 6

形 **安定した** (≒steady) (⇔unstable)
名stability：安定(性)
動stabilize：～を安定させる

☐ 0341
peculiar
/pikjúːljər/
Part 2, 3

形 ❶**奇妙な**、風変わりな (≒strange, odd, queer, eccentric)　❷(be peculiar toで)～に特有[独特、固有]である (≒be proper to)
名peculiarity：❶特性、特質　❷奇癖
副peculiarly：❶特に、特別に　❷奇妙に

☐ 0342
delicate
/délikət/
❶発音注意
Part 5, 6

形 ❶**壊れやすい** (≒fragile)　❷細心の注意を要する (≒sensitive)　❸繊細な
名delicacy：❶ごちそう　❷繊細さ　❸傷つきやすさ
副delicately：❶繊細[優美]に　❷微妙に　❸上品に

☐ 0343
humble
/hʌ́mbl/
Part 5, 6

形 ❶**謙虚な** (≒modest) (⇔proud)　❷質素な
名humility：謙遜、謙虚

☐ 0344
remarkable
/rimάːrkəbl/
Part 4

形 (～で)**注目すべき**、顕著な (for ～)
名remark：(～についての)見解、発言、所見、感想 (about [on] ～)
動remark：～と述べる、言う

continued
▼

勉強する気分になれないときは、CDを「聞き流す」だけでもOK。家で、車内で、いつでもどこでも語彙に「触れる」時間を作ってみよう。

- ☐ 聞くだけモード　Check 1
- ☐ しっかりモード　Check 1 ▶ 2
- ☐ かんぺきモード　Check 1 ▶ 2 ▶ 3

Check 2　Phrase

☐ a controversial issue [plan]（議論の余地がある問題[計画]）
☐ a controversial figure（物議を醸す人物）

☐ compulsory education（義務教育）

☐ internal organs（内臓）
☐ internal affairs（国内問題）

☐ a stable job（安定した仕事）

☐ a peculiar noise（奇妙な音）
☐ be peculiar to the region（[風習などが]その地域に特有である）

☐ delicate porcelain（壊れやすい磁器）
☐ a delicate operation（細心の注意を要する手術[作業]）

☐ a humble attitude（謙虚な態度）
☐ lead a humble life（質素な生活を送る）

☐ a remarkable discovery（注目すべき発見）

Check 3　Sentence

☐ The movie was controversial because of its violent scenes.（その映画は暴力シーンのため議論の的になった）

☐ Attendance at the seminar is compulsory.（そのセミナーへの出席は義務となっている）

☐ The company had conducted an internal investigation into an alleged embezzlement.（その会社は横領疑惑の内部調査をした）

☐ The patient remains in stable condition.（その患者の容体は安定したままだ）

☐ It is peculiar that he didn't tell me he was quitting the company.（奇妙なことに会社を辞めることを彼は私に言わなかった）

☐ Wrap delicate items in newspaper.（壊れやすい品物は新聞紙でくるんでください）

☐ She is humble about her talents.（彼女は自分の才能に対して謙虚だ）

☐ He made remarkable achievements in the field of education.（彼は教育分野で顕著な業績を残した）

continued
▼

Day 22

Check 1　Listen))) CD-A22

□ 0345
brief
/bríːf/
Part 4

形 ❶**短時間の**（≒short）　❷（話などが）簡潔な
名 簡潔な説明
動 (brief A on Bで)AにBの概要を伝える
名 briefing：簡単な報告[発表]
副 briefly：❶少しの間、しばらく　❷簡潔に、手短に

□ 0346
steep
/stíːp/
Part 7

形 ❶（増加などが）**急激な**　❷（坂などが）険しい、急な
❸（値段が）不当に高い
名 steeple：（教会などの）尖塔
副 steeply：❶急に　❷急勾配に

□ 0347
primary
/práimeri/
Part 5, 6

形 ❶**最も重要な**；主要な　❷（学校などが）初級[初等]の（≒elementary）
名 prime：最盛[全盛]期
形 prime：❶最も重要な　❷最良の
副 primarily：❶主に、主として　❷第一に

□ 0348
abstract
/ǽbstrækt/
Part 7

形 **抽象的な**（⇔concrete：具体的な）
名 (/ǽbstrækt/) ❶抽象（概念）　❷要約、摘要
名 abstraction：❶抽象概念[観念]　❷放心（状態）

□ 0349
inevitable
/inévətəbl/
Part 5, 6

形 **避けられない**、不可避の、必然の（≒unavoidable）
名 (the ～)避けられないこと[もの]
副 inevitably：必然的に、必ず

□ 0350
corporate
/kɔ́ːrpərət/
ビジネス問題

形 ❶**企業[会社、法人]の**　❷共同の　✚cooperate（協力する）と混同しないように注意
名 corporation：❶株式会社；企業　❷法人

□ 0351
overall
/óuvərɔ̀ːl/
Part 4

形 **全体[全部]の**、総合的な
副 (/óuvərɔ́ːl/)全体としては

□ 0352
upward
/ʌ́pwərd/
ビジネス問題

形 **上向きの**、上方への（⇔downward）
副 上方へ、上向きに

Day 21))) CD-A21
Quick Review
答えは右ページ下

□ 勤勉な　□ 有名な　□ 生産力のある　□ 十分な
□ 首尾一貫した　□ 豊富な　□ 控えめな　□ 居心地のよい
□ 柔軟な　□ 激しい　□ 有益な　□ 独占的な
□ 地域の　□ かなりの　□ 微妙な　□ 空いている

Check 2 Phrase

- a brief stay（短時間の滞在）
- a brief speech（簡潔なスピーチ）

- a steep increase in prices（物価の急激な上昇）
- a steep hill（険しい丘）

- the primary objective（最も重要な目標）
- primary education（初等教育）

- an abstract concept [painting]（抽象概念[画]）

- an inevitable result [consequence, outcome]（必然の結果）

- a corporate image（企業イメージ）
- take corporate responsibility for ～（～の共同責任を取る）

- the overall impression of ～（～の全体的な印象）

- an upward current（上昇気流）

Check 3 Sentence

- We will be making a brief stop at Shin-Osaka.（新大阪でしばらくの間停車します）⊕電車のアナウンス

- There was a steep rise in unemployment last year.（昨年、失業者数の急激な増加があった）

- The primary role of parents is to protect their children.（親の最も重要な役割は子どもを守ることだ）

- "Happiness" and "peace" are abstract nouns.（「幸福」と「平和」は抽象名詞だ）

- Without government assistance, the company's collapse would be inevitable.（政府の支援がなければ、その会社の倒産は避けられないだろう）

- As the recession gets worse, corporate bankruptcies will increase.（景気後退が悪化するにつれて、企業の倒産は増えるだろう）

- The overall cost of the project is estimated at $20 million.（そのプロジェクトの総経費は2000万ドルと見積もられている）

- Food prices are on an upward trend.（食品価格は上昇傾向にある）

Day 21))) CD-A21
Quick Review
答えは左ページ下

- diligent
- consistent
- flexible
- regional
- distinguished
- abundant
- acute
- substantial
- productive
- conservative
- beneficial
- subtle
- ample
- cozy
- exclusive
- vacant

Day 23　形容詞5

Check 1　Listen))) CD-A23

☐ 0353
artificial
/ɑ̀ːrtəfíʃəl/
Part 7

形 ❶**人工の**、人工的な(⇔natural)　❷不自然な、わざとらしい

☐ 0354
minimum
/mínəməm/
ビジネス問題

形 **最低[最小]限の**(⇔maximum)
名 最低[最小]限
動 minimize：❶〜を最小限にする　❷〜を最小限に評価する、軽視する

☐ 0355
potential
/pəténʃəl/
Part 4

形 **潜在的な**、可能性のある(≒possible)
名 (〜の)可能性、潜在力(for 〜)

☐ 0356
splendid
/spléndid/
Part 4

形 ❶**素晴らしい**、素敵な(≒fine)　❷豪華な、見事な
名 splendor：❶豪華さ　❷雄大さ

☐ 0357
secure
/sikjúər/
Part 7

形 (〜に対して)**安全な**(from [against] 〜)(≒safe)
動 ❶〜を確保する　❷〜を(…から)守る(from . . .)
名 security：❶警備　❷安全　❸(〜ies)有価証券

☐ 0358
illegal
/ilíːgəl/
Part 2, 3

形 **違法[不法]の**(≒unlawful)(⇔legal)
副 illegally：不法に

☐ 0359
genuine
/dʒénjuin/
❶アクセント注意
Part 2, 3

形 ❶(物などが)**本物の**(≒real)(⇔fake：偽の)　❷誠実な(≒sincere)
副 genuinely：誠実に、心から；純粋に

☐ 0360
contemporary
/kəntémpərèri/
❶アクセント注意
Part 5, 6

形 ❶**現代の**(≒modern)　❷同時代の
名 同時代[同時期]の人

continued
▼

見出し語の下にある「❶アクセント注意」や「❶発音注意」を見てる？ 少しの違いで相手に伝わらないこともあるので要チェック！

- ☐ 聞くだけモード　Check 1
- ☐ しっかりモード　Check 1 ▶ 2
- ☐ かんぺきモード　Check 1 ▶ 2 ▶ 3

Check 2　Phrase

☐ artificial sweeteners（人工甘味料）
☐ an artificial smile（作り笑い）

☐ the minimum wage（最低賃金）

☐ a potential customer（見込み客、潜在客）

☐ splendid weather（素晴らしい天気）
☐ a splendid view of Mt. Fuji（富士山の見事な眺め）

☐ secure investment（安全な投資）
☐ be secure from [against] theft（盗難に遭う恐れがない）

☐ illegal drugs（違法薬物）
☐ It is illegal to do ~.（~することは違法だ）

☐ genuine leather（本革）
☐ a genuine person（誠実な人）

☐ contemporary music（現代音楽）
☐ be contemporary with ~（~と同時代の人である）

Check 3　Sentence

☐ The product contains no artificial colors or flavors.（その製品には人工着色料や人工香味料は含まれていない）

☐ A minimum order of $20 is required if you want free delivery.（無料配達を希望する場合は20ドルの最低注文量が必要である）

☐ Properly targeting potential buyers is an important part of the selling process.（適切に潜在購買者を絞ることが販売過程の重要な要素だ）

☐ We had a splendid holiday in France.（私たちはフランスで素晴らしい休暇を過ごした）

☐ Keep your valuables in a secure place.（貴重品は安全な場所にしまっておいてください）

☐ The minimum fine for illegal parking is $50.（違法駐車に対する最低罰金は50ドルだ）

☐ I don't know whether the painting is genuine or not.（私はその絵画が本物かどうか分からない）

☐ I'm interested in contemporary art.（私は現代美術に関心がある）

continued
▼

Day 23

Check 1　Listen)) CD-A23

□ 0361
prompt
/prámpt/
Part 5, 6

形 ❶**即座[即刻]の**(≒quick)　❷時間を守る(≒punctual)
動 ❶〜を引き起こす　❷(prompt A to do で)A に〜するよう促す
副 promptly：❶即座に、敏速に　❷(ある時刻)ちょうど、きっかり

□ 0362
terrific
/tərífik/
Part 2, 3

形 ❶**素晴らしい**、非常によい(≒marvelous)　❷(程度が)ものすごい、猛烈な　✚terrible は「極めてひどい；恐ろしい」

□ 0363
environmental
/invàiərənméntl/
Part 2, 3

形 **環境(上)の**、周囲の
名 environment：❶(the 〜)自然環境　❷環境、周囲の状況
名 environmentalist：自然保護論者
副 environmentally：環境保護に関して

□ 0364
crucial
/krúːʃəl/
Part 7

形 (〜にとって)**非常に重要[重大]な**(≒vital)；決定的な(to [for] 〜)
副 crucially：決定的に

□ 0365
vital
/váitl/
Part 7

形 ❶(〜にとって)**極めて重要[重大]な**、不可欠な(to [for] 〜)(≒crucial)　❷活気のある、生き生きとした
名 vitality：❶活力、生命力　❷(制度などの)持続力
副 vitally：極めて重大に；絶対に

□ 0366
federal
/fédərəl/
Part 7

形 ❶**連邦政府[国家]の**　❷(国家が)連邦(制)の
名 federalism：連邦主義
名 federalist：連邦主義者
名 federation：❶連合、連盟　❷連邦政府[制度]

□ 0367
prominent
/prámənənt/
Part 7

形 ❶(〜の点で)**著名[有名]な**、卓越した(in 〜)(≒famous)　❷目立った、重要な　❸(歯などが)突き出た
名 prominence：❶目立つこと、卓越　❷突出物

□ 0368
sole
/sóul/
Part 7

形 ❶(通例 the 〜)**唯一の**　❷独占的な(≒exclusive)
副 solely：❶専ら、全く　❷ただ1人で、単独で

Day 22)) CD-A22
Quick Review
答えは右ページ下

- □ 議論の余地のある
- □ 義務的な
- □ 内部の
- □ 安定した
- □ 奇妙な
- □ 壊れやすい
- □ 謙虚な
- □ 注目すべき
- □ 短時間の
- □ 急激な
- □ 最も重要な
- □ 抽象的な
- □ 避けられない
- □ 企業の
- □ 全体の
- □ 上向きの

Check 2 Phrase

- a prompt reply（即答）
- try to be prompt（時間を守るように努める）

- a terrific idea（素晴らしいアイデア）
- at terrific speed（猛スピードで）

- environmental pollution（環境汚染）
- the environmental movement（環境保護運動）

- a crucial moment [point]（決定的な瞬間[点]）
- It is crucial that ~.（~ということは非常に重要である）

- play a vital role in ~（~で極めて重要な役割を果たす）
- a vital man（元気のよい男性）

- federal law（連邦法）
- a federal state（連邦国家）

- a prominent scientist（著名な科学者）
- occupy a prominent place [position]（重要な場所を占める）

- the sole purpose [reason]（唯一の目的[理由]）
- the sole right（独占権）

Check 3 Sentence

- We must take prompt action to prevent global warming.（地球温暖化を食い止めるために私たちはすぐに行動を起こさなければならない）

- We had a terrific dinner at the restaurant last night.（私たちは昨晩、そのレストランで素晴らしい夕食を食べた）

- The government should tackle environmental problems more aggressively.（政府はもっと積極的に環境問題に取り組むべきだ）

- New policy is crucial to the development of our company.（新しい方針が我が社の発展にとって非常に重要だ）

- It is vital that you attend the meeting.（あなたがその会議に出席することが極めて重要だ）

- They are trying to reduce the federal deficit by 10 percent.（彼らは連邦政府の赤字を10パーセント減らそうと努力している）

- Mr. Dawson is a prominent business leader.（ドーソン氏は卓越した経済界のリーダーだ）

- She was the sole survivor of the accident.（彼女はその事故の唯一の生存者だった）

Day 22))) CD-A22
Quick Review
答えは左ページ下

- controversial
- compulsory
- internal
- stable
- peculiar
- delicate
- humble
- remarkable
- brief
- steep
- primary
- abstract
- inevitable
- corporate
- overall
- upward

Day 24　形容詞6

Check 1　Listen 》CD-A24

0369
extensive
/iksténsiv/
Part 5, 6

形 ❶(調査などが)**広範囲にわたる**(⇔intensive：集中的な)　❷(損害などが)大規模な、甚だしい
名 extension：❶(電話の)内線　❷延期　❸拡張
動 extend：❶〜を延長する　❷〜を拡張する
副 extensively：広範囲に、広く

0370
gloomy
/glúːmi/
ビジネス問題

形 ❶**悲観的な**(≒depressing)　❷薄暗い　❸憂うつな

0371
deliberate
/dilíbərət/
❶アクセント注意
Part 5, 6

形 ❶**意図**[計画]**的な**、故意の(≒intentional, willful)　❷(〜の点で)慎重な(in 〜)(≒careful)
動 (/dilíbərèit/) ❶〜を熟考する(≒consider)　❷(deliberate about [on, over]で)〜について熟考する
副 deliberately：❶故意に　❷慎重に

0372
rigid
/rídʒid/
Part 5, 6

形 ❶**厳格な**、厳しい(≒strict, rigorous, stringent)　❷柔軟性のない(⇔flexible)　❸堅い(≒firm, stiff)
副 rigidly：❶厳格に　❷堅く

0373
sophisticated
/səfístəkèitid/
Part 2, 3

形 ❶**洗練された**、教養のある　❷(機械などが)精巧な
名 sophistication：❶洗練　❷精巧
名 sophisticate：洗練された人；教養人
動 sophisticate：〜を洗練させる

0374
deserted
/dizə́ːrtid/
Part 1

形 ❶**人けのない**、人通りのない
動 desert：〜を見捨てる、捨てる

0375
tremendous
/triméndəs/
Part 5, 6

形 ❶**ものすごい**、すさまじい　❷素晴らしい(≒excellent)

0376
competent
/kámpətənt/
Part 7

形 ❶(仕事などに)**有能な**(at [in] 〜)(≒skilled)；(〜する)能力のある(to do)(≒able, capable)；(〜するのに)適格な(to do)　❷(仕事が)満足のいく(≒satisfactory)
名 competence：❶能力、力量　❷法的権限

continued
▼

今日でChapter 3は最後！ 時間に余裕があったら、章末のReviewにも挑戦しておこう。忘れてしまった単語も結構あるのでは?!

☐ 聞くだけモード　Check 1
☐ しっかりモード　Check 1 ▶ 2
☐ かんぺきモード　Check 1 ▶ 2 ▶ 3

Check 2　Phrase

☐ extensive research（広範囲にわたる調査）
☐ extensive damage（大規模な被害）

☐ a gloomy economic outlook（悲観的な景気見通し）
☐ a gloomy room（薄暗い部屋）

☐ a deliberate lie（意図的なうそ）
☐ deliberate speech（慎重な発言）

☐ rigid methods（厳格な方法）
☐ rigid rules（柔軟性のない規則）

☐ a sophisticated woman（洗練された女性）
☐ a highly sophisticated machine（非常に精巧な機械）

☐ a deserted beach（人けのない海岸）

☐ tremendous appetite（ものすごい食欲）
☐ a tremendous athlete（素晴らしい運動選手）

☐ a competent mechanic（有能な機械工）
☐ a competent job（満足のいく仕事）

Check 3　Sentence

☐ He has extensive knowledge of classical literature.（彼は古典文学の広範な知識を持っている）

☐ The view for the country's economic future is gloomy.（その国の経済の見通しは暗い）

☐ His comment was a deliberate insult to her.（彼のコメントは彼女を意図的に侮辱するものだった）

☐ He maintains a rigid separation of private and public life.（彼は私的な生活と公的な生活を厳密に分けている）

☐ The district is one of the most sophisticated areas in the city.（その地区は市の中で最も洗練された地域の1つだ）

☐ The street is deserted.（通りには人けがない）

☐ The progress in information technology is tremendous.（情報技術の進歩はすさまじい）

☐ I don't think he is competent to manage the company.（彼に会社を経営する力があるとは私は思わない）

continued
▼

Day 24

Check 1　Listen))) CD-A24

0377 vigorous
/vígərəs/
Part 5, 6

形 ❶**精力[積極]的な**　❷健康[丈夫]な　+rigorous(厳格な)と混同しないように注意
- 名 vigor: 精力、活力
- 副 vigorously: 精力的に、力強く

0378 decent
/dí:snt/
❶発音注意
Part 5, 6

形 ❶**まずまずの**、まあまあの　❷礼儀正しい、慎み深い(⇔indecent)　❸(服装が)まともな
- 名 decency: ❶礼儀正しさ、上品さ　❷良識
- 副 decently: ❶相当に　❷見苦しくなく

0379 preliminary
/prilímənèri/
Part 5, 6

形 (〜の)**予備[準備]の** (to 〜) (≒preparatory)
名 (通例〜ies) ❶予備段階；準備　❷予選

0380 grand
/grǽnd/
Part 4

形 ❶**壮大[雄大]な** (≒magnificent)　❷偉大[崇高]な

0381 harsh
/há:rʃ/
Part 7

形 ❶**(気候などが)厳しい**(⇔mild, comfortable)；過酷[残酷]な(≒cruel)　❷(色・光などが)不快な、どぎつい；(声・音などが)耳[目]障りな
- 副 harshly: ❶厳しく　❷耳[目]障りになるほど

0382 alike
/əláik/
Part 7

形 **似ている** (≒similar)　+叙述用法のみ
副 同様に (≒equally)

0383 maximum
/mǽksəməm/
Part 5, 6

形 **最大限の**、最高の(⇔minimum)
名 最大限、最高
- 動 maximize: 〜を最大にする

0384 detailed
/dí:teild/
Part 2, 3

形 **詳細な**
- 名 detail: ❶(〜s)詳細　❷細部
- 動 detail: 〜を詳しく述べる

Day 23))) CD-A23
Quick Review
答えは右ページ下

- □ 人工の
- □ 最低限の
- □ 潜在的な
- □ 素晴らしい
- □ 安全な
- □ 違法の
- □ 本物の
- □ 現代の
- □ 即座の
- □ 素晴らしい
- □ 環境の
- □ 非常に重要な
- □ 極めて重要な
- □ 連邦政府の
- □ 著名な
- □ 唯一の

Check 2　Phrase

- a vigorous debate（活発な議論）
- a vigorous old man（健康な老人）

- a decent income（まずまずの収入）
- a decent young man（礼儀正しい若者）

- a preliminary examination（予備試験）

- on a grand scale（大規模に）
- a grand idea（崇高な考え）

- a harsh winter（厳しい冬）
- a harsh voice（耳障りな声）

- be exactly alike（全くよく似ている）

- for maximum effect（最大の効果を得るために）

- a detailed explanation [account]（詳細な説明）

Check 3　Sentence

- He is a vigorous opponent of a tax increase.（彼は増税の猛烈な反対者だ）

- I had a decent sleep last night.（昨夜はまあまあ眠れた）

- The construction is still in the preliminary stages.（建設はまだ準備段階にある）

- You can enjoy a grand view of the Rocky Mountains from the hotel windows.（ホテルの窓からはロッキー山脈の壮大な眺めを楽しむことができる）

- The movie has received harsh reviews from critics.（その映画は評論家たちから厳しい批評を受けた）

- The twin sisters are so much alike that it's difficult to tell one from the other.（その双子の姉妹は非常によく似ているので、区別がつきにくい）

- You should make maximum use of this opportunity.（あなたはこの機会を最大限に活用したほうがいい）

- Could you write a detailed report of the meeting?（その会議の詳細な報告書を書いてくれますか?）

Day 23 》CD-A23
Quick Review
答えは左ページ下

- artificial
- minimum
- potential
- splendid
- secure
- illegal
- genuine
- contemporary
- prompt
- terrific
- environmental
- crucial
- vital
- federal
- prominent
- sole

Chapter 3 Review

左ページの(1)〜(20)の形容詞の同意・類義語（≒）、反意・反対語（⇔）を右ページのA〜Tから選び、カッコの中に答えを書き込もう。意味が分からないときは、見出し番号を参照して復習しておこう（答えは右ページ下）。

- □ (1) significant (0289) ≒は? (　　)
- □ (2) generous (0292) ⇔は? (　　)
- □ (3) initial (0294) ≒は? (　　)
- □ (4) numerous (0302) ≒は? (　　)
- □ (5) valid (0306) ⇔は? (　　)
- □ (6) enormous (0312) ≒は? (　　)
- □ (7) urban (0320) ⇔は? (　　)
- □ (8) consistent (0322) ≒は? (　　)
- □ (9) abundant (0326) ≒は? (　　)
- □ (10) vacant (0336) ≒は? (　　)
- □ (11) compulsory (0338) ≒は? (　　)
- □ (12) peculiar (0341) ≒は? (　　)
- □ (13) delicate (0342) ≒は? (　　)
- □ (14) abstract (0348) ⇔は? (　　)
- □ (15) artificial (0353) ⇔は? (　　)
- □ (16) terrific (0362) ≒は? (　　)
- □ (17) prominent (0367) ≒は? (　　)
- □ (18) deliberate (0371) ≒は? (　　)
- □ (19) preliminary (0379) ≒は? (　　)
- □ (20) grand (0380) ≒は? (　　)

A. huge
B. natural
C. obligatory
D. rural
E. marvelous
F. plentiful
G. important
H. magnificent
I. strange
J. void
K. intentional
L. empty
M. stingy
N. concrete
O. many
P. famous
Q. coherent
R. fragile
S. preparatory
T. first

【解答】 (1) G (2) M (3) T (4) O (5) J (6) A (7) D (8) Q (9) F (10) L
(11) C (12) I (13) R (14) N (15) B (16) E (17) P (18) K (19) S (20) H

CHAPTER 4

名詞：必修192

Chapter 4では、TOEIC「必修」の名詞192をマスターします。「超」が抜けても、どれも重要な単語ばかり。本テストで慌てることがないよう、1語1語を着実に身につけていきましょう。

TOEIC的格言

Don't count your chickens before they are hatched.

捕らぬ狸の皮算用。
[直訳] 孵化する前にひよこを数えるな。

Day 25 【名詞13】
▶ 122
Day 26 【名詞14】
▶ 126
Day 27 【名詞15】
▶ 130
Day 28 【名詞16】
▶ 134
Day 29 【名詞17】
▶ 138
Day 30 【名詞18】
▶ 142
Day 31 【名詞19】
▶ 146
Day 32 【名詞20】
▶ 150
Day 33 【名詞21】
▶ 154
Day 34 【名詞22】
▶ 158
Day 35 【名詞23】
▶ 162
Day 36 【名詞24】
▶ 166
Chapter 4 Review
▶ 170

Day 25　名詞13

Check 1　Listen))) CD-A25

□ 0385
apparatus
/ǽpərǽtəs/
Part 7

名 **器具**、装置(≒equipment)　●複数形はapparatus(単数と同形)とapparatusesの2つある

□ 0386
poll
/póul/
Part 5, 6

名 ❶**世論調査**(の結果)　❷(the ~s)投票；投票所
動 (人々)の世論調査をする

□ 0387
earning
/ə́:rniŋ/
ビジネス問題

名 (~s)**所得**、収入(≒income)；(企業の)収益、利益
動 earn：❶(金など)を稼ぐ　❷(名声など)を得る

□ 0388
surgeon
/sə́:rdʒən/
Part 5, 6

名 **外科医**　●「内科医」はphysician
名 surgery：❶(外科)手術　❷外科

□ 0389
architect
/ɑ́:rkətèkt/
Part 2, 3

名 **建築家**
名 architecture：❶建築様式　❷建築
形 architectural：建築上の；建築学[術]の

□ 0390
garbage
/gɑ́:rbidʒ/
Part 2, 3

名 **生ごみ**、くず(≒trash, litter, refuse, rubbish)

□ 0391
consumption
/kənsʌ́mpʃən/
ビジネス問題

名 **消費**(⇔production)；消費量[高]
名 consumer：消費者
動 consume：❶~を消費する　❷~を摂取する

□ 0392
barn
/bɑ́:rn/
Part 1

名 **納屋**：家畜小屋

continued
▼

Chapter 4では、12日をかけて必修名詞192をチェック。まずはCDでチャンツを聞いて、単語を「耳」からインプット！

- □ 聞くだけモード　Check 1
- □ しっかりモード　Check 1 ▶ 2
- □ かんぺきモード　Check 1 ▶ 2 ▶ 3

Check 2　Phrase

□ an electric [a heating] **apparatus**（電気器具[暖房装置]）

□ take [conduct, do] a **poll**（世論調査を行う）
□ go to the **polls**（投票に行く）

□ future **earnings**（将来の収入）
□ company **earnings**（企業収益）

□ an orthopedic **surgeon**（整形外科医）

□ a competent **architect**（有能な建築家）

□ a **garbage** can [truck]（ごみ入れ[収集車]）
□ take out the **garbage**（ごみを出す）

□ fuel **consumption**（燃料消費）

□ shelter in a **barn**（納屋の中に避難する）

Check 3　Sentence

□ Ambulances are equipped with the necessary **apparatus**, medicines, and stores.（救急車には必要な器具、薬、そして備品が備えられている）

□ According to a recent **poll**, the prime minister's approval rating has fallen below 30 percent.（最近の世論調査によると、首相の支持率は30パーセントを割り込んだ）

□ The average worker's **earnings** were up only 0.3 percent over the previous year's.（労働者の平均所得は昨年よりわずかに0.3パーセント上昇した）

□ Dr. Davis is a first-rate **surgeon**.（デービス医師は一流の外科医だ）

□ Frank Lloyd Wright was one of the greatest **architects** of the 20th century.（フランク・ロイド・ライトは20世紀の最も偉大な建築家の1人だった）

□ Take out the **garbage** when you go.（出かける時にごみを出してください）

□ Generally, electricity **consumption** increases during the summer.（一般に電気消費量は夏の間増加する）

□ The man is painting the **barn**.（男性は納屋にペンキを塗っている）

continued
▼

Day 25

Check 1　Listen)) CD-A25

□ 0393
unemployment
/ʌ́nimplɔ́imənt/
ビジネス問題

- 名 ❶**失業率**、失業者数；失業(状態)(⇔employment) ❷失業手当
- 名 unemployed：(the ~)失業者
- 形 unemployed：失業した

□ 0394
preference
/préfərəns/
Part 4

- 名 ❶(~に対する)**好み**(for ~) ❷優先
- 動 prefer：❶(…より)~を好む(to ...) ❷(prefer to do で)~することが好きである
- 形 preferable：(~より)好ましい(to ~)
- 副 preferably：好んで、むしろ

□ 0395
recipe
/résəpi/
Part 7

- 名 ❶(~の)**調理法**、レシピ(for ~) ❷(~の)原因(for ~)

□ 0396
commitment
/kəmítmənt/
Part 2, 3

- 名 ❶(~の／…するという)**約束**、誓約(to ~/to do) ❷(~への)献身(to ~)(≒devotion)
- 名 commission：❶(代理業務に対する)手数料、歩合(on ~) ❷(任務の)委任 ❸(集合的に)委員会
- 動 commit：(commit A to B で)A を B に委託する

□ 0397
appreciation
/əpriːʃiéiʃən/
Part 2, 3

- 名 ❶**感謝** ❷(~の)正しい理解(of ~)(≒understanding) ❸(資産などの)値上がり(⇔depreciation)
- 動 appreciate：❶~を感謝する ❷~を正当に評価する ❸価格[相場]が上がる

□ 0398
terminal
/tə́ːrmənl/
Part 2, 3

- 名 ❶(コンピューターの)**端末** ❷(鉄道・バスなどの)ターミナル
- 形 ❶(病気が)末期の ❷絶望的な ❸最終の
- 動 terminate：❶~を終わらせる ❷終わる
- 名 termination：終了、終結；満了

□ 0399
fatigue
/fətíːg/
❶発音注意
Part 5, 6

- 名 (心身の)**疲労**(≒tiredness, weariness)

□ 0400
summary
/sʌ́məri/
Part 4

- 名 (~の)**要約**、概略(of ~)
- 形 ❶略式の、即決の ❷要約した、手短な
- 動 summarize：~を要約する

Day 24)) CD-A24 Quick Review 答えは右ページ下

- □ 広範囲にわたる
- □ 悲観的な
- □ 意図的な
- □ 厳格な
- □ 洗練された
- □ 人けのない
- □ ものすごい
- □ 有能な
- □ 精力的な
- □ まずまずの
- □ 予備の
- □ 壮大な
- □ 厳しい
- □ 似ている
- □ 最大限の
- □ 詳細な

Check 2　Phrase

- □ high [low] unemployment(高い[低い]失業率)
- □ be on unemployment(失業手当を受けている)

- □ have a preference for fish over meat(肉より魚のほうが好きだ)
- □ give [show] preference to ~(~を優先する)

- □ a recipe book(料理本)
- □ be a recipe for disaster([事が]災害の原因である)

- □ a lifelong commitment(一生の約束)
- □ commitment to one's work(仕事への献身)

- □ in appreciation of ~(~に感謝して)
- □ have an appreciation of the situation(状況を正しく理解している)

- □ a computer terminal(コンピューター端末)
- □ an airport terminal(空港ターミナル)

- □ physical fatigue(体の疲れ)

- □ in summary(要約すると)

Check 3　Sentence

- □ The government is seeking solutions to the problem of unemployment.(政府は失業問題の解決策を探している)

- □ Don't impose your personal preferences on others.(自分の好みを他人に押しつけてはならない)

- □ This recipe feeds three to four.(この調理法は3、4人分だ)

- □ The author made a commitment to write two new books in the next two years.(その作家は今後2年で2冊の新作を書くと約束した)

- □ I'd like to show my appreciation for your cooperation.(あなたのご協力に感謝の意を表したいと思います)

- □ Can you help me with hooking up the terminal?(端末を接続するのを手伝ってくれますか?)

- □ Fever, headache, coughing, and fatigue are common symptoms of flu.(熱、頭痛、せき、そして疲労はインフルエンザの一般的な症状だ)

- □ Can you give me a brief summary of yesterday's meeting?(昨日の会議の概要を簡単に教えてくれますか?)

Day 24))) CD-A24
Quick Review
答えは左ページ下

- □ extensive
- □ gloomy
- □ deliberate
- □ rigid
- □ sophisticated
- □ deserted
- □ tremendous
- □ competent
- □ vigorous
- □ decent
- □ preliminary
- □ grand
- □ harsh
- □ alike
- □ maximum
- □ detailed

Day 26　名詞14

Check 1　Listen ») CD-A26

☐ 0401
receptionist
/rɪsépʃənɪst/
Part 2, 3

名 (会社・ホテルなどの)**受付係**
名 reception：❶歓迎会、宴会　❷受け入れること　❸(会社などの)受付、フロント
動 receive：❶～を(…から)受け取る(from ...)　❷(意見など)を受け入れる

☐ 0402
nuisance
/njúːsns/
❶発音注意
Part 2, 3

名 **迷惑**[不愉快]**な人**[物、こと]；迷惑

☐ 0403
trash
/trǽʃ/
Part 4

名 **ごみ**、くず(≒garbage, litter, refuse, rubbish)

☐ 0404
registration
/rèdʒɪstréɪʃən/
Part 2, 3

名 **登録**、登記、記録
名 register：登録[記録](簿)
動 register：❶～を(…として)登録[記録]する(as ...)　❷(郵便物)を書留にする　❸(register forで)～の入学[受講]手続きをする

☐ 0405
retail
/ríːteɪl/
ビジネス問題

名 **小売り**(⇔wholesale：卸売り)
動 (～の値で)小売りされる(for [at] ～)
副 小売(価格)で
名 retailer：小売業者

☐ 0406
fluid
/flúːɪd/
Part 4

名 **水分**、飲み物；流体(≒liquid)(⇔solid：固体)
形 ❶(動作などが)流れるような、滑らかな　❷(状況などが)流動的な

☐ 0407
cargo
/káːrɡoʊ/
Part 1

名 **積み荷**、貨物(≒freight)

☐ 0408
withdrawal
/wɪðdrɔ́ːəl/
Part 7

名 ❶**預金の引き出し**　❷撤退、撤兵　❸(約束などの)撤回
動 withdraw：❶(預金など)を(…から)引き出す(from ...)　❷～を撤回する　❸(～から)撤退する(from ～)

continued
▼

見出し語下の「Part 1」マークの単語には、Check 3でPart 1型の例文を用意している。情景を頭に浮かべながら、音読してみよう！

- □ 聞くだけモード　Check 1
- □ しっかりモード　Check 1 ▶ 2
- □ かんぺきモード　Check 1 ▶ 2 ▶ 3

Check 2　Phrase

□ a hotel receptionist（ホテルの受付係）

□ make a nuisance of oneself（人に迷惑をかける、厄介者になる）
□ a public nuisance（公的不法妨害；はた迷惑な人）

□ trash collection（ごみ収集）
□ take out the trash（ごみを出す）

□ voter registration（選挙人登録）

□ retail trade（小売業）
□ a retail outlet（小売店）

□ fluid replacement（水分補給）

□ a cargo ship [train, plane]（貨物船［列車、輸送機］）

□ make a withdrawal（預金を引き出す）
□ a withdrawal of the troops（軍隊の撤退）

Check 3　Sentence

□ Lisa got a job as a receptionist.（リーサは受付係の仕事を見つけた）

□ Monkeys can be a nuisance to farmers.（サルは農民の迷惑者になることもある）

□ Bottles and cans are picked up with the regular trash collection.（瓶と缶は定期的なごみ収集で回収される）

□ The registration fee is $100.（登録［登記］料は100ドルだ）

□ Retail sales have been slow this year.（今年は小売りの売上高が不振だ）

□ Drink plenty of fluids after exercise.（運動した後は水分を十分に取ってください）

□ Cargo is being unloaded from a truck.（積み荷がトラックから降ろされている）

□ Cash withdrawals from ATMs can't be made on December 1.（12月1日はATMからの現金の引き出しはできない）

continued
▼

Day 26

Check 1　Listen 》CD-A26

0409 discrimination /dɪskrɪ̀mənéɪʃən/ Part 5, 6
名(～に対する)**差別**(待遇)(against ～) ⊕「偏見」は prejudice

0410 theft /θéft/ Part 4
名**窃盗**、盗み(≒stealing)
名thief：泥棒

0411 transmission /trænzmíʃən/ Part 4
名❶(自動車の)**変速装置**、トランスミッション　❷伝達　❸送信、放送
動transmit：❶(ニュースなど)を放送する、伝える　❷(病気など)を伝染させる、うつす

0412 outbreak /áʊtbrèɪk/ Part 2, 3
名(戦争などの)**勃発**、突発(of ～)
動break out：(戦争などが)勃発する、急に発生する

0413 counterpart /káʊntərpɑ̀ːrt/ Part 5, 6
名(～に)**相当**[対応]**するもの**[人](of [to] ～)(≒equivalent)

0414 odor /óʊdər/ Part 7
名(通例不快な)**におい**、悪臭(≒smell) ⊕「香気」は scent, fragrance, aroma

0415 storage /stɔ́ːrɪdʒ/ Part 7
名❶**保管**、貯蔵　❷保管[貯蔵]量　❸保管[貯蔵]所
名store：❶(しばしば～s)蓄え　❷店
動store：❶～をしまい込む　❷～を(…に備えて)蓄える(for …)

0416 apology /əpɑ́lədʒi/ Part 4
名(～に対する)**謝罪**、おわび(for ～)
動apologize：(apologize to A for Bで)AにBのことでわびる、謝る

Day 25 》CD-A25　Quick Review
答えは右ページ下

- □ 器具
- □ 世論調査
- □ 所得
- □ 外科医
- □ 建築家
- □ 生ごみ
- □ 消費
- □ 納屋
- □ 失業率
- □ 好み
- □ 調理法
- □ 約束
- □ 感謝
- □ 端末
- □ 疲労
- □ 要約

Check 2　Phrase

☐ racial discrimination（人種差別）
☐ discrimination against women（女性に対する差別）

☐ car theft（自動車窃盗）
☐ be charged with theft（窃盗容疑で告発される）

☐ an automatic transmission（自動の変速装置）
☐ the transmission of knowledge（知識の伝承）

☐ the outbreak of World War I（第1次世界大戦の勃発）

☐ the Japanese counterpart of the US Senate（日本でアメリカの上院に相当するもの）➕参議院

☐ body odor（体臭）

☐ keep food in storage（食料を保管している）
☐ data storage（[コンピューターの]データ保存量）

☐ make an apology for ～（～のことを謝る）
☐ demand an apology from ～（～からの謝罪を要求する）

Check 3　Sentence

☐ Job discrimination based on sex or age is prohibited.（性別や年齢に基づいた雇用差別は禁止されている）

☐ The man was arrested for theft.（その男は窃盗の容疑で逮捕された）

☐ My car has a six-speed manual transmission.（私の車は6段変速の手動トランスミッションだ）

☐ The government is preparing for an outbreak of flu.（政府はインフルエンザの突発に備えて準備している）

☐ This Japanese word has no counterpart in English.（この日本語に相当する英語はない）

☐ The residents in the area have complained about odors from the chemical plant.（その地域の住民たちは化学工場からの悪臭について苦情を述べている）

☐ The storage of radioactive material is done with extreme care.（放射性物質の保管は細心の注意を払って行われる）

☐ Please accept my apologies.（ここにおわびいたします）

Day 25))CD-A25
Quick Review
答えは左ページ下

☐ apparatus
☐ poll
☐ earning
☐ surgeon
☐ architect
☐ garbage
☐ consumption
☐ barn
☐ unemployment
☐ preference
☐ recipe
☐ commitment
☐ appreciation
☐ terminal
☐ fatigue
☐ summary

Day 27　名詞15

Check 1　Listen)) CD-A27

0417
laundry
/lɔ́:ndri/
Part 2, 3

名❶(集合的に)**洗濯物**；洗濯　❷クリーニング店

0418
scenery
/sí:nəri/
Part 4

名(集合的に)(通例美しい)**景色**、風景　⊕不可算名詞であることに注意

0419
resistance
/rizístəns/
Part 5, 6

名❶(～に対する)**抵抗**、反抗(to ～)　❷(～に対する)抵抗力(to ～)
動resist：❶(通例否定文で)～を我慢する、こらえる　❷～に抵抗[反抗]する
形resistant：(～に)抵抗力のある(to ～)

0420
disaster
/dizǽstər/
Part 4

名❶**災害**、惨事(≒calamity, catastrophe)　❷大失敗(≒fiasco)
形disastrous：災害[災難]を引き起こす、破滅を招く

0421
instinct
/ínstiŋkt/
Part 5, 6

名(～しようとする／…に対する)**本能**(to do/for . . .)；直感(≒intuition)
形instinctive：本能的な、本能の
副instinctively：本能的に；直感的に

0422
gulf
/gʌ́lf/
❶定義注意
Part 5, 6

名❶(～の間の)**大きな隔たり**、超え難い溝(between ～)　❷湾

0423
shortage
/ʃɔ́:rtidʒ/
Part 4

名(～の)**不足**(of ～)(≒lack, want, dearth)　⊕absenceは「完全な欠如」
形short：❶短い　❷(be short of [on])で)～が不足している
副shortly：❶間もなく、すぐに　❷少し(後、前)に

0424
intent
/intént/
Part 7

名(～する)**意図**、意志(to do)(≒aim, purpose)
形(be intent on [upon]で)❶～を決意している　❷～に没頭[専念]している
名intention：(～する)意図(of doing [to do])
動intend：(intend to doで)～するつもりである

continued
▼

Quick Reviewは使ってる? 昨日覚えた単語でも、記憶に残っているとは限らない。学習の合間に軽くチェックするだけでも効果は抜群!

☐ 聞くだけモード　Check 1
☐ しっかりモード　Check 1 ▶ 2
☐ かんぺきモード　Check 1 ▶ 2 ▶ 3

Check 2　Phrase

☐ fold laundry（洗濯物を畳む）
☐ do the laundry（洗濯をする）

☐ magnificent scenery（壮大な景色）

☐ meet with resistance from ~（~からの抵抗に遭う）
☐ resistance to cold [colds]（寒さ[風邪]に対する抵抗力）

☐ a natural disaster（天災）
☐ a total disaster（完全な失敗）

☐ maternal instinct（母性本能）
☐ My instinct tells me that ~.（私の直感では~だ）

☐ a gulf between the rich and poor（大きな貧富の差）
☐ the Gulf of Mexico（メキシコ湾）

☐ a shortage of water [labor]（水[労働力]不足）

☐ good [evil] intent（善意[悪意]）
☐ with intent to do ~（~するつもりで）

Check 3　Sentence

☐ Can you help me with the laundry?（洗濯を手伝ってくれますか?）

☐ We were overwhelmed by the breathtaking scenery of the mountains.（私たちは山々の息をのむような景色に圧倒された）

☐ There was little resistance to the new economic plan.（新しい経済計画に対する反対はほとんどなかった）

☐ Five million dollars were allocated as disaster relief for the hurricane victims.（ハリケーン被災者への災害救助として500万ドルが割り当てられた）

☐ Every creature has an instinct for self-preservation.（すべての生物は自衛本能を持っている）

☐ There is a wide gulf between the two parties' opinions on a health care system.（医療制度に関する両党間の考えには大きな隔たりがある）

☐ The country is facing severe food shortages.（その国は深刻な食糧不足に直面している）

☐ The CEO announced his intent to resign.（そのCEOは辞職する意向を発表した）

continued
▼

Day 27

Check 1　Listen))) CD-A27

☐ 0425
housing
/háuziŋ/
Part 4

名 ❶(集合的に)**住宅**、家　❷住宅供給

☐ 0426
barrel
/bǽrəl/
Part 1

名 ❶**たる**　❷バレル　✚石油容量の単位＝159リットル

☐ 0427
prosperity
/prɑspérəti/
ビジネス問題

名 (特に財政的な)**繁栄**、繁盛
動 prosper：繁栄する；成功する
形 prosperous：繁栄している；(経済的に)成功している

☐ 0428
possession
/pəzéʃən/
Part 4

名 ❶(通例～s)**所有物**；財産　❷所有、所持
動 possess：～を所有する、持っている
形 possessive：所有[独占]欲の強い

☐ 0429
wildlife
/wáildlàif/
Part 4

名 (集合的に)**野生生物**

☐ 0430
efficiency
/ifíʃənsi/
ビジネス問題

名 **効率**、能率
形 efficient：❶効率[能率]的な　❷有能な
副 efficiently：能率[効果]的に

☐ 0431
congress
/káŋgris/
Part 7

名 (C～)(米国の)**国会**、連邦議会　✚英国の「国会」はParliament、日本の「国会」はDiet
名 congressman：(しばしばC～)(米国の)国会議員、(特に)下院議員　✚「上院議員」はsenator
形 congressional：(通例C～)(米国の)国会の

☐ 0432
infant
/ínfənt/
Part 7

名 (通例1歳未満の)**乳児**；幼児
形 初期(段階)の
名 infancy：❶幼時　❷(発達の)初期

Day 26))) CD-A26
Quick Review
答えは右ページ下

☐ 受付係　☐ 小売り　☐ 差別　☐ 相当するもの
☐ 迷惑な人　☐ 水分　☐ 窃盗　☐ におい
☐ ごみ　☐ 積み荷　☐ 変速装置　☐ 保管
☐ 登録　☐ 預金の引き出し　☐ 勃発　☐ 謝罪

Check 2　Phrase

- ☐ housing construction（住宅建設）
- ☐ a shortage of housing（住宅不足）

- ☐ a barrel of beer（1たるのビール）
- ☐ an increase of oil prices by $2 per barrel（1バレル2ドルの石油価格の上昇）

- ☐ national prosperity（国の繁栄）

- ☐ the most prized possession（最も大切な所有物）
- ☐ be in possession of ～（～を所有している）

- ☐ a wildlife preservation（野生生物保護区）
- ☐ a wildlife habitat（野生生物の生息地）

- ☐ energy [fuel] efficiency（エネルギー[燃料]効率）
- ☐ improve [increase] efficiency（効率を高める）

- ☐ an act [a law] of Congress（国会制定法）

- ☐ an infant daughter [son]（女[男]の赤ん坊）

Check 3　Sentence

- ☐ There has been a sharp decrease in housing prices in some metropolitan areas.（都心部のいくつかの地域では住宅価格の急激な低下が続いている）

- ☐ The barrels are lined up neatly in a warehouse.（倉庫の中にたるがきちんと並べられている）

- ☐ The country is experiencing a period of economic prosperity.（その国は経済的繁栄期を経験している）

- ☐ They lost their homes and all their possessions in the hurricane.（彼らは家と全所有物をそのハリケーンで失った）

- ☐ Increasingly, people are getting interested in wildlife conservation.（人々は野生生物の保護にますます関心を持つようになってきている）

- ☐ Increasing efficiency is the best way to increase productivity.（効率を上げることが生産性を上げる最良の方法だ）

- ☐ Congress approved the new tax on tobacco.（国会はたばこに課す新しい税を可決した）

- ☐ Infants start to learn to walk when they are about a year old.（乳児は1歳くらいで歩くことを学び始める）

Day 26))) CD-A26
Quick Review
答えは左ページ下

- ☐ receptionist
- ☐ nuisance
- ☐ trash
- ☐ registration
- ☐ retail
- ☐ fluid
- ☐ cargo
- ☐ withdrawal
- ☐ discrimination
- ☐ theft
- ☐ transmission
- ☐ outbreak
- ☐ counterpart
- ☐ odor
- ☐ storage
- ☐ apology

CHAPTER 4

Day 28　名詞16

Check 1　Listen)) CD-A28

0433
tension
/ténʃən/
Part 5, 6

名❶(～の間の)**緊張関係**[状態](between ～)　❷緊張、不安
動tense：❶(筋肉など)を緊張させる　❷緊張する
形tense：❶緊張[緊迫]した　❷(筋肉などが)ぴんと張った

0434
outcome
/áutkàm/
Part 5, 6

名(～の)(最終的な)**結果**(of ～)(≒result, consequence, effect)

0435
poverty
/pávərti/
Part 5, 6

名❶**貧困**、貧乏　❷(～の)欠乏、不足(of ～)(≒lack)
形poor：❶貧しい　❷(～に)乏しい(in ～)
副poorly：❶まずく、下手に　❷貧しく　❸乏しく

0436
command
/kəmǽnd/
Part 4

名❶(言語の)**運用力**　❷命令(≒order)　❸指揮、統率(≒control)
動❶(command A to doで)Aに～するよう命令する(≒order A to do)　❷～を指揮する
名commander：指揮者、指導者、司令官

0437
residence
/rézədəns/
Part 5, 6

名❶**居住**、滞在　❷邸宅、住宅(≒house, home)
名resident：居住者、在住者
形resident：居住[在住]している
形residential：住宅[居住]の

0438
fame
/féim/
Part 7

名**名声**(≒reputation, renown)
形famous：(～で/…として)有名な(for ～/as …)

0439
expectation
/èkspektéiʃən/
Part 7

名**期待**、予想(≒anticipation)
動expect：❶～を期待する；～を予期[予想]する　❷(expect A to doで)Aが～するだろうと思う　❸(expect to doで)～すると思っている、～するつもりである

0440
acceptance
/ækséptəns/
Part 7

名❶(～の)**受け入れ**、受諾(of ～)(⇔offer：申し出)；合格[採用]通知　❷承認、容認、賛成
動accept：❶～を受け入れる　❷～を受け取る
形acceptable：(～にとって)受け入れられる、満足できる(to ～)

continued
▼

「声に出す」練習は続けている？ えっ、周りに人がいてできない?! そんなときは「口パク」でもOK。「耳＋口」の練習を忘れずに！

- ☐ 聞くだけモード　Check 1
- ☐ しっかりモード　Check 1 ▶ 2
- ☐ かんぺきモード　Check 1 ▶ 2 ▶ 3

Check 2　Phrase

☐ racial tension(人種間の緊張状態)
☐ get rid of tension(緊張を取り除く)

☐ the eventual outcome of the war(その戦争の最終的な結果)
☐ the outcome of a negotiation(交渉の結果)

☐ live in poverty(貧困生活を送る)
☐ poverty of imagination(想像力の欠如)

☐ a command of reading(読解力)
☐ give [issue] a command(命令を出す)

☐ temporary residence(一時的な滞在)
☐ the official residence(公邸、官邸)

☐ win [gain, achieve] fame(名声を得る)
☐ at the height of one's fame(名声の絶頂期で)

☐ below [beyond] expectation(s)(期待[予想]以下[以上]で)
☐ in expectation of ~(～を見越して、期待して)

☐ the acceptance of economic aid(経済援助の受け入れ)
☐ the acceptance of the plan(その計画の承認)

Check 3　Sentence

☐ The UN's mediation lessened the tension between the two countries.(国連の調停によって両国間の緊張関係は弱まった)

☐ The candidate and his supporters are waiting for the outcome of the election.(その候補者と支持者たちは選挙の結果を待っている)

☐ Nearly a half of the country's citizens live below the poverty line.(その国の国民の半数近くは貧困ライン以下で暮らしている)

☐ He has a good command of Chinese.(彼は中国語を上手に使いこなすことができる)

☐ Sachiko has permanent residence in the US.(サチコはアメリカの永住権を持っている)

☐ I don't want fame or wealth.(私は名声や富は欲しくない)

☐ The concert has exceeded my expectations.(そのコンサートは私の期待を上回るものだった)

☐ He has had acceptances from five universities.(彼は5つの大学から合格通知をもらった)

continued
▼

Day 28

Check 1　Listen 》CD-A28

☐ 0441
capacity
/kəpǽsəti/
ビジネス問題

名 ❶**生産能力**；収容能力　❷容量　❸能力
名 capability：(〜できる)能力、才能(of doing [to do])
形 capable：(be capable ofで)〜の能力[才能]がある

☐ 0442
scholarship
/skάlərʃìp/
Part 4

名 ❶**奨学金**(≒grant)　❷学識
名 scholar：❶学者　❷奨学生
形 scholarly：❶学術[専門]的な　❷学者の

☐ 0443
adjustment
/ədʒʌ́stmənt/
Part 2, 3

名 ❶**調整**、調節　❷適応
動 adjust：❶(機械など)を調節[整備]する　❷〜を(…に)適合させる(to...)　❸(adjust toで)(環境など)に適応[順応]する
形 adjustable：調節[調整]できる

☐ 0444
priority
/praiɔ́ːrəti/
Part 4

名 ❶**優先事項**　❷優先(権)
形 prior：❶(prior toで)〜より前に、〜に先立って　❷前の、先の　❸(〜に)優先する、(〜より)重要な(to 〜)

☐ 0445
mess
/més/
Part 2, 3

名 **めちゃくちゃな状態**[様子]、乱雑、混乱(≒chaos, confusion)
動 (mess upで)❶〜を台無しにする(≒spoil, ruin)　❷〜を散らかす
形 messy：散らかった、乱雑な

☐ 0446
institute
/ínstətjùːt/
Part 4

名 (学術などの)**研究機関**、学会；(理工系の)大学
動 ❶(制度など)を制定する、設ける　❷(調査など)を始める(≒start)
名 institution：❶機関、団体　❷(孤児院などの)施設　❸(社会的)制度

☐ 0447
establishment
/istǽbliʃmənt/
Part 5, 6

名 ❶(会社・病院・学校などの)**社会的機関**、公共施設　❷設立　❸(通例the E〜)(既成の)体制、権力機構
動 establish：〜を設立[創立]する、〜を樹立する

☐ 0448
sidewalk
/sáidwɔ̀ːk/
Part 1

名 **歩道**

Day 27 》CD-A27
Quick Review
答えは右ページ下

☐ 洗濯物　☐ 本能　☐ 住宅　☐ 野生生物
☐ 景色　☐ 大きな隔たり　☐ たる　☐ 効率
☐ 抵抗　☐ 不足　☐ 繁栄　☐ 国会
☐ 災害　☐ 意図　☐ 所有物　☐ 乳児

Check 2　Phrase

- at full capacity（フル操業で）
- a seating capacity of 1,000（1000人分の座席）

Check 3　Sentence

- The factory has the capacity to manufacture 500 cars a day.（その工場は1日に500台の車を作る生産能力がある）

- win a scholarship（奨学金を受ける）
- a work of great scholarship（卓越した学術研究）

- She applied for a college scholarship.（彼女は大学の奨学金を申し込んだ）

- a slight [minor] adjustment（微調整）
- adjustment to a new environment（新しい環境への適応）

- Do you think we'll have to make any adjustments to the schedule?（スケジュールを少々調整する必要があると思いますか？）

- establish priorities（優先事項を設ける）
- have [take, get] priority over ～（～に優先する）

- The government's first priority now is to stimulate the domestic economy.（政府の今の最優先事項は国内経済を刺激することだ）

- make a mess of ～（～を散らかす）
- in a mess（散らかって）

- His room was an absolute mess.（彼の部屋は散らかり放題だった）

- a language institute（語学研究所）
- the Massachusetts Institute of Technology（マサチューセッツ工科大学）●略語はMIT

- He works at a research institute at the university.（彼はその大学の研究所に勤務している）

- a financial establishment（金融機関）
- the establishment of a new hospital（新しい病院の設立）

- Yale University is one of the most prestigious educational establishments in the US.（エール大学はアメリカで最も権威ある教育機関の1つだ）

- walk along the sidewalk（歩道を歩く）

- There is a fence along the sidewalk.（歩道に沿ってフェンスがある）

Day 27 》CD-A27
Quick Review
答えは左ページ下

- laundry
- scenery
- resistance
- disaster
- instinct
- gulf
- shortage
- intent
- housing
- barrel
- prosperity
- possession
- wildlife
- efficiency
- congress
- infant

CHAPTER 1
CHAPTER 2
CHAPTER 3
CHAPTER 4
CHAPTER 5
CHAPTER 6
CHAPTER 7
CHAPTER 8
CHAPTER 9
CHAPTER 10

Day 29　名詞17

Check 1　Listen 》CD-A29

☐ 0449
charity
/tʃǽrəti/
Part 2, 3

名 ❶**慈善団体**[施設]；慈善事業　❷義援金
形 charitable：❶慈善(事業)の　❷寛大な；慈悲深い

☐ 0450
popularity
/pɑ̀pjulǽrəti/
Part 2, 3

名 **人気**、評判；流行
形 popular：❶(〜に)人気のある、評判のよい(with [among] ...)　❷一般人の、一般民衆の

☐ 0451
scholar
/skɑ́lər/
Part 7

名 ❶**学者**　➡通例、人文学系の「学者」を指す。理科系の「学者」はscientist　❷奨学金受給者、奨学生
名 scholarship：❶奨学金　❷学識
形 scholarly：❶学術[専門]的な　❷学者の

☐ 0452
crisis
/kráisis/
ビジネス問題

名 **危機**、重大局面
形 critical：❶(〜にとって)重大な(to 〜)　❷批判[批評]的な

☐ 0453
elderly
/éldərli/
Part 4

名 (the 〜) **年配**[初老]**の人々**、老人層(≒senior citizens)
形 年配[初老]の(≒old, aged)

☐ 0454
rage
/réidʒ/
Part 5, 6

名 (〜に対する)**激怒**(at [against] 〜)(≒anger, fury)
動 ❶(〜に対して)激怒する(at [against] 〜)　❷(悪天候などが)荒れ狂う

☐ 0455
scheme
/skíːm/
❶発音注意
Part 7

名 ❶**計画**、案(≒plan)　❷たくらみ、陰謀(≒plot, conspiracy)　❸体系
動 (〜しようと／…に対して)たくらむ(to do/against ...)

☐ 0456
invention
/invénʃən/
Part 4

名 **発明**；発明品
動 invent：〜を発明[考案]する

continued
▼

「分散学習」も効果的。朝起きたらCheck 1、昼食後にCheck 2、寝る前にCheck 3といった具合に、学習時間を作る工夫をしてみよう。

☐ 聞くだけモード　Check 1
☐ しっかりモード　Check 1 ▶ 2
☐ かんぺきモード　Check 1 ▶ 2 ▶ 3

Check 2　Phrase

☐ leave one's estate to a charity（財産を慈善団体に遺贈する）
☐ accept charity（義援金を受け取る）

☐ have a popularity among ～（～の間で人気がある）
☐ gain [grow, increase] in popularity（人気が高まる）

☐ a classical scholar（古典学者）
☐ a Rhodes scholar（ローズ奨学生）➡英国オックスフォード大学のローズ奨学金の受給者

☐ an energy [a financial] crisis（エネルギー[金融]危機）

☐ crimes against the elderly（年配の人々を狙った犯罪）

☐ in a rage（激怒して、かんかんに怒って）
☐ fly into a rage（激怒する、かっとなる）

☐ a business scheme（事業計画）
☐ come up with a scheme（たくらみを思いつく）

☐ the invention of the television（テレビの発明）
☐ a wonderful invention（素晴らしい発明品）

Check 3　Sentence

☐ She donated $10,000 to the charity.（彼女はその慈善団体に1万ドルを寄付した）

☐ That singer's popularity has started to fade.（その歌手の人気は薄れ始めている）

☐ Dr. Hamilton is a distinguished scholar.（ハミルトン博士は著名な学者だ）

☐ Things are coming [drawing] to a crisis.（事態は重大な局面へと向かっている）

☐ The number of elderly is increasing rapidly in Japan.（日本では高齢者の数が急速に増えている）

☐ Her face turned red with rage.（彼女の顔は怒りで赤くなった）

☐ This get-rich-quick scheme is bound to fail.（この一獲千金的な計画は必ず失敗する）

☐ The Internet is one of the greatest inventions in the 20th century.（インターネットは20世紀最大の発明の1つだ）

continued ▼

Day 29

Check 1 Listen)) CD-A29

0457 incident
/ínsədənt/
Part 4

名 出来事、事件、事故(≒accident)
形 (〜に)ありがちな、起こりがちな(to 〜)
名 incidence：(病気・事件などの)発生(率)
名 incidental：●(〜s)雑費 ●付随的な事柄
形 incidental：(〜に)付随して起こる(to 〜)

0458 treaty
/tríːti/
Part 5, 6

名 (国家間の)**条約**、協定(≒agreement, pact)；条約[協定]文書

0459 provision
/prəvíʒən/
Part 7

名 ●(〜の)**供給**(of 〜)；(〜への)用意、準備(for [against] 〜) **❷**条項、規定 **❸**(〜s)食糧
動 provide：**●**(provide A with Bで)AにBを提供[供給]する **❷**(provide forで)〜に備える
接 provided：もし〜ならば、〜という条件で

0460 errand
/érənd/
Part 2, 3

名 使い走り

0461 profile
/próufail/
●定義注意
Part 5, 6

名 ●注目度；(会社などの)評判、イメージ **❷**(新聞などでの)人物紹介 **❸**横顔、輪郭
動 〜のプロフィールを紹介する

0462 conservation
/kànsərvéiʃən/
Part 7

名 (自然環境などの)**保護**、保存
名 conservative：保守的な人
形 conservative：**●**(評価などが)控えめな **❷**保守的な
動 conserve：〜を保護[保存]する；(エネルギーなど)を節約して使う

0463 immigrant
/ímigrənt/
Part 7

名 (外国からの)**移民**、移住者 **✚**外国への「移民、移住者」はemigrant
名 immigration：**●**移住、移民 **❷**入国管理[審査]
動 immigrate：(〜から／…へ)移住する(from 〜/to ...)

0464 prejudice
/prédʒudis/
Part 5, 6

名 (〜に対する)**偏見**、先入観(against 〜)(≒bias) **✚**「差別」はdiscrimination
動 ●(prejudice A against Bで)AにBに対して偏見を抱かせる **❷**〜に損害を与える(≒damage)

Day 28)) CD-A28
Quick Review
答えは右ページ下

- □ 緊張関係
- □ 結果
- □ 貧困
- □ 運用力
- □ 居住
- □ 名声
- □ 期待
- □ 受け入れ
- □ 生産能力
- □ 奨学金
- □ 調整
- □ 優先事項
- □ めちゃくちゃな状態
- □ 研究機関
- □ 社会的機関
- □ 歩道

Check 2　Phrase

- a strange incident（奇妙な出来事）
- without incident（無事に、何事もなく）

- conclude [make] a treaty with ~（~と条約を結ぶ）
- the nuclear non-proliferation treaty（核不拡散条約）

- the provision of food（食料の供給）
- penal provisions（罰則）

- send her on an errand（彼女を使い走りに出す）

- a high-profile trial（注目度の高い裁判）
- a biographical profile（伝記風の人物紹介）

- conservation of nature（自然保護）

- Irish immigrants（アイルランド人移民）
- receive immigrants（移民を受け入れる）

- racial [religious] prejudice（人種[宗教]的偏見）
- without prejudice（偏見なしで）

Check 3　Sentence

- The incident was recorded on a surveillance camera.（その事件は監視カメラで撮影されていた）

- The leaders of the two countries signed a peace treaty.（両国の首脳は平和条約に署名した）

- We need to make provision for old age.（私たちは老後に備えておく必要がある）

- Can you run [do] an errand for me?（使い走りをしてくれますか?）

- We have to increase our company's profile in China.（私たちは中国における当社の注目度を上げなければならない）

- The NPO works on the conservation of forest resources.（そのNPOは森林資源の保護に取り組んでいる）

- Australia has a lot of immigrants from Greece.（オーストラリアにはギリシャからの移民が多くいる）

- Few people are free from prejudice.（偏見のない人はほとんどいない）

Day 28))) CD-A28
Quick Review
答えは左ページ下

- tension
- outcome
- poverty
- command
- residence
- fame
- expectation
- acceptance
- capacity
- scholarship
- adjustment
- priority
- mess
- institute
- establishment
- sidewalk

Day 30 名詞18

Check 1　Listen)) CD-A30

0465 similarity /sìməlǽrəti/ Part 2, 3
名 (〜の間の／…との) **類似点** (⇔difference：相違点)；類似(性) (≒resemblance, likeness) (between 〜/with ...)
形 similar：(〜と) 同じような、似ている、類似した (to 〜)

0466 exploration /èkspləréiʃən/ Part 4
名 ❶ **探査**、探検　❷ (〜の) 調査、探求 (into 〜) (≒investigation)
名 explorer：探検家
動 explore：❶〜を探検する　❷〜を調査[探求]する
形 exploratory：(手術などが) 予備的な

0467 shipping /ʃípiŋ/ ビジネス問題
名 **発送**、出荷
名 shipment：❶出荷、発送　❷積み荷、発送品
名 ship：船
動 ship：(商品を) 発送[出荷]する；〜を輸送する

0468 phenomenon /finámənàn/ Part 5, 6
名 **現象**、事象　● 複数形はphenomena

0469 obligation /àbləgéiʃən/ Part 5, 6
名 (〜に対する／…する) (道徳的・法律的な) **義務**、責任 (to 〜/to do) (≒duty)
動 oblige：(be obliged to do で) 〜せざるを得ない
形 obligatory：(〜にとって) 義務[強制]的な (for [on] 〜)；必須の

0470 theme /θíːm/ ❶ 発音注意 Part 5, 6
名 **主題**、テーマ (≒subject)

0471 confusion /kənfjúːʒən/ Part 2, 3
名 ❶ (〜についての) **混乱** (about [over, as to] 〜)　❷ (〜との／…の間の) 混同 (with 〜/between ...)
動 confuse：❶ (confuse A with B で) A を B と間違える　❷ (be confused with で) 〜に困惑[当惑] している
形 confusing：紛らわしい、混乱[当惑] させる

0472 uncertainty /ʌnsə́ːrtnti/ Part 5, 6
名 **不確実性**、不明確
形 uncertain：(be uncertain about [of] で) 〜について確信[自信] がない
副 uncertainly：❶不確実に　❷自信がなく

continued

定義が分かっていても、その単語を「使える」とは限らない。Check 2と3の和訳を見て、英語がすぐに出てくれば「使える」レベルは目前！

☐ 聞くだけモード　Check 1
☐ しっかりモード　Check 1 ▶ 2
☐ かんぺきモード　Check 1 ▶ 2 ▶ 3

Check 2　Phrase

☐ similarities between the two products(2つの製品の類似点)
☐ points of similarity(類似点)

☐ oil exploration(石油探査)
☐ under exploration(調査中の[で])

☐ shipping charges(発送料)

☐ a psychological phenomenon(心理現象)

☐ be under no obligation to do ~(~する義務はない)
☐ a sense of obligation(責任感)

☐ the theme of the conference(その会議のテーマ)

☐ in confusion(混乱して；ろうばいして)
☐ confusion between Iran and Iraq(イランとイラクの混同)

☐ the uncertainty of life(人生の不確実性)

Check 3　Sentence

☐ There are many similarities between Spanish and Italian.(スペイン語とイタリア語には類似点が多い)

☐ The US has spent a lot of money on space exploration.(アメリカは宇宙探査に多くの金を使ってきている)

☐ Shipping by sea is less expensive than by air.(船便での発送は航空便よりも安い)

☐ Homelessness is not only an urban phenomenon.(ホームレスは都市に特有の現象ではない)

☐ Parents have an obligation to their children.(親は子どもに対する責任がある)

☐ Birth and death have been a consistent theme in his novels.(生と死は彼の小説における一貫した主題になっている)

☐ There is some confusion about when we will start the project.(そのプロジェクトをいつ開始するかに関して少々混乱がある)

☐ There is a lot of uncertainty about the future of the economy.(経済の将来に関しては不確実なことが多い)

continued ▼

Day 30

Check 1　Listen CD-A30

□ 0473
routine
/ruːtíːn/
Part 2, 3

名 ❶**決まりきった仕事**、日課　❷いつもの手順
形 いつもの、日常の
副 routinely：いつものように、定期的に

□ 0474
garment
/gáːrmənt/
Part 7

名 **衣服**；(〜s)衣類(≒clothes, clothing, wear, apparel)

□ 0475
margin
/máːrdʒin/
ビジネス問題

名 ❶**利ざや**、販売利益、マージン　❷(ページの)余白、欄外　❸(得票数などの)差
形 marginal：❶取るに足らない、重要でない　❷(人が)影響力を持っていない　❸限界収益点の

□ 0476
surgery
/sə́ːrdʒəri/
Part 5, 6

名 ❶(外科)**手術**(≒operation)　❷外科　❸手術室
名 surgeon：外科医

□ 0477
outlook
/áutlùk/
Part 5, 6

名 ❶(〜の)**見通し**、見込み(for 〜)　❷(〜に対する)見解、態度(on 〜)　❸展望台

□ 0478
investor
/invéstər/
ビジネス問題

名 **投資家**、投資者
名 investment：(〜への)投資、出資(in 〜)
動 invest：(invest A in Bで)A(金など)をBに投資する

□ 0479
advertising
/ǽdvərtàiziŋ/
ビジネス問題

名 ❶(集合的に)**広告**　❷広告業
形 広告の
名 advertisement：広告、宣伝
動 advertise：❶〜を宣伝[広告]する　❷(〜を求める)広告を出す(for 〜)

□ 0480
restriction
/ristríkʃən/
Part 2, 3

名 (〜に対する)**制限**、制約、限定(on 〜)
動 restrict：〜を(…に)制限[限定]する(to …)
形 restricted：(〜に)制限された、限られた(to 〜)

Day 29　CD-A29
Quick Review
答えは右ページ下

□ 慈善団体　□ 年配の人々　□ 出来事　□ 注目度
□ 人気　□ 激怒　□ 条約　□ 保護
□ 学者　□ 計画　□ 供給　□ 移民
□ 危機　□ 発明　□ 使い走り　□ 偏見

Check 2　Phrase

- a daily routine（日課）
- according to routine（いつもの手順に従って）

- a sports garment（スポーツ着）
- the garment industry（衣料産業）

- profit margin（利幅）
- leave a margin（余白を空ける）

- heart surgery（心臓手術）
- cosmetic surgery（美容外科）

- the short-term [long-term] outlook（短期[長期]的見通し）
- an outlook on life（人生観）

- an individual [institutional] investor（個人[機関]投資家）
- investor relations（投資家への広報活動）

- corporate advertising（企業広告）
- a career in advertising（広告業の仕事）

- impose restrictions on ～（～に対して制限を課す）
- lift restrictions on ～（～に対する制限を解除する）

Check 3　Sentence

- I'm getting tired of the routines at work.（私は職場での決まりきった仕事に飽き始めている）

- The store carries suits, dresses, and other garments.（その店はスーツ、ドレス、そしてその他の衣類を扱っている）

- Don't you think we'd better widen the margin of the product a bit more?（その製品の利ざやをもう少し大きくしたほうがいいと思いませんか？）

- My father underwent surgery for the cancer last week.（先週、私の父はがんの手術を受けた）

- The outlook for the country's economy is very bright.（その国の経済の見通しは非常に明るい）

- Investors are becoming more cautious in the present economic conditions.（現在の経済状況の中で、投資家たちはより慎重になってきている）

- Tobacco advertising on TV is not allowed.（テレビでのたばこの宣伝は認められていない）

- The government will lift restrictions on foreign property investment.（政府は外国からの不動産投資に対する制限を解除する予定だ）

Day 29 ») CD-A29
Quick Review
答えは左ページ下

- charity
- popularity
- scholar
- crisis
- elderly
- rage
- scheme
- invention
- incident
- treaty
- provision
- errand
- profile
- conservation
- immigrant
- prejudice

CHAPTER 1
CHAPTER 2
CHAPTER 3
CHAPTER 4
CHAPTER 5
CHAPTER 6
CHAPTER 7
CHAPTER 8
CHAPTER 9
CHAPTER 10

Day 31　名詞19

Check 1　Listen)) CD-A31

□ 0481
significance
/sɪgnífɪkəns/
Part 5, 6

名❶**重要性**、重大性(≒importance)　❷意味、意義(≒meaning)
形significant：❶重要な　❷かなりの　❸意味のある
副significantly：❶著しく　❷(more [most] ～で)さらに[最も]重要なことに(は)

□ 0482
intervention
/ìntərvénʃən/
Part 7

名❶(～への)**介入**、干渉(in ～)　❷(～への)仲裁、調停(in ～)
動intervene：(intervene inで)❶～に干渉する、割り込む　❷～を調停する、とりなす

□ 0483
consultation
/kànsəltéiʃən/
Part 4

名(～との／…についての)**相談**、協議(with ～/on [about] …)
名consultant：(会社などの)コンサルタント、顧問
動consult：❶～に助言を求める　❷(本など)を調べる　❸(consult withで)～と話し合う、相談する

□ 0484
utility
/ju:tíləti/
Part 2, 3

名❶(通例～ies)(水道などの)**公共料金**；公共施設　❷有用性[実用性](≒usefulness)
名utilization：利用
動utilize：～を(…のために)利用する、役立たせる(for …)

□ 0485
perspective
/pərspéktiv/
Part 5, 6

名❶(～についての)**観点**、視点(on ～)(≒viewpoint)
❷総体的な見方　❸遠近法

□ 0486
inheritance
/inhérətəns/
Part 5, 6

名❶**遺産**、相続財産(≒heritage)　❷(前代などから)受け継いだもの；(無形の)遺産
動inherit：(財産など)を(…から)相続する、受け継ぐ(from …)

□ 0487
defendant
/diféndənt/
Part 7

名**被告**(人)(≒accused)(⇔plaintiff：原告)　❶「容疑者」はsuspect

□ 0488
gratitude
/grǽtətjù:d/
Part 7

名(～への)**感謝の気持ち**；謝意(for ～)(⇔ingratitude：忘恩)
動gratify：(be gratified byで)～に喜んでいる
形grateful：(be grateful to A for Bで)AにBのことで感謝している

continued
▼

英字紙・英字雑誌などを使って、語彙との出合いを増やそう。学習した語彙ともきっと遭遇するはず。出合いの数と定着度は正比例する！

- □ 聞くだけモード　Check 1
- □ しっかりモード　Check 1 ▶ 2
- □ かんぺきモード　Check 1 ▶ 2 ▶ 3

Check 2　Phrase

- □ be of great [little] significance(非常に重要である[ほとんど重要でない])
- □ the significance of the poem(その詩の意味)

- □ foreign intervention(外国からの介入)
- □ the intervention of the court(裁判所の仲裁)

- □ in consultation with ~(~と協議中で[に])

- □ a utility company(公益事業会社)
- □ be of no utility(役に立たない)

- □ from a historical perspective(歴史的な観点から)
- □ get the situation in perspective(状況を総体的にとらえる)

- □ a quarrel over an inheritance(遺産争い)
- □ literary inheritance(文学的遺産)

- □ represent a defendant(被告の代理人を務める)

- □ owe a debt of gratitude to ~(~に恩がある)
- □ with gratitude(感謝して)

Check 3　Sentence

- □ The prime minister stressed the significance of economic reforms.(首相は経済改革の重要性を強調した)

- □ The senator opposed the US military intervention in Iraq.(その上院議員はイラクへのアメリカの軍事介入に反対した)

- □ Our operators are available for consultation by phone from 9 a.m. to 7 p.m.(当社のオペレーターは午前9時から午後7時まで電話で相談に対応可能だ)

- □ The rent includes utilities.(その家賃には公共料金が含まれている)

- □ The construction of the nuclear plant seems to be a bad thing from an environmental perspective.(その原子力発電所の建設は環境の観点からは悪いことのように思える)

- □ He has used up his inheritance on gambling.(彼は遺産をギャンブルに使い果たしてしまった)

- □ The jury found the defendant guilty.(陪審員団はその被告を有罪と評決した)

- □ I would like to express my gratitude for your cooperation.(皆さんのご協力に対して感謝申し上げます)

continued
▼

Day 31

Check 1　Listen)) CD-A31

☐ 0489
checkup
/tʃékʌp/
Part 2, 3

名 ❶健康診断　❷(機械などの)検査

☐ 0490
stimulus
/stímjuləs/
ビジネス問題

名 刺激(するもの)　❶複数形はstimuli
名 stimulation：刺激、興奮
動 stimulate：~を刺激する、活気づける

☐ 0491
postage
/póustidʒ/
Part 2, 3

名 郵便料金
名 post：❶柱　❷職、地位　❸郵便
動 post：❶(ビラなど)を(…に)貼る(on …)　❷(手紙など)をポストに入れる、郵便局に出す

☐ 0492
formula
/fɔ́ːrmjulə/
Part 7

名 ❶製法、調理法　❷(~の)解決[打開]策(for ~)　❸(~の)公式(for ~)　❹複数形はformulasとformulaeの2つある
動 formulate：❶(考えなど)を編み出す、練り上げる　❷(考えなど)を明確に述べる　❸~を公式化する

☐ 0493
violation
/vàiəléiʃən/
Part 7

名 ❶(法律などの)違反(of ~)　❷(権利などの)侵害(of ~)
動 violate：❶(法律など)に違反する　❷(私生活など)を侵害する

☐ 0494
microscope
/máikrəskòup/
Part 1

名 顕微鏡　❶「望遠鏡」はtelescope
形 microscopic：❶非常に小さい、微細な　❷顕微鏡の

☐ 0495
proceeding
/prəsíːdiŋ/
ビジネス問題

名 ❶(~s)議事録(≒minutes)　❷(~s)(法的)手続き　❸進行
名 proceed：(~s)収益、売上高
動 proceed：❶(proceed toで)~へ進む、向かう　❷(proceed withで)~を続ける

☐ 0496
indication
/ìndikéiʃən/
Part 5, 6

名 (~の/…という)兆候、しるし(of ~/that節 …)
動 indicate：~を示す、表す

Day 30)) CD-A30
Quick Review
答えは右ページ下

☐ 類似点　☐ 義務　☐ 決まりきった仕事　☐ 見通し
☐ 探査　☐ 主題　☐ 衣服　☐ 投資家
☐ 発送　☐ 混乱　☐ 利ざや　☐ 広告
☐ 現象　☐ 不確実性　☐ 手術　☐ 制限

Check 2 Phrase	Check 3 Sentence
☐ a regular checkup(定期的な健康診断) ☐ give ~ a checkup(~を検査する)	☐ Have you already had this year's checkup?(今年の健康診断はもう受けましたか?)
☐ respond to stimuli(刺激に反応する)	☐ The tax cuts will be a stimulus to the economy.(減税は経済への刺激になるだろう)
☐ postage free [due](郵便料金無料[不足])	☐ Postage is extra.(郵便料金は別途必要だ)
☐ a formula for wine(ワインの製法) ☐ a magic formula([何でも解決してくれる]魔法の解決策)	☐ Coca-Cola's formula is patented.(コカコーラの製法は特許を受けている)
☐ in violation of ~(~に違反して) ☐ a violation of human rights(人権の侵害)	☐ The country has heavy penalties for drug violations.(その国は麻薬違反に重罰を課している)
☐ an electron [optical] microscope([電子]光学顕微鏡)	☐ The woman is looking through a microscope.(女性は顕微鏡をのぞいている)
☐ the proceedings of the meeting(その会議の議事録) ☐ divorce proceedings(離婚手続き)	☐ He looked through the proceedings of the annual conference.(彼は年次会議の議事録に目を通した)
☐ indications of the disease(その病気の兆候)	☐ There is every indication that the economy is slowing.(経済が減速している十分な兆候がある)

Day 30))) CD-A30
Quick Review
答えは左ページ下

☐ similarity ☐ obligation ☐ routine ☐ outlook
☐ exploration ☐ theme ☐ garment ☐ investor
☐ shipping ☐ confusion ☐ margin ☐ advertising
☐ phenomenon ☐ uncertainty ☐ surgery ☐ restriction

CHAPTER 1
CHAPTER 2
CHAPTER 3
CHAPTER 4
CHAPTER 5
CHAPTER 6
CHAPTER 7
CHAPTER 8
CHAPTER 9
CHAPTER 10

Day 32　名詞20

Check 1　Listen)) CD-A32

□ 0497
hospitality
/hὰspətǽləti/
Part 5, 6

名**親切なもてなし**、歓待
名hospital：病院
形hospitable：❶(客などを)親切に[手厚く]もてなす ❷(環境などが)快適な

□ 0498
cashier
/kæʃíər/
❶アクセント注意
Part 1

名❶(店などの)**レジ係** ❷(会社などの)会計[出納]係
名cash：現金
動cash：(小切手など)を現金に換える

□ 0499
completion
/kəmplíːʃən/
Part 5, 6

名**完成**、完了
動complete：〜を完成させる
形complete：❶完全な ❷全部の
副completely：完全に、すっかり

□ 0500
offender
/əféndər/
Part 4

名**犯罪者**、違反者(≒criminal)
名offense：❶(〜に対する)違反、犯罪(against 〜) ❷気分を害すること[もの]
動offend：❶〜の気分を害する ❷罪を犯す
形offensive：❶不快な、無礼な ❷攻撃側の

□ 0501
boom
/búːm/
❶定義注意
ビジネス問題

名❶(〜の)**にわか景気**(in 〜)(⇔slump：不況) ❷(〜の)大流行、ブーム(in 〜)
動にわかに景気づく

□ 0502
carrier
/kǽriər/
ビジネス問題

名❶**運送**[輸送、運輸]**会社** ❷配達人 ❸保菌者 ❹保険会社 ❺長距離通信会社
動carry：❶(店が)(商品)を扱っている、売っている ❷〜を運ぶ

□ 0503
remainder
/riméindər/
Part 7

名(the 〜)(集合的に)(〜の)**残り**、残りの物[人](of 〜)
名remain：(通例 〜s)残り(物)
動remain：❶(依然として)〜のままである ❷(ある場所に)とどまる

□ 0504
circulation
/sə̀ːrkjuléiʃən/
❶定義注意
Part 4

名❶**発行部数** ❷(貨幣の)流通 ❸(血液の)循環
動circulate：❶循環する ❷〜を循環させる ❸(うわさなどが)広がる ❹(うわさなど)を流布させる

continued
▼

「書いて覚える」のも効果的。「聞く＋音読する」に加えて、「書く」学習もしてみよう。そう、語彙学習は「あの手この手」が大切！

□ 聞くだけモード　Check 1
□ しっかりモード　Check 1 ▶ 2
□ かんぺきモード　Check 1 ▶ 2 ▶ 3

Check 2　Phrase

□ give hospitality to guests（客を親切にもてなす）

□ a cashier at a convenience store（コンビニエンスストアのレジ係）
□ a cashier's window（出納窓口）

□ be near completion（完成間近である）
□ on completion of ~（~の完了時に）

□ a drug offender（麻薬犯）
□ a repeat offender（常習犯）

□ a war boom（軍需景気）
□ a fitness boom（健康ブーム）

□ an air carrier（空輸会社）
□ a newspaper [mail] carrier（新聞[郵便]配達人）

□ the remainder of the day [loan]（その日[ローン]の残り）

□ a newspaper with a daily circulation of 50,000（1日の発行部数が5万部の新聞）
□ in circulation（[貨幣が]流通して）

Check 3　Sentence

□ Thank you so much for your hospitality.（ご歓待いただき、どうもありがとうございます）

□ The cashier is standing behind the counter.（レジ係はカウンターの後ろに立っている）

□ The construction of the bridge is scheduled for completion in February.（その橋の建設は2月に完了する予定だ）

□ We must prevent juvenile offenders from becoming repeat criminals.（私たちは未成年犯罪者が常習犯になるのを防がなければならない）

□ I don't think this property boom will last much longer.（この不動産景気がさらに長く続くとは私は思わない）

□ I use a carrier whose rates are lower than the others.（私はほかの会社よりも料金が安い運送会社を使っている）

□ The remainder of the climbers are still missing.（残りの登山者たちは依然として行方不明となっている）

□ The magazine has a circulation of 200,000.（その雑誌の発行部数は20万部だ）

continued
▼

Day 32

Check 1　Listen))) CD-A32

0505
manuscript
/mǽnjuskrɪpt/
Part 7

名 (手書き・タイプの)**原稿**

0506
flexibility
/flèksəbíləti/
Part 7

名 **柔軟[融通]性**
形 flexible：❶(考えなどが)柔軟な；(予定が)融通の利く　❷曲げやすい

0507
generosity
/dʒènərάsəti/
Part 4

名 **気前のよさ**；寛大
形 generous：❶(金などに)気前のよい(with ～)；(～に対して)寛大な(to ～)　❷たくさんの
副 generously：❶気前よく　❷寛大にも　❸たっぷり

0508
monopoly
/mənάpəli/
ビジネス問題

名 ❶(～の)**独占**(権)、専売(権)(on [of, in] ～)　❷独占企業
動 monopolize：(事業など)を独占する

0509
attendance
/əténdəns/
Part 4

名 ❶(～への)**出席**(at ～)　❷(～への)出席者数(at ～)
名 attendant：❶店員、接客係　❷従者
形 attendant：❶付随する　❷つき添いの
動 attend：❶～に出席する　❷(attend toで)～を処理する；～の世話をする；～に注意を払う

0510
jury
/dʒúəri/
Part 7

名 ❶(集合的に)**陪審**(員団)　❷(集合的に)(競技会などの)審査員団(≒panel)
名 juror：❶陪審員　❷(競技会などの)審査員

0511
assessment
/əsésmənt/
Part 7

名 ❶**評価**(≒evaluation, appraisal)　❷査定
動 assess：❶～を評価する　❷～を(…と)査定する(at …)

0512
prediction
/prɪdíkʃən/
Part 5, 6

名 (～についての)**予測**、予報、予言、予想(about [of] ～)
動 predict：～を予測[予言、予想]する

Day 31))) CD-A31
Quick Review
答えは右ページ下

- □ 重要性
- □ 介入
- □ 相談
- □ 公共料金
- □ 観点
- □ 遺産
- □ 被告
- □ 感謝の気持ち
- □ 健康診断
- □ 刺激
- □ 郵便料金
- □ 製法
- □ 違反
- □ 顕微鏡
- □ 議事録
- □ 兆候

Check 2　Phrase

- ☐ an unpublished manuscript（未発表の原稿）
- ☐ be in manuscript（原稿のままである、未発表である）

- ☐ flexibility of thought（思考の柔軟性）

- ☐ imperial generosity（大変な気前のよさ[寛大さ]）
- ☐ show one's generosity（気前のよさを見せる）

- ☐ have a monopoly on [of, in] ～（～の独占[専売]権を持つ）
- ☐ a state-run monopoly（国営の独占企業）

- ☐ take attendance（出席を取る）
- ☐ a large [poor] attendance（多い[少ない]出席者数）

- ☐ sit on a jury（陪審員を務める）
- ☐ the jury of a speech contest（弁論大会の審査員団）

- ☐ environmental assessment（環境アセスメント、環境影響評価）
- ☐ a tax assessment（税額の査定）

- ☐ make a prediction about ～（～について予測する）
- ☐ weather prediction（天気予報）

Check 3　Sentence

- ☐ The editor made a lot of corrections to the manuscript.（その編集者は原稿に多くの修正を入れた）

- ☐ Flexibility is the key to success.（柔軟性は成功へのかぎだ）

- ☐ I was overwhelmed by his generosity.（私は彼の気前のよさに圧倒された）

- ☐ Microsoft virtually has a monopoly on desktop operating systems.（マイクロソフト社はデスクトップコンピューターのオペレーティングシステムを実質的に独占している）

- ☐ Attendance at the conference is optional.（その会議への出席は随意となっている）

- ☐ The jury debated for three days before reaching a verdict.（評決をまとめる前に陪審団は3日間討議した）

- ☐ His assessment of the situation was fairly accurate.（彼の状況評価はまあまあ正確だった）

- ☐ His economic predictions for this year were half right.（彼の今年の経済予測は半分は正しかった）

Day 31))) CD-A31
Quick Review
答えは左ページ下

- ☐ significance
- ☐ intervention
- ☐ consultation
- ☐ utility
- ☐ perspective
- ☐ inheritance
- ☐ defendant
- ☐ gratitude
- ☐ checkup
- ☐ stimulus
- ☐ postage
- ☐ formula
- ☐ violation
- ☐ microscope
- ☐ proceeding
- ☐ indication

Day 33　名詞21

Check 1　Listen))) CD-A33

☐ 0513
speculation
/spèkjuléiʃən/
Part 7

名 ❶(～についての)**推測**、推量(about [on] ～)(≒guess) ❷(～への)投機、思惑買い(in ～)
動 speculate：❶(～について)推測する(about ～)　❷～だと推測する　❸(～に)投機する(in ～)

☐ 0514
donation
/dounéiʃən/
Part 4

名 ❶(～への)**寄付**、寄贈(to ～)　❷(～への)寄付金、寄贈品(to ～)(≒contribution)
動 donate：(donate A to Bで)AをBに寄付[寄贈]する

☐ 0515
interruption
/ìntərʌ́pʃən/
Part 2, 3

名 **妨害**、遮ること；妨害物、遮る物
動 interrupt：～を遮る、妨げる

☐ 0516
insight
/ínsàit/
Part 5, 6

名 (～への/…についての)**洞察**(力)、見識(into ～/about …)

☐ 0517
faculty
/fǽkəlti/
❶アクセント注意
Part 5, 6

名 ❶(集合的に)**学部教授陣**；学部　❷(～の)才能(for [of] ～)(≒ability, talent, gift)　⊕facility(施設)と混同しないように注意

☐ 0518
perishable
/périʃəbl/
Part 2, 3

名 (～s)**生鮮食品**、腐りやすい物[食品]
形 (食べ物が)腐りやすい
動 perish：❶死ぬ　❷滅びる

☐ 0519
cellphone
/sélfòun/
Part 2, 3

名 **携帯電話**(≒cellular phone, mobile phone, mobile)

☐ 0520
mall
/mɔ́ːl/
Part 2, 3

名 **ショッピングセンター**(≒shopping center)

continued ▼

本を持ち歩かなくても、語彙学習はできる！
特に復習はCDを「聞き流す」だけでもOK。
通勤・通学時などの「細切れ時間」を活用しよう。

- ☐ 聞くだけモード　Check 1
- ☐ しっかりモード　Check 1 ▶ 2
- ☐ かんぺきモード　Check 1 ▶ 2 ▶ 3

Check 2　Phrase

- ☐ wild [idle] speculation（いい加減な推測）
- ☐ on speculation（投機的に、思惑で）

- ☐ make a donation to ~（~に寄付する）
- ☐ beg for donations（寄付金を請う）

- ☐ without interruption（間断なく）
- ☐ constant interruption（繰り返される妨害）

- ☐ a man of great insight（洞察力の鋭い人）
- ☐ have an insight into ~（~に見識がある）

- ☐ the faculty of law（法学部）
- ☐ have a great faculty for [of] ~（~の素晴らしい才能がある）

- ☐ use up perishables（生鮮食品を使い切る）

- ☐ talk on one's cellphone（携帯電話で話す）

- ☐ shop at the mall（ショッピングセンターで買い物をする）

Check 3　Sentence

- ☐ The report is based on speculation rather than facts.（その報告書は事実よりもむしろ推測に基づいている）

- ☐ She made a donation of $200,000 to the local hospital.（彼女は地元の病院に20万ドルを寄付した）

- ☐ I can't stand these continual interruptions by phone calls.（こう頻繁にかかってくる電話に邪魔されては我慢できない）

- ☐ I was impressed with his knowledge and insight.（私は彼の知識と洞察力に感心した）

- ☐ The faculty will have a meeting tomorrow.（教授陣は明日、会議を開く予定だ）

- ☐ Keep perishables in the refrigerator.（生鮮食品を冷蔵庫にしまっておいてください）

- ☐ Can I use your cellphone?（あなたの携帯電話を使っていいですか？）

- ☐ Why don't we go to the mall later?（後でショッピングセンターに行きませんか？）

continued ▼

Day 33

Check 1　Listen)) CD-A33

□ 0521
deregulation
/dì:régjulèiʃən/
ビジネス問題

名**規制緩和**[撤廃]、自由化
動deregulate：〜の規制を緩和[撤廃]する、〜を自由化する

□ 0522
workout
/wə́:rkàut/
Part 2, 3

名(練習)**運動**、トレーニング(≒exercise)
動work out：練習[運動]をする、体を鍛える

□ 0523
booklet
/búklit/
Part 4

名**小冊子**、パンフレット(≒pamphlet, brochure)

□ 0524
pavement
/péivmənt/
Part 1

名**舗装道路**
動pave：(道路など)を(…で)舗装する(with . . .)
形paved：舗装された

□ 0525
origin
/ɔ́:rədʒin/
❶アクセント注意
Part 7

名❶(しばしば〜s)(〜の)**起源**；由来(of 〜)　❷(しばしば〜s)生まれ、血統
名original：(the 〜)原物、原作
形original：❶最初の　❷独創的な　❸原作の
動originate：(〜から)起こる、生じる(in [from] 〜)

□ 0526
plot
/plɑ́t/
Part 7

名❶(小説などの)**筋**、構想　❷(〜しようとする／…に対する)陰謀、策略(to do/against . . .)(≒scheme, conspiracy)
動❶〜をたくらむ　❷(plot to doで)〜しようとたくらむ　❸(〜に対して)陰謀を企てる(against 〜)

□ 0527
container
/kəntéinər/
Part 1

名❶**容器**、入れ物(≒receptacle)　❷(貨物用)コンテナ
動contain：❶〜を含む　❷(通例否定語を伴って)(感情など)を抑える

□ 0528
particle
/pɑ́:rtikl/
Part 7

名**微粒子**、小さな粒
名particular：(〜s)詳細、明細
形particular：❶特別[格別]の　❷特定の　❸(be particular aboutで)〜について好みがうるさい
副particularly：特に

Day 32)) CD-A32
Quick Review
答えは右ページ下

- □ 親切なもてなし
- □ レジ係
- □ 完成
- □ 犯罪者
- □ にわか景気
- □ 運送会社
- □ 残り
- □ 発行部数
- □ 原稿
- □ 柔軟性
- □ 気前のよさ
- □ 独占
- □ 出席
- □ 陪審
- □ 評価
- □ 予測

Check 2 Phrase

☐ the effect of the deregulation（規制緩和の効果）

☐ an aerobic workout（エアロビクスの運動）
☐ a daily workout（毎日の運動）

☐ a test booklet（試験答案冊子）

☐ a concrete pavement（コンクリートの舗装道路）

☐ the origins of the universe（宇宙の起源）
☐ an American of Irish origin（アイルランド系のアメリカ人）

☐ the plot of the novel（その小説の筋）
☐ a plot against the government（反政府の陰謀）

☐ a plastic container（プラスチック製の容器）
☐ a container ship（コンテナ船）

☐ particles of dust（粉塵、細かいほこり）

Check 3 Sentence

☐ More than 100 carriers have gone bankrupt since deregulation.（規制緩和以降、100を超える運送会社が倒産している）

☐ He has a light workout every day.（彼は毎日、軽い運動をしている）

☐ The booklet provides information about hotel accommodations in the city.（その小冊子には市内の宿泊施設に関する情報が載っている）

☐ There are fallen leaves on the pavement.（舗道に落ち葉がある）

☐ The origin of life is still unknown.（生命の起源はまだ分かっていない）

☐ The movie's plot was hard to follow.（その映画の筋はつかみにくかった）

☐ The cookies are stored in a container.（クッキーが容器にしまってある）

☐ Electrons are atomic particles.（電子は原子の粒子だ）

Day 32 》CD-A32
Quick Review
答えは左ページ下

☐ hospitality ☐ boom ☐ manuscript ☐ attendance
☐ cashier ☐ carrier ☐ flexibility ☐ jury
☐ completion ☐ remainder ☐ generosity ☐ assessment
☐ offender ☐ circulation ☐ monopoly ☐ prediction

Day 34　名詞22

Check 1　Listen)) CD-A34

□ 0529
expedition
/èkspədíʃən/
Part 5, 6

名 ❶(〜への)**探検**、遠征、調査旅行(to 〜)　❷(〜への)ちょっとした外出(to 〜)　❸探検[遠征]隊

□ 0530
plunge
/plʌ́ndʒ/
ビジネス問題

名 ❶(価値などの)**急落**(in 〜)　❷飛び込み
動 ❶(価格などが)急落する　❷(〜に)飛び込む、落ち込む(in [into] 〜)

□ 0531
involvement
/inválvmənt/
Part 5, 6

名 (〜への)**関与**、参加(in 〜)(≒participation)
動 involve：❶〜を(議論などに)巻き込む(in ...)　❷(be involved in [with]で)〜に参加している；〜と関係している

□ 0532
premise
/prémis/
Part 7

名 ❶(〜s)(建物を含む)**敷地**、土地、構内　❷(〜という)前提、仮定(that節 〜)

□ 0533
diversity
/divə́ːrsəti/
Part 5, 6

名 **多様性**(≒variety)；相違(≒difference)
動 diversify：❶〜を多様化する　❷(投資)を多角的にする　❸事業を広げる
形 diverse：多様な、さまざまの

□ 0534
plague
/pléig/
Part 7

名 **疫病**、伝染病(≒epidemic)；(the 〜)ペスト
動 〜を苦しめる、悩ます

□ 0535
restoration
/rèstəréiʃən/
Part 7

名 ❶**回復**　❷修復　❸返還(≒return)
動 restore：❶〜を修復[復元]する　❷(信頼など)を取り戻す

□ 0536
fraction
/frǽkʃən/
Part 7

名 ❶(全体の)**一部**、小部分；(ある物の)何分の1(of 〜)　❷分数

continued

1日の「サボり」が挫折につながる。語彙習得論的にも、2日分(=32語)を1日で覚えるのは難しい。1日1日の「積み重ね」を大切に！

- ☐ 聞くだけモード　Check 1
- ☐ しっかりモード　Check 1 ▶ 2
- ☐ かんぺきモード　Check 1 ▶ 2 ▶ 3

Check 2　Phrase

☐ an expedition to the South Pole(南極への探検)
☐ a shopping expedition(買い出し)

☐ a plunge in oil prices(石油価格の急落)
☐ take a plunge into ～(～に飛び込む)

☐ his involvement in the crime(その犯罪への彼の関与)

☐ on [off] the premises(敷地内[外]で)
☐ on the premise that ～(～という前提で)

☐ ethnic diversity(民族的多様性)
☐ a diversity of opinions(さまざまな意見)

☐ a visitation of plague(疫病の襲来)

☐ one's restoration from illness(病気からの回復)
☐ the restoration of the building(その建物の修復)

☐ a fraction of the work(その仕事の一部分)
☐ a proper [an improper] fraction(真[仮]分数)

Check 3　Sentence

☐ The expedition discovered many new species of plants.(その調査旅行では多くの植物の新種が発見された)

☐ There was a nearly 8 percent plunge in stock prices today.(今日は株価が8パーセント近く急落した)

☐ The politician denied any involvement in the scandal.(その政治家は汚職事件への関与を否定した)

☐ Smoking is not permitted on the premises.(敷地内では喫煙は認められていない)

☐ New York is famous for its cultural diversity.(ニューヨークは文化的多様性で有名だ)

☐ Millions lost their lives in the plague.(その疫病で何百万人もの人々が命を落とした)

☐ The country's first priority is the restoration of law and order.(その国の最優先事項は治安の回復だ)

☐ She bought the dress at a fraction of the original price.(彼女は元値の数分の1でそのドレスを買った)

continued
▼

Day 34

Check 1　Listen 》CD-A34

□ 0537
penetration
/pènətréiʃən/
ビジネス問題

  名 **進出**、普及；浸透
  動 penetrate：❶(市場)に浸透する　❷～を貫通する　❸(～を)貫く(into ～)

□ 0538
correspondent
/kɔ̀:rəspándənt/
Part 5, 6

  名 (新聞・テレビなどの)**特派員**；通信員
  名 correspondence：❶一致　❷文通、通信
  動 correspond：❶(correspond to [with]で)～に一致する　❷(correspond toで)～に相当する　❸(correspond withで)～と文通する

□ 0539
rally
/rǽli/
❶定義注意
ビジネス問題

  名 ❶(株価などの)**反発**、持ち直し　❷集会、大会
  動 ❶(支持など)を集める　❷集まる、結集する　❸(株価が)反発する、持ち直す

□ 0540
participation
/pɑ:rtìsəpéiʃən/
Part 7

  名 (～への)**参加**、加入(in ～)
  名 participant：(～の)参加者、当事者(in ～)
  動 participate：(participate inで)～に参加する

□ 0541
horn
/hɔ́:rn/
Part 4

  名 **クラクション**、警笛

□ 0542
collar
/kάlər/
Part 1

  名 **襟**　●color(色)と混同しないように注意

□ 0543
wage
/wéidʒ/
ビジネス問題

  名 (しばしば～s)**賃金**、給料(≒salary, pay)

□ 0544
alarm
/əlά:rm/
❶定義注意
Part 2, 3

  名 ❶**心配**、不安　❷警報器[装置]　❸目覚まし時計
  動 ❶～を心配させる、不安にさせる　❷(be alarmed by [at, over]で)～に驚いている、不安を感じている

Day 33 》CD-A33
Quick Review
答えは右ページ下

- ☐ 推測
- ☐ 寄付
- ☐ 妨害
- ☐ 洞察
- ☐ 学部教授陣
- ☐ 生鮮食品
- ☐ 携帯電話
- ☐ ショッピングセンター
- ☐ 規制緩和
- ☐ 運動
- ☐ 小冊子
- ☐ 舗装道路
- ☐ 起源
- ☐ 筋
- ☐ 容器
- ☐ 微粒子

Check 2 Phrase

- the penetration rate of the Internet(インターネットの普及率)

- a foreign correspondent(海外特派員)

- a rally on the stock market(株式市場の持ち直し)
- a peace rally(平和集会)

- participation in volunteer activities(ボランティア活動への参加)

- sound [blow, honk] a horn(クラクションを鳴らす)

- a stand-up collar(立ち襟)

- a wage increase(賃上げ)

- a look of alarm(不安の表情)
- a burglar alarm(盗難警報器)

Check 3 Sentence

- The company is trying to increase its penetration into the Chinese market.(その会社は中国市場への進出を高めようと努力している)

- The newspaper has five correspondents in Japan.(その新聞社には5人の日本在住特派員がいる)

- There was a rally in stock prices today.(今日は株価が反発した)

- Thank you very much for your participation.(ご参加いただき誠にありがとうございます)

- He sounded his horn at the car that was driving too slow.(彼はあまりにゆっくり走っている車に対してクラクションを鳴らした)

- The woman is ironing a shirt collar.(女性はシャツの襟にアイロンをかけている)

- He earns an hourly wage of $20.(彼は時給20ドルをもらっている)

- There is no cause for alarm.(心配はいりません)

Day 33 》CD-A33
Quick Review
答えは左ページ下

- speculation
- donation
- interruption
- insight
- faculty
- perishable
- cellphone
- mall
- deregulation
- workout
- booklet
- pavement
- origin
- plot
- container
- particle

Day 35　名詞23

Check 1　Listen)) CD-A35

□ 0545
setting
/sétiŋ/
Part 5, 6

名 ❶**環境**、周囲の状態(≒ environment)　❷(小説などの)舞台、背景

□ 0546
neighborhood
/néibərhùd/
Part 2, 3

名 ❶(ある特定の)**地域**　❷近所、近隣　❸(集合的に)近所の人々　❹(the ~)(~に)近いこと(of ~)
名 neighbor：近所の人；隣国
形 neighboring：近所の、近隣の

□ 0547
breed
/bríːd/
Part 5, 6

名 (動植物の)**品種**；血統
動 ❶~を飼育[栽培]する；~を品種改良する　❷繁殖する　❸~を引き起こす
名 breeding：❶繁殖　❷品種改良
名 breeder：繁殖させる人；品種改良家

□ 0548
statue
/stǽtʃuː/
Part 1

名 **像**、彫像　⊕ 「彫刻」はsculpture

□ 0549
drawing
/dróːiŋ/
Part 1

名 ❶**スケッチ**、デッサン　❷くじ引き、抽選
名 drawer：引き出し；(~s)たんす
動 draw：❶~を引く　❷~を描く

□ 0550
selection
/silékʃən/
❶定義注意
ビジネス問題

名 ❶**品ぞろえ**　❷選択、選抜　❸(~から)選ばれた物[人](from ~)
動 select：❶~を(…のために)選ぶ(for . . .)　❷(select A as Bで)AをBとして選出する
形 select：えり抜きの、選ばれた

□ 0551
threat
/θrét/
❶発音注意
Part 7

名 ❶**脅迫**、脅し、脅威(≒ menace)　❷(悪いことの)兆し、前兆、恐れ(of ~)
動 threaten：❶~を(…で)脅す、脅迫する(with . . .)　❷(threaten to doで)~するぞと脅す、脅迫する　❸~の恐れがある

□ 0552
edition
/idíʃən/
Part 2, 3

名 (本などの)**版**
名 editor：編集者
名 editorial：(新聞などの)社説、論説
形 editorial：❶編集(上)の　❷社説[論説]の
動 edit：❶~を編集する　❷~を校訂する

continued
▼

今日で『キクタンTOEIC Test Score 800』は前半戦が終了！ ここまで一緒に学習を続けてくれてありがとう！ あと5週間、頑張ろう！

- □ 聞くだけモード　Check 1
- □ しっかりモード　Check 1 ▶ 2
- □ かんぺきモード　Check 1 ▶ 2 ▶ 3

Check 2　Phrase

- □ a social setting（社会的環境）
- □ the setting of the movie（その映画の舞台）

- □ a dangerous neighborhood（危険地域）
- □ live in the neighborhood of ~（~の近くに住んでいる）

- □ a rare breed（珍しい品種）

- □ a gigantic statue（巨大な像）
- □ the Statue of Liberty（自由の女神像）

- □ a drawing pad（スケッチブック）
- □ prize drawing（賞品［賞金］の抽選）

- □ a wide selection of ~（~の幅広い品ぞろえ）
- □ make a selection from ~（~から選択する）

- □ an empty threat（口だけの脅し）
- □ the threat of rain（雨の兆し）

- □ the first edition（初版）
- □ the evening edition（夕刊）

Check 3　Sentence

- □ The hotel is located in a marvelous natural setting.（そのホテルは素晴らしい自然環境の中にある）

- □ Do you know any good restaurants in the neighborhood?（この辺りにいいレストランを知っていますか?）

- □ Chihuahuas are my favorite breed of dog.（チワワは私の大好きな犬種だ）

- □ There are statues on both sides of the gate.（門の両側に像がある）

- □ The woman is making a drawing of the view.（女性は景色をスケッチしている）

- □ The store has a wide selection of winter items.（その店は冬物を数多く取りそろえている）

- □ Nuclear weapons are a threat to the human race.（核兵器は人類にとって脅威だ）

- □ The textbook is now in its fifth edition.（その教科書は現在、第5版だ）

continued
▼

Day 35

Check 1 Listen))) CD-A35

0553
panel
/pǽnl/
Part 5, 6

名 ❶(集合的に)**委員会**；(コンテストなどの)審査員団 ❷陪審団(≒jury) ❸パネル
動(壁など)に(…で)鏡板を張る(with ...)
名panelist：(公開討論会の)討論者

0554
bite
/báit/
Part 2, 3

名 ❶**軽い食事**、(食べ物の)一口(分) ❷かむこと
動〜をかむ

0555
electrician
/ilektríʃən/
Part 2, 3

名**電気技師**、電気工
名electricity：❶電気 ❷電力
形electric：❶電気の ❷電動の ❸わくわくさせる
形electrical：電気に関する、電気関係の

0556
crosswalk
/krɔ́:swɔ̀:k/
Part 1

名**横断歩道**(≒crossing, pedestrian crossing)

0557
partnership
/pá:rtnərʃìp/
ビジネス問題

名(〜との)**提携**、共同、協力(with 〜)
名partner：❶共同経営[事業]者 ❷配偶者 ❸相手、協力者
動partner：〜と提携する、パートナーを組む

0558
accomplishment
/əkámpliʃmənt/
ビジネス問題

名 ❶**業績**、功績、実績(≒achievement) ❷完成、成就、達成
動accomplish：(仕事など)を成し遂げる、完遂[成就]する

0559
dock
/dák/
Part 1

名**波止場**、埠頭(≒wharf, pier)

0560
justification
/dʒʌ̀stəfikéiʃən/
Part 5, 6

名**正当化**；(〜を)正当とする理由(for 〜)；(〜に対する)弁明(for 〜)
動justify：〜を正当化する

Day 34))) CD-A34
Quick Review
答えは右ページ下

- ☐ 探検
- ☐ 急落
- ☐ 関与
- ☐ 敷地
- ☐ 多様性
- ☐ 疫病
- ☐ 回復
- ☐ 一部
- ☐ 進出
- ☐ 特派員
- ☐ 反発
- ☐ 参加
- ☐ クラクション
- ☐ 襟
- ☐ 賃金
- ☐ 心配

Check 2　Phrase

- a **panel** of experts（専門家委員会）
- serve on a **panel**（陪審員を務める）

- have [get, grab] a **bite**（軽い食事を取る）
- take a **bite** at ~（~にかみつく、食いつく）

- a skilled **electrician**（腕のよい電気技師）

- cross at the **crosswalk**（横断歩道を渡る）

- work in **partnership** with ~（~と提携[共同、協力]して働く）
- go into **partnership** with ~（~と提携[協力]する）

- a major **accomplishment**（偉大な業績）
- a sense of **accomplishment**（達成感）

- unload the cargo at the **dock**（埠頭で積み荷を降ろす）

- in **justification** of [for] ~（~を正当化[弁明]して）

Check 3　Sentence

- Some of the **panel**'s members disagreed with the decision.（委員会の何人かの委員はその決定に異議を唱えた）

- Can I take a **bite** of your sandwich?（あなたのサンドイッチを一口食べてもいいですか?）

- Two **electricians** are coming to rewire the office tomorrow.（明日、2人の電気技師が事務所の配線変更工事に来る予定だ）

- There is no traffic light at the **crosswalk**.（この横断歩道には信号がない）

- We entered into a business **partnership** agreement with the firm.（私たちはその会社と事業提携契約を結んだ）

- Employees should be evaluated according to their **accomplishments**.（従業員はそれぞれの業績に従って評価されるべきだ）

- The boat is heading for the **dock**.（ボートは波止場へ向かっている）

- There is no **justification** for abuse.（虐待を正当化する理由などない）

Day 34　CD-A34　Quick Review　答えは左ページ下

- expedition
- plunge
- involvement
- premise
- diversity
- plague
- restoration
- fraction
- penetration
- correspondent
- rally
- participation
- horn
- collar
- wage
- alarm

Day 36　名詞24

Check 1　Listen 》CD-B1

□ 0561
staircase
/stéərkèis/
Part 1

名 **階段**(≒ stairs, stairway)

□ 0562
diagram
/dáiəgræm/
Part 2, 3

名 **図**、設計図

□ 0563
preservation
/prèzərvéiʃən/
Part 5, 6

名 **保存**、保護、維持(≒ conservation)　●reservation(予約)と混同しないように注意
名 preservative：保存料、防腐剤
動 preserve：～を(…から)保護[保存]する(from . . .)

□ 0564
transformation
/trænsfərméiʃən/
Part 5, 6

名 (～から／…への)**変化**、変形、変質(from ～/to . . .)(≒ change)
動 transform：(transform A into Bで)AをBに変形[変質]させる

□ 0565
masterpiece
/mǽstərpì:s/
Part 4

名 (最高)**傑作**、代表作(≒ masterwork)

□ 0566
standpoint
/stǽndpòint/
Part 7

名 **観点**、視点、立場(≒ viewpoint)

□ 0567
lodging
/lɑ́dʒiŋ/
Part 7

名 (一時的な)**宿泊[滞在]場所**
名 lodge：山小屋、バンガロー
動 lodge：❶(～に)泊まる(at [in] ～)　❷～を泊める

□ 0568
blueprint
/blú:prìnt/
Part 2, 3

名 ❶(建築物・機械などの)**設計図**、図面　❷(～の)(詳細な)計画(for ～)

continued
▼

今日でChapter 4は最後！ 時間に余裕があったら、章末のReviewにも挑戦しておこう。忘れてしまった単語も結構あるのでは?!

- ☐ 聞くだけモード　Check 1
- ☐ しっかりモード　Check 1 ▶ 2
- ☐ かんぺきモード　Check 1 ▶ 2 ▶ 3

Check 2　Phrase

☐ a moving staircase(エスカレーター)

☐ draw a diagram(図を描く)
☐ a diagram of the building(その建物の設計図)

☐ nature preservation(自然保護)
☐ the preservation of peace(平和の維持)

☐ the rapid transformation of the world economy(世界経済の急激な変化)

☐ a masterpiece of Picasso's "blue period"(ピカソの「青の時代」の代表作)

☐ from an economic [a historical] standpoint(経済[歴史]的観点から見ると)

☐ a lodging for the night(一夜の宿)

☐ a blueprint of the new city hall(新しい市庁舎の設計図)
☐ a blueprint for success(成功への計画)

Check 3　Sentence

☐ The woman is sweeping the staircase.(女性は階段を掃除している)

☐ See the diagram on page 54.(54ページの図を見てください)

☐ The old temple is in a good state of preservation.(その古い寺は保存状態がよい)

☐ The country experienced a political transformation from socialism to democracy.(その国は社会主義から民主主義への政治的変化を経験した)

☐ Beethoven's ninth symphony is regarded as one of his masterpieces.(ベートーベンの交響曲第9番は彼の傑作の1つと見なされている)

☐ The doctor recommended surgery from a professional standpoint.(その医者は専門家としての立場から手術を勧めた)

☐ You can find information on lodging at the tourist center.(その観光案内所で宿泊場所の情報を見つけることができる)

☐ The architect showed us a blueprint of our new house.(その建築家は新居の設計図を私たちに見せた)

continued
▼

Day 36

Check 1　Listen))) CD-B1

□ 0569
ritual
/rítʃuəl/
Part 5, 6

- 名 **儀式**(≒ceremony, rite)
- 形 儀式の、儀式的な

□ 0570
exhaustion
/ɪgzɔ́ːstʃən/
Part 7

- 名 ❶**極度の疲労** ❷使い尽くすこと、枯渇
- 名 exhaust：排気ガス
- 動 exhaust：❶～を疲れさせる ❷～を使い尽くす
- 形 exhausted：❶(～で)疲れ切った、力尽きた(from [with] ～) ❷使い尽くされた

□ 0571
newsletter
/njúːzlètər/
Part 2, 3

- 名 **会報**、公報(≒bulletin)

□ 0572
assembly
/əsémbli/
ビジネス問題

- 名 ❶(機械の)**組み立て**(作業) ❷集会、会合
- 動 assemble：❶(機械など)を組み立てる ❷集まる ❸～を集める

□ 0573
holding
/hóuldɪŋ/
ビジネス問題

- 名 (しばしば～s)(不動産・株などの)**所有財産**(≒property)
- 動 hold：❶(会など)を催す、行う ❷電話を切らずに待つ ❸～を持っている、握っている

□ 0574
ornament
/ɔ́ːrnəmənt/
Part 1

- 名 ❶**装飾品**、装身具 ❷装飾
- 動 ～を(…で)飾る(with ...)(≒decorate, adorn, garnish)

□ 0575
cathedral
/kəθíːdrəl/
❶発音注意
Part 4

- 名 **大聖堂**

□ 0576
outskirt
/áutskəːrt/
Part 4

- 名 (～s)(～の)**郊外**、町外れ(of ～)(≒suburb)

Day 35))) CD-A35
Quick Review
答えは右ページ下

□ 環境	□ スケッチ	□ 委員会	□ 提携
□ 地域	□ 品ぞろえ	□ 軽い食事	□ 業績
□ 品種	□ 脅迫	□ 電気技師	□ 波止場
□ 像	□ 版	□ 横断歩道	□ 正当化

Check 2 Phrase

- conduct [perform, carry out] a ritual（儀式を行う）

- mental exhaustion（精神的疲労）
- the exhaustion of water resources（水資源の枯渇）

- a monthly newsletter（月刊の会報）

- an assembly line（組み立て[生産]ライン）
- freedom of assembly（集会の自由）

- real estate holdings（不動産）

- Christmas ornaments（クリスマスの装飾品）
- by way of ornament（装飾として）

- a magnificent cathedral（荘厳な大聖堂）

- live on the outskirts of ～（～の郊外に住む）

Check 3 Sentence

- Many traditional rituals are still alive in this region.（この地域では多くの伝統儀式がいまだに残っている）

- I'm feeling ill from exhaustion.（私は疲れ切っていて気持ちが悪い）

- Do you subscribe to our weekly online newsletter?（当社の週刊のオンライン会報を定期購読していますか？）

- The automaker announced that it would close its two assembly plants in Europe.（その自動車会社はヨーロッパにある2つの組み立て工場の閉鎖を発表した）

- The company had to sell some of its holdings because of lack of funds.（資金不足のため、その会社は自社の所有財産の一部を売却しなければならなかった）

- The girl is wearing various ornaments.（少女はさまざまな装身具を身につけている）

- The tour includes a visit to the famous St. Paul's Cathedral.（そのツアーには有名なセント・ポール大聖堂の観光が含まれている）

- The university is on the outskirts of Tokyo.（その大学は東京の郊外にある）

Day 35))CD-A35
Quick Review
答えは左ページ下

- setting
- neighborhood
- breed
- statue
- drawing
- selection
- threat
- edition
- panel
- bite
- electrician
- crosswalk
- partnership
- accomplishment
- dock
- justification

CHAPTER 1
CHAPTER 2
CHAPTER 3
CHAPTER 4
CHAPTER 5
CHAPTER 6
CHAPTER 7
CHAPTER 8
CHAPTER 9
CHAPTER 10

Chapter 4 Review

左ページの(1)〜(20)の名詞の同意・類義語（≒）、反意・反対語（⇔）を右ページのA〜Tから選び、カッコの中に答えを書き込もう。意味が分からないときは、見出し番号を参照して復習しておこう（答えは右ページ下）。

- [ ] (1) earning (0387) ≒は? (　　)
- [ ] (2) garbage (0390) ≒は? (　　)
- [ ] (3) retail (0405) ⇔は? (　　)
- [ ] (4) cargo (0407) ≒は? (　　)
- [ ] (5) shortage (0423) ≒は? (　　)
- [ ] (6) outcome (0434) ≒は? (　　)
- [ ] (7) expectation (0439) ≒は? (　　)
- [ ] (8) rage (0454) ≒は? (　　)
- [ ] (9) prejudice (0464) ≒は? (　　)
- [ ] (10) similarity (0465) ⇔は? (　　)
- [ ] (11) surgery (0476) ≒は? (　　)
- [ ] (12) perspective (0485) ≒は? (　　)
- [ ] (13) defendant (0487) ⇔は? (　　)
- [ ] (14) boom (0501) ⇔は? (　　)
- [ ] (15) speculation (0513) ≒は? (　　)
- [ ] (16) plague (0534) ≒は? (　　)
- [ ] (17) setting (0545) ≒は? (　　)
- [ ] (18) threat (0551) ≒は? (　　)
- [ ] (19) ritual (0569) ≒は? (　　)
- [ ] (20) newsletter (0571) ≒は? (　　)

A. income
B. bulletin
C. viewpoint
D. difference
E. consequence
F. slump
G. guess
H. trash
I. menace
J. anticipation
K. anger
L. plaintiff
M. operation
N. lack
O. epidemic
P. bias
Q. freight
R. ceremony
S. wholesale
T. environment

【解答】 (1) A (2) H (3) S (4) Q (5) N (6) E (7) J (8) K (9) P (10) D
(11) M (12) C (13) L (14) F (15) G (16) O (17) T (18) I (19) R (20) B

CHAPTER 5
動詞：必修96

Chapter 5 では、TOEIC 必修の動詞96を見ていきます。ところで、学習が単調になってきていませんか？「800点を突破する！」という「初心」を胸に、いつもフレッシュな気持ちで学習に取り組んでいきましょう！

Day 37【動詞7】
▶ 174
Day 38【動詞8】
▶ 178
Day 39【動詞9】
▶ 182
Day 40【動詞10】
▶ 186
Day 41【動詞11】
▶ 190
Day 42【動詞12】
▶ 194
Chapter 5 Review
▶ 198

TOEIC的格言

Don't forget your first resolution.

初心忘るべからず。
[直訳] 最初の決意を忘れてはならない。

Day 37　動詞7

Check 1　Listen))) CD-B2

0577 resemble
/rizémbl/
Part 5, 6

動 **～に似ている**
名 resemblance：(～と／…の間で)似ていること；(～との／…との間の)類似[相似](点) (to ～/between . . .)

0578 spot
/spát/
❶定義注意
Part 2, 3

動 ❶ **～を見つける**、発見する(≒notice)；～を(…と)見抜く(as [for] . . .)　❷～に(…の)染みをつける(with . . .)
名 ❶場所　❷斑点；染み

0579 construct
/kənstrákt/
Part 4

動 **～を**(…で)**建設する** (of [from] . . .) (≒build)
(⇔destroy：～を破壊する)
名 construction：❶建設；建築工事　❷構造
形 constructive：(考えなどが)建設的な

0580 investigate
/invéstəgèit/
❶アクセント注意
Part 4

動 **～を**(詳細に)**調査する**、取り調べる
名 investigation：(～の)調査；捜査(into [of] ～)
名 investigator：調査員；(犯罪の)調査官

0581 alter
/ɔ́:ltər/
Part 5, 6

動 ❶ **～を変える**、改める　❷変わる(≒change)
名 alteration：変更、修正

0582 recall
/rikɔ́:l/
ビジネス頻出

動 ❶ (不良品など) **を回収する**　❷～を思い出す(≒remember, recollect)
名 ❶ (欠陥商品の)回収；リコール　❷思い出す能力

0583 doubt
/dáut/
❶発音注意
Part 5, 6

動 **～でないと思う**；～かどうか疑問に思う
名 (～についての／…かどうかの)疑い (about [as to] ～/wh-[if]節 . . .)
形 doubtful：疑わしい、不確かな
副 doubtless：疑いもなく、確かに

0584 analyze
/ǽnəlàiz/
Part 5, 6

動 **～を分析する**(⇔synthesize：～を総合する)
名 analysis：(～の)分析(of ～)
名 analyst：分析家、アナリスト；(情勢などの)解説者
形 analytical：分析の、分析的な

continued ▼

Chapter 5では、6日をかけて必修動詞96をチェック。まずはCDでチャンツを聞いて、単語を「耳」からインプット！

- □ 聞くだけモード　Check 1
- □ しっかりモード　Check 1 ▶ 2
- □ かんぺきモード　Check 1 ▶ 2 ▶ 3

Check 2　Phrase

□ closely resemble（〜とよく似ている）

□ spot mistakes in the report（その報告書の中に間違いを見つける）
□ a carpet spotted with coffee（コーヒーの染みがついたじゅうたん）

□ construct a bridge（橋を建設する）

□ investigate the murder（その殺人事件を調査する）
□ investigate the suspect（その容疑者を取り調べる）

□ alter one's hairstyle（髪型を変える）
□ alter in appearance（外見が変わる）

□ recall defective products（欠陥商品を回収する）
□ recall meeting him（彼に会ったことを思い出す）

□ doubt that he will come（彼が来るとは思わない）
□ doubt if she will succeed（彼女が成功するかどうか疑問に思う）

□ analyze the statistics（統計を分析する）

Check 3　Sentence

□ Jack and Tom resemble each other.（ジャックとトムは互いに似ている）

□ The police spotted him driving over the speed limit.（警察は彼が制限速度を超えて運転しているところを発見した）

□ The house is constructed of bricks.（その家はれんがで建てられている）

□ Police are investigating the cause of the fire.（警察はその火事の原因を調査中だ）

□ We had to alter some of our travel plans because of bad weather.（悪天候のため、私たちは旅行計画の一部を変更しなければならなかった）

□ The food company recalled some of its canned goods because of the risk of food poisoning.（その食品会社は食中毒の危険があるため、自社製の缶詰商品の一部を回収した）

□ I doubt that the project will be completed on schedule.（そのプロジェクトが予定通りに完了するとは私は思わない）

□ The researcher analyzed economic growth and income inequality in China.（その研究者は中国の経済成長と所得格差を分析した）

continued
▼

Day 37

Check 1　Listen 》CD-B2

0585
conquer
/kάŋkər/
Part 5, 6

動 ❶〜を征服する　❷(困難など)を克服する
名 conquest：征服、克服
名 conqueror：征服者、勝利者

0586
file
/fáil/
❶定義注意
Part 2, 3

動 ❶(書類など)を整理(保存)する、ファイルに入れる　❷(告訴など)を(正式に)提出する　❸(file forで)〜を申請する、願い出る
名 ファイル

0587
absorb
/æbsɔ́ːrb/
Part 4

動 ❶〜を吸収する　❷(be absorbed inで)〜に夢中になっている、没頭している　❸(be absorbed intoで)〜に合併[吸収]される
名 absorption：❶吸収　❷(〜への)没頭(in 〜)
形 absorbing：非常に面白い

0588
accomplish
/əkάmpliʃ/
Part 7

動 (仕事など)を成し遂げる、完遂[成就]する(≒achieve)
名 accomplishment：❶業績、功績、実績　❷完成、成就、達成

0589
grasp
/grǽsp/
❶定義注意
Part 5, 6

動 ❶〜を理解[把握]する(≒understand)　❷〜を(しっかり)握る、つかむ
名 ❶理解(力)(≒understanding)　❷握ること

0590
justify
/dʒΛ́stəfài/
Part 5, 6

動 〜を正当化する
名 justification：正当化；(〜を)正当とする理由(for 〜)；(〜に対する)弁明(for 〜)

0591
capture
/kǽptʃər/
Part 5, 6

動 ❶〜を捕まえる(≒catch)　❷(人の心など)をとらえる　❸〜を占領する
名 ❶逮捕(≒arrest)　❷占領
名 captive：❶捕虜、囚人　❷とりこ
形 captive：❶捕虜になった　❷とりこになった

0592
evaluate
/ivǽljuèit/
Part 2, 3

動 〜を評価する(≒assess, appraise)
名 evaluation：評価、査定

Day 36 》CD-B1
Quick Review
答えは右ページ下

☐ 階段　☐ 傑作　☐ 儀式　☐ 所有財産
☐ 図　☐ 観点　☐ 極度の疲労　☐ 装飾品
☐ 保存　☐ 宿泊場所　☐ 会報　☐ 大聖堂
☐ 変化　☐ 設計図　☐ 組み立て　☐ 郊外

Check 2 Phrase

- □ conquer a nation(国を征服する)
- □ conquer difficulties(困難を克服する)

- □ file the documents(書類を整理する)
- □ file a suit against ～(～を相手取って訴訟を起こす)

- □ absorb water(水を吸収する)
- □ be absorbed in classical music(クラシック音楽に夢中になっている)

- □ accomplish the task(その仕事をやり遂げる)
- □ accomplish one's purpose(目的を達成する)

- □ grasp the main points of the lecture(講義の要点を理解する)
- □ grasp the rope(ロープを握る)

- □ justify one's crime(自分の犯罪を正当化する)

- □ capture a burglar(強盗を捕まえる)
- □ capture his attention(彼の注意を引く)

- □ evaluate her work(彼女の仕事を評価する)

Check 3 Sentence

- □ France was conquered by Germany in 1940 and liberated in 1944.(フランスは1940年にドイツに征服され、1944年に解放された)

- □ Could you file these reports?(これらの報告書を整理してしまっておいてくれますか?)

- □ A child absorbs knowledge like a sponge.(子どもはスポンジのように知識を吸収する)

- □ Professor Wise has accomplished much in the field of education.(ワイズ教授は教育の分野で多くの業績を残した)

- □ Do you grasp my meaning clearly?(私の言っていることの意味がちゃんと分かりますか?)

- □ The government official tried to justify Japan's military actions during World War II.(その政府高官は第2次世界大戦中の日本の軍事行動を正当化しようとした)

- □ Their mission is to capture the remaining enemy soldiers.(彼らの任務は敵兵の残党を捕らえることだ)

- □ How do you evaluate the employees' abilities?(従業員の能力をどのように評価しますか?)

Day 36))) CD-B1
Quick Review
答えは左ページ下

- □ staircase
- □ diagram
- □ preservation
- □ transformation
- □ masterpiece
- □ standpoint
- □ lodging
- □ blueprint
- □ ritual
- □ exhaustion
- □ newsletter
- □ assembly
- □ holding
- □ ornament
- □ cathedral
- □ outskirt

Day 38 動詞8

Check 1　Listen 》CD-B3

0593
house
/háuz/
❶定義注意
Part 4

動 ❶〜を収容する　❷〜に住居を供給する
名 (/háus/) 家
名housing：❶(集合的に)住宅、家　❷住宅供給

0594
consult
/kənsÁlt/
Part 4

動 ❶〜に助言[意見、情報]を求める　❷(本など)を調べる　❸(consult withで)〜と話し合う
名consultation：(〜との/…についての)相談、協議(with 〜/on [about]…)
名consultant：(会社などの)コンサルタント、顧問

0595
vacuum
/vǽkjuəm/
❶定義注意
Part 4

動 ❶掃除機をかける　❷〜に掃除機をかける
名 ❶電気掃除機(≒vacuum cleaner)　❷真空

0596
advertise
/ǽdvərtàiz/
❶発音注意
ビジネス問題

動 ❶〜を宣伝[広告]する　❷(〜を求める)広告を出す(for 〜)
名advertisement：広告、宣伝
名advertising：❶(集合的に)広告　❷広告業
形advertising：広告の

0597
restrict
/ristríkt/
Part 5, 6

動 〜を(…に)制限[限定]する(to …)(≒limit, confine)
名restriction：(〜に対する)制限、限定(on 〜)
形restricted：(〜に)制限された(to 〜)

0598
convey
/kənvéi/
Part 7

動 ❶(思想・感情など)を(…に)伝える(to …)(≒communicate)　❷〜を運ぶ(≒carry)
名conveyance：❶乗り物、輸送機関　❷運搬、輸送　❸(不動産などの)譲渡

0599
suspend
/səspénd/
Part 5, 6

動 ❶〜を一時停止[中止]する　❷〜を(…から)停学[停職、出場停止]にする(from …)　❸〜をつるす
名suspension：❶(活動などの)一時停止、中止(of 〜)　❷停職、停学、出場停止
名suspense：懸念、不安、気掛かり

0600
insure
/infúər/
Part 5, 6

動 〜に(…に備えて)保険をかける(against …)
⊕ensure(〜を保証する)と混同しないように注意
名insurance：保険

continued ▼

見出し語下の「❶定義注意」マークに気をつけてる？ このマークがついた単語の用法はTOEIC独特のもの。定義をしっかりチェック！

- ☐ 聞くだけモード　Check 1
- ☐ しっかりモード　Check 1 ▶ 2
- ☐ かんぺきモード　Check 1 ▶ 2 ▶ 3

Check 2　Phrase

☐ be housed in ~(~に収容[所蔵]されている)
☐ house refugees(難民たちに住居を供給する)

☐ consult a lawyer(弁護士に助言を求める)
☐ consult a map(地図を調べる)

☐ vacuum the floor(床に掃除機をかける)

☐ advertise a house for sale(売り家の広告を出す)
☐ advertise for a sales manager(販売部長の募集広告を出す)

☐ restrict freedom of expression(表現の自由を制限する)

☐ convey one's apologies to her(謝罪の言葉を彼女に伝える)
☐ convey passengers(乗客を運ぶ)

☐ suspend payment(支払いを一時停止する)
☐ suspend the student for ten days(その生徒を10日間停学にする)

☐ insure a house against fire(火事に備えて家に保険をかける)

Check 3　Sentence

☐ The hotel houses 100 rooms with sea views.(そのホテルには海が見える100の部屋がある)

☐ For further information on vaccinations, consult your doctor or pharmacist.(予防接種に関するさらなる情報については、かかりつけの医師または薬剤師にご相談ください)

☐ How often do you vacuum?(どのくらいよく掃除機で掃除をしますか?)

☐ We advertised our products in the newspaper.(私たちは当社の製品の新聞広告を出した)

☐ Speed is restricted to 25 mph in school zones.(スクールゾーンでは速度は時速25マイルに制限されている)

☐ If you see Paul, please convey my regards to him.(ポールに会ったら、よろしくお伝えください)

☐ The game was suspended due to darkness.(その試合は日没のため一時中止となった)

☐ Transported luggage and personal belongings are insured against theft.(輸送手荷物と所持品は盗難に備えて保険がかけられている)

continued
▼

Day 38

Check 1　Listen)) CD-B3

☐ 0601
execute
/éksikjù:t/
❶アクセント注意
Part 7

動 ❶(計画など)**を実行する**(≒carry out, implement)
❷～を死刑にする
名execution：❶死刑執行　❷実行、実施
名executive：重役、経営幹部
形executive：❶実施[事務]の　❷重役の

☐ 0602
hail
/héil/
Part 1

動 **～を呼び止める**
名ひょう、あられ

☐ 0603
cite
/sáit/
Part 7

動 ❶**～に言及する**(≒mention, refer to)、～を(…として)引き合いに出す(as ...)　❷～を引用する(≒quote)
名citation：❶(裁判所への)召還　❷表彰　❸引用

☐ 0604
foster
/fɔ́:stər/
Part 7

動 ❶**～を促進[育成]する**(≒promote, encourage)
❷～を(里子として)育てる、養育する　❹「～を養子にする」はadopt
形里親[里子]の

☐ 0605
water
/wɔ́:tər/
❶定義注意
Part 1

動 **～に水をまく**、かける
名水

☐ 0606
leak
/lí:k/
Part 7

動 ❶(水などが)(～から)**漏れる**(from ～)　❷(秘密など)を漏らす
名❶漏れ口　❷漏れること　❸(秘密などの)漏えい、リーク
名leakage：❶漏れ　❷(秘密の)漏えい、リーク

☐ 0607
fascinate
/fǽsənèit/
Part 5, 6

動 ❶**～を魅了[魅惑]する**　❷(be fascinated by [with] ～で)～にうっとりしている、引きつけられている
名fascination：魅了[魅惑](された状態)
形fascinating：魅力[魅惑]的な

☐ 0608
double
/dʌ́bl/
Part 5, 6

動 ❶**～を2倍にする**　❷2倍になる
名2倍
形2倍の
副2倍に、2重に

Day 37)) CD-B2
Quick Review
答えは右ページ下

☐ ～に似ている　☐ ～を変える　☐ ～を征服する　☐ ～を理解する
☐ ～を見つける　☐ ～を回収する　☐ ～を整理する　☐ ～を正当化する
☐ ～を建設する　☐ ～でないと思う　☐ ～を吸収する　☐ ～を捕まえる
☐ ～を調査する　☐ ～を分析する　☐ ～を成し遂げる　☐ ～を評価する

Check 2　Phrase

- execute an order（命令を実行する）
- be executed for ~（~のかどで処刑される）

- hail a bus（バスを呼び止める）

- cite a few examples（2、3の例を挙げる）
- cite a passage from ~（~から一節を引用する）

- foster democracy（民主主義を促進する）
- foster an orphan（孤児を養育する）

- water the lawn（芝生に水をまく）

- leak from the engine（[オイルなどが]エンジンから漏れる）
- leak the details of the contract（その契約の詳細を漏らす）

- fascinate baseball fans（野球ファンを魅了する）
- be fascinated by the scenery（景色にうっとりしている）

- double the number of employees（従業員数を2倍にする）
- double in price（価格が2倍になる）

Check 3　Sentence

- The plan will be executed in three phases.（その計画は3段階で行われる予定だ）

- The woman is hailing a cab.（女性はタクシーを呼び止めようとしている）

- The CEO cited several reasons for his resignation.（そのCEOは辞職の理由についていくつか言及した）

- The program aims to foster better communication among the staff.（その計画は社員間のよりよいコミュニケーションの促進を目指している）

- The man is watering the plants.（男性は植物に水をまいている）

- Water was leaking from the ceiling.（水が天井から漏れていた）

- The concert fascinated its audience.（そのコンサートは聴衆を魅了した）

- The company is planning to double revenues within three years.（その会社は3年以内に収益を2倍にすることを計画している）

Day 37))) CD-B2
Quick Review
答えは左ページ下

- resemble
- spot
- construct
- investigate
- alter
- recall
- doubt
- analyze
- conquer
- file
- absorb
- accomplish
- grasp
- justify
- capture
- evaluate

Day 39　動詞9

Check 1　Listen 》CD-B4

□ 0609
clap
/klǽp/
Part 1

動 ❶ **拍手する**(≒applaud)　❷(手)をたたく
名 clapping：拍手、手拍子

□ 0610
stage
/stéidʒ/
❶定義注意
Part 7

動 ❶(ストライキなど)**を実施する**、企てる、計画する　❷～を上演する
名 ❶(発達などの)段階、時期(≒phase)　❷舞台、ステージ

□ 0611
matter
/mǽtər/
❶定義注意
Part 4

動 (通例itを主語にして)(～に)**重要[重大]である**、重大な関係がある(to ～)
名 ❶問題、事柄　❷物質(≒material, stuff, substance)(⇔spirit, mind)

□ 0612
prolong
/prəlɔ́ːŋ/
Part 7

動 **～を延長する**、長くする(≒lengthen)

□ 0613
mount
/máunt/
❶定義注意
Part 7

動 ❶(運動など)**を実施する**、～に取りかかる　❷～を(…に)据える、置く(on . . .)　❸(数量が)増す(≒increase)　❹～に登る
名 (M～)(固有名詞につけて)～山

□ 0614
drop
/drάp/
❶定義注意
Part 2, 3

動 ❶(計画など)**をやめる**、中止する　❷～を落とす　❸落ちる　❹(価値などが)下落する
名 ❶しずく　❷(液体の)少量　❸下落

□ 0615
resist
/rizíst/
❶定義注意
Part 2, 3

動 ❶(通例否定文で)**～を我慢する**、こらえる　❷～に抵抗[反抗]する(≒oppose)
名 resistance：❶(～に対する)抵抗、反抗(to ～)　❷(～に対する)抵抗力(to ～)
形 resistant：(～に)抵抗力のある(to ～)

□ 0616
slip
/slíp/
❶定義注意
ビジネス問題

動 ❶(質などが)**悪化[低下]する**(≒worsen)　❷(誤って)滑る、滑って転ぶ　➕意図的に「滑る」はslide　❸こっそりと動く
名 ❶伝票、スリップ　❷(ちょっとした)間違い
形 slippery：❶滑りやすい　❷理解しにくい

continued
▼

つらくて挫折しそうになったら、Check 1の「聞くだけモード」だけでもOK。少しずつでもいいので、「継続する」ことを大切にしよう！

- ☐ 聞くだけモード　Check 1
- ☐ しっかりモード　Check 1 ▶ 2
- ☐ かんぺきモード　Check 1 ▶ 2 ▶ 3

Check 2　Phrase

☐ clap and cheer（拍手喝さいする）
☐ clap one's hands（手をたたく）

☐ stage a demonstration（デモを実施する）
☐ stage a play（劇を上演する）

☐ It doesn't matter.（重要でない、関係ない、構わない）

☐ prolong life（寿命を長くする）

☐ mount a campaign against ～（～に反対する運動を行う）
☐ mount a mirror on the wall（壁に鏡を据える）

☐ drop everything（すべてを中止する）
☐ drop a vase from a table（テーブルから花瓶を落とす）

☐ resist the impulse [temptation, urge] to do ～（～したい衝動を抑える）
☐ resist arrest（逮捕に抵抗する）

☐ slip noticeably（著しく悪化する）
☐ slip on the icy sidewalk（氷が張った歩道で滑って転ぶ）

Check 3　Sentence

☐ The audience is clapping in time to the music.（聴衆は音楽に合わせて手をたたいている）

☐ The union will stage a strike tomorrow.（その労働組合は明日、ストライキを行う予定だ）

☐ It doesn't matter to me what others think.（他人がどう考えようと私には重要ではない）

☐ He decided to prolong his stay in Tokyo for another week.（彼は東京での滞在をもう1週間延ばすことにした）

☐ The residents in the area are mounting a protest against the construction of the building.（その地域の住民はビルの建設に反対する抗議運動を行うつもりだ）

☐ Can you drop what you're doing and help me?（していることをやめて、私を手伝ってくれますか？）

☐ I couldn't resist buying new clothes.（私は新しい服を買うのを我慢できなかった）

☐ Sales slipped from $3 million to $2.5 million last year.（昨年、売上高は300万ドルから250万ドルに下がった）

continued ▼

Day 39

Check 1　Listen 》CD-B4

0617 define
/difáin/
Part 7

動 ❶〜を(…と)**定義する**(as …)　❷〜を明確にする、明らかにする
名 definition：❶定義　❷明確さ
形 definite：明確な；明白な
副 definitely：❶確かに　❷はっきりと、明確に

0618 screen
/skríːn/
❶定義注意
Part 7

動 ❶**〜を選別する**　❷〜を(…から)守る；隠す(from …)
名 ❶画面　❷スクリーン　❸網戸
名 screening：❶選別　❷上映

0619 overflow
/òuvərflóu/
Part 1

動 ❶(〜で)**あふれる**(with 〜)　❷(川などが)氾濫する　❸〜を越えて氾濫する
名 (/óuvərflòu/)❶氾濫、洪水　❷あふれ出た物、あふれた群衆

0620 strengthen
/stréŋkθən/
Part 5, 6

動 ❶**〜を強化する**　❷強くなる(⇔weaken)
名 strength：力、強さ
形 strong：強い

0621 inhabit
/inhǽbit/
Part 5, 6

動 **〜に住む**、生息する(≒live in, dwell in)　❶他動詞なので(×)inhabit inのように後に前置詞はつかない。inhibit(〜を妨げる)と混同しないように注意
名 inhabitant：住民、居住者

0622 near
/níər/
❶定義注意
Part 7

動 **〜に近づく**(≒approach)
形 (〜に)近い(to 〜)
副 近くに
前 〜の近くに
副 nearly：ほとんど、ほぼ

0623 portray
/pɔːrtréi/
Part 5, 6

動 **〜を**(絵・彫刻などで)**描く**、表現する(≒describe, represent, depict)
名 portrait：❶肖像画　❷描写
名 portrayal：描写

0624 commence
/kəméns/
Part 5, 6

動 ❶**〜を開始する**、始める　❷(〜で)始まる(with 〜)(≒begin, start)
名 commencement：❶開始、始まり　❷(大学・高校の)卒業式

Day 38 》CD-B3　Quick Review　答えは右ページ下

- □ 〜を収容する
- □ 〜に助言を求める
- □ 掃除機をかける
- □ 〜を宣伝する
- □ 〜を制限する
- □ 〜を伝える
- □ 〜を一時停止する
- □ 〜に保険をかける
- □ 〜を実行する
- □ 〜を呼び止める
- □ 〜に言及する
- □ 〜を促進する
- □ 〜に水をまく
- □ 漏れる
- □ 〜を魅了する
- □ 〜を2倍にする

Check 2　Phrase

- ☐ define a new word(新語を定義する)
- ☐ define one's responsibility(責任を明確にする)

- ☐ screen job applicants(求職者たちを選別する)
- ☐ screen one's eyes from the sun(太陽から目を守る)

- ☐ overflow with shoppers([店が]買い物客であふれかえる)
- ☐ overflow the banks(堤防を越えて氾濫する)

- ☐ strengthen the economy(経済を強化する)
- ☐ strengthen against ~(~に対して強くなる)

- ☐ inhabit a remote island(離島に住む)

- ☐ near an end(終わりに近づく)

- ☐ portray life in the raw(ありのままの人生を描く)

- ☐ commence the meeting(会議を開始する)
- ☐ commence with a keynote address([会議などが]基調演説で始まる)

Check 3　Sentence

- ☐ In this dictionary, January is defined as "the first month of the year, between December and February."(この辞書では、1月は「1年の最初の月で、12月と2月の間」と定義されている)

- ☐ Candidates will be screened on the following knowledge, skills, and abilities.(候補者たちは以下の知識、技能、そして能力において選別される予定だ)

- ☐ The bathtub is overflowing with water.(バスタブは水であふれている)

- ☐ The company needs to strengthen its financial base.(その会社は財政基盤を強化する必要がある)

- ☐ The region was once inhabited by several Native American tribes.(その地域にはかつて、アメリカ先住民のいくつかの種族が住んでいた)

- ☐ The construction of the new mall is nearing completion.(新しいショッピングセンターの建設は完成に近づいている)

- ☐ The painting portrays the world 100 years from now.(その絵は今から100年後の世界を描いている)

- ☐ The factory will commence production early next year.(その工場は来年早々に生産を開始する予定だ)

Day 38))) CD-B3
Quick Review
答えは左ページ下

- ☐ house
- ☐ consult
- ☐ vacuum
- ☐ advertise
- ☐ restrict
- ☐ convey
- ☐ suspend
- ☐ insure
- ☐ execute
- ☐ hail
- ☐ cite
- ☐ foster
- ☐ water
- ☐ leak
- ☐ fascinate
- ☐ double

CHAPTER 1
CHAPTER 2
CHAPTER 3
CHAPTER 4
CHAPTER 5
CHAPTER 6
CHAPTER 7
CHAPTER 8
CHAPTER 9
CHAPTER 10

Day 40　動詞10

Check 1　Listen 》CD-B5

☐ 0625
tackle
/tǽkl/
❶定義注意
Part 7

- 動 ❶（難しい仕事など）**に取り組む**（≒ deal with）　❷〜にタックルする
- 名 ❶タックル　❷器具、用具；釣り道具

☐ 0626
applaud
/əplɔ́ːd/
Part 1

- 動 ❶**〜に拍手を送る**　❷拍手する（≒ clap）　❸〜を称賛する（≒ praise）
- 名 applause：❶拍手　❷称賛

☐ 0627
complicate
/kɑ́mpləkèit/
Part 5, 6

- 動 ❶（事）**を複雑にする**　❷（病気）を悪化させる
- 名 complication：❶（通例〜s）合併症　❷面倒な事態[問題]
- 形 complicated：❶困難な　❷複雑な

☐ 0628
extract
/ikstrǽkt/
Part 5, 6

- 動 ❶**〜を**（…から）**引き抜く**、引き出す（from ...）　❷〜を（…から）抽出する（from ...）
- 名 (/ékstrækt/) ❶抽出物、エキス　❷（〜からの）抜粋（from 〜）
- 名 extraction：❶摘出、抽出　❷家系、血統

☐ 0629
evolve
/ivɑ́lv/
Part 5, 6

- 動 ❶（〜から／…へ）**進化[発展]する**（from 〜/into ...）　❷〜を進化[発展]させる　⊕revolve（回転する）と混同しないように注意
- 名 evolution：❶進化、進化論　❷発展、進展

☐ 0630
subcontract
/sʌ̀bkəntrǽkt/
ビジネス問題

- 動 **〜の下請け契約をする**
- 名 (/sʌ̀bkɑ́ntrækt/) 下請負、下請契約
- 名 contract：（〜との）契約（書）（with 〜）
- 動 contract：（〜と）契約を結ぶ（with 〜）

☐ 0631
refuel
/riːfjúːəl/
Part 4

- 動 ❶**〜に燃料を補給する**　❷燃料の補給を受ける
- 名 fuel：（〜の）燃料（for 〜）
- 動 fuel：❶〜に燃料を供給する　❷〜を刺激[助長]する

☐ 0632
deregulate
/diːrégjulèit/
ビジネス問題

- 動 **〜の規制を緩和[撤廃]する**、〜を自由化する
- 名 deregulation：規制緩和[撤廃]、自由化
- 動 regulate：〜を規制[統制、管理]する

continued
▼

毎日繰り返しチャンツCDを聞いていれば、リスニング力もアップしているはず。英語ニュースなどを聞いて、効果を確認してみては？

- □ 聞くだけモード　Check 1
- □ しっかりモード　Check 1 ▶ 2
- □ かんぺきモード　Check 1 ▶ 2 ▶ 3

Check 2　Phrase

- □ tackle a difficult task（難しい仕事に取り組む）
- □ tackle a burglar（強盗にタックルする）

- □ applaud the orchestra（オーケストラに拍手を送る）
- □ applaud repeatedly（繰り返し拍手する）

- □ to complicate matters（厄介なことには）
- □ complicate the disease（病気を悪化させる）

- □ extract a cork from a bottle（瓶からコルクを引き抜く）
- □ extract DNA from bones（骨からDNAを抽出する）

- □ evolve into a leading company（一流企業へと進化する）
- □ evolve technology（技術を進化させる）

- □ subcontract the whole of the works（その仕事のすべての下請け契約をする）

- □ refuel a plane（飛行機に燃料を補給する）
- □ refuel in midair（[飛行機が]上空で燃料補給を受ける）

- □ deregulate the banking industry（銀行業の規制を緩和する）

Check 3　Sentence

- □ The government should continue to tackle economic problems.（政府は経済問題に取り組み続けるべきだ）

- □ The audience is applauding the speaker.（聴衆は演説者に拍手を送っている）

- □ It will only complicate the situation if you do something.（あなたが何かをしても、状況を複雑にするだけだろう）

- □ You had better have your wisdom teeth extracted.（あなたは親知らずを抜いてもらったほうがいい）

- □ Humans evolved from apes.（ヒトは類人猿から進化した）

- □ Most of the construction of the house was subcontracted to a local builder.（その家の建築のほとんどは地元の建設会社に下請けされた）

- □ Refuel the car before returning it to the rental company.（レンタル会社に返す前に、車に燃料を補給してください）

- □ The government plans to deregulate the communications market.（政府は通信市場の規制を緩和する予定だ）

continued ▼

Day 40

Check 1　Listen)) CD-B5

□ 0633
remodel
/ríːmɑ́dl/
Part 2, 3

🔵 **〜を改築[改装]する**、模様替えする

□ 0634
finalize
/fáɪnəlàɪz/
ビジネス問題

🔵 **〜に決着をつける**、〜を仕上げる、完結させる(≒ complete, conclude)
🔶 final: ❶最終試験　❷(しばしばthe 〜s)決勝戦
🔶 final: 最後[最終]の
🔶 finally: ❶ついに、とうとう　❷最後に

□ 0635
question
/kwéstʃən/
❶ 定義注意
Part 4

🔵 ❶**〜を疑う**　❷〜に(…について)質問する(about [as to] ...)
🔶 ❶質問(≒ query)(⇔ answer)　❷問題(≒ problem, matter, issue)　❸(〜についての)疑問(about 〜)(≒ doubt)

□ 0636
multiply
/mʌ́ltəplàɪ/
Part 5, 6

🔵 ❶**〜を(どんどん)増やす**　❷増える(≒ increase)　❸(multiply A by Bで)AにBを掛ける　➕「AをBで割る」はdivide A by B、「AとBを足す」はadd A and B、「AをBから引く」はsubtract A from B
🔶 multiplication: ❶増加　❷掛け算

□ 0637
negotiate
/nɪɡóʊʃièɪt/
ビジネス問題

🔵 ❶(〜と／…のことで)**交渉する**(with 〜/for [about, over] ...)　❷(契約など)を(…と)取り決める(with ...)
🔶 negotiation: (〜に関する)交渉(on 〜)
🔶 negotiable: 交渉の余地がある

□ 0638
triple
/trípl/
Part 7

🔵 ❶**〜を3倍にする**　❷3倍になる
🔶 3倍
🔶 3倍の

□ 0639
cap
/kǽp/
❶ 定義注意
Part 5, 6

🔵 (価格など)**の上限を定める**
🔶 帽子

□ 0640
expose
/ɪkspóʊz/
Part 7

🔵 ❶**〜を(…に)暴露する**、ばらす(to ...)(≒ reveal, disclose, uncover)(⇔ conceal: 〜を秘密にする)　❷(expose A to Bで)AをB(危険など)にさらす；AをBに触れさせる
🔶 exposure: (危険などに)身をさらすこと(to 〜)

Day 39)) CD-B4　Quick Review
答えは右ページ下

- □ 拍手する
- □ 〜を実施する
- □ 重要である
- □ 〜を延長する
- □ 〜を実施する
- □ 〜をやめる
- □ 〜を我慢する
- □ 悪化する
- □ 〜を定義する
- □ 〜を選別する
- □ あふれる
- □ 〜を強化する
- □ 〜に住む
- □ 〜に近づく
- □ 〜を描く
- □ 〜を開始する

Check 2 Phrase

- □ remodel the kitchen(台所を改装する)

- □ finalize a deal(取引をまとめる)

- □ question her story(彼女の話を疑う)
- □ question the man about the theft(その男性に窃盗について質問する)

- □ multiply the possibilities of ~(~の可能性を増す)
- □ multiply rapidly(急速に増加する)

- □ sit at the negotiating table(交渉のテーブルにつく)
- □ negotiate a ceasefire with ~(~との停戦を取り決める)

- □ triple the output(生産高を3倍にする)
- □ triple in size(規模が3倍になる)

- □ cap enrollment(入学者数の上限を定める)

- □ expose the truth(真実を暴露する)
- □ expose employees to danger(従業員たちを危険にさらす)

Check 3 Sentence

- □ We're remodeling our house next year.(私たちは来年、自宅を改築するつもりだ)

- □ The budget for the project has not been finalized yet.(そのプロジェクトの予算はまだ決まっていない)

- □ The authenticity of the painting has been questioned.(その絵が本物であるかどうかが疑われている)

- □ We need to multiply the productivity of our employees.(私たちは従業員の生産力を高める必要がある)

- □ The management refused to negotiate with the union.(経営陣は労働組合と交渉することを拒んだ)

- □ The company has tripled its profits over the past five years.(その会社はこの5年で収益を3倍にした)

- □ The interest rate of the loan is capped at 10 percent.(そのローンの金利の上限は10パーセントに定められている)

- □ The informant exposed corruption in the food company.(情報提供者はその食品会社内の違法行為を暴露した)

Day 39))CD-B4
Quick Review
答えは左ページ下

- □ clap
- □ stage
- □ matter
- □ prolong
- □ mount
- □ drop
- □ resist
- □ slip
- □ define
- □ screen
- □ overflow
- □ strengthen
- □ inhabit
- □ near
- □ portray
- □ commence

Day 41　動詞11

Check 1　Listen ») CD-B6

□ 0641
sustain
/səstéin/
Part 7

動 ❶**〜を維持する**、持続させる(≒maintain)　❷(損失など)を被る(≒suffer)　❸〜を養う
形 sustainable：持続可能な、環境を破壊しない

□ 0642
spell
/spél/
❶定義注意
Part 7

動 ❶**〜の結果をもたらす**、〜ということになる　❷〜をつづる
名 ❶呪文、魔法　❷一続き(の期間)
名 spelling：❶つづり　❷つづり方

□ 0643
squeeze
/skwíːz/
Part 5, 6

動 ❶**〜を(…に)押し[詰め]込む**(into . . .)　❷〜を強く握る　❸(水分など)を(…から)絞り出す(from . . .)、〜を絞る
名 ❶ぎゅうぎゅう詰め　❷強く握ること　❸経済的圧迫[引き締め]

□ 0644
air
/ɛ́ər/
❶定義注意
Part 4

動 ❶**〜を放送する**　❷放送される(≒broadcast)
名 ❶空気　❷放送

□ 0645
spark
/spáːrk/
❶定義注意
Part 4

動 ❶**〜を誘発する**、〜への引き金となる　❷(興味など)を刺激する　❸火花を出す
名 火花

□ 0646
assess
/əsés/
Part 7

動 ❶**〜を評価する**(≒evaluate, appraise)　❷〜を(…と)査定する(at . . .)
名 assessment：❶評価　❷査定

□ 0647
tap
/tǽp/
❶定義注意
ビジネス問題

動 (資源・土地など)**を開発[開拓、利用]する**
名 蛇口(≒faucet)

□ 0648
accumulate
/əkjúːmjulèit/
Part 7

動 ❶(金など)**を(徐々に)ためる**、蓄積する　❷たまる
名 accumulation：❶蓄積　❷蓄積物

continued ▼

今日は「❶定義注意」の単語が続出！ TOEICならではの意味を、しっかりと押さえておこう。それでは、チャンツからスタート！

- ☐ 聞くだけモード　Check 1
- ☐ しっかりモード　Check 1 ▶ 2
- ☐ かんぺきモード　Check 1 ▶ 2 ▶ 3

Check 2　Phrase

☐ sustain one's health(健康を維持する)
☐ sustain a severe injury(重傷を負う)

☐ spell danger(危険をもたらす)
☐ be spelled wrong([名前などが]間違ってつづられている)

☐ squeeze clothes into a bag(服をかばんの中に押し込む)
☐ squeeze her hand(彼女の手を強く握る)

☐ be aired live(生放送される)

☐ spark a national debate(全国的な議論を引き起こす)
☐ spark his curiosity(彼の好奇心を刺激する)

☐ assess his performance(彼の実績を評価する)
☐ assess the house at $1 million(その家を100万ドルと査定する)

☐ tap a new market(新しい市場を開拓する)

☐ accumulate money(金をためる)
☐ accumulate on the floor([ほこりなどが]床にたまる)

Check 3　Sentence

☐ The country will sustain economic growth of close to 9 percent.(その国は9パーセント近い経済成長を維持するだろう)

☐ Droughts could spell disaster for the country's agriculture.(干ばつはその国の農業に災いを及ぼすかもしれない)

☐ I squeezed everything into my car.(私はすべての物を車の中へ詰め込んだ)

☐ The movie will be aired on channel 4 at 9 p.m. tonight.(その映画は今夜9時から4チャンネルで放送される)

☐ The country's determination to develop a nuclear weapon could spark a war.(核兵器を開発するというその国の決断は戦争を誘発するかもしれない)

☐ Examinations are not the only method of assessing students' abilities.(試験は生徒の能力を評価する唯一の方法ではない)

☐ The area has the potential to tap solar energy.(その地域は太陽エネルギーを利用できる可能性がある)

☐ The company has accumulated $4 million in debt.(その会社は借金を400万ドルまで増やしてしまった)

continued
▼

Day 41

Check 1 Listen)) CD-B6

0649
repay
/ripéi/
ビジネス問題

動 (金)**を返済する**、返す

0650
exercise
/éksərsàiz/
❶定義注意
Part 5, 6

動 ❶(権利など)**を行使する** ❷運動する
名 ❶運動 ❷(権力などの)行使(of ~)

0651
skip
/skíp/
❶定義注意
Part 2, 3

動 ❶**~を抜かす**、飛ばす ❷(授業など)を休む、サボる ❸軽く跳ぶ ❹~を軽く跳び越える
名 スキップ

0652
uncover
/ʌnkʌ́vər/
Part 7

動 ❶(秘密など)**を暴露する**、打ち明ける(≒reveal, disclose, expose);~を発見する ❷~の覆い[ふた]を取る

0653
omit
/oumít/
Part 5, 6

動 (うっかり・故意に)**~を**(…から)**省略[除外]する** (from ...)(≒leave out)
名 omission:省略;省略された物

0654
rinse
/ríns/
❶定義注意
Part 1

動 (コップ・口など)**をゆすぐ**、すすぐ;(汚れなど)をすすぎ落とす
名 ❶ゆすぐこと ❷リンス液

0655
illustrate
/íləstrèit/
Part 5, 6

動 ❶**~を説明する**、明らかにする(≒explain) ❷~に挿絵を入れる;(illustrate A with Bで)A(本など)にB(挿絵など)を入れる
名 illustration:❶挿絵、イラスト ❷実例;説明

0656
erect
/irékt/
Part 5, 6

動 (家・像など)**を建てる**(≒build) ❶elect(~を選ぶ)と混同しないように注意
形 直立した、真っすぐな
名 erection:建設

Day 40)) CD-B5
Quick Review
答えは右ページ下

- □ ~に取り組む
- □ ~に拍手を送る
- □ ~を複雑にする
- □ ~を引き抜く
- □ 進化する
- □ ~の下請け契約をする
- □ ~に燃料を補給する
- □ ~の規制を緩和する
- □ ~を改築する
- □ ~に決着をつける
- □ ~を疑う
- □ ~を増やす
- □ 交渉する
- □ ~を3倍にする
- □ ~の上限を定める
- □ ~を暴露する

Check 2 Phrase

- ☐ repay a debt（借金を返済する）

- ☐ exercise caution（注意[用心、警戒]する）
- ☐ exercise regularly（定期的に運動する）

- ☐ skip a page（1ページ飛ばす）
- ☐ skip math class（数学の授業をサボる）

- ☐ uncover a scheme（陰謀を暴露する）
- ☐ uncover the box（箱のふたを取る）

- ☐ omit details（詳細を省く）

- ☐ rinse one's mouth（口をゆすぐ）

- ☐ illustrate the main point（要点を説明する）
- ☐ be illustrated with photos（[本などに]写真が入っている）

- ☐ erect a monument（記念碑を建てる）

Check 3 Sentence

- ☐ We have to repay the home loan within 20 years.（私たちはその住宅ローンを20年以内に返済しなければならない）

- ☐ We should exercise our right to vote.（私たちは投票する権利を行使すべきだ）

- ☐ It's not a good thing to skip breakfast to lose weight.（減量するために朝食を抜くのはいいことではない）

- ☐ Police still haven't uncovered any new evidence in the case.（警察はその事件における新しい証拠をまだ見つけていない）

- ☐ His name was omitted from the attendance list.（彼の名前は出席者リストに入っていなかった）

- ☐ The man is rinsing the dishes.（男性は皿をすすいでいる）

- ☐ The chart illustrates how gas prices have climbed in the US.（その図はガソリン価格がどのようにアメリカで上昇したかを表している）

- ☐ The statue was erected in 1880.（その像は1880年に建てられた）

Day 40))) CD-B5
Quick Review
答えは左ページ下

☐ tackle	☐ evolve	☐ remodel	☐ negotiate
☐ applaud	☐ subcontract	☐ finalize	☐ triple
☐ complicate	☐ refuel	☐ question	☐ cap
☐ extract	☐ deregulate	☐ multiply	☐ expose

Day 42　動詞12

Check 1　Listen 》CD-B7

☐ 0657
tighten
/táitn/
Part 5, 6

動 ❶(制限など)**をきつくする**、厳しくする　❷〜をしっかり締める(⇔loosen)
形 tight：❶(物などが)不足している；(金融が)ひっ迫した　❷(予定などが)ぎっしり詰まった　❸きつい

☐ 0658
overtake
/òuvərtéik/
Part 5, 6

動 **〜を追い越す**、追い抜く；〜に追いつく(≒catch up with)

☐ 0659
plow
/pláu/
❶発音注意
Part 1

動 **〜をすきで耕す**
名 (農耕用の)すき

☐ 0660
highlight
/háilàit/
Part 7

動 **〜を強調する**、目立たせる(≒emphasize, stress)
名 (催し物などの)ハイライト、呼び物

☐ 0661
salute
/səlú:t/
Part 1

動 ❶**〜に敬礼する**　❷敬礼する
名 敬礼

☐ 0662
deepen
/dí:pən/
Part 5, 6

動 ❶**〜を深める**、深くする　❷深くなる
形 deep：深い
副 deeply：深く

☐ 0663
cooperate
/kouápərèit/
Part 2, 3

動 ❶(〜と)**協力する**(with 〜)　❷(cooperate to doで)〜するために協力する、協力して〜する　✚corporate(企業の)と混同しないように注意
名 cooperation：協力
形 cooperative：❶協力的な　❷協同の

☐ 0664
graze
/gréiz/
Part 1

動 ❶(家畜が)**牧草を食べる**　❷(家畜)に牧草を食べさせる

continued
▼

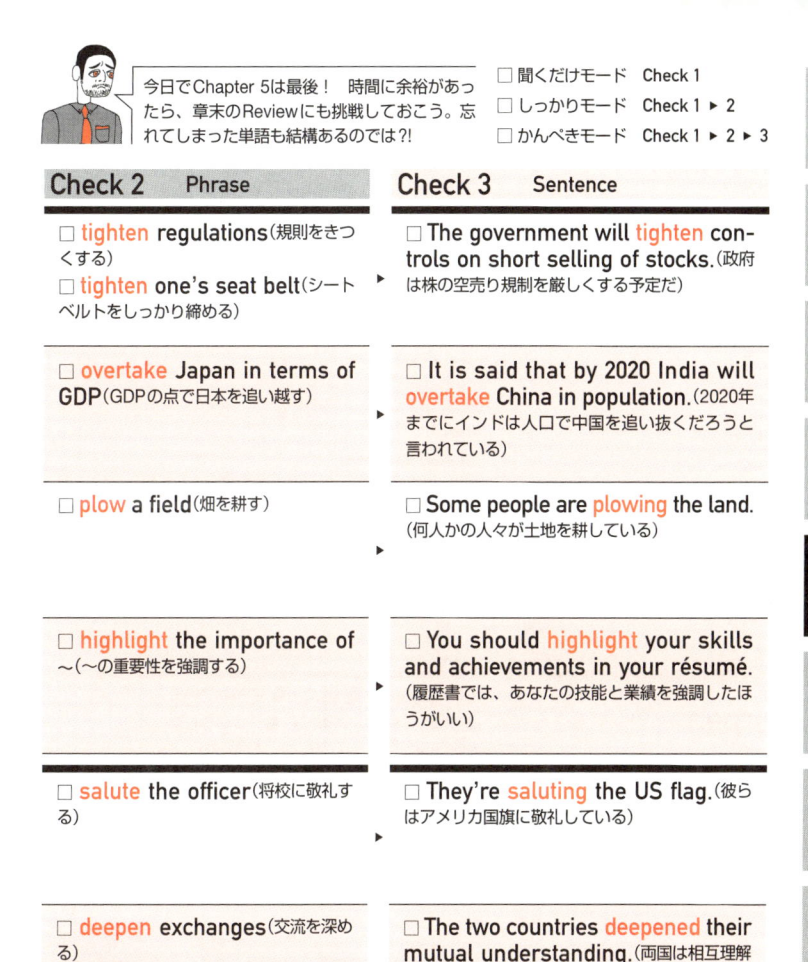

今日でChapter 5は最後！ 時間に余裕があったら、章末のReviewにも挑戦しておこう。忘れてしまった単語も結構あるのでは?!

☐ 聞くだけモード　Check 1
☐ しっかりモード　Check 1 ▶ 2
☐ かんぺきモード　Check 1 ▶ 2 ▶ 3

Check 2　Phrase

☐ tighten regulations（規則をきつくする）
☐ tighten one's seat belt（シートベルトをしっかり締める）

☐ overtake Japan in terms of GDP（GDPの点で日本を追い越す）

☐ plow a field（畑を耕す）

☐ highlight the importance of ～（～の重要性を強調する）

☐ salute the officer（将校に敬礼する）

☐ deepen exchanges（交流を深める）
☐ a deepening recession（深まる景気後退）

☐ refuse to cooperate（協力するのを拒む）
☐ cooperate to achieve the goal（目標を達成するために協力する）

☐ graze the sheep（ヒツジに牧草を食べさせる）

Check 3　Sentence

☐ The government will tighten controls on short selling of stocks.（政府は株の空売り規制を厳しくする予定だ）

☐ It is said that by 2020 India will overtake China in population.（2020年までにインドは人口で中国を追い抜くだろうと言われている）

☐ Some people are plowing the land.（何人かの人々が土地を耕している）

☐ You should highlight your skills and achievements in your résumé.（履歴書では、あなたの技能と業績を強調したほうがいい）

☐ They're saluting the US flag.（彼らはアメリカ国旗に敬礼している）

☐ The two countries deepened their mutual understanding.（両国は相互理解を深めた）

☐ The residents in the area cooperated with the police to find the missing girl.（その地域の住民たちは行方不明の少女を見つけるために警察と協力した）

☐ The cows are grazing in the pasture.（ウシたちは牧草地で草を食べている）

continued
▼

Day 42

Check 1 Listen)) CD-B7

□ 0665
reproduce
/rìːprədjúːs/
Part 5, 6

動 ❶ **〜を複製**[複写、再現]**する** ❷繁殖する ❸〜を繁殖させる
名 reproduction：❶繁殖、生殖 ❷複製

□ 0666
defy
/difái/
Part 5, 6

動 ❶（物事が）（解決・理解など）**を拒む**、受け入れない ❷（人が）〜を無視する、物ともしない

□ 0667
utilize
/júːtəlàiz/
Part 5, 6

動 〜を（…として）**利用する**、役立たせる（as ...）(≒ use)
名 utilization：利用
名 utility：❶（通例〜ies）(水道などの）公共料金；公共施設 ❷有用[実用]性

□ 0668
comprehend
/kàmprihénd/
❶ アクセント注意
Part 5, 6

動 〜を（十分に）**理解する**（≒ understand）
名 comprehension：理解（力）
形 comprehensive：包括的な；広範囲な

□ 0669
sharpen
/ʃáːrpən/
Part 7

動 ❶（技術など）**を磨く** ❷〜を鋭くする
形 sharp：❶鋭い ❷急な ❸くっきりした
副 sharp：❶時間きっかりに ❷鋭く
副 sharply：❶急に、突然 ❷鋭く ❸厳しく

□ 0670
rebuild
/riːbíld/
Part 7

動 ❶ **〜を再建**[改築]**する** ❷〜を強化[補強]する

□ 0671
shorten
/ʃɔ́ːrtn/
Part 4

動 ❶ **〜を短くする** ❷短くなる（⇔ lengthen）
名 shortage：(〜の)不足（of 〜）
形 short：❶短い ❷（be short of [on]で）〜が不足している
副 shortly：❶間もなく、すぐに ❷少し（後、前）に

□ 0672
memorize
/méməràiz/
Part 2, 3

動 〜を暗記[記憶]**する**
名 memory：記憶

Day 41)) CD-B6
Quick Review
答えは右ページ下

- □ 〜を維持する
- □ 〜の結果をもたらす
- □ 〜を押し込む
- □ 〜を放送する
- □ 〜を誘発する
- □ 〜を評価する
- □ 〜を開発する
- □ 〜をためる
- □ 〜を返済する
- □ 〜を行使する
- □ 〜を抜かす
- □ 〜を暴露する
- □ 〜を省略する
- □ 〜をゆずる
- □ 〜を説明する
- □ 〜を建てる

Check 2 Phrase

- [ ] reproduce the picture(その絵を複写する)
- [ ] reproduce oneself(繁殖する)

- [ ] defy understanding([物事が]理解できない)
- [ ] defy the law(法律を無視する)

- [ ] utilize the sun as a heat source(太陽を熱源として利用する)
- [ ] utilize solar energy for household use(家庭で太陽エネルギーを利用する)

- [ ] comprehend the phenomenon(その現象を理解する)

- [ ] sharpen one's business senses(ビジネス感覚を磨く)
- [ ] sharpen a pencil(鉛筆を削る)

- [ ] rebuild an old house(古い家を建て直す)
- [ ] rebuild the domestic economy(国内経済を強化する)

- [ ] shorten the length of ~(~の長さを短くする)
- [ ] shorten in winter([昼が]冬は短くなる)

- [ ] memorize the lyrics of the song(その歌の歌詞を暗記する)
- [ ] be good at memorizing ~(~を記憶するのが得意である)

Check 3 Sentence

- [ ] These speakers can reproduce orchestral sounds.(これらのスピーカーはオーケストラの音を再現することができる)

- [ ] The beauty of the stars defies description.(星々の美しさは表現することができない)

- [ ] The building could be utilized as a library.(その建物は図書館として利用できるかもしれない)

- [ ] He fully comprehends the importance of the job.(彼はその仕事の重要性を十分に理解している)

- [ ] This course will serve to sharpen your computer skills.(このコースはあなたのコンピューター技能を磨くのに役立つだろう)

- [ ] The cathedral was rebuilt in 1657.(その大聖堂は1657年に再建された)

- [ ] I shortened my stay in Beijing by two days.(私は北京での滞在を2日短縮した)

- [ ] She is trying to memorize 100 new English words per week.(彼女は1週間に100の新しい英単語を暗記しようと努力している)

Day 41))) CD-B6
Quick Review
答えは左ページ下

- [ ] sustain
- [ ] spell
- [ ] squeeze
- [ ] air
- [ ] spark
- [ ] assess
- [ ] tap
- [ ] accumulate
- [ ] repay
- [ ] exercise
- [ ] skip
- [ ] uncover
- [ ] omit
- [ ] rinse
- [ ] illustrate
- [ ] erect

CHAPTER 1
CHAPTER 2
CHAPTER 3
CHAPTER 4
CHAPTER 5
CHAPTER 6
CHAPTER 7
CHAPTER 8
CHAPTER 9
CHAPTER 10

Chapter 5 Review

左ページの(1)〜(20)の動詞の同意・類義語［熟語］(≒)、反意・反対語(⇔)を右ページのA〜Tから選び、カッコの中に答えを書き込もう。意味が分からないときは、見出し番号を参照して復習しておこう（答えは右ページ下）。

- [ ] (1) alter (0581) ≒は? (　)
- [ ] (2) grasp (0589) ≒は? (　)
- [ ] (3) evaluate (0592) ≒は? (　)
- [ ] (4) restrict (0597) ≒は? (　)
- [ ] (5) cite (0603) ≒は? (　)
- [ ] (6) clap (0609) ≒は? (　)
- [ ] (7) prolong (0612) ≒は? (　)
- [ ] (8) near (0622) ≒は? (　)
- [ ] (9) commence (0624) ≒は? (　)
- [ ] (10) tackle (0625) ≒は? (　)
- [ ] (11) multiply (0636) ≒は? (　)
- [ ] (12) expose (0640) ≒は? (　)
- [ ] (13) sustain (0641) ≒は? (　)
- [ ] (14) air (0644) ≒は? (　)
- [ ] (15) omit (0653) ≒は? (　)
- [ ] (16) illustrate (0655) ≒は? (　)
- [ ] (17) erect (0656) ≒は? (　)
- [ ] (18) tighten (0657) ⇔は? (　)
- [ ] (19) highlight (0660) ≒は? (　)
- [ ] (20) utilize (0667) ≒は? (　)

A. maintain
B. lengthen
C. loosen
D. understand
E. broadcast
F. refer to
G. deal with
H. approach
I. disclose
J. use
K. appraise
L. explain
M. begin
N. limit
O. increase
P. build
Q. applaud
R. leave out
S. emphasize
T. change

【解答】 (1) T (2) D (3) K (4) N (5) F (6) Q (7) B (8) H (9) M (10) G
(11) O (12) I (13) A (14) E (15) R (16) L (17) P (18) C (19) S (20) J

CHAPTER 6
形容詞：必修96

Chapter 6 では、TOEIC 必修の形容詞96をマスターします。単語は「繰り返しの学習」で身につけるもの。目・耳・口をフル動員して、あきらめることなく学習を続けていきましょう！

Day 43【形容詞7】
▶202
Day 44【形容詞8】
▶206
Day 45【形容詞9】
▶210
Day 46【形容詞10】
▶214
Day 47【形容詞11】
▶218
Day 48【形容詞12】
▶222
Chapter 6 Review
▶226

TOEIC的格言

He that falls today may rise tomorrow.

七転び八起き。
[直訳] 今日転んだ者は、明日は立ち上がるだろう。

Day 43　形容詞7

Check 1　Listen 》CD-B8

□ 0673
monetary
/mánətèri/
ビジネス問題

形 ❶**通貨**[貨幣]**の**　❷金融[財政]の；金銭的な

□ 0674
concerned
/kənsə́ːrnd/
Part 4

形 ❶(通例名詞の後に置いて)**関係**[関与]**している**　❷心配そうな　❸(be concerned about [for]で)〜を心配している　❹(be concerned with [in]で)〜に関係している
名 concern：懸念；関心事
動 concern：❶〜を心配させる　❷〜に関係する

□ 0675
overseas
/óuvərsíːz/
Part 2, 3

形 **海外の**、外国への
副 (/ðuvərsíːz/)海外へ[に](≒abroad)

□ 0676
innovative
/ínəvèitiv/
Part 4

形 **革新**[刷新]**的な**；創意に富んだ
名 innovation：革新、刷新；斬新な考え
動 innovate：刷新[革新]する

□ 0677
principal
/prínsəpəl/
Part 5, 6

形 **主な**、主要な、(最も)重要な(≒main, chief)
名 ❶校長　❷元金　❸主役、主演者　❹principle(主義)と混同しないように注意
副 principally：主に、主として

□ 0678
tight
/táit/
❗定義注意
Part 2, 3

形 ❶(物などが)**不足している**；(金融が)ひっ迫した　❷(予定などが)ぎっしり詰まった　❸きつい(⇔loose)
動 tighten：❶(制限など)をきつくする、厳しくする　❷〜をしっかり締める

□ 0679
severe
/səvíər/
Part 5, 6

形 ❶(天候・痛みなどが)**ひどい**、厳しい、激しい(≒serious)　❷厳格な(≒harsh, stern)
名 severity：厳しさ；激しさ、重大さ
副 severely：厳しく、激しく

□ 0680
harmful
/háːrmfəl/
Part 4

形 (〜に)**有害な**、害を及ぼす(to 〜)(⇔harmless)
名 harm：害、損害
動 harm：〜を害する、傷つける

continued
▼

Chapter 6では、6日をかけて必修形容詞96をチェック。まずはCDでチャンツを聞いて、単語を「耳」からインプット!

- ☐ 聞くだけモード　Check 1
- ☐ しっかりモード　Check 1 ▶ 2
- ☐ かんぺきモード　Check 1 ▶ 2 ▶ 3

Check 2　Phrase

☐ the monetary system(貨幣制度)
☐ a monetary policy(金融政策)

☐ the party concerned(関係当事者)
☐ with a concerned look(心配そうな顔つきで)

☐ overseas travel(海外旅行)
☐ an overseas student(海外留学生)

☐ innovative technology(革新的な技術)

☐ the principal cities(主要都市)
☐ the principal reason(主な理由)

☐ a tight job market(厳しい就職市場)
☐ a tight schedule(ぎっしり詰まった予定)

☐ severe pain(激痛)
☐ a severe penalty(厳罰)

☐ the harmful effects of global warming(地球温暖化の有害な影響)

Check 3　Sentence

☐ The monetary unit in Germany is the euro.(ドイツの通貨単位はユーロだ)

☐ The closure of the factory was a shock to all concerned.(その工場の閉鎖は関係者全員にとってショックだった)

☐ The company is expanding rapidly in overseas markets.(その会社は海外市場で急速に拡大している)

☐ Innovative ideas are essential to business success.(革新的なアイデアはビジネスの成功に不可欠だ)

☐ The country's principal export is oil.(その国の主要な輸出品は石油だ)

☐ Money is tight right now.(今はお金が不足している)

☐ Australia has experienced severe drought over recent years.(オーストラリアはここ数年ひどい干ばつを経験している)

☐ Greenhouse gas emissions are harmful to the environment.(温室効果ガスの放出は自然環境に害を及ぼす)

continued
▼

Day 43

Check 1　Listen)) CD-B8

0681
amazing
/əméiziŋ/
Part 2, 3

形 **驚くべき**、すごい、見事な(≒astonishing)
動 amaze：❶〜をびっくりさせる　❷(be amazed atで)〜にびっくりしている　❸(be amazed to doで)〜してびっくりしている
副 amazingly：驚くべきことに；驚くほど

0682
radical
/rǽdikəl/
Part 5, 6

形 ❶**急進的な**、過激な(⇔conservative：保守的な)　❷根本的な(≒fundamental)　❸徹底的な(≒thorough)
名 過激派、急進論者

0683
unexpected
/ʌ̀nikspéktid/
Part 5, 6

形 **思いがけない**、予期しない(⇔expected)
動 expect：〜を期待する；〜を予期[予想]する
副 unexpectedly：❶突然に　❷意外なことに

0684
impressive
/imprésiv/
Part 4

形 **印象的な**、深い感銘を与える
名 impression：❶印象　❷(〜という)考え、感じ(that節 〜)
動 impress：❶〜に感銘を与える、〜を感動させる　❷(be impressed by [with]で)〜に感動[感心]している

0685
evident
/évədənt/
Part 5, 6

形 **明らかな**、明白な(≒clear, apparent, obvious)
名 evidence：(〜の)証拠、根拠(of [for] 〜)
副 evidently：❶明らかに　❷見たところ〜らしい

0686
fortunate
/fɔ́ːrtʃənət/
Part 4

形 (〜の点で／…するとは)**幸運な**、運のよい(in 〜/to do)(≒lucky)(⇔unfortunate)
名 fortune：❶財産、大金；富　❷運
副 fortunately：幸いにも、運よく

0687
fancy
/fǽnsi/
❶定義注意
Part 2, 3

形 ❶**高級な**、一流の　❷装飾の多い、装飾的な(⇔plain：質素な)
名 ❶好み　❷空想、想像
動 〜を想像する

0688
desirable
/dizáiərəbl/
Part 7

形 **望ましい**、好ましい(⇔undesirable)
名 desire：(〜に対する／…したいという)願望；欲望(for 〜/to do)
動 desire：❶〜を強く望む　❷(desire to doで)〜することを望む、欲する

Day 42)) CD-B7
Quick Review
答えは右ページ下

- □ 〜をきつくする
- □ 〜を追い越す
- □ 〜をすきで耕す
- □ 〜を強調する
- □ 〜に敬礼する
- □ 〜を深める
- □ 協力する
- □ 牧草を食べる
- □ 〜を複製する
- □ 〜を拒む
- □ 〜を利用する
- □ 〜を理解する
- □ 〜を磨く
- □ 〜を再建する
- □ 〜を短くする
- □ 〜を暗記する

Check 2 Phrase

- China's amazing economic growth(中国の驚くべき経済成長)
- It is amazing that ~.(~ということは驚くべきことだ)

- radical ideas(過激思想)
- a radical change(根本的な変更)

- an unexpected pleasure(思いがけない喜び)
- an unexpected result(予期せぬ結果)

- an impressive speech(感動的な演説)

- become evident(明らかになる)
- It is evident that ~.(~ということは明らかだ)

- a fortunate circumstance(幸運な状況)

- a fancy hotel(高級ホテル)
- a fancy cake(デコレーションケーキ)

- a desirable result(望ましい結果)
- It is desirable that ~.(~ということが望ましい)

Check 3 Sentence

- The movie was really amazing.(その映画は本当に素晴らしかった)

- He is known as a radical politician.(彼は急進的な政治家として知られている)

- I was surprised at her unexpected visit.(彼女の思いがけない訪問に私は驚いた)

- The view from the mountaintop was impressive.(山頂からの眺めは印象的だった)

- The disappointment was evident on his face.(失望していることは彼の表情から明らかだった)

- She was fortunate to have won the lottery.(宝くじに当たるとは彼女は幸運だった)

- We had dinner at a fancy restaurant last night.(私たちは昨晩、高級レストランでディナーを食べた)

- An accounting degree is desirable but not required.(会計学の学位があるのが望ましいが、必須ではない) ●求人広告の表現

Day 42 》CD-B7
Quick Review
答えは左ページ下

- tighten
- overtake
- plow
- highlight
- salute
- deepen
- cooperate
- graze
- reproduce
- defy
- utilize
- comprehend
- sharpen
- rebuild
- shorten
- memorize

CHAPTER 1
CHAPTER 2
CHAPTER 3
CHAPTER 4
CHAPTER 5
CHAPTER 6
CHAPTER 7
CHAPTER 8
CHAPTER 9
CHAPTER 10

Day 44　形容詞8

Check 1　Listen 》CD-B9

☐ 0689
acceptable
/ækséptəbl/
Part 5, 6

形 (〜にとって)**受け入れられる**、満足できる(to 〜)
名 acceptance：❶(〜の)受け入れ、受諾(of 〜) ❷承認、容認、賛成
動 accept：❶〜を受け入れる ❷〜を受け取る

☐ 0690
emotional
/imóuʃənl/
Part 5, 6

形 ❶**感情の**、情緒の ❷感動的な ❸感情的な(⇔rational：理性的な)
名 emotion：❶感情 ❷感動

☐ 0691
missing
/mísiŋ/
Part 4

形 **行方不明の**、欠けている、紛失した
動 miss：❶〜に乗り遅れる ❷〜を見逃す ❸〜がいないのを寂しく思う

☐ 0692
visible
/vízəbl/
Part 5, 6

形 ❶**目に見える**(⇔invisible) ❷見た目に明らかな
名 visibility：❶可視性；視界 ❷知名度
名 vision：❶(〜の)理想像；想像(図)(of 〜) ❷視力 ❸想像力 ❹幻覚

☐ 0693
neat
/níːt/
Part 2, 3

形 ❶**きちんとした**、小ぎれいな(≒tidy)(⇔messy：散らかった) ❷素晴らしい、すごい
副 neatly：きちんと、小ぎれいに；手際よく

☐ 0694
registered
/rédʒistərd/
Part 2, 3

形 ❶**登録[登記]された** ❷(郵便が)書留の
名 registration：登録、登記、記録
名 register：登録[記録](簿)
動 register：❶〜を登録[記録]する ❷〜を書留にする ❸(register forで)〜の入学[受講]手続きをする

☐ 0695
favorable
/féivərəbl/
Part 7

形 ❶**好意的な** ❷(〜のために/…にとって)好都合な(for 〜/to …)
名 favor：❶親切な行為，恩恵 ❷支持、援助
形 favorite：お気に入りの、大好きな
副 favorably：好意的に

☐ 0696
frequent
/fríːkwənt/
Part 5, 6

形 **たびたびの**、頻繁に起こる(⇔occasional：時々の)
動 〜によく行く
名 frequency：❶頻度 ❷頻発 ❸周波数；振動数
副 frequently：頻繁に、しばしば

continued
▼

「声に出す」練習もずいぶん慣れてきたのでは？次はチャンツの「単語」だけでなく、Check 2 の「フレーズ」の音読にも挑戦してみよう！

- ☐ 聞くだけモード　Check 1
- ☐ しっかりモード　Check 1 ▶ 2
- ☐ かんぺきモード　Check 1 ▶ 2 ▶ 3

Check 2　Phrase

☐ an acceptable decision（受諾し得る決定）
☐ an acceptable level [amount] of ~（~の許容水準[量]）

☐ a child's emotional development（子どもの情緒の発達）
☐ an emotional scene in the movie（その映画の感動的なシーン）

☐ a missing person（行方不明者）
☐ a missing page（抜けているページ）

☐ barely visible（ほとんど見えない）
☐ visible signs of ~（見た目に明らかな~の兆し）

☐ a neat room（整頓された部屋）
☐ a neat idea（素晴らしいアイデア）

☐ a registered trademark（登録商標）
☐ by registered mail（書留郵便で）

☐ a favorable response（好意的な反応）
☐ favorable weather（好天）

☐ a frequent visitor to Japan（たびたび訪日する人）

Check 3　Sentence

☐ They came to an arrangement that was acceptable to both sides.（彼らは両者にとって満足できる合意に達した）

☐ My boss has emotional ups and downs.（私の上司は感情の起伏がある）

☐ The boy went missing on his way home from school.（その少年は学校から家へ帰る途中に行方不明になった）

☐ Jupiter is visible to the naked eye.（木星は肉眼でも見える）

☐ Her house is always so neat.（彼女の家はいつでもよく片づいている）

☐ Mr. James is the registered owner of the house.（ジェームズ氏がその家の登録名義人だ）

☐ The play has received favorable reviews from critics.（その劇は批評家たちから好評を受けている）

☐ Thefts are frequent in this area.（この地域では窃盗がたびたび起こる）

continued
▼

Day 44

Check 1　Listen)) CD-B9

□ 0697
sound
/sáund/
❶定義注意
Part 5, 6

形 ❶**適切な**、信頼できる　❷(財政的に)堅実な、安定した　❸健全な、健康な
名 音
動 ❶鳴る　❷〜を鳴らす　❸〜に聞こえる；〜に思われる

□ 0698
extraordinary
/ikstrɔ́ːrdənèri/
Part 5, 6

形 **並外れた**、驚くべき；異常な；風変わりな
形 ordinary：❶普通の、通常の　❷平凡な

□ 0699
nuclear
/njúːkliər/
Part 7

形 **原子力の**、核兵器の；核の
名 核兵器

□ 0700
ambitious
/æmbíʃəs/
Part 2, 3

形 ❶**野心[大望]のある**　❷(計画などが)野心[意欲]的な、大がかりな
名 ambition：(〜しようとする)野心、大望(to do)

□ 0701
handsome
/hǽnsəm/
❶定義注意
Part 4

形 ❶**見事な**、見栄えのする　❷(数量的に)相当の、かなりの(≒considerable)　❸(男性が)ハンサムな(≒good-looking)；(女性が)きりっとした

□ 0702
occasional
/əkéiʒənəl/
Part 5, 6

形 ❶**時々[時折]の**(⇔frequent：たびたびの)
名 occasion：❶(特定の)時、場合　❷(〜のための／…する)機会(for 〜/to do)　❸(特別な)出来事
動 occasion：〜を生じさせる
副 occasionally：時々、時折

□ 0703
horrible
/hɔ́ːrəbl/
Part 2, 3

形 ❶**ひどく不快[嫌]な**　❷恐ろしい(≒awful, terrible)
名 horror：❶恐怖　❷憎悪、嫌悪

□ 0704
ethnic
/éθnik/
Part 5, 6

形 **民族の**、民族[人種]的な　◆「人種の」はracial
名 ethnicity：民族性

Day 43)) CD-B8
Quick Review
答えは右ページ下

- □ 通貨の
- □ 関係している
- □ 海外の
- □ 革新的な
- □ 主な
- □ 不足している
- □ ひどい
- □ 有害な
- □ 驚くべき
- □ 急進的な
- □ 思いがけない
- □ 印象的な
- □ 明らかな
- □ 幸運な
- □ 高級な
- □ 望ましい

Check 2　Phrase

- sound advice（適切なアドバイス）
- a sound investment（堅実な投資）

- extraordinary beauty（並外れた美しさ）
- extraordinary weather（異常な天候）

- a nuclear power station [plant]（原子力発電所）
- nuclear fission [fusion]（核分裂[融合]）

- an ambitious entrepreneur（野心のある起業家）
- an ambitious plan（大胆な計画）

- a handsome painting（見事な絵）
- a handsome profit（相当な利益）

- have occasional headaches（時々頭痛がする）
- an occasional traveler（時々旅行をする人）

- a horrible odor（ひどく不快なにおい）
- a horrible crime（恐ろしい犯罪）

- an ethnic minority（[ある社会の]少数派民族）
- ethnic cooking（民族料理）

Check 3　Sentence

- He can make sound judgments and decisions.（彼は適切な判断と決定を下すことができる）

- She has an extraordinary talent for music.（彼女には並外れた音楽の才能がある）

- Renewed interest in nuclear energy is linked to concern about global warming.（原子力エネルギーに再び関心が集まっているのは、地球温暖化への懸念と関係している）

- He is an ambitious and hard-working employee.（彼は大望のある、勤勉な従業員だ）

- He was dressed in a handsome suit.（彼は見事なスーツで正装していた）

- I make occasional visits to art museums.（私は美術館に時々行く）

- The weather is horrible today.（今日はひどい天気だ）

- Hispanics are the largest ethnic group in the US.（ラテン系アメリカ人はアメリカで最大の民族集団だ）

Day 43 》CD-B8
Quick Review
答えは左ページ下

- monetary
- concerned
- overseas
- innovative
- principal
- tight
- severe
- harmful
- amazing
- radical
- unexpected
- impressive
- evident
- fortunate
- fancy
- desirable

Day 45　形容詞9

Check 1　Listen)) CD-B10

□ 0705
organic
/ɔːrgǽnik/
Part 4

形 ❶**有機栽培**[農法]**の**　❷有機体の(⇔inorganic：無機物の)　❸有機的な
名 organism：❶有機体；生物　❷有機的組織体

□ 0706
massive
/mǽsiv/
Part 5, 6

形 ❶**巨大な**、大きくて重い(≒huge, enormous, immense)　❷(程度が)甚だしい、大きい
名 mass：❶(〜の)固まり、集まり(of 〜)　❷(a mass of 〜で)多数[多量]の〜

□ 0707
widespread
/wáidspréd/
Part 5, 6

形 **広く行き渡った**、普及した；広範囲に及ぶ
名 spread：普及
動 spread：❶〜を広げる　❷広がる　❸〜を広める　❹広まる

□ 0708
ridiculous
/ridíkjuləs/
❶アクセント注意
Part 2, 3

形 **ばかげた**、途方もない(≒stupid, foolish, silly)
名 ridicule：あざ笑い、嘲笑
動 ridicule：〜をあざ笑う、嘲笑する

□ 0709
aggressive
/əgrésiv/
Part 2, 3

形 ❶**積極的な**　❷攻撃的な(⇔defensive)
名 aggression：❶攻撃性　❷攻撃
副 aggressively：❶積極的に　❷攻撃的に

□ 0710
skilled
/skíld/
ビジネス問題

形 (〜に)**熟練した**、腕のいい(at [in] 〜)(⇔unskilled)
名 skill：技術、技能
形 skillful：上手な

□ 0711
honorable
/ánərəbl/
Part 7

形 ❶**立派な**、尊敬すべき　❷名誉ある　❸(the H〜)閣下
名 honor：❶光栄　❷名誉　❸尊敬
動 honor：❶〜を尊敬する　❷(be honored for [by]で)〜を光栄に思う

□ 0712
vivid
/vívid/
Part 7

形 (記憶・表現などが)**鮮明な**、生き生きとした
副 vividly：鮮明に、はっきりと

continued
▼

疲れているときは、「聞き流す」学習だけでもOK。大切なのは途中で挫折しないこと。でもテキストを使った復習も忘れずにね！

☐ 聞くだけモード　Check 1
☐ しっかりモード　Check 1 ▶ 2
☐ かんぺきモード　Check 1 ▶ 2 ▶ 3

Check 2　Phrase

☐ organic farming（有機農業）
☐ organic matter（有機物）

☐ a massive meteorite（巨大な隕石）
☐ on a massive scale（大規模に）

☐ a widespread superstition（広く行き渡った迷信）
☐ a widespread influence（広範囲に及ぶ影響）

☐ It is ridiculous to do ～．（～するとはばかげている）
☐ That's ridiculous．（ばかげた話だ）

☐ an aggressive promotion campaign（積極的な販売促進運動）
☐ get aggressive（攻撃的になる）

☐ a highly skilled surgeon（非常に腕のいい外科医）

☐ honorable conduct（立派な行為）
☐ an honorable death（名誉ある死）

☐ a vivid description（生き生きとした描写）

Check 3　Sentence

☐ Demand for organic vegetables is increasing．（有機栽培野菜への需要が増えている）

☐ The massive Buddha statue was completed in 752．（その巨大な仏像は752年に完成した）

☐ The use of illegal drugs is widespread among young people．（違法薬物の使用が若者の間で広まっている）

☐ Where did you come up with such a ridiculous idea?（どこでそんなばかげた考えを思いついたんだい？）

☐ The company has aggressive plans to expand overseas．（その会社には海外への積極的な拡大計画がある）

☐ The shortage of skilled labor is particularly acute in the country．（その国では熟練労働者の不足が特に深刻になっている）

☐ Miss Thompson is an honorable person．（トンプソンさんは尊敬すべき人物だ）

☐ I still have vivid memories of my first day at work．（私は職場での初日のことを今でも鮮明に覚えている）

continued
▼

Day 45

Check 1 Listen)) CD-B10

0713 industrious
/indʌ́striəs/
Part 5, 6

形 **勤勉な**(≒hardworking, diligent)　⊕industrial(産業の)と混同しないように注意
名 industry: ❶産業;(産業各部門の)〜業　❷勤勉
名 industriousness: 勤勉さ

0714 superior
/səpíəriər/
Part 5, 6

形 ❶**優れた**、優秀な　❷(be superior toで)〜より優れている、勝っている(⇔be inferior to)
名 上司、上役
名 superiority:(〜に対する/…における)優越、優勢(to [over] 〜/in ...)

0715 dedicated
/dédikèitid/
Part 4

形 ❶**熱心な**、献身的な、ひたむきな(≒devoted)　❷(装置などが)ある特定の目的用の、専用の
名 dedication:(〜への)献身(to 〜)
動 dedicate: ❶(dedicate A to Bで)AをBにささげる　❷(be dedicated toで)〜に専念[熱中]している

0716 green
/gríːn/
❶定義注意
Part 7

形 ❶(政策などが)**環境保護の**、環境にやさしい　❷緑(色)の
名 緑色

0717 optional
/ɑ́pʃənl/
Part 7

形 **随意[任意]の**、自由選択の(⇔compulsory, obligatory:義務的な)
名 option:(〜する)選択;選択肢、選択権(of doing [to do])

0718 administrative
/ædmínəstrèitiv/
ビジネス問題

形 ❶**管理の**、経営上の　❷行政上の
名 administration: ❶管理、経営　❷行政;(しばしばthe A〜)政府、内閣
動 administer: ❶〜を管理[運営]する　❷〜を治める　❸(処罰など)を執行する

0719 voluntary
/vɑ́ləntèri/
Part 5, 6

形 **ボランティアの**、自発的な(⇔compulsory, obligatory:強制的な)
名 volunteer: 志願者、ボランティア
動 volunteer: ❶(〜を)進んで引き受ける(for 〜)　❷(volunteer to doで)〜しようと進んで申し出る

0720 coarse
/kɔ́ːrs/
Part 5, 6

形 ❶**下品な**、粗野な(≒crude)　❷(生地・粒などが)きめの粗い(⇔fine)

Day 44)) CD-B9
Quick Review
答えは右ページ下

☐ 受け入れられる
☐ 感情の
☐ 行方不明の
☐ 目に見える

☐ きちんとした
☐ 登録された
☐ 好意的な
☐ たびたびの

☐ 適切な
☐ 並外れた
☐ 原子力の
☐ 野心のある

☐ 見事な
☐ 時々の
☐ ひどく不快な
☐ 民族の

Check 2 Phrase

- an industrious pupil(勤勉な生徒)

- a superior doctor(優れた医者)
- be superior to anything(どんなものより優れている)

- a dedicated teacher(熱心な教師)
- a dedicated line(専用回線)

- the green movement(環境保護運動)

- an optional subject(選択科目)

- administrative ability(管理能力)
- administrative reform(行政改革)

- a voluntary donation(自発的な寄付)
- on a voluntary basis(ボランティアとして)

- a coarse joke(下品な冗談)
- coarse sand(きめの粗い砂)

Check 3 Sentence

- He is a competent and industrious employee.(彼は有能で勤勉な従業員だ)

- She graduated from the university with a superior academic record.(彼女は優れた学業成績でその大学を卒業した)

- Mr. Perez has been a dedicated firefighter for 30 years.(ペレス氏は30年にわたる献身的な消防士だ)

- I'm interested in green issues.(私は環境問題に関心がある)

- Attendance at the workshop is optional.(その研修会への出席は随意となっている)

- We need to reduce administrative costs.(私たちは管理費を削る必要がある)

- She does voluntary work for a local charity.(彼女は地元の慈善団体でボランティア活動をしている)

- Don't use coarse language in front of children.(子どもたちの前では下品な言葉遣いをしないでください)

Day 44 》CD-B9
Quick Review
答えは左ページ下

- acceptable
- emotional
- missing
- visible
- neat
- registered
- favorable
- frequent
- sound
- extraordinary
- nuclear
- ambitious
- handsome
- occasional
- horrible
- ethnic

Day 46　形容詞10

Check 1　Listen))) CD-B11

□ 0721
hostile
/hάstl/
Part 7

形 ❶ (〜に)**敵意[反感]を持った**(to [toward] 〜) (⇔friendly)　❷敵[敵国]の
名 hostility：❶(〜に対する／…の間の)敵意(to [toward] 〜/between . . .)　❷(〜に対する)反対(to 〜)　❸(〜ies)戦争行為

□ 0722
elaborate
/ilǽbərət/
Part 5, 6

形 ❶**精巧[精密]な**、手の込んだ　❷入念な
動 (/ilǽbərèit/)(〜について)詳しく述べる(on 〜)
名 elaboration：念入りに作ること；推敲
副 elaborately：精巧に、入念に

□ 0723
spectacular
/spektǽkjulər/
Part 5, 6

形 **見事な**、壮大な、壮観の、目覚ましい
名 ❶(大々的な)見せ物　❷豪華ショー[番組]
名 spectacle：❶(大仕掛けな)見せ物、ショー　❷壮観、奇観

□ 0724
residential
/rèzədénʃəl/
Part 5, 6

形 **住宅[居住]の**
名 residence：❶居住、滞在　❷邸宅、住宅
名 resident：居住者、在住者
形 resident：居住[在住]している

□ 0725
exceptional
/iksépʃənl/
Part 4

形 ❶**非常に優れた**　❷例外的な
名 exception：例外
副 exceptionally：非常に、例外的に
前 except：〜を除いて、〜以外は

□ 0726
striking
/stráikiŋ/
Part 7

形 **際立った**、著しい、印象的な
名 strike：❶打つこと、打撃　❷(〜を求める／…に反対する)ストライキ(for 〜/against . . .)
動 strike：❶〜を打つ　❷(考えなどが)〜の心に浮かぶ　❸ストライキを行う

□ 0727
satisfactory
/sæ̀tisfǽktəri/
Part 5, 6

形 (〜にとって)**満足な**、納得のいく(to [for] 〜)
名 satisfaction：満足、充足
動 satisfy：❶〜を満足させる　❷(必要など)を満たす　❸(be satisfied withで)〜に満足している

□ 0728
advanced
/ædvǽnst/
Part 4

形 ❶(国などが)**先進の**、進歩した　❷(知識・技術などが)上級の、高等の(⇔elementary：初歩の)
名 advance：❶進歩　❷前進　❸前払い金
動 advance：❶進歩する　❷前進する　❸〜を前進させる

continued
▼

なかなか覚えられないときこそ「音読」を！面倒くさがっていては、いつになっても語彙は身につかない。口を積極的に動かそう！

☐ 聞くだけモード　Check 1
☐ しっかりモード　Check 1 ▶ 2
☐ かんぺきモード　Check 1 ▶ 2 ▶ 3

Check 2　Phrase

☐ hostile buyout（敵対的買収）
☐ hostile territory（敵地）

☐ an elaborate machine（精巧な機械）
☐ elaborate preparations（入念な準備）

☐ a spectacular performance（見事な演奏）
☐ spectacular growth（目覚ましい成長）

☐ a residential area（住宅地域）

☐ an exceptional student（非常に優秀な学生）
☐ an exceptional situation（異例の事態）

☐ a striking difference（際立った違い）
☐ striking features（印象的な特徴）

☐ a satisfactory answer [explanation]（納得のいく回答［説明］）

☐ advanced technology（先進技術）
☐ an advanced English course（上級英語コース）

Check 3　Sentence

☐ He is hostile to the idea of laying off staff.（彼は社員を解雇するという考えに反対している）

☐ Elaborate ornamentation is characteristic of the Victorian style.（手の込んだ装飾はビクトリア朝様式の特徴である）

☐ The mountaintop provides a spectacular view of the whole city.（山頂からは市全体の見事な景色を見渡せる）

☐ The site is developed for residential purposes.（その用地は居住用に開発されている）

☐ Dinner at the restaurant was exceptional.（そのレストランのディナーは非常に素晴らしかった）

☐ There are striking similarities between the two incidents.（その2つの事件の間には顕著な類似点がある）

☐ The student obtained a satisfactory mark in the examination.（その生徒は試験で満足のいく点数を取った）

☐ The leaders of several advanced countries gathered to discuss the current economic crisis.（現在の経済危機について話し合うために先進諸国の首脳たちが集まった）

continued
▼

Day 46

Check 1　Listen 》CD-B11

□ 0729
experienced
/ikspíəriənst/
Part 4

形(〜の)**経験豊かな**(in 〜)(⇔inexperienced)
名experience：経験
動experience：〜を経験する

□ 0730
immense
/iméns/
Part 5, 6

形**巨大な**、多大な(≒huge, enormous, massive)
副immensely：非常に、とても

□ 0731
fascinating
/fǽsənèitiŋ/
Part 4

形**魅力[魅惑]的な**
名fascination：魅了[魅惑](された状態)
動fascinate：❶〜を魅了[魅惑]する ❷(be fascinated by [with] 〜で)〜にうっとりしている、引きつけられている

□ 0732
conventional
/kənvénʃənl/
Part 5, 6

形❶**従来の**、慣例[慣習]の ❷月並みな、平凡な(⇔un-conventional)
名convention：❶代表者会議[大会] ❷慣習、慣例

□ 0733
suspicious
/səspíʃəs/
Part 7

形❶**怪しい**、疑わしい、疑いを起こさせる ❷(〜について)疑わしく思っている(of [about] 〜)
名suspicion：(〜に対する)疑い、容疑(about [against, for] 〜)
副suspiciously：❶疑い深く ❷いやに、やけに

□ 0734
exhausted
/igzɔ́:stid/
Part 5, 6

形❶(〜で)**疲れ切った**、力尽きた(from [with, by] 〜)(≒tired) ❷使い尽くされた
名exhaust：排気ガス
動exhaust：❶〜を疲れさせる ❷〜を使い尽くす
名exhaustion：❶極度の疲労 ❷使い尽くすこと

□ 0735
devoted
/divóutid/
Part 7

形(〜に)**献身的な**；愛情深い(to 〜)(≒dedicated)
名devotion：(〜への)献身、専念(to 〜)
動devote：❶(devote A to Bで)A(時間など)をB(仕事・目的など)にささげる、充てる ❷(devote oneself toで)〜に専念する、一身をささげる

□ 0736
classified
/klǽsəfàid/
Part 7

形❶**分類された** ❷(文書などが)機密[極秘]扱いの
名classification：❶分類 ❷範疇
動classify：❶(classify A as [into] Bで)AをBに分類する ❷(文書など)を機密扱いにする

Day 45 》CD-B10
Quick Review
答えは右ページ下

□ 有機栽培の
□ 巨大な
□ 広く行き渡った
□ ばかげた

□ 積極的な
□ 熟練した
□ 立派な
□ 鮮明な

□ 勤勉な
□ 優れた
□ 熱心な
□ 環境保護の

□ 随意の
□ 管理の
□ ボランティアの
□ 下品な

Check 2　Phrase

- ☐ an experienced teacher（経験豊かな教師）

- ☐ an immense palace（巨大な宮殿）
- ☐ an immense debt（多大な借金）

- ☐ a fascinating man（魅力的な男性）
- ☐ It is fascinating to do ~.（~するのはとても面白い）

- ☐ a conventional method（従来の方法）
- ☐ (the) conventional wisdom（世間の通念）

- ☐ under [in] suspicious circumstances（不審な状況下で）
- ☐ be suspicious of his story（彼の話を疑わしく思っている）

- ☐ be exhausted from studying（勉強で疲れ切っている）
- ☐ an exhausted oil field（枯渇した油田）

- ☐ a devoted wife（献身的な妻）

- ☐ a classified telephone directory（職業別電話帳）
- ☐ classified documents [information]（機密文書[情報]）

Check 3　Sentence

- ☐ We are looking for someone who is very experienced in marketing.（私たちはマーケティング分野での経験が非常に豊かな人を探している）

- ☐ Illegal immigration into the US has become an immense issue.（アメリカへの不法移住は大きな問題になっている）

- ☐ I found the movie fascinating.（私はその映画をとても面白いと思った）

- ☐ Organic farming is labor-intensive, whereas conventional farming is capital-intensive.（有機農業が労働集約的なのに対し、従来農業は資本集約的である）

- ☐ Please report any suspicious people or activities immediately to the police.（不審者や不審な行為を見つけた場合はすぐに警察に連絡してください）

- ☐ I'm exhausted from working all day.（私は1日中働いて疲れ切っている）

- ☐ Mike is a devoted family man.（マイクは家庭を大切にする献身的な男性だ）

- ☐ Many employers use classified ads to find employees.（多くの雇用主は従業員を見つけるために分類広告を使っている）

Day 45))) CD-B10
Quick Review
答えは左ページ下

- ☐ organic
- ☐ massive
- ☐ widespread
- ☐ ridiculous
- ☐ aggressive
- ☐ skilled
- ☐ honorable
- ☐ vivid
- ☐ industrious
- ☐ superior
- ☐ dedicated
- ☐ green
- ☐ optional
- ☐ administrative
- ☐ voluntary
- ☐ coarse

Day 47 形容詞11

Check 1　Listen))) CD-B12

□ 0737
dizzy
/dízi/
Part 2, 3

形 (暑さなどで)**目まいがする**、ふらふらする(from ~)

□ 0738
admirable
/ǽdmərəbl/
❶アクセント注意
Part 5, 6

形 **称賛に値する**；見事な
名 admiration：(~に対する)感嘆；称賛(の気持ち)(for ~)
動 admire：❶ ~に感心[感嘆]する　❷(admire A for Bで)AをBの点で称賛する

□ 0739
transparent
/trænspéərənt/
Part 5, 6

形 **透明な**、透き通った(⇔opaque：不透明な)　❶「半透明の」はtranslucent
名 transparency：透明(度)；透明性

□ 0740
countless
/káuntlis/
Part 4

形 **数え切れない**(ほどの)、無数の
名 count：計算
動 count：❶ ~を数える　❷ ~を勘定[数、考慮]に入れる　❸(count onで)~に頼る、~を当てにする

□ 0741
disappointing
/dìsəpɔ́intiŋ/
Part 2, 3

形 **期待外れの**、失望[がっかり]させる
名 disappointment：失望
動 disappoint：❶ ~を失望させる、がっかりさせる　❷(be disappointed with [at, about]で)~に失望している、がっかりしている

□ 0742
racial
/réiʃəl/
Part 7

形 **人種の**　❶「民族の」はethnic
名 race：人種
名 racism：人種差別(主義)
名 racist：人種差別主義者

□ 0743
influential
/ìnfluénʃəl/
Part 5, 6

形 ❶**影響力の大きい**　❷(~に)影響力を及ぼす(in ~)
名 influence：(~への)影響(on ~)
動 influence：~に(間接的な)影響を及ぼす

□ 0744
intermediate
/ìntərmíːdiət/
Part 7

形 ❶**中級の**　❷中間の

continued
▼

Quick Reviewは使ってる？ 昨日覚えた単語でも、記憶に残っているとは限らない。学習の合間に軽くチェックするだけでも効果は抜群！

☐ 聞くだけモード　Check 1
☐ しっかりモード　Check 1 ▶ 2
☐ かんぺきモード　Check 1 ▶ 2 ▶ 3

Check 2　Phrase	Check 3　Sentence
☐ feel dizzy（目まいがする） ☐ suffer from dizzy spells（目まいに苦しむ）	☐ I feel dizzy from lack of sleep.（私は寝不足で目まいがする）
☐ an admirable achievement（称賛に値する業績）	☐ He did an admirable job on the project.（彼はそのプロジェクトで称賛に値する仕事をした）
☐ a transparent plastic box（透明なプラスチックの箱）	☐ The water in the lake was transparent and very deep.（その湖の水は透んでいて、とても深かった）
☐ countless times（数え切れないほど何度も）	☐ She spent countless hours to find a solution to the problem.（彼女はその問題の解決策を見つけるために数え切れないほどの時間を費やした）
☐ a disappointing result（期待外れの結果）	☐ The movie was somewhat disappointing.（その映画は少し期待外れだった）
☐ racial equality（人種的平等）	☐ America has deep-rooted racial problems.（アメリカは根深い人種問題を抱えている）
☐ an influential figure（影響力のある人物） ☐ be influential in making foreign policy（外交政策の作成に影響力を及ぼす）	☐ *The Times* is one of the most influential newspapers in the world.（『タイムズ』は世界で最も影響力の大きい新聞の1つだ）
☐ an intermediate golfer（中級のゴルファー） ☐ an intermediate color（中間色）	☐ The English course is divided into three classes, elementary, intermediate, and advanced.（その英語コースは、初級、中級、そして上級の3つのクラスに分けられている）

continued ▼

Day 47

Check 1　Listen 》CD-B12

☐ 0745
mere
/míər/
Part 5, 6

形 **単なる**、ほんの、ただの〜にすぎない
副 merely：単に、ただ

☐ 0746
unreasonable
/ʌnríːzənəbl/
Part 2, 3

形 ❶(値段などが) **法外な**、常軌を逸した　❷不当な、不合理な　❸(人などが)理性的でない(⇔reasonable)

☐ 0747
oral
/ɔ́ːrəl/
Part 5, 6

形 ❶**口頭**[口述]**の**(≒verbal)(⇔written)　❷口の、口腔の

☐ 0748
insufficient
/ìnsəfíʃənt/
Part 5, 6

形 (〜に／…するのに)**不十分な**、不足な(for 〜/to do)
(⇔sufficient, enough)

☐ 0749
fundamental
/fʌ̀ndəméntl/
Part 5, 6

形 ❶**基本**[根本]**的な**　❷(〜にとって)重要な、必須の(to 〜)(≒important, necessary)
名 (通例〜s)基礎、基本
副 fundamentally：基本[根本]的に

☐ 0750
utmost
/ʌ́tmòust/
Part 5, 6

形 **最大(限)の**
名 (the [one's] 〜)(程度などの)最大限

☐ 0751
destructive
/distrʌ́ktiv/
Part 5, 6

形 **破壊的な**(⇔constructive：建設的な)
名 destruction：破壊(行為)
動 destroy：❶〜を破壊する　❷(敵など)を滅ぼす

☐ 0752
accessible
/æksésəbl/
Part 7

形 (〜にとって)**入手**[利用、入場、接近]**可能な**(to 〜)
(⇔inaccessible)
名 access：❶(〜への)接近(方法)(to 〜)　❷(〜を)利用[入手]する権利[機会](to 〜)
動 access：❶〜にアクセスする　❷〜に接近する

| Day 46 》CD-B11
Quick Review
答えは右ページ下 | ☐ 敵意を持った
☐ 精巧な
☐ 見事な
☐ 住宅の | ☐ 非常に優れた
☐ 際立った
☐ 満足な
☐ 先進の | ☐ 経験豊かな
☐ 巨大な
☐ 魅力的な
☐ 従来の | ☐ 怪しい
☐ 疲れ切った
☐ 献身的な
☐ 分類された |

Check 2 Phrase

- ☐ a mere rumor（単なるうわさ）

- ☐ unreasonable price（法外な値段）
- ☐ unreasonable demands（不当な要求）

- ☐ an oral examination（口頭試験）
- ☐ oral hygiene（口腔衛生）

- ☐ insufficient information（不十分な情報）

- ☐ a fundamental mistake（基本的な間違い）
- ☐ elements fundamental to success（成功に必要な要素）

- ☐ with the utmost care（最大の注意を払って）
- ☐ of the utmost importance（最も重要な）

- ☐ the destructive force of an earthquake（地震の破壊力）

- ☐ a healthcare system accessible to everyone（誰でも利用可能な医療制度）

Check 3 Sentence

- ☐ The ticket for the concert costs a mere $5.（そのコンサートのチケットはほんの5ドルだ）

- ☐ The current price of oil is unreasonable.（現在の石油価格は常軌を逸している）

- ☐ Agreements must be written, not oral.（契約は口頭ではなく、文書でなければならない）

- ☐ There is insufficient scientific evidence to attribute climatic disasters to global warming.（気候災害を地球温暖化の原因とする科学的な証拠は十分ではない）

- ☐ The company needs to make fundamental changes in the way it does its business.（その会社はビジネス手法を根本的に変える必要がある）

- ☐ He has the utmost respect for Abraham Lincoln.（彼はエイブラハム・リンカーンを最も尊敬している）

- ☐ World War I was one of the most destructive wars in European history.（第1次大戦はヨーロッパ史における最も破壊的な戦争の1つだった）

- ☐ The Internet has made information readily accessible to people.（インターネットは人々が容易に情報を入手できるようにした）

Day 46 》CD-B11
Quick Review
答えは左ページ下

- ☐ hostile
- ☐ elaborate
- ☐ spectacular
- ☐ residential
- ☐ exceptional
- ☐ striking
- ☐ satisfactory
- ☐ advanced
- ☐ experienced
- ☐ immense
- ☐ fascinating
- ☐ conventional
- ☐ suspicious
- ☐ exhausted
- ☐ devoted
- ☐ classified

CHAPTER 1
CHAPTER 2
CHAPTER 3
CHAPTER 4
CHAPTER 5
CHAPTER 6
CHAPTER 7
CHAPTER 8
CHAPTER 9
CHAPTER 10

Day 48 形容詞12

Check 1 Listen 》CD-B13

☐ 0753
prosperous
/prɑ́spərəs/
ビジネス問題

▶ 形 **繁栄している**(≒thriving)；(経済的に)成功している(≒successful)
名 prosperity：(特に財政的な)繁栄、繁盛
動 prosper：繁栄する；成功する

☐ 0754
successive
/səksésiv/
Part 5, 6

▶ 形 **連続する**、継続的な(≒consecutive)
名 succession：❶連続 ❷(〜の)継承(to 〜)
名 successor：後継[後任]者、相続者
動 succeed：❶(succeed inで)〜に成功する ❷(succeed toで)〜を継承[相続]する；〜の後任となる

☐ 0755
uncommon
/ʌnkɑ́mən/
Part 2, 3

▶ 形 **珍しい**、まれな(≒rare, unusual)(⇔common)

☐ 0756
irritating
/írətèitiŋ/
Part 4

▶ 形 **腹の立つ**、いらいらさせる
名 irritation：❶立腹、いら立ち ❷炎症、過敏症
動 irritate：❶〜をいらいらさせる、怒らせる ❷(be irritated about [at, with, by]で)〜にいらいらしている、〜に怒っている ❸〜をひりひりさせる

☐ 0757
partial
/pɑ́ːrʃəl/
Part 5, 6

▶ 形 ❶**部分**[局部]**的な**(⇔total：全体的な) ❷(〜が)とても好きな(to 〜) ❸(〜を)えこひいきする(to [toward] 〜)
名 part：❶部分 ❷役目；役
副 partially：部分的に、不十分に

☐ 0758
tiring
/táiəriŋ/
Part 7

▶ 形 (仕事などが)**骨の折れる**、疲れさせる
動 tire：❶〜を疲れさせる ❷疲れる
形 tired：❶(〜で)疲れている(from 〜) ❷(〜に)飽きている、うんざりしている(of 〜)
形 tiresome：(演説などが)退屈な、飽き飽きする

☐ 0759
inadequate
/inǽdikwət/
Part 5, 6

▶ 形 (〜にとって)**不十分な**、不適切な(for 〜)(⇔adequate)
副 inadequately：不十分に

☐ 0760
respectful
/rispéktfəl/
Part 5, 6

▶ 形 (〜に)**敬意を表する**、礼儀正しい、丁寧な(of [to] 〜) ✚respective(それぞれの)と混同しないように注意
名 respect：❶尊敬、敬意 ❷尊重；配慮
動 respect：〜を尊敬[尊重]する

continued
▼

今日でChapter 6は最後！ 時間に余裕があったら、章末のReviewにも挑戦しておこう。忘れてしまった単語も結構あるのでは?!

- ☐ 聞くだけモード　Check 1
- ☐ しっかりモード　Check 1 ▶ 2
- ☐ かんぺきモード　Check 1 ▶ 2 ▶ 3

Check 2　Phrase

☐ a prosperous business [region]（繁盛している商売[繁栄している地域]）

☐ for five successive days（5日間連続して）
☐ successive governments（歴代政府）

☐ an uncommon name（珍しい名前）

☐ irritating noise（いらいらする騒音）
☐ find ~ irritating（~にいらいらする）

☐ a partial solution（部分的な解決策）
☐ be partial to wine（ワインが大好きである）

☐ a tiring job（骨の折れる仕事）

☐ inadequate supply of food（不十分な食糧供給）
☐ totally [woefully] inadequate（全く不十分な）

☐ be respectful of other cultures（異文化を尊重する）
☐ a respectful tone of voice（礼儀正しい口調）

Check 3　Sentence

☐ Sweden is one of the most prosperous countries in the world.（スウェーデンは世界で最も繁栄している国の1つだ）

☐ The politician has won three successive elections.（その政治家は3回連続で選挙に勝っている）

☐ It is not uncommon for her to work until midnight.（彼女が夜の12時まで働くのは珍しいことではない）

☐ Everyone is tired of his irritating behavior.（みんなが彼の腹立たしい態度にうんざりしている）

☐ They reached partial agreement on the issue.（彼らはその問題に関して部分的な合意に達した）

☐ I had a very tiring day yesterday.（昨日は本当に疲れる1日だった）

☐ The current minimum wage is inadequate to cover the costs of living.（現在の最低賃金は生活費を賄うのに十分ではない）

☐ We should be respectful of others.（私たちは他者に敬意を表するべきだ）

continued ▼

Day 48

Check 1　Listen))) CD-B13

☐ 0761
unlikely
/ʌnláikli/
Part 2, 3

形 **ありそうもない**、起こりそうもない；(~)しそうもない(to do)(⇔likely)
前 unlike：❶~と違って　❷~らしくない

☐ 0762
rosy
/róuzi/
ビジネス問題

形 (前途などが)**明るい**、楽観的な、ばら色の

☐ 0763
plentiful
/pléntifəl/
Part 5, 6

形 **豊富な**、多くの(≒abundant, ample, affluent)(⇔scarce：不十分な)
名 plenty：❶たくさん、十分　❷豊富さ、豊かさ
副 plenty：❶十分に　❷たくさん、かなり

☐ 0764
conditional
/kəndíʃənl/
Part 5, 6

形 ❶**条件つきの**、暫定的な(⇔unconditional：無条件の)　❷(~を)条件として、(~)次第で(on [upon] ~)
名 condition：❶(通例~s)(~の)(必要)条件(of [for] ~)　❷(~s)状況、事情；状態

☐ 0765
retired
/ritáiərd/
Part 4

形 **退職[引退]した**
名 retiree：退職[引退]者
動 retire：(~を)退職[引退]する(from ~)

☐ 0766
lasting
/læstiŋ/
Part 7

形 **長続き[長持ち]する**、耐久力のある
動 last：❶続く、継続する　❷長持ちする

☐ 0767
structural
/strʌ́ktʃərəl/
Part 5, 6

形 **構造(上)の**
名 structure：❶構造、構成　❷建造[構造]物
動 structure：~を組織[構造]化する

☐ 0768
grim
/grím/
ビジネス問題

形 (状況などが)**厳しい**、暗い

Day 47))) CD-B12
Quick Review
答えは右ページ下

☐ 目まいがする
☐ 称賛に値する
☐ 透明な
☐ 数え切れない

☐ 期待外れの
☐ 人種の
☐ 影響力の大きい
☐ 中級の

☐ 単なる
☐ 法外な
☐ 口頭の
☐ 不十分な

☐ 基本的な
☐ 最大の
☐ 破壊的な
☐ 入手可能な

Check 2　Phrase

- ☐ an unlikely story(ありそうもない話)
- ☐ an unlikely pair [couple](意外なペア[カップル])

- ☐ a rosy future(明るい未来)
- ☐ paint a rosy picture of ~(~を楽観的に述べる)

- ☐ a plentiful harvest(豊作)
- ☐ a plentiful supply(豊富な供給)

- ☐ conditional approval(条件つきの許可)
- ☐ be conditional on weather([行事の開催などが]天気次第である)

- ☐ a retired school teacher(退職した学校教師)

- ☐ a lasting peace(恒久平和)
- ☐ leave a lasting impression on ~(~にいつまでも消えない印象を残す)

- ☐ structural defects(構造上の欠陥)

- ☐ grim news(暗いニュース)
- ☐ look grim(厳しそうである)

Check 3　Sentence

- ☐ It is unlikely that we will achieve our sales target this year.(今年は売上目標を達成しそうもない)

- ☐ The economic situation will become less rosy in the next few years.(今後数年間は、経済状況は明るさが弱まるだろう)

- ☐ Job opportunities for qualified technicians are plentiful.(資格を持った技術者の就職の機会は豊富にある)

- ☐ The owner of the site entered into a conditional contract with the developer.(その用地の所有者は開発業者と暫定契約を結んだ)

- ☐ Mr. Sato is a retired police officer.(サトウさんは退職した警察官だ)

- ☐ I formed a lasting friendship with him.(私は彼と永遠の友情を結んだ)

- ☐ The bridge suffered structural damage due to the heavy rain.(豪雨のため、その橋は構造的な損傷を受けた)

- ☐ The current economic situation is especially grim for small businesses.(現在の経済状況は中小企業にとって特に厳しい)

Day 47))CD-B12
Quick Review
答えは左ページ下

- ☐ dizzy
- ☐ admirable
- ☐ transparent
- ☐ countless
- ☐ disappointing
- ☐ racial
- ☐ influential
- ☐ intermediate
- ☐ mere
- ☐ unreasonable
- ☐ oral
- ☐ insufficient
- ☐ fundamental
- ☐ utmost
- ☐ destructive
- ☐ accessible

CHAPTER 1
CHAPTER 2
CHAPTER 3
CHAPTER 4
CHAPTER 5
CHAPTER 6
CHAPTER 7
CHAPTER 8
CHAPTER 9
CHAPTER 10

Chapter 6 Review

左ページの(1)〜(20)の形容詞の同意・類義語（≒）、反意・反対語（⇔）を右ページのA〜Tから選び、カッコの中に答えを書き込もう。意味が分からないときは、見出し番号を参照して復習しておこう（答えは右ページ下）。

- [ ] (1) principal (0677) ≒は? (　　)
- [ ] (2) severe (0679) ≒は? (　　)
- [ ] (3) radical (0682) ⇔は? (　　)
- [ ] (4) evident (0685) ≒は? (　　)
- [ ] (5) neat (0693) ⇔は? (　　)
- [ ] (6) frequent (0696) ⇔は? (　　)
- [ ] (7) massive (0706) ≒は? (　　)
- [ ] (8) ridiculous (0708) ≒は? (　　)
- [ ] (9) industrious (0713) ≒は? (　　)
- [ ] (10) optional (0717) ⇔は? (　　)
- [ ] (11) exhausted (0734) ≒は? (　　)
- [ ] (12) devoted (0735) ≒は? (　　)
- [ ] (13) transparent (0739) ⇔は? (　　)
- [ ] (14) oral (0747) ⇔は? (　　)
- [ ] (15) insufficient (0748) ⇔は? (　　)
- [ ] (16) destructive (0751) ⇔は? (　　)
- [ ] (17) prosperous (0753) ≒は? (　　)
- [ ] (18) successive (0754) ≒は? (　　)
- [ ] (19) uncommon (0755) ≒は? (　　)
- [ ] (20) partial (0757) ⇔は? (　　)

A. messy
B. written
C. opaque
D. conservative
E. total
F. compulsory
G. enormous
H. constructive
I. dedicated
J. serious
K. enough
L. stupid
M. thriving
N. clear
O. consecutive
P. hardworking
Q. tired
R. occasional
S. rare
T. main

【解答】(1) T (2) J (3) D (4) N (5) A (6) R (7) G (8) L (9) P (10) F
(11) Q (12) I (13) C (14) B (15) K (16) H (17) M (18) O (19) S (20) E

CHAPTER 7

副詞：必修48

Chapter 7 では、TOEIC 必修の副詞48をチェック。このChapterが終われば、単語編は終了です。せっかく覚えた単語も、使わなければ「宝の持ち腐れ」です。何かの機会に使ってみては？

Day 49【副詞1】
▶ 230
Day 50【副詞2】
▶ 234
Day 51【副詞3】
▶ 238
Chapter 7 Review
▶ 242

TOEIC的格言

A book that remains shut is but a block.

宝の持ち腐れ。
[直訳] 閉じたままの本は塊でしかない。

Day 49　副詞1

Check 1　Listen 》CD-B14

☐ 0769
approximately
/əpráksəmətli/
Part 5, 6

副 **おおよそ**、約（≒about）
動 approximate：おおよそ～になる、～に近い
形 approximate：おおよその

☐ 0770
eventually
/ivéntʃuəli/
Part 5, 6

副 **結局は**、ついに；いつかは
名 event：❶出来事；行事　❷(the ~)結果、成り行き
形 eventual：いつかは起こる[生じる]；最後の

☐ 0771
promptly
/prάmptli/
Part 5, 6

副 ❶**即座に**、敏速に（≒quickly）　❷(ある時刻)ちょうど、きっかり（≒punctually, on time）
形 prompt：❶即座[即刻]の　❷時間を守る
動 prompt：❶～を引き起こす　❷(prompt A to doで)Aに～するよう促す

☐ 0772
fairly
/féərli/
Part 5, 6

副 ❶**まあまあ**、まずまず　➕「平均以上だが『very』ではない」というニュアンス　❷公正[公平]に
形 fair：❶公正[公平]な　❷まあまあの、普通の
副 fair：公正に、フェアに

☐ 0773
steadily
/stédili/
Part 5, 6

副 **徐々に**、だんだん；着実に、着々と
形 steady：❶安定した、固定された　❷着実な、堅実な

☐ 0774
practically
/prǽktikəli/
Part 2, 3

副 ❶**ほとんど**（≒almost）　❷実際的に　❸実質的に、事実上
名 practice：❶習慣、慣例　❷練習　❸実行、実施
動 practice：❶～を習慣的に行う　❷～を実行する
形 practical：❶現実[実際]的な　❷実用的な

☐ 0775
apparently
/əpǽrəntli/
Part 2, 3

副 **どうやら**[見たところでは]**～らしい**
名 appearance：❶外見、外観　❷出現　❸出席
動 appear：❶～のように見える[思える]　❷(appear to doで)～するように見える　❸現れる
形 apparent：❶明らかな　❷見かけ上の

☐ 0776
beforehand
/bifɔ́ːrhænd/
Part 4

副 **あらかじめ**、前もって（≒in advance）（⇔afterward：後で）

continued
▼

Chapter 7では、3日をかけて必修副詞48をチェック。まずはCDでチャンツを聞いて、単語を「耳」からインプット!

- ☐ 聞くだけモード　Check 1
- ☐ しっかりモード　Check 1 ▶ 2
- ☐ かんぺきモード　Check 1 ▶ 2 ▶ 3

Check 2　Phrase & Sentence

☐ approximately correct(ほぼ正しい)

☐ Eventually, he agreed with the plan.(結局、彼はその計画に賛成した)

☐ do things promptly(物事を迅速にこなす)
☐ arrive promptly at 1 p.m.(午後1時ちょうどに到着する)

☐ fairly cheap(まあまあ安い)
☐ treat people fairly(人々を公平に扱う)

☐ develop steadily(徐々に[着実に]発展する)

☐ practically impossible(ほとんど不可能な)
☐ think practically(実際に即して考える)

☐ Apparently, we're having snow tomorrow.(どうやら明日は雪が降るらしい)

☐ reserve a hotel room beforehand(あらかじめホテルの部屋を予約する)

Check 3　Sentence

☐ The construction of the condominium will be completed in approximately 24 months.(そのマンションの建設はおおよそ24カ月後に完了する予定だ)

☐ She will eventually marry someone.(彼女はいつかは誰かと結婚するだろう)

☐ You should answer customers' e-mails as promptly as possible.(顧客からの電子メールにはできるだけ早く返事を出したほうがいい)

☐ She speaks Chinese fairly well.(彼女は中国語をまあまあうまく話す)

☐ The unemployment rate has risen steadily since 2000.(失業率は2000年以降、徐々に上昇している)

☐ The company is practically bankrupt.(その会社は破産しているのも同然だ)

☐ Apparently, the situation is still getting worse.(見たところでは、状況はまだ悪化しているようだ)

☐ I told her beforehand that I would be late.(私は遅れることを彼女にあらかじめ伝えた)

continued ▼

Day 49

Check 1　Listen 》CD-B14

□ 0777
consequently
/kάnsəkwèntli/
❶アクセント注意
Part 5, 6

副 **その結果**、従って（≒as a result, therefore, thus）
名consequence：(通例～s)(～の)結果、影響(of ～)
形consequent：(～の)結果として起こる(on [upon, to] ～)

□ 0778
fully
/fúlli/
Part 5, 6

副 ❶**完全に**、全く（≒completely）　❷(数詞の前に置いて)丸々
形full：❶(～で)いっぱいの、満ちた(of ～)　❷完全な、詳細な　❸最大[最高]限度の

□ 0779
currently
/kə́ːrəntli/
Part 5, 6

副 **現在は**、現在のところ（≒now）
名current：❶(川などの)流れ　❷電流
形current：現在の、今の
名currency：通貨、貨幣

□ 0780
simultaneously
/sàiməltéiniəsli/
Part 5, 6

副 **同時に**、一斉に（≒at once）
形simultaneous：(～と)同時の、同時に起こる(with ～)

□ 0781
nearly
/níərli/
Part 5, 6

副 **ほとんど**、ほぼ（≒almost）
動near：～に近づく
形near：(～に)近い(to ～)
副near：近くに
前near：～の近くに

□ 0782
unfortunately
/ʌnfɔ́ːrtʃənətli/
Part 2, 3

副 **残念ながら**、あいにく、不運にも（⇔fortunately）
名unfortunate：不運[不幸]な人
形unfortunate：不運[不幸]な

□ 0783
rather
/rǽðər/
Part 5, 6

副 ❶**かなり**；幾分　❷(A rather than Bで)BよりもむしろA；BではなくてA

□ 0784
relatively
/rélətɪvli/
Part 5, 6

副 **比較的**、割合に
名relative：親戚、親類
形relative：❶ある程度の　❷(～に)関連した(to ～)

| Day 48 》CD-B13
Quick Review
答えは右ページ下 | □ 繁栄している
□ 連続する
□ 珍しい
□ 腹の立つ | □ 部分的な
□ 骨の折れる
□ 不十分な
□ 敬意を表する | □ ありそうもない
□ 明るい
□ 豊富な
□ 条件つきの | □ 退職した
□ 長続きする
□ 構造の
□ 厳しい |

Check 2 Phrase & Sentence

- ☐ He was late for work so many times, and consequently got fired. (彼は何度も仕事に遅刻した結果、首になった)

- ☐ fully recover from an illness (病気から完全に回復する)
- ☐ for fully 20 years (丸20年間)

- ☐ Eric is currently staying in Hong Kong. (エリックは現在、香港に滞在中だ)

- ☐ Three terrorist bombings occurred almost simultaneously today. (今日、3件の爆破テロがほぼ同時に起きた)

- ☐ nearly always (ほとんどいつも)
- ☐ nearly everyone (ほぼ全員)

- ☐ Unfortunately, racial discrimination still exists. (残念ながら、人種差別はいまだに存在する)

- ☐ rather hot (かなり暑い)
- ☐ want wine rather than beer (ビールよりもワインが飲みたい)

- ☐ a relatively expensive hotel (比較的高いホテル)
- ☐ relatively speaking (比較して言えば)

Check 3 Sentence

- ☐ It started to rain heavily and consequently the baseball game was called off. (雨が激しく降り始めたので、その野球の試合は中止になった)

- ☐ It seemed that he fully understood what I had said. (彼は私の言ったことを完全に理解しているようだった)

- ☐ The issue is currently under consideration. (その問題は現在のところ検討中だ)

- ☐ I can't do two things simultaneously. (私は2つのことを同時にできない)

- ☐ It's been nearly three months since she quit the job. (彼女がその仕事を辞めてからほぼ3カ月になる)

- ☐ Unfortunately, she was out when I called. (私が電話をした時、彼女はあいにく外出中だった)

- ☐ He speaks Spanish rather well. (彼はスペイン語をかなり上手に話す)

- ☐ It was relatively warm today. (今日は比較的暖かかった)

Day 48))) CD-B13
Quick Review
答えは左ページ下

- ☐ prosperous
- ☐ successive
- ☐ uncommon
- ☐ irritating
- ☐ partial
- ☐ tiring
- ☐ inadequate
- ☐ respectful
- ☐ unlikely
- ☐ rosy
- ☐ plentiful
- ☐ conditional
- ☐ retired
- ☐ lasting
- ☐ structural
- ☐ grim

Day 50　副詞2

Check 1　Listen 》CD-B15

□ 0785 definitely
/défənitli/
Part 2, 3

副 ❶(返事として)**確かに**、全くその通り　❷はっきりと、明確に
名 definition：❶定義　❷明確さ
動 define：❶〜を(…と)定義する(as . . .)　❷〜を明確にする、明らかにする
形 definite：明確な；明白な

□ 0786 therefore
/ðéərfɔ̀ːr/
Part 5, 6

副 **従って**、それ故に(≒as a result, consequently, thus)

□ 0787 regularly
/régjulərli/
Part 5, 6

副 ❶**定期的に**、規則正しく　❷いつも(≒often)
名 regular：常連、お得意
形 regular：❶通常の；普通の　❷規則的な
名 regulation：❶規則　❷規制
動 regulate：❶〜を規制する　❷〜を調節する

□ 0788 clearly
/klíərli/
Part 5, 6

副 ❶**明らかに**　❷はっきりと
動 clear：❶(clear upで)(問題など)を解決する；〜を片づける；(天気が)晴れ上がる　❷(clear A of Bで)AからBを取り除く；A(人)のB(疑いなど)を晴らす
形 clear：❶(道が)すいている　❷澄んだ　❸はっきりした

□ 0789 absolutely
/æ̀bsəlúːtli/
Part 2, 3

副 ❶**完全に**、全く(≒completely)　❷(返事として)その通り；(否定文で)絶対に
名 absolute：絶対的なもの
形 absolute：完全な；全くの

□ 0790 previously
/príːviəsli/
❶発音注意
Part 5, 6

副 **以前に**[は]
形 previous：以前の、前の

□ 0791 yet
/jét/
Part 5, 6

副 ❶(通例and yet、but yetの形で)**それにもかかわらず**、けれども　❷(否定文で)まだ　❸(疑問文で)もう

□ 0792 diligently
/dílədʒəntli/
Part 5, 6

副 **勤勉に**、こつこつと
名 diligence：(〜での)勤勉、不断の努力(in 〜)
形 diligent：(〜に)勤勉な(in [about] 〜)

continued
▼

本書も残すところあと3週間=21日！ TOEICで「800点」を突破する日も少しずつ近づいている！ この調子で頑張っていこう。

- □ 聞くだけモード　Check 1
- □ しっかりモード　Check 1 ▶ 2
- □ かんぺきモード　Check 1 ▶ 2 ▶ 3

Check 2　Phrase & Sentence

□ "Are you coming to the party tonight?" "Definitely."(「今夜、パーティーに来るよね?」「もちろんよ」)

□ I think, therefore I am.(我思う、故に我あり)✚フランスの哲学者デカルト(1596-1650)の言葉

□ attend school regularly(規則正しく学校に通う)
□ regularly occur([事故などが]よく起こる)

□ It is clearly his fault.(それは明らかに彼の責任だ)

□ She knows absolutely nothing about sports.(彼女はスポーツのことを全く何も知らない)

□ a previously read book(以前に読んだ本)
□ three months previously(3カ月前に)

□ The movie is horrifying, and yet funny.(その映画は怖いが面白い)

□ work diligently(勤勉に働く)

Check 3　Sentence

□ The prime minister definitely said that he would resign.(首相は辞職すると明言した)

□ I missed the train and therefore was late for school.(私は電車に乗り遅れたので、学校に遅刻した)

□ The doctor advised me to exercise regularly to prevent obesity.(肥満にならないために定期的に運動するようその医者は私に勧めた)

□ Can you speak a bit more clearly?(もう少しはっきり話してくれますか?)

□ "Can I go out tonight?" "Absolutely not."(「今夜、外出してもいい?」「絶対にだめよ」)

□ The country's famine is far worse than previously reported.(その国の飢饉は以前に報告されていたよりもはるかに悪化している)

□ I haven't finished the task yet.(私はその仕事をまだ終えていない)

□ He studied diligently and finally received his doctorate.(彼は勤勉に勉強し、ついに博士号を取得した)

continued
▼

Day 50

Check 1 Listen 》CD-B15

□ 0793
significantly
/sɪɡnífɪkəntli/
Part 5, 6

副 ❶**著しく** ❷(more [most] ~で)さらに[最も]重要なことに(は)
名 significance：❶重要性、重大性　❷意味、意義
形 significant：❶(~にとって)重要な、重大な(for [to] ~)　❷かなりの　❸意味のある

□ 0794
adequately
/ǽdɪkwətli/
Part 5, 6

副 **十分に**、適切に
形 adequate：❶(~のために)十分な(量の)(for ~)　❷(~に)適した(for [to] ~)

□ 0795
annually
/ǽnjuəli/
Part 4

副 **毎年**、年1度
形 annual：年1回の、毎年の、年次の；1年間の

□ 0796
collectively
/kəléktɪvli/
Part 5, 6

副 **集団[集合]的に**、団結して(≒jointly)
名 collective：共同[集合]体
形 collective：共同[共通、集団]の

□ 0797
efficiently
/ɪfíʃəntli/
Part 2, 3

副 **能率[効果]的に**
名 efficiency：効率、能率
形 efficient：❶効率[能率]的な　❷有能な

□ 0798
extensively
/ɪksténsɪvli/
Part 4

副 **広範囲に**、広く
名 extension：❶(電話の)内線　❷延期　❸拡張
動 extend：❶~を延長する　❷~を拡張する
形 extensive：❶(調査などが)広範囲にわたる　❷(損害などが)大規模な、甚だしい

□ 0799
favorably
/féɪvərəbli/
Part 5, 6

副 ❶**好意的に**　❷優位に；有利に
名 favor：❶親切な行為；恩恵　❷支持、援助
形 favorable：❶好意的な　❷(~のために/…にとって)好都合な(for ~/to …)
形 favorite：お気に入りの、大好きな

□ 0800
precisely
/prɪsáɪsli/
Part 5, 6

副 **正確に**、ちょうど(≒exactly)
名 precision：正確さ
形 precise：正確な

Day 49 》CD-B14
Quick Review
答えは右ページ下

□ おおよそ
□ 結局は
□ 即座に
□ まあまあ

□ 徐々に
□ ほとんど
□ どうやら~らしい
□ あらかじめ

□ その結果
□ 完全に
□ 現在は
□ 同時に

□ ほとんど
□ 残念ながら
□ かなり
□ 比較的

Check 2 Phrase

- increase [decrease] significantly（著しく増加［減少］する）
- perhaps most significantly（恐らく最も重要なことは）

- be adequately prepared to do ~（~する用意が十分にできている）

- an annually held event（毎年開催される行事）

- work collectively（共同で働く）

- run a business efficiently（能率的に事業を経営する）

- research the subject extensively（その問題を幅広く研究する）

- speak favorably of him（彼のことを好意的に言う）
- compare favorably with ~（~より優れている、~に引けを取らない）

- at 8 p.m. precisely（午後8時ちょうどに）

Check 3 Sentence

- Home prices have dropped significantly over the past year.（住宅価格はこの1年で著しく下落した）

- Japanese students are not adequately educated to communicate in English.（日本の生徒は英語で意志疎通する教育を十分に受けていない）

- Your salary will be reviewed annually.（あなたの給料は年に1度見直される）

- Workers have the right to bargain collectively.（労働者は団体交渉をする権利を持っている）

- The financial system is functioning efficiently.（金融システムは能率的に機能している）

- The town was extensively damaged by the earthquake.（その町は地震で広範囲にわたって被害を受けた）

- Most critics reviewed the movie favorably.（ほとんどの評論家はその映画を好意的に論評した）

- I can't remember precisely what she said to me.（私は彼女が私に言ったことを正確に思い出せない）

Day 49 》CD-B14
Quick Review
答えは左ページ下

- approximately
- eventually
- promptly
- fairly
- steadily
- practically
- apparently
- beforehand
- consequently
- fully
- currently
- simultaneously
- nearly
- unfortunately
- rather
- relatively

CHAPTER 1
CHAPTER 2
CHAPTER 3
CHAPTER 4
CHAPTER 5
CHAPTER 6
CHAPTER 7
CHAPTER 8
CHAPTER 9
CHAPTER 10

Day 51　副詞3

Check 1　Listen 》CD-B16

☐ 0801
readily
/rédəli/
Part 5, 6

副 ❶**容易に**(≒easily)；すぐに(≒quickly)　❷喜んで、快く(≒willingly)
形 ready：(be ready to do で)❶〜する用意[準備]ができている　❷喜んで[進んで]〜する

☐ 0802
increasingly
/inkríːsiŋli/
Part 5, 6

副 **ますます**、いよいよ(≒more and more)
名 increase：増加
動 increase：❶増加する　❷〜を増やす

☐ 0803
originally
/ərídʒənəli/
Part 7

副 ❶**最初は**、初めは(≒at first)　❷出身は
名 origin：❶(しばしば〜s)(〜の)起源；由来(of 〜)　❷(しばしば〜s)生まれ、血統
名 original：(the 〜)原物、原作
形 original：❶最初の　❷独創的な　❸原作の

☐ 0804
thoroughly
/θə́ːrouli/
❶発音注意
Part 5, 6

副 **徹底的に**、完全に
形 thorough：徹底的な、完全な、周到な

☐ 0805
accurately
/ǽkjurətli/
Part 5, 6

副 **正確[精密]に**
名 accuracy：正確さ、精密さ
形 accurate：❶正確な　❷精密な

☐ 0806
occasionally
/əkéiʒənəli/
Part 2, 3

副 **時々**、時折(≒at times, now and then)
名 occasion：❶(特定の)時、場合　❷(〜のための/…する)機会(for 〜/to do)　❸(特別な)出来事
動 occasion：〜を生じさせる
形 occasional：時々[時折]の

☐ 0807
primarily
/praimérəli/
Part 7

副 ❶**主に**、主として(≒mainly)　❷最初に、本来
名 prime：最盛[全盛]期
形 prime：❶最も重要な　❷最良の
形 primary：❶最も重要な；主要な　❷(学校などが)初級[初等]の

☐ 0808
nevertheless
/nèvərðəlés/
❶アクセント注意
Part 5, 6

副 **それにもかかわらず**(≒nonetheless, however)

continued
▼

今日でChapter 7は最後！ 時間に余裕があったら、章末のReviewにも挑戦しておこう。忘れてしまった単語も結構あるのでは?!

- □ 聞くだけモード　Check 1
- □ しっかりモード　Check 1 ▶ 2
- □ かんぺきモード　Check 1 ▶ 2 ▶ 3

Check 2　Phrase & Sentence

- □ readily understand the problem（その問題を容易に理解する）
- □ readily agree to do ~（~することを快く認める）

- □ become increasingly important（ますます重要になる）

- □ as originally expected（最初に期待したように）
- □ originally came from Italy（イタリアの出身である）

- □ thoroughly investigate the cause of the accident（その事故の原因を徹底的に調査する）

- □ play a piece accurately（曲を正確に演奏する）

- □ meet her occasionally（彼女に時々会う）

- □ This course is primarily for people who are seeking a career in teaching English.（このコースは英語を教える仕事を目指している人を主に対象にしている）

- □ a small but nevertheless significant change（わずかだが、それにもかかわらず重要な変化）

Check 3　Sentence

- □ An enormous amount of information is readily available on the Internet.（莫大な量の情報がインターネットで容易に手に入る）

- □ Japan's economy is increasingly dependent on China.（日本経済はますます中国に依存するようになっている）

- □ I was originally against the plan but changed my mind.（私は最初はその計画に反対だったが、考えを変えた）

- □ Wash your hands thoroughly before and after food preparation.（食事の準備の前後には手をしっかりと洗ってください）

- □ It is difficult to predict the weather accurately more than three days in advance.（3日より先の天気を正確に予測するのは難しい）

- □ Everyone makes a mistake occasionally.（誰でも時々失敗はする）

- □ He is primarily a doctor, not a writer.（彼は本来は作家ではなく医者だ）

- □ It was raining; nevertheless she went shopping.（雨が降っていたにもかかわらず、彼女は買い物に出かけた）

continued ▼

Day 51

Check 1　Listen))) CD-B16

□ 0809 finely
/fáinli/
Part 4

副 ❶細かく　❷精巧[精密]に
形 fine：❶素晴らしい　❷細かい　❸十分な　❹元気な
副 fine：立派に、見事に

□ 0810 exclusively
/iksklú:sivli/
Part 5, 6

副 専ら、全く～のみ；独占[排他]的に
名 exclusion：(～からの)除外、排除(from ～)
動 exclude：(exclude A from Bで)AをBから締め出す、排除する
形 exclusive：❶独占的な　❷排他的な　❸高級な

□ 0811 surprisingly
/sərpráiziŋli/
Part 2, 3

副 ❶驚くほど(に)　❷意外にも、驚いたことに
名 surprise：❶驚き　❷驚くべき事[物]
動 surprise：❶～を驚かす　❷(be surprised at [by]で)～に驚く　❸(be surprised to doで)～して驚く
形 surprising：驚くべき

□ 0812 frequently
/frí:kwəntli/
Part 2, 3

副 頻繁に、しばしば(≒ often, a lot)
名 frequency：❶頻度　❷頻発　❸周波数；振動数
動 frequent：～によく行く
形 frequent：たびたびの、頻繁に起こる

□ 0813 overtime
/óuvərtàim/
Part 2, 3

副 時間外に
名 ❶残業　❷残業手当

□ 0814 strictly
/stríktli/
Part 7

副 ❶厳しく　❷厳密に
形 strict：(～に対して／…に関して)厳しい、厳格な(with ～/about [on] ...)

□ 0815 furthermore
/fə́:rðərmɔ̀:r/
Part 5, 6

副 その上、さらに(≒ moreover, besides, in addition)

□ 0816 shortly
/ʃɔ́:rtli/
Part 4

副 ❶間もなく、すぐに(≒ soon)　❷少し(後、前)に
名 shortage：(～の)不足(of ～)
動 shorten：❶～を短くする　❷短くなる
形 short：❶短い　❷(be short of [on]で)～が不足している

Day 50))) CD-B15　Quick Review　答えは右ページ下

□ 確かに　□ 完全に　□ 著しく　□ 能率的に
□ 従って　□ 以前に　□ 十分に　□ 広範囲に
□ 定期的に　□ それにもかかわらず　□ 毎年　□ 好意的に
□ 明らかに　□ 勤勉に　□ 集団的に　□ 正確に

Check 2　Phrase & Sentence

- ☐ finely decorated furniture（細かく装飾を施された家具）
- ☐ a finely tuned car（よく整備された車）

- ☐ be exclusively available to ~（～のみ利用[入手]できる）

- ☐ surprisingly cheap [expensive]（驚くほど安い[高い]）
- ☐ Not surprisingly, ~.（～ということはもっともなことだ）

- ☐ frequently asked questions（よくある質問）❶FAQはこの頭文字を取ったもの

- ☐ work overtime（残業する）

- ☐ be strictly enforced（[規則などが]厳格に実施されている）
- ☐ strictly speaking（厳密に言えば）

- ☐ She is intelligent and furthermore she is very kind.（彼女は頭がいい上に、とても優しい）

- ☐ be back shortly（もうすぐ帰ってくる）
- ☐ shortly before 8 a.m.（午前8時少し前に）

Check 3　Sentence

- ☐ Finely chop the onions in a food processor.（フードプロセッサーでタマネギをみじん切りにしてください）

- ☐ This restaurant is exclusively for guests staying at our hotel.（このレストランは当ホテルの宿泊客専用だ）

- ☐ It is surprisingly warm today.（今日は驚くほど暖かい）

- ☐ My computer crashes frequently.（私のコンピューターは頻繁にクラッシュする）

- ☐ The company forced employees to work overtime without pay.（その会社は従業員たちにサービス残業するように強制した）

- ☐ The use of cellphones in the library is strictly forbidden.（図書館内での携帯電話の使用は厳しく禁止されている）

- ☐ This meal is delicious; furthermore it's good for your health.（この料理はおいしい上に、健康にいい）

- ☐ We will shortly be landing at Hong Kong International Airport.（当機は間もなく香港国際空港に着陸します）❶機内のアナウンス

Day 50 》CD-B15
Quick Review
答えは左ページ下

- ☐ definitely
- ☐ therefore
- ☐ regularly
- ☐ clearly
- ☐ absolutely
- ☐ previously
- ☐ yet
- ☐ diligently
- ☐ significantly
- ☐ adequately
- ☐ annually
- ☐ collectively
- ☐ efficiently
- ☐ extensively
- ☐ favorably
- ☐ precisely

CHAPTER 1
CHAPTER 2
CHAPTER 3
CHAPTER 4
CHAPTER 5
CHAPTER 6
CHAPTER 7
CHAPTER 8
CHAPTER 9
CHAPTER 10

Chapter 7 Review

左ページの(1)〜(18)の副詞の同意・類義語［熟語］（≒）、反意・反対語（⇔）を右ページのA〜Rから選び、カッコの中に答えを書き込もう。意味が分からないときは、見出し番号を参照して復習しておこう（答えは右ページ下）。

- [ ] (1) approximately (0769) ≒は？（　）
- [ ] (2) promptly (0771) ≒は？（　）
- [ ] (3) practically (0774) ≒は？（　）
- [ ] (4) beforehand (0776) ⇔は？（　）
- [ ] (5) consequently (0777) ≒は？（　）
- [ ] (6) fully (0778) ≒は？（　）
- [ ] (7) currently (0779) ≒は？（　）
- [ ] (8) simultaneously (0780) ≒は？（　）
- [ ] (9) collectively (0796) ≒は？（　）
- [ ] (10) precisely (0800) ≒は？（　）
- [ ] (11) readily (0801) ≒は？（　）
- [ ] (12) increasingly (0802) ≒は？（　）
- [ ] (13) originally (0803) ≒は？（　）
- [ ] (14) occasionally (0806) ≒は？（　）
- [ ] (15) primarily (0807) ≒は？（　）
- [ ] (16) frequently (0812) ≒は？（　）
- [ ] (17) furthermore (0815) ≒は？（　）
- [ ] (18) shortly (0816) ≒は？（　）

A. almost
B. at once
C. about
D. as a result
E. jointly
F. quickly
G. at times
H. afterward
I. now
J. completely
K. easily
L. more and more
M. exactly
N. at first
O. moreover
P. mainly
Q. soon
R. often

【解答】(1) C (2) F (3) A (4) H (5) D (6) J (7) I (8) B (9) E (10) M
(11) K (12) L (13) N (14) G (15) P (16) R (17) O (18) Q

CHAPTER 8
動詞句

Chapter 8からは「熟語編」が始まります。このChapterでは、動詞表現240を見ていきましょう。本書でも最も長い、まさに「胸突き八丁」のChapter。ここを乗り切れば、ゴールはすぐそこに見えてくる！

TOEIC的格言

Everything comes to him who waits.

待てば海路の日和あり。
[直訳] 待つ者にはすべてがやって来る。

Day 52 【動詞句1】「動詞＋副詞［前置詞］」型1
▶ 246
Day 53 【動詞句2】「動詞＋副詞［前置詞］」型2
▶ 250
Day 54 【動詞句3】「動詞＋副詞［前置詞］」型3
▶ 254
Day 55 【動詞句4】「動詞＋副詞［前置詞］」型4
▶ 258
Day 56 【動詞句5】「動詞＋副詞［前置詞］」型5
▶ 262
Day 57 【動詞句6】「動詞＋A＋前置詞＋B」型1
▶ 266
Day 58 【動詞句7】「動詞＋A＋前置詞＋B」型2
▶ 270
Day 59 【動詞句8】「動詞＋A＋前置詞＋B」型3
▶ 274
Day 60 【動詞句9】「動詞＋to do [doing]」型1
▶ 278
Day 61 【動詞句10】「動詞＋to do [doing]」型2
▶ 282
Day 62 【動詞句11】「動詞＋A＋to do [from doing]」型
▶ 286
Day 63 【動詞句12】「be動詞＋形容詞＋前置詞」型1
▶ 290
Day 64 【動詞句13】「be動詞＋形容詞＋前置詞」型2
▶ 294
Day 65 【動詞句14】「be動詞＋形容詞＋to do」型
▶ 298
Day 66 【動詞句15】その他
▶ 302
Chapter 8 Review
▶ 306

Day 52 動詞句1
「動詞＋副詞［前置詞］」型1

Check 1　Listen 》CD-B17

□ 0817
comply with
Part 5, 6

（規則など）**に従う**、応じる（≒ obey, follow, conform to [with], abide by）
名 compliance：法令遵守；（命令などに）従うこと（with ～）

□ 0818
account for
Part 5, 6

❶（ある割合）**を占める**　❷～（の理由・原因）を説明する
名 account：❶（銀行）口座　❷（金銭の）計算書
名 accountant：会計士
名 accounting：会計（学）、経理

□ 0819
specialize in
Part 5, 6

～を専門にする、専攻する　➕通例、大学院レベルで「専攻する」ことを表す。学部レベルで「～を専攻する」は major in
名 special：❶特別料理；特売品　❷特別番組
形 special：特別な

□ 0820
apply for
Part 2, 3

～を申し込む、～を志願する　➕apply toは「（規則などが）～に適用される」
名 application：❶（～への）申し込み（書）、申請（書）(for ～)　❷（コンピューターの）アプリケーション
名 applicant：（～への）志願者、応募者(for ～)

□ 0821
refrain from
Part 4

～を差し控える、慎む（≒ abstain from）

□ 0822
hang up
Part 4

❶**電話を切る**（⇔ hold on：電話を切らないでおく）　❷（電話）を切る

□ 0823
lean against [on]
Part 1

～に寄りかかる、もたれる
形 lean：❶細身で健康な　❷（肉が）脂肪の少ない

□ 0824
proceed with
Part 5, 6

～を続ける（≒ continue）
名 proceed：(～s)収益、売上高
名 proceeding：❶(～s)議事録　❷(～s)（法的）手続き　❸進行
名 procedure：❶手順、順序　❷（正式な）手続き

continued
▼

Chapter 8では、動詞句240をチェック。まずは、5日をかけて「動詞＋副詞[前置詞]」型の表現を見ていこう。

□ 聞くだけモード　Check 1
□ しっかりモード　Check 1 ▶ 2
□ かんぺきモード　Check 1 ▶ 2 ▶ 3

Check 2　Phrase

□ comply with the law（法律に従う）

□ account for a half [third]（半分[3分の1]を占める）
□ account for the accident（その事故の原因を説明する）

□ specialize in economics（経済学を専攻する）

□ apply for unemployment benefits（失業手当を申請する）

□ refrain from sweets（甘い物を我慢する）

□ hang up on him（彼との電話を切る）
□ hang up the phone（電話を切る）

□ lean against the wall（壁に寄りかかる）

□ proceed with one's work（仕事を続ける）

Check 3　Sentence

□ There are fines and penalties for failure to comply with the regulations.（規則に従わなかった場合は罰金と罰則がある）

□ Hispanics account for approximately 15 percent of the US population.（ラテン系アメリカ人はアメリカの人口の約15パーセントを占める）

□ The restaurant specializes in seafood.（そのレストランはシーフードを専門にしている）

□ Have you applied for the job yet?（その仕事にもう応募しましたか?）

□ Please refrain from using cellphones.（携帯電話の使用はご遠慮ください）

□ The number you have dialed is busy. Please hang up and dial again.（おかけになった電話番号は込み合っています。電話を切っておかけ直しください）❶電話の録音メッセージ

□ The bicycle is leaning against the railing.（自転車がさくに寄りかかっている）

□ The plaintiff decided not to proceed with the case.（原告は裁判を続けないことを決定した）

continued
▼

Day 52

Check 1 Listen))) CD-B17

0825
fill out [in]
Part 4
〜に必要事項を記入する

0826
cope with
Part 7
(問題など)に(うまく)対処する、〜を(うまく)処理する

0827
count on
Part 2, 3
〜に頼る、〜を当てにする、〜を期待する(≒depend on, rely on, look to, turn to)
名count：計算
形countless：数え切れない(ほどの)、無数の

0828
inquire about
Part 2, 3
(…に)〜について尋ねる、問い合わせる(of …)
名inquiry：❶(〜についての)問い合わせ、質問(about 〜) ❷(事件などの)調査(into 〜)

0829
embark on [upon]
ビジネス問題
❶(事業など)に着手する、乗り出す ❷〜に搭乗[乗船]する
名embarkation：❶乗船、搭乗；積み込み ❷(事業などへの)乗り出し、進出(on [upon] 〜)

0830
object to
Part 5, 6
〜に反対[抗議]する
名object：❶物体 ❷(〜の)対象(of 〜) ❸(〜の)目的(of 〜)
名objection：(〜に対する)反対(to [against] 〜)
名objective：(達すべき)目標、目的

0831
consent to
Part 7
〜に同意する、〜を承諾[許可]する
名consent：(〜に対する)同意、許可(to 〜)
名consensus：❶合意 ❷(意見などの)一致、コンセンサス

0832
contribute to
Part 5, 6
〜に貢献[寄与]する；〜の一因[一助]となる
名contribution：❶(〜への)貢献、寄与(to [toward] 〜) ❷(〜への)寄付(金)(to [toward] 〜)

Day 51))) CD-B16
Quick Review
答えは右ページ下

- □ 容易に
- □ ますます
- □ 最初は
- □ 徹底的に
- □ 正確に
- □ 時々
- □ 主に
- □ それにもかかわらず
- □ 細かく
- □ 専ら
- □ 驚くほど
- □ 頻繁に
- □ 時間外に
- □ 厳しく
- □ その上
- □ 間もなく

Check 2　Phrase

- ☐ **fill out** a questionnaire(アンケート用紙に記入する)

- ☐ **cope with** difficulties(難局にうまく対処する)

- ☐ **count on** others for help(他人の助けに頼る)

- ☐ **inquire about** prices(価格について尋ねる)

- ☐ **embark on** a new business(新事業に着手する)
- ☐ **embark on** a plane(飛行機に搭乗する)

- ☐ **object to** war(戦争に反対する)

- ☐ **consent to** his plan(彼の計画に同意する)

- ☐ **contribute to** the victory(勝利に貢献する)
- ☐ **contribute to** someone's death([病気などが]~の死の一因となる)

Check 3　Sentence

- ☐ Please **fill out** this form before the school year begins.(学年が始まる前に、この用紙に必要事項を記入してください)

- ☐ Many companies are struggling to **cope with** a deepening recession.(多くの企業は深刻化する景気後退に対処しようと努力している)

- ☐ You can **count on** me to work with you.(あなたと一緒に働くことを私に期待していい)

- ☐ I'm calling to **inquire about** the job opening in the newspaper ad.(新聞広告に載っていた求人についてお尋ねしたくお電話しております)

- ☐ The government is **embarking on** a major reform of education.(政府は教育の大改革に着手しようとしている)

- ☐ The opposition parties strongly **objected to** the economic measures.(野党はその経済対策に強く反対した)

- ☐ He didn't **consent to** his daughter's marriage.(彼は娘の結婚に同意しなかった)

- ☐ Japan has been **contributing to** world peace and security.(日本は世界の平和と安全に貢献してきた)

Day 51))CD-B16　Quick Review
答えは左ページ下

- ☐ readily
- ☐ increasingly
- ☐ originally
- ☐ thoroughly
- ☐ accurately
- ☐ occasionally
- ☐ primarily
- ☐ nevertheless
- ☐ finely
- ☐ exclusively
- ☐ surprisingly
- ☐ frequently
- ☐ overtime
- ☐ strictly
- ☐ furthermore
- ☐ shortly

CHAPTER 1
CHAPTER 2
CHAPTER 3
CHAPTER 4
CHAPTER 5
CHAPTER 6
CHAPTER 7
CHAPTER 8
CHAPTER 9
CHAPTER 10

Day 53 動詞句2
「動詞＋副詞［前置詞］」型2

Check 1　Listen))) CD-B18

0833
aim at
Part 5, 6

～を目指す、狙う
名aim：❶(～の)目標；目的(of ～)　❷狙い

0834
register for
Part 2, 3

～の入学[受講]手続きをする
名register：登録[記録] (簿)
名registration：登録、登記、記録
形registered：❶登録[登記]された　❷(郵便が)書留の

0835
approve of
Part 2, 3

～に賛成する
名approval：承認、賛成、認可

0836
make out
Part 4

❶(小切手など)を(…あてに)作成する、書く(to . . .)
❷(通例canを伴って)～を理解する(≒understand)

0837
respond to
Part 2, 3

❶～に応答[返答]する　❷～に反応する(≒react to)
名response：(～への)返答、応答(to ～)
名respondent：応答[回答]者

0838
file for
Part 2, 3

～を申請する、願い出る

0839
benefit from [by]
ビジネス問題

～によって利益を得る
名benefit：❶(通例～s)給付金、手当　❷利益
形beneficial：(～にとって)有益な、(～の)ためになる(to ～)

0840
compensate for
Part 5, 6

(損失など)の埋め合わせをする、～を償う、補う(≒make up for)
名compensation：❶(～に対する)補償[賠償] (金) (for ～)　❷報酬

continued
▼

「動詞＋副詞[前置詞]」型の表現は「丸ごと1つの動詞」として覚えることが大切。そのためにも「聞いて音読する」ことを忘れずに！

- ☐ 聞くだけモード　Check 1
- ☐ しっかりモード　Check 1 ▶ 2
- ☐ かんぺきモード　Check 1 ▶ 2 ▶ 3

Check 2 Phrase

☐ aim at reducing costs（経費の削減を目指す）
☐ aim at the target（標的を狙う）

☐ register for the university（その大学の入学手続きをする）

☐ approve of the plan（その計画に賛成する）

☐ make out a bill（請求書を作成する）
☐ can hardly make out what he is saying（彼の言っていることがほとんど理解できない）

☐ respond to a question（質問に答える）
☐ respond to stimuli（刺激に反応する）

☐ file for divorce（離婚を申請する）

☐ benefit from investments（投資によって利益を得る）

☐ compensate for lack of experience（経験不足を補う）

Check 3 Sentence

☐ The talks aimed at ending North Korea's nuclear weapons programs.（その会談では北朝鮮の核兵器計画を終了させることが目標とされた）

☐ Have you already registered for the workshop?（研修会の受講手続きをもうしましたか?）

☐ His parents didn't approve of his decision to quit the company.（彼の両親はその会社を辞めるという彼の決心に賛成しなかった）

☐ To donate money, please make out a check to the Red Cross.（献金するには、赤十字あてに小切手を作成してください）

☐ Nearly 100 people have responded to our job ads.（100人近い人々が私たちの求人広告に応募してきた）

☐ The company filed for bankruptcy with nearly $10 billion of debt.（その会社は100億ドル近い借金を抱えて破産を申請した）

☐ Consumers will benefit from a reduction in income tax.（消費者は所得減税によって利益を得るだろう）

☐ The construction period will be extended for another week to compensate for the lost time.（損失時間を埋め合わせるために、建設期間はもう1週間延長される予定だ）

continued
▼

Day 53

Check 1　Listen))) CD-B18

0841 qualify as [for]
ビジネス問題
〜の資格を得る、〜として適任である
名qualification：❶(〜する)資格(to do)　❷(〜の)適性、資質(for 〜)

0842 call in
Part 2, 3
❶電話で報告[通報]する　❷(医者・専門家など)を呼ぶ

0843 consist of
Part 5, 6
〜から成り立つ、構成される(≒be comprised of, be composed of, be made up of)
名consistency：❶一貫性　❷(液体などの)濃度
形consistent：❶首尾一貫した　❷堅実な、安定した　❸(be consistent withで)〜と一致[調和、両立]している

0844 succeed to
Part 5, 6
〜を継承[相続]する；〜の後任となる　⊕succeed inは「〜に成功する」
名succession：❶連続　❷(〜の)継承(to 〜)
名successor：後継[後任]者、相続者
形successive：連続する、継続的な

0845 abide by
Part 7
(規則・決定など)に従う(≒obey, follow, comply with, conform to [with])；(約束など)を忠実に守る

0846 correspond to [with]
Part 5, 6
❶〜に一致する　❷(correspond toで)〜に相当する　❸(correspond withで)〜と文通する
名correspondent：(新聞・テレビなどの)特派員；通信員
名correspondence：❶一致　❷文通、通信

0847 report to
❶定義注意
Part 7
❶〜の部下である、監督下にある　❷〜に出頭する
名report：❶報告(書)　❷報道

0848 attend to
Part 4
❶(仕事など)を処理する(≒deal with)　❷〜の世話をする(≒take care of)　❸〜に注意を払う(≒pay attention to)
名attention：❶(〜への)注意(to 〜)　❷(〜への)配慮(to 〜)

Day 52))) CD-B17　Quick Review
答えは右ページ下

- □ 〜に従う
- □ 〜を占める
- □ 〜を専門にする
- □ 〜を申し込む
- □ 〜を差し控える
- □ 電話を切る
- □ 〜に寄りかかる
- □ 〜を続ける
- □ 〜に必要事項を記入する
- □ 〜に対処する
- □ 〜に頼る
- □ 〜について尋ねる
- □ 〜に着手する
- □ 〜に反対する
- □ 〜に同意する
- □ 〜に貢献する

Check 2 Phrase

- qualify as a doctor(医師の資格を取る)

- call in to say that she will be late(彼女が遅刻することを伝えるために電話をする)
- call in a doctor(医者を呼ぶ)

- consist of 40 students([クラスなどが]40人で構成されている)

- succeed to the throne [presidency](王位[大統領職]を継承する)

- abide by the decision(決定に従う)

- correspond to [with] one's words([行動などが]発言と一致する)
- correspond with one's pen pal(ペンフレンドと文通する)

- report directly to ~(~の直属の部下である)
- report to the police(警察に出頭する)

- attend to one's work(仕事を処理する)
- attend to a patient(患者の世話をする)

Check 3 Sentence

- Practical training is compulsory to qualify as a nurse.(看護師になるには実地研修が必須だ)

- Why don't you call in sick today?(今日は病欠すると電話で伝えたらどうですか?)

- The mall consists of nearly 200 shops.(そのショッピングセンターは200近くの店から成っている)

- Robert succeeded to his father's estate.(ロバートは父親の財産を相続した)

- Every member company must abide by the code of ethics.(すべての会員企業はその倫理規定に従わなければならない)

- The defendant's statement corresponded to the facts.(被告人の供述は事実と一致していた)

- In your new post, you will report to Mr. Wright.(新しい職場では、あなたはライト氏の部下になる)

- We should attend to the problem immediately.(私たちはその問題にすぐに対処したほうがいい)

Day 52))CD-B17
Quick Review
答えは左ページ下

- comply with
- account for
- specialize in
- apply for
- refrain from
- hang up
- lean against
- proceed with
- fill out
- cope with
- count on
- inquire about
- embark on
- object to
- consent to
- contribute to

CHAPTER 1
CHAPTER 2
CHAPTER 3
CHAPTER 4
CHAPTER 5
CHAPTER 6
CHAPTER 7
CHAPTER 8
CHAPTER 9
CHAPTER 10

Day 54　動詞句3
「動詞＋副詞［前置詞］」型3

Check 1　　Listen)) CD-B19

0849 wear out
Part 5, 6
❶**擦り減る**、擦り切れる　❷～を擦り減らす、～を擦り切らす　❸～を疲れ果てさせる(≒exhaust)

0850 lay off
ビジネス問題
～を一時解雇する
名layoff：一時解雇、レイオフ

0851 recover from
Part 5, 6
～から回復する(≒get better from)
名recovery：❶(～からの)回復(from ～)　❷(～を)取り戻すこと(of ～)

0852 insist on
Part 5, 6
～を強く要求する
名insistence：強い主張、断言
形insistent：ぜひ(～)したい(on doing [that節 ～])；(要求などが)執拗な、しつこい

0853 consult with
Part 5, 6
～と話し合う、相談する
名consultation：(～との／…についての)相談、協議(with ～/on [about]…)
名consultant：(会社などの)コンサルタント、顧問

0854 keep up with
Part 5, 6
～に(遅れないで)**ついていく**　●catch up withは「～に追いつく」

0855 come down with
Part 5, 6
(風邪など)**にかかる**、(病気)で倒れる

0856 result in
Part 7
～という結果になる　●result fromは「～に起因[由来]する」
名result：❶(～の)結果(of ～)　❷(～s)成果

continued
▼

Check 2の「フレーズ」の音読をやってる？慣れてきたら、Check 3の「センテンス」にも挑戦してみよう。定着度がさらにアップするよ！

☐ 聞くだけモード　Check 1
☐ しっかりモード　Check 1 ▶ 2
☐ かんぺきモード　Check 1 ▶ 2 ▶ 3

Check 2　Phrase

☐ begin to wear out（擦り切れ始める）
☐ wear out a carpet（じゅうたんを擦り減らす）

☐ lay off employees（従業員たちを一時解雇する）

☐ recover from an illness（病気から回復する）

☐ insist on attendance at lectures（講義への出席を強く要求する）

☐ consult with a lawyer（弁護士と話し合う）

☐ keep up with current events（最近の出来事についていく）

☐ come down with a cold（風邪をひく）

☐ result in success [failure]（成功[失敗]に終わる）

Check 3　Sentence

☐ Tires wear out faster when they do not have the correct air pressure.（正しい空気圧がない場合、タイヤはより早く擦り減る）

☐ More than 500 workers were laid off following the closure of the factory.（その工場の閉鎖の後で、500人以上の労働者が解雇された）

☐ The country is recovering from its economic crisis.（その国は経済危機から立ち直ろうとしている）

☐ Shareholders insist on a high return on their investments.（株主たちは投資に対する高い利回りを強く要求する）

☐ You should consult with a healthcare professional before starting any diet.（ダイエットをする前には、医療専門家に相談したほうがいい）

☐ Keeping up with demand is our biggest challenge.（需要についていくことが我が社の最大の課題だ）

☐ Unfortunately, he has come down with the flu.（残念なことに、彼はインフルエンザにかかってしまった）

☐ The earthquake resulted in the loss of more than 6,400 lives.（その地震によって6400人以上の命が奪われた）

continued ▼

Day 54

Check 1　Listen))) CD-B19

☐ 0857
look up
Part 2, 3

(単語など)**を**(辞書などで)**調べる**(in ...)

☐ 0858
shut down
ビジネス問題

❶(工場など)**を閉鎖する**　❷(工場などが)操業[営業]を停止する

☐ 0859
turn down
Part 2, 3

❶(申し出など)**を断る**、はねつける(≒reject, refuse)
❷(ラジオなど)の音を低く[小さく]する(⇔turn up)

☐ 0860
fail in
Part 5, 6

❶**～に失敗する**(⇔succeed in)　❷(試験など)に落ちる
图failure：❶(～での)失敗(in [of] ～)　❷(～)しない[できない]こと(to do)

☐ 0861
break out
Part 5, 6

(戦争・病気などが)**勃発する**、急に発生する
图outbreak：(戦争などの)勃発、突発(of ～)

☐ 0862
look through
Part 1

(書類など)**に目を通す**、～を詳しく調べる

☐ 0863
sum up
Part 2, 3

❶**～を要約する**(≒summarize)　❷要約する

☐ 0864
conflict with
Part 5, 6

～と対立[矛盾、衝突]**する**(≒disagree with)
图conflict：❶(～との／…の間の)対立、葛藤(with ～/between ...)　❷(～／…の間の)争い(with ～/between ...)

Day 53))) CD-B18
Quick Review
答えは右ページ下

- ☐ ～を目指す
- ☐ ～の入学手続きをする
- ☐ ～に賛成する
- ☐ ～を作成する
- ☐ ～に応答する
- ☐ ～を申請する
- ☐ ～によって利益を得る
- ☐ ～の埋め合わせをする
- ☐ ～の資格を得る
- ☐ 電話で報告する
- ☐ ～から成り立つ
- ☐ ～を継承する
- ☐ ～に従う
- ☐ ～に一致する
- ☐ ～の部下である
- ☐ ～を処理する

Check 2　Phrase

- look up "capitalism" in the encyclopedia(「資本主義」を百科事典で調べる)

- shut down an airport(空港を閉鎖する)
- shut down temporarily(一時的に操業を中止する)

- turn down his offer(彼の申し出を断る)
- turn down the radio(ラジオの音を低くする)

- fail in business(事業に失敗する)
- fail in a college entrance exam(大学の入試に落ちる)

- break out all over the country([暴動などが]国中で発生する)

- look through a newspaper(新聞に目を通す)

- sum up the speech(そのスピーチを要約する)
- to sum up(要約すれば、要するに)

- conflict with public opinion(世論と対立する)

Check 3　Sentence

- If you don't know the word, why don't you look it up in the dictionary?(その言葉を知らないなら、辞書で調べたらどうですか?)

- The company announced plans to shut down three factories as a part of restructuring.(その会社はリストラの一環として3つの工場を閉鎖する計画を発表した)

- She turned down his invitation to dinner.(彼女は彼の夕食への誘いを断った)

- He failed in his attempt to break the world record.(彼は世界記録を破る試みに失敗した)

- World War I broke out in August, 1914.(第1次世界大戦は1914年の8月に勃発した)

- They are looking through the documents.(彼らは書類に目を通している)

- Can you sum up the main points in a sentence or two?(要点を1、2文でまとめてくれますか?)

- These two laws conflict with each other.(これらの2つの法律は互いに矛盾している)

Day 53))) CD-B18
Quick Review
答えは左ページ下

- aim at
- register for
- approve of
- make out

- respond to
- file for
- benefit from
- compensate for

- qualify as
- call in
- consist of
- succeed to

- abide by
- correspond to
- report to
- attend to

CHAPTER 1
CHAPTER 2
CHAPTER 3
CHAPTER 4
CHAPTER 5
CHAPTER 6
CHAPTER 7
CHAPTER 8
CHAPTER 9
CHAPTER 10

Day 55 動詞句4
「動詞＋副詞［前置詞］」型4

Check 1　Listen))) CD-B20

□ 0865
prevail over [against]
Part 5, 6

〜に勝つ、勝る（≒ win）　●prevail among [in]は「〜に普及している」
形prevailing：広く行き渡っている、一般的な
形prevalent：広く行き渡っている

□ 0866
show up
Part 2, 3

到着する、姿を現す（≒ arrive, appear）
名show：❶番組　❷見せ物、ショー　❸展示会

□ 0867
bring together
Part 4

〜を呼び集める：〜を寄せ集める

□ 0868
pay off
ビジネス問題

❶（借金など）**を完済する**　❷うまくいく、成功する（≒ succeed）

□ 0869
add to
Part 5, 6

〜を増やす（≒ increase）
名addition：❶追加　❷追加分　❸足し算
形additional：追加の

□ 0870
live up to
Part 2, 3

（期待など）**に応える**、添う

□ 0871
withdraw from
ビジネス問題

〜から退く、撤退する
名withdrawal：❶預金の引き出し　❷撤退、撤兵　❸（約束などの）撤回

□ 0872
get together
Part 2, 3

集まる、（〜と）会う（with 〜）
名get-together：親睦［懇親］会；（非公式の）会合、集まり

continued ▼

チャンツを聞いているだけでは、正しい発音はなかなか身につかない。つぶやくだけでもOKなので、必ず口を動かそう！

- ☐ 聞くだけモード　Check 1
- ☐ しっかりモード　Check 1 ▶ 2
- ☐ かんぺきモード　Check 1 ▶ 2 ▶ 3

Check 2　Phrase

☐ prevail over the enemy（敵に勝つ）

☐ show up late for work（仕事に遅刻する）

☐ bring information together（情報を集める）

☐ pay off one's debt（借金を完済する）
☐ finally pay off（やっとうまくいく）

☐ add to one's savings（貯金を増やす）
☐ add to the problem（問題を大きくする）

☐ live up to one's promise（約束を果たす）

☐ withdraw from Iraq（[軍が]イラクから撤退する）
☐ withdraw from the tournament（トーナメントを棄権する）

☐ get together annually（年に1度集まる）
☐ get together with old friends（旧友たちと会う）

Check 3　Sentence

☐ Logic should always prevail over emotion.（道理は常に感情に勝るべきだ）

☐ What time is Richard showing up?（リチャードは何時にやって来ますか？）

☐ Experts were brought together to work on the project.（そのプロジェクトに取り組むために専門家たちが集められた）

☐ I will pay off my mortgage in 20 years.（私は住宅ローンを20年で完済する予定だ）

☐ The economic stimulus plan would only add to budget deficits.（その経済刺激計画は財政赤字を増やすだけになるかもしれない）

☐ The movie lived up to my expectations.（その映画は私の期待に応えるものだった）

☐ The automaker decided to withdraw from the Japanese market.（その自動車メーカーは日本市場から撤退することを決定した）

☐ Why don't we get together for lunch sometime?（いつかお会いして昼食というのはどうですか？）

continued ▼

Day 55

Check 1　Listen))) CD-B20

☐ 0873
run short of
Part 4

〜を切らす、〜に不足する(≒run out of)
名shortage：(〜の)不足(of 〜)
形short：❶短い　❷(be short of [on]で)〜が不足している

☐ 0874
comment on
Part 5, 6

〜について論評[コメント]する
名comment：(〜についての)論評、コメント(about [on] 〜)

☐ 0875
proceed to
Part 4

〜へ進む、向かう　➕proceed withは「〜を続ける」
名proceed：(〜s)収益、売上高
名proceeding：❶(〜s)議事録　❷(〜s)(法的)手続き　❸進行
名procedure：❶手順、順序　❷(正式な)手続き

☐ 0876
coincide with
Part 5, 6

❶**〜と同時に起こる**　❷(意見などが)〜と一致する
名coincidence：(偶然の)一致

☐ 0877
look to
Part 5, 6

〜に(…を)**頼る**(for …)、〜を当てにする(≒depend on, rely on, count on, turn to)

☐ 0878
set off
Part 7

❶(〜に向けて)**出発する**(for 〜)(≒depart, set out)
❷〜を作動させる

☐ 0879
go into
Part 2, 3

❶**〜を**(詳しく)**調査[説明]する**　❷(職業など)に就く

☐ 0880
throw away
Part 2, 3

❶**〜を捨てる**(≒get rid of, throw out)　❷(機会など)をふいにする、見逃す

Day 54))) CD-B19
Quick Review
答えは右ページ下

☐ 擦り減る
☐ 〜を一時解雇する
☐ 〜から回復する
☐ 〜を強く要求する
☐ 〜と話し合う
☐ 〜についていく
☐ 〜にかかる
☐ 〜という結果になる
☐ 〜を調べる
☐ 〜を閉鎖する
☐ 〜を断る
☐ 〜に失敗する
☐ 勃発する
☐ 〜に目を通す
☐ 〜を要約する
☐ 〜と対立する

Check 2 Phrase

- run short of money(金を切らす)

- comment on the current economic situation(現在の経済状況について論評する)

- proceed to the next subject(次の議題に進む)

- happen to coincide with ~(偶然~と同時に起こる)
- coincide with his opinion(彼の意見と一致する)

- look to the UN for help(国連に支援を頼る)

- set off on foot(歩いて出発する)
- set off an alarm(警報器を鳴らす)

- go into the cause of the incident(その事故の原因を詳しく調査する)
- go into business(事業を始める)

- throw away old clothes(古着を捨てる)
- throw away the best chance(最高のチャンスを逃す)

Check 3 Sentence

- We are running short of time to complete the project.(そのプロジェクトを完了するための時間がなくなってきている)

- The president refused to comment on specifics in the report.(大統領はその報告書の詳細についてコメントするのを拒んだ)

- All passengers for flight BA104 please proceed to gate 15.(BA104便にご搭乗のお客様は15番ゲートへお進みください)●空港のアナウンス

- Unfortunately, my holiday coincided with heavy rain.(残念なことに、私の休日は豪雨と同じ日になってしまった)

- The world is looking to America to solve the economic crisis.(世界はアメリカが経済危機を解決することを期待している)

- We set off for Philadelphia the next morning.(翌朝、私たちはフィラデルフィアに向けて出発した)

- I don't want to go into details now.(今は詳しいことは話したくない)

- Why don't you throw away those old magazines of yours?(その古い雑誌は捨てたらどうですか?)

Day 54 》CD-B19
Quick Review
答えは左ページ下

- wear out
- lay off
- recover from
- insist on

- consult with
- keep up with
- come down with
- result in

- look up
- shut down
- turn down
- fail in

- break out
- look through
- sum up
- conflict with

Day 56 動詞句5
「動詞＋副詞［前置詞］」型5

Check 1　Listen 》CD-B21

☐ 0881
hold on
Part 4
→ **電話を切らないでおく**、待つ（≒hang on）（⇔hang up：電話を切る）

☐ 0882
turn out
Part 5, 6
→ ❶**〜であることが判明する**、結局は〜になる　❷（〜に）出席する、出かける（for 〜）
名turnout：❶出席者数　❷投票数；投票率

☐ 0883
come out
ビジネス問題
→ （商品が）**市場［店頭］に出る**；（本が）出版される

☐ 0884
take out
Part 2, 3
→ （保険）**をかける**、（ローン）を受ける、（免許など）を取得する

☐ 0885
hear from
Part 2, 3
→ **〜から連絡**［手紙、電話］**をもらう**　❶hear ofは「〜について伝え聞く、〜のうわさを聞く」

☐ 0886
take on
Part 2, 3
→ （仕事など）**を引き受ける**；（責任など）を負う

☐ 0887
turn to
Part 2, 3
→ **〜に**(…を)**頼る**、求める（for 〜）（≒depend on, rely on, count on, look to）

☐ 0888
get along with
Part 4
→ **〜と仲よくやっていく**

continued
▼

Quick Reviewは使ってる？ 昨日覚えた表現でも、記憶に残っているとは限らない。学習の合間に軽くチェックするだけでも効果は抜群！

- ☐ 聞くだけモード　Check 1
- ☐ しっかりモード　Check 1 ▶ 2
- ☐ かんぺきモード　Check 1 ▶ 2 ▶ 3

Check 2　Phrase

☐ hold on a minute（[電話を切らないで]しばらくの間待つ）

☐ turn out (to be) true（本当であることが判明する）
☐ turn out for the event（その行事に出かける）

☐ come out on schedule（予定通り市場に出る[出版される]）

☐ take out a life insurance policy on 〜（〜に生命保険をかける）
☐ take out a mortgage（住宅ローンを組む）

☐ hear from an old friend（旧友から連絡をもらう）

☐ take on new responsibilities（新たな責任を負う）

☐ turn to him for advice（彼にアドバイスを求める）

☐ get along with coworkers（同僚たちと仲よくやっていく）

Check 3　Sentence

☐ Please hold on while I transfer you.（おつなぎする間、電話を切らずにお待ちください）

☐ Unfortunately, his efforts turned out to be ineffective.（残念ながら、彼の努力は結局無駄になった）

☐ When will the new iPod come out?（新しいiPodが発売されるのはいつですか？）

☐ Did you take out fire insurance on your house?（自宅に火災保険はかけましたか？）

☐ Have you heard from Carol recently?（最近、キャロルから連絡はありましたか？）

☐ No one wants to take on the job.（誰もその仕事を引き受けたがらない）

☐ You can always turn to me for help.（いつでも私に助けを求めてください）

☐ Do you get along with your neighbors?（近所の人たちとはうまくいっていますか？）

continued
▼

Day 56

Check 1　Listen 》CD-B21

□ 0889
rest with
Part 5, 6

(決定などが)**〜に委ねられている**、かかっている、〜次第である

□ 0890
come by
Part 2, 3

❶**立ち寄る**　❷〜に立ち寄る　❸〜を(努力して)手に入れる(≒obtain)

□ 0891
bring in
Part 2, 3

❶**〜を(…してもらうように)参加させる**、導入する(to do)　❷(金額)を稼ぐ

□ 0892
seal off
Part 5, 6

(地域など)**を封鎖する**、立入禁止にする
名seal：❶印章、紋章　❷封印、封

□ 0893
clear up
Part 2, 3

❶(問題など)**を解決する**、解く　❷〜を片づける　❸(天気が)晴れ上がる
形clear：❶(道が)すいている　❷澄んだ　❸はっきりした
副clearly：❶明らかに　❷はっきりと

□ 0894
kneel down
Part 1

ひざをつく、ひざまずく
名knee：ひざ

□ 0895
back up
Part 4

❶(交通など)**を渋滞[停滞]させる**　❷渋滞する　❸〜のバックアップを取る　❹後退する
名backup：❶(コンピューターの)バックアップ　❷交代要員、代替物

□ 0896
substitute for
Part 5, 6

〜の代わりをする、〜の代用[代理]になる
名substitute：❶代理人　❷代用品
形substitute：代理[代用]の
名substitution：❶代理、代用　❷代理人、代用品

Day 55 》CD-B20
Quick Review
答えは右ページ下

- □ 〜に勝つ
- □ 到着する
- □ 〜を呼び集める
- □ 〜を完済する
- □ 〜を増やす
- □ 〜に応える
- □ 〜から退く
- □ 集まる
- □ 〜を切らす
- □ 〜について論評する
- □ 〜へ進む
- □ 〜と同時に起こる
- □ 〜に頼る
- □ 出発する
- □ 〜を調査する
- □ 〜を捨てる

Check 2 Phrase

- □ rest with him to decide（[itを主語にして]決定するのを彼に委ねる）

- □ come by his house（彼の家に立ち寄る）
- □ be difficult [hard] to come by（[商品などが]手に入れるのが難しい）

- □ bring in an expert to deal with the situation（事態に対処してもらうよう専門家を参加させる）

- □ seal off the area（その地域を立入禁止にする）

- □ clear up a mystery（謎を解く）
- □ clear up the kitchen（台所を片づける）

- □ kneel down on one knee（片ひざをつく）

- □ back up traffic（交通を渋滞させる）
- □ back up an important file（大切なファイルのバックアップを取る）

- □ substitute for someone's mother（～の母親代わりをする）

Check 3 Sentence

- □ The final decision rests with the governor.（最終決定は知事に委ねられている）

- □ You can come by anytime you want.（いつでもお好きな時にお立ち寄りください）

- □ More than 100 police officers were brought in to guard the event.（そのイベントを警備するために100人以上の警官が動員された）

- □ Police sealed off the airport shortly after the terrorist attack.（テロ攻撃のすぐ後に、警察はその空港を封鎖した）

- □ The murder case was cleared up in a short time.（その殺人事件は短期間で解決した）

- □ The man is kneeling down on the floor.（男性は床にひざをつけている）

- □ The traffic on Highway 82 is backed up due to an accident.（事故のため82号線は渋滞している）

- □ The understudy will substitute for the actress who is sick.（代役が病気の女優の代わりをする予定だ）

Day 55))) CD-B20
Quick Review
答えは左ページ下

- □ prevail over
- □ show up
- □ bring together
- □ pay off
- □ add to
- □ live up to
- □ withdraw from
- □ get together
- □ run short of
- □ comment on
- □ proceed to
- □ coincide with
- □ look to
- □ set off
- □ go into
- □ throw away

Day 57 動詞句6
「動詞＋A＋前置詞＋B」型1

Check 1　Listen)) CD-B22

0897
assign A to B
ビジネス問題

❶**AをB**（地位など）**に任命する**、就かせる（≒appoint A as [to] B）　❷AをBに割り当てる
名assignment：❶任務；（仕事などの）割り当て　❷宿題、研究課題

0898
impose A on B
Part 7

❶**A**（義務・税など）**をBに課す**、負わす　❷A（意見など）をBに押しつける
名imposition：❶（税・重荷などを）課すこと　❷賦課物、義務、負担
形imposing：堂々とした、印象的な

0899
furnish A with B
Part 7

❶**A**（部屋など）**にB**（家具など）**を備えつける**　❷AにBを供給する（≒provide A with B, supply A with B）
名furniture：（集合的に）家具

0900
familiarize A with B
Part 7

AをBに精通させる、慣れさせる
名familiarity：❶（～に）精通していること（with ～）　❷気安さ
形familiar：❶（be familiar withで）～に精通している　❷（be familiar toで）～によく知られている

0901
classify A as [into] B
Part 5, 6

AをBに分類する
名classification：❶分類　❷範疇
形classified：❶分類された　❷（文書などが）機密[極秘]扱いの

0902
put A through to B
Part 2, 3

Aの電話をBにつなぐ；A（電話）をBにつなぐ（≒connect A to [with] B）

0903
transform A into B
Part 5, 6

AをBに変形[変質]**させる**（≒change A into B）
名transformation：（～から／…への）変化、変形、変質（from ～/to ...）

0904
link A to [with] B
Part 7

AをBに関連させる、関連づける
名link：❶（～との／…の間の）関連、つながり、きずな（with ～／between ...）　❷（鎖の）輪
名linkage：（～との／…の間の）結合、つながり（with ～／between ...）

continued ▼

今日から3日間は、「動詞＋A＋前置詞＋B」型の表現をチェック！　まずはCDでチャンツを聞いて、表現を「耳」からインプットしよう

- ☐ 聞くだけモード　Check 1
- ☐ しっかりモード　Check 1 ▶ 2
- ☐ かんぺきモード　Check 1 ▶ 2 ▶ 3

Check 2　　Phrase

☐ assign him to the newly created post（彼を新しく作られた職に任命する）

☐ impose a fine on him（彼に罰金を課す）
☐ impose one's ideas on others（自分の考えを他人に押しつける）

☐ furnish the room with a bed（部屋にベッドを備えつける）
☐ furnish him with information（彼に情報を提供する）

☐ familiarize students with the Internet（生徒たちをインターネットに精通させる）
☐ familiarize oneself with ~（~に精通する、慣れる）

☐ classify an injury as serious（けがを重度に分類する）

☐ put a call through to the public relations（電話を広報部につなぐ）

☐ transform clay into a vase（粘土から花瓶を作る）

☐ link the rise in hurricanes to global warming（ハリケーンの増加を地球温暖化に関連づける）

Check 3　　Sentence

☐ I was assigned to the R&D department last month.（先月、私は研究開発部に配属された）

☐ The US has imposed economic sanctions on North Korea and Iran.（アメリカは北朝鮮とイランに経済制裁を課した）

☐ The house is fully furnished with brand-new furniture.（その家には新品の家具が全室備えつけられている）

☐ Cathy readily familiarized herself with the new surroundings on campus.（キャシーはすぐにキャンパスの新しい環境に慣れた）

☐ Whales are classified as mammals.（クジラは哺乳類に分類される）

☐ Could you put me through to the sales department?（販売部に電話をつないでいただけますか？）

☐ The building will be transformed into a city museum.（その建物は市立美術館に変わる予定だ）

☐ One third of all cancers can be linked to smoking.（すべてのがんの3分の1は喫煙と関連がある可能性がある）

continued
▼

Day 57

Check 1　Listen 》CD-B22

0905　charge A with B　Part 4
AをBのかどで告発する、非難する(≒accuse A of B, blame A for B)
图charge：❶料金　❷責任　❸(～に対する)告発(against ～)

0906　dedicate A to B　Part 4
A(一生など)をB(目的など)にささげる
图dedication：(～への)献身(to ～)
形dedicated：❶熱心な、ひたむきな、献身的な　❷(装置などが)ある特定の目的用の、専用の

0907　insert A in [into] B　Part 1
AをBに差し込む、挿入する
图insert：❶折り込み広告　❷挿入物
图insertion：❶挿入　❷挿入物；書き込み

0908　elect A to B　Part 5, 6
AをB(役職・地位)に選ぶ、選任する
图election：❶選挙　❷選ぶ[選ばれる]こと
图elector：選挙人、有権者
图electorate：(集合的に)選挙民、有権者
形electoral：❶選挙の　❷選挙人の

0909　identify A as B　Part 5, 6
AをBであると確認[認定]する
图identity：❶身元、正体　❷同一性、アイデンティティー
图identification：身分証明書；身元確認

0910　sue A for B　Part 2, 3
AをBで訴える、告訴する
图suit：訴訟

0911　invest A in B　ビジネス問題
A(金など)をBに投資する
图investment：(～への)投資、出資(in ～)
图investor：投資家、投資者

0912　prefer A to B　Part 2, 3
AをBより好む
图preference：❶(～に対する)好み(for ～)　❷優先
形preferable：(～より)好ましい(to ～)
副preferably：好んで、むしろ

Day 56 》CD-B21
Quick Review
答えは右ページ下

- 電話を切らないでおく
- ～であることが判明する
- 市場に出る
- ～をかける
- ～から連絡をもらう
- ～を引き受ける
- ～に頼る
- ～と仲よくやっていく
- ～に委ねられている
- 立ち寄る
- ～を参加させる
- ～を封鎖する
- ～を解決する
- ひざをつく
- ～を渋滞させる
- ～の代わりをする

Check 2 Phrase

- ☐ **charge** him **with** theft(窃盗のかどで彼を告発する)
- ☐ **charge** her **with** lying(うそを言ったと彼女を非難する)

- ☐ **dedicate** one's life **to** music(音楽に一生をささげる)

- ☐ **insert** one's card **in** an ATM(ATMにカードを入れる)

- ☐ **elect** him **to** the chair(彼を議長に選ぶ)

- ☐ **identify** the bill **as** counterfeit(その紙幣を偽物と確認する)

- ☐ **sue** the publisher **for** libel(その出版社を名誉毀損で訴える)

- ☐ **invest** $1,000 **in** stocks(1000ドルを株に投資する)

- ☐ **prefer** soccer **to** baseball(野球よりもサッカーが好きである)

Check 3 Sentence

- ☐ The suspect was **charged with** robbery.(その容疑者は強盗罪で告発された)

- ☐ She **dedicated** her life **to** helping the sick and poor.(彼女は病人や貧者の救済に一生をささげた)

- ☐ The man is **inserting** the key **in** the lock.(男性は錠に鍵を差し込んでいる)

- ☐ Mr. Obama was **elected to** the office of US President in 2008.(オバマ氏は2008年にアメリカ大統領の職に選ばれた)

- ☐ The suspect was **identified as** the former boyfriend of the victim.(容疑者は被害者のかつてのボーイフレンドだと確認された)

- ☐ My boss was **sued for** sexual harassment.(私の上司はセクハラで訴えられた)

- ☐ The company **invested** $800 million **in** constructing five overseas plants.(その会社は5つの海外工場の建設に8億ドルを投資した)

- ☐ I **prefer** chicken **to** beef.(私は牛肉よりも鶏肉のほうが好きだ)

Day 56)) CD-B21
Quick Review
答えは左ページ下

- ☐ hold on
- ☐ turn out
- ☐ come out
- ☐ take out
- ☐ hear from
- ☐ take on
- ☐ turn to
- ☐ get along with
- ☐ rest with
- ☐ come by
- ☐ bring in
- ☐ seal off
- ☐ clear up
- ☐ kneel down
- ☐ back up
- ☐ substitute for

Day 58　動詞句7
「動詞＋A＋前置詞＋B」型2

Check 1　　Listen ») CD-B23

□ 0913
focus A **on** B
Part 7

A（注意など）をBに集中させる
名 focus：❶焦点　❷（興味・注目などの）中心、焦点
形 focal：❶焦点の　❷重要な

□ 0914
select A **as** B
Part 4

AをBとして選出する
名 selection：❶品ぞろえ　❷選択、選抜　❸（〜から）選ばれた物［人］（from 〜）
形 select：えり抜きの、選ばれた

□ 0915
appropriate A **for** B
Part 5, 6

A（金など）をBのために充てる、使用する
形 appropriate：❶適切な　❷（be appropriate forで）〜に適している、ふさわしい

□ 0916
name A **after** B
Part 4

AにBの名を取って名づける
名 name：❶名前　❷評判；名声

□ 0917
associate A **with** B
Part 5, 6

AをBと結びつけて考える、AからBを連想する（≒ connect A with B）
名 associate：同僚、仲間
名 association：❶（共通の目的のための）協会、団体　❷（〜との）提携、つき合い（with 〜）

□ 0918
keep A **away from** B
Part 4

AをBから遠ざけておく、AをBに近づけない

□ 0919
load A **with** B
Part 1

A（トラックなど）にB（荷）を積む　● load A into [onto] Bは「A（荷）をB（トラックなど）に積む」
名 load：積み荷

□ 0920
show A **around** B
Part 2, 3

AにB（場所）を案内して回る、見学させる
名 show：❶番組　❷見せ物、ショー　❸展示会

continued
▼

「動詞＋A＋前置詞＋B」型の表現は、Aを主語にした受け身の文で使われることも多い。その場合の語順もしっかり押さえておこう

- ☐ 聞くだけモード　Check 1
- ☐ しっかりモード　Check 1 ▶ 2
- ☐ かんぺきモード　Check 1 ▶ 2 ▶ 3

Check 2　Phrase

☐ **focus** one's attention [mind] **on** ~（~に注意[気持ち]を集中させる）

☐ **select** him **as** a candidate（彼を候補者として選ぶ）

☐ **appropriate** funds **for** new product development（資金を新製品の開発のために充てる）

☐ **name** the baby girl Alice **after** her grandmother（祖母の名を取ってその女の赤ちゃんにアリスと名づける）

☐ **associate** hay fever **with** spring（花粉症から春を連想する）

☐ **keep** children **away from** danger（子どもたちを危険から遠ざけておく）

☐ **load** a ship **with** cargo ＝ load cargo onto a ship（船に貨物を積む）

☐ **show** tourists **around** Tokyo（観光客たちに東京を案内して回る）

Check 3　Sentence

☐ The government should **focus** its efforts **on** conservation of the environment.（政府は自然環境の保護に努力を集中するべきだ）

☐ Miss Gordon was **selected as** mayor last year.（ゴードンさんは昨年、市長に選ばれた）

☐ Approximately $500 billion is **appropriated for** defense programs annually.（毎年、約5000億ドルが防衛計画に充てられている）

☐ He was **named** Aaron **after** his grandfather.（彼は祖父の名を取ってアーロンと名づけられた）

☐ People tend to **associate** poverty **with** crime.（人々は貧困を犯罪と結びつけて考える傾向がある）

☐ Always **keep** valuables **away from** windows so burglars can't see them from outside.（強盗に外から見られないように貴重品は常に窓から遠ざけておきましょう）

☐ They are **loading** the truck **with** furniture.（彼らはトラックに家具を積んでいる）

☐ Let me **show** you **around** our factory.（当社の工場をご案内しましょう）

continued

Day 58

Check 1　Listen 》CD-B23

0921 clear A of B
Part 1

❶**A(場所)からBを取り除く**、排除する(≒clear B from A)　❷A(人)のB(疑いなど)を晴らす
形clear：❶(道が)すいている　❷澄んだ　❸はっきりした
副clearly：❶明らかに　❷はっきりと

0922 divide A by B
Part 5, 6

A(数)をB(数)で割る　➕「AにBを掛ける」はmultiply A by B、「AとBを足す」はadd A and B、「AをBから引く」はsubtract A from B
名division：❶(会社などの)部局、部門　❷(〜への)分割(into 〜)　❸割り算

0923 replace A as B
Part 5, 6

BとしてAに取って代わる、BとしてAの後任になる
名replacement：(〜の)後任[後継]者；取り換え品(for 〜)

0924 confuse A with B
Part 5, 6

AをBと間違える、混同する(≒mistake A for B)
名confusion：❶(〜についての)混乱(about [over, as to] 〜)　❷(〜との／…の間の)混同(with 〜/between …)

0925 trace A (back) to B
Part 7

A(事柄など)をBまでたどる、追跡[調査]する
名trace：❶痕跡、形跡　❷(a trace of 〜で)微量の〜、ほんのわずかの〜

0926 combine A with B
Part 5, 6

AをBと結合[合体]させる
名combine：❶企業連合、合同企業　❷コンバイン
名combination：結合、組み合わせ

0927 convince A of B
Part 2, 3

AにBを確信[納得]させる(≒persuade A of B)
名conviction：❶確信、信念　❷(犯罪に対する)有罪判決(for 〜)
形convincing：❶説得力のある　❷もっともらしい　❸(勝利などが)圧倒的な

0928 relocate A to B
ビジネス問題

AをBに移転[移動]させる；AをBに転勤させる
名relocation：移転；配置転換、転勤

Day 57 》CD-B22　Quick Review
答えは右ページ下

- □ AをBに任命する
- □ AをBに課す
- □ AにBを備えつける
- □ AをBに精通させる
- □ AをBに分類する
- □ Aの電話をBにつなぐ
- □ AをBに変形させる
- □ AをBに関連させる
- □ AをBのかどで告発する
- □ AをBにささげる
- □ AをBに差し込む
- □ AをBに選ぶ
- □ AをBであると確認する
- □ AをBで訴える
- □ AをBに投資する
- □ AをBより好む

Check 2 Phrase

- clear the table of dishes（テーブルから皿を片づける）
- be cleared of the charge of murder（殺人の容疑が晴れる）

- divide 36 by 6（36を6で割る）

- replace agriculture as the main industry（[製造業などが]主産業として農業に取って代わる）

- confuse her with her sister（彼女を彼女の姉と間違える）

- trace one's ancestry to ～（祖先を～までたどる）

- combine one's hobby with one's job（趣味と仕事を兼ねる）

- convince the jury of one's innocence（陪審員団に無罪を納得させる）
- convince oneself of ～（～を確信している）

- relocate headquarters to Tokyo（本社を東京に移転する）

Check 3 Sentence

- The man is clearing the road of snow.（男性は道の雪かきをしている）

- 20 divided by 5 is [equals] 4.（20割る5は4）

- Mr. Scott will replace Mr. Thompson as the new CEO of the company.（スコット氏はトンプソン氏に代わってその会社の新CEOになる予定だ）

- Some people confuse Iran with Iraq.（イランをイラクと間違える人もいる）

- The practice of applying fertilizer can be traced to the ancient Greeks and Romans.（肥料の使用の習慣は古代ギリシャ人とローマ人までたどることができる）

- Diet should be combined with exercise.（ダイエットは運動と組み合わされるべきだ）

- We are convinced of the importance of environmental issues.（私たちは環境問題の重要性を確信している）

- She will be relocated to Los Angeles next month.（彼女は来月、ロサンゼルスに転勤になる予定だ）

Day 57 ») CD-B22
Quick Review
答えは左ページ下

- assign A to B
- impose A on B
- furnish A with B
- familiarize A with B
- classify A as B
- put A through to B
- transform A into B
- link A to B
- charge A with B
- dedicate A to B
- insert A in B
- elect A to B
- identify A as B
- sue A for B
- invest A in B
- prefer A to B

Day 59　動詞句8
「動詞＋A＋前置詞＋B」型3

Check 1　Listen)) CD-B24

0929 trade A for B　Part 5, 6
AをB(物)と交換する(≒exchange A for B)　❶「AをB(人)と交換する」はtrade A with B
- 名trade：❶(〜との)貿易、通商(with 〜)　❷商売；(the 〜)(修飾語と共に)〜業
- 名trader：商人；貿易商

0930 assist A with [in] B　Part 5, 6
A(人)のB(仕事など)を助ける、手伝う(≒help A with B, aid A with B)
- 名assistance：援助
- 名assistant：助手、アシスタント
- 形assistant：補佐[補助]の、副〜

0931 confine A to B　Part 5, 6
❶**AをB(の範囲)に制限[限定]する**(≒limit A to B, restrict A to B)　❷AをBに閉じ込める、監禁する
- 名confinement：監禁
- 形confined：(場所が)限られた、狭い

0932 scold A for B　Part 5, 6
A(主に子ども)をBの理由でしかる、説教する(≒blame A for B, reproach A for B, rebuke A for B)

0933 connect A with B　Part 5, 6
AをBと関係づける(≒associate A with B)
- 名connection：❶(〜との／…の間の)関係、つながり(with 〜/between ...)　❷接続

0934 forgive A for B　Part 5, 6
AのB(罪など)を許す(≒excuse A for B)
- 名forgiveness：許すこと、容赦

0935 reproach A for B　Part 5, 6
AをBのことで非難する、とがめる、しかる(≒blame A for B, scold A for B, rebuke A for B)
- 名reproach：❶非難　❷非難の言葉

0936 blame A on B　Part 5, 6
AをBの責任[せい]にする：Aのことでbを非難する、責める　❶blame A on B＝blame B for A
- 名blame：(〜に対する)非難；責任(for 〜)

continued ▼

熟語がなかなか身につかないのは、表現の「幅」が長いから。そんなときこそ、繰り返しの音読が不可欠だよ！

- □ 聞くだけモード　Check 1
- □ しっかりモード　Check 1 ▶ 2
- □ かんぺきモード　Check 1 ▶ 2 ▶ 3

Check 2　Phrase

- □ trade one's old car for a new one（古い車を新車に代える）

- □ assist her with her homework（彼女の宿題を手伝う）

- □ confine one's efforts to ~（~に努力を集中する）
- □ confine him to prison（彼を投獄する）

- □ scold the student for being late（遅刻を理由にその生徒をしかる）

- □ confidential information connected with national security（国の安全保障に関連した機密情報）

- □ forgive him for his sins（彼の［道徳上の］罪を許す）

- □ have nothing to reproach oneself for（非難されることは何もない）

- □ blame the accident on her（その事故を彼女の責任にする）

Check 3　Sentence

- □ If you could trade your life for someone else's, who's life would you want?（自分の人生を誰かの人生と交換できるとしたら、誰の人生がいいですか？）

- □ The NPO assists immigrants with applications for citizenship.（そのNPOは移民たちの市民権の申請を支援している）

- □ The use of controlled drugs is confined to medical and scientific purposes.（規制薬物の使用は医療・科学目的に制限されている）

- □ She scolded her daughter for her late hours.（彼女は娘の夜更かしをしかった）

- □ There was little evidence to connect the defendant with the crime.（被告をその犯罪と関係づける証拠はほとんどなかった）

- □ Please forgive me for not having written you for a long time.（長い間お手紙を出さなくて申し訳ありません）

- □ His teacher reproached him for his behavior.（彼の先生は彼の振る舞いをとがめた）

- □ Don't blame your failures on others.（自分の失敗を他人のせいにしてはいけません）

continued
▼

Day 59

Check 1　Listen)) CD-B24

0937 relieve A of B Part 5, 6
❶**AからB(責任など)を取り除く**、軽減する　❷AをB(職)から解任[解雇]する
名relief：❶安心　❷(苦痛などの)緩和　❸救済
形relieved：(be relieved to doで)〜して安心[ほっと]している

0938 excuse A for B Part 5, 6
AのB(行為)を許す(≒forgive A for B)
名excuse：(〜に対する)言い訳、弁解(for 〜)

0939 rescue A from B Part 5, 6
AをBから救助[救出]する(≒save A from B)
名rescue：救助、救出

0940 couple A to [with] B　❶定義注意　Part 7
AをBにつなぐ、連結する(≒connect A to B, join A to B, link A to B)
名couple：❶(同種類の)2つ、2人　❷夫婦、恋人同士

0941 aim A at B Part 5, 6
AをBに向ける
名aim：❶(〜の)目標；目的(of 〜)　❷狙い

0942 guard A against B Part 5, 6
AをBから守る、保護する(≒protect A against B)
名guard：❶警備員；看守　❷見張り、監視

0943 commit A to B Part 5, 6
AをBに委託[委任]する
名commitment：❶(〜の/…するという)約束、誓約(to 〜/to do)　❷(〜への)献身(to 〜)
名commission：❶(代理業務に対する)手数料、歩合(on 〜)　❷(任務の)委任　❸(集合的に)委員会

0944 dismiss A as B Part 4
A(提案など)をBだとして退ける、忘れてしまう
名dismissal：❶(〜からの)解雇、免職(from 〜)　❷(考えなどの)放棄；(告訴などの)却下

Day 58)) CD-B23　Quick Review　答えは右ページ下

□ AをBに集中させる　□ AをBと結びつけて考える　□ AからBを取り除く　□ AをBまでたどる
□ AをBとして選出する　□ AをBから遠ざけておく　□ AをBで割る　□ AをBと結合させる
□ AをBのために充てる　□ AにBを積む　□ BとしてAに取って代わる　□ AをBに確信させる
□ AにBの名を取って名づける　□ AにBを案内して回る　□ AをBと間違える　□ AをBに移転させる

Check 2　Phrase

- relieve the patient of pain(患者から痛みを取り除く)
- be relieved of the post of governor(知事職から解任される)

- excuse her for being late for work(彼女が仕事に遅刻したことを許す)

- rescue the company from bankruptcy(その会社を倒産から救う)

- couple a video camera to a television(ビデオカメラをテレビにつなぐ)

- aim a gun at a target(銃を標的に向ける)

- guard the nation against terrorist threats(テロの脅威から国を守る)

- commit one's life to God(運命を神に託す)

- dismiss the idea as silly [ridiculous](その考えをばかげているとして退ける)

Check 3　Sentence

- They are seeking ways to relieve the company of its massive debt.(彼らは会社の巨額の負債を軽減する方法を探っている)

- We'll excuse you for what you did this time.(今回は、あなたのしたことを大目に見るつもりだ)

- The firefighter rescued a child from a burning house.(その消防士は燃え盛る家から子どもを救助した)

- The network server is coupled to a backup drive.(そのネットワークサーバーはバックアップドライブにつながっている)

- This movie is aimed at kids.(この映画は子ども向けだ)

- The government has announced plans to guard the public against bird flu.(政府は鳥インフルエンザから国民を守る計画を発表した)

- The property was committed to his care.(その財産は彼の管理に託された)

- His proposal was dismissed as unrealistic.(彼の提案は非現実的だとして退けられた)

Day 58 》CD-B23
Quick Review
答えは左ページ下

- [ ] focus A on B
- [ ] select A as B
- [ ] appropriate A for B
- [ ] name A after B
- [ ] associate A with B
- [ ] keep A away from B
- [ ] load A with B
- [ ] show A around B
- [ ] clear A of B
- [ ] divide A by B
- [ ] replace A as B
- [ ] confuse A with B
- [ ] trace A to B
- [ ] combine A with B
- [ ] convince A of B
- [ ] relocate A to B

CHAPTER 1
CHAPTER 2
CHAPTER 3
CHAPTER 4
CHAPTER 5
CHAPTER 6
CHAPTER 7
CHAPTER 8
CHAPTER 9
CHAPTER 10

Day 60　動詞句9
「動詞＋to do [doing]」型1

Check 1　Listen)) CD-B25

0945
hesitate to do
Part 4

〜するのをためらう　➕この意味では(×)hesitate doingとは言えない
图hesitation：(〜することの)ためらい、躊躇(in 〜)

0946
bother to do [doing]
Part 2, 3

(通例否定文で)**わざわざ〜する**
图bother：悩みの種、厄介(者)

0947
attempt to do
Part 2, 3

〜しようと試みる(≒try to do)　➕この意味ではattempt doingと言うのはまれ
图attempt：(〜する)試み、企て(to do [at doing])

0948
refuse to do
Part 5, 6

〜することを拒む(≒decline to do)　➕この意味では(×)refuse doingとは言えない
图refusal：(〜することの)拒絶、拒否(to do)

0949
resolve to do
Part 5, 6

〜しようと決心[決意]する(≒decide to do, determine to do)　➕この意味では(×)resolve doingとは言えない
图resolve：決心、決意
图resolution：❶決議(案)　❷(問題などの)解決(of [to] 〜)　❸(〜しようという)決意、決心(to do)

0950
tend to do
Part 7

〜しがちである、〜する傾向がある(≒be likely to do, be apt to do, be liable to do, be inclined to do)　➕この意味では(×)tend doingとは言えない
图tendency：(〜への／…する)傾向；性向(toward [to] 〜/to do)

0951
regret to do
Part 4

残念ながら〜する(≒be sorry to do)　➕regret doingは「〜したことを後悔する」
图regret：後悔
形regrettable：残念[遺憾]な
副regrettably：遺憾ながら、残念なことには

0952
strive to do
Part 5, 6

〜しようと努力する(≒try to do)　➕この意味では(×)strive doingとは言えない
图strife：争い、紛争

continued
▼

この型の表現は、Part 5, 6で頻出！ 不定詞・動名詞のどちらを使うか、もしくは、どちらも使えるかを正確に押さえておこう。

- ☐ 聞くだけモード　Check 1
- ☐ しっかりモード　Check 1 ▶ 2
- ☐ かんぺきモード　Check 1 ▶ 2 ▶ 3

Check 2　Phrase

☐ hesitate to speak to her（彼女に話しかけるのをためらう）

☐ bother to visit him（わざわざ彼を訪問する）

☐ attempt to climb the mountain（その山に登ろうと試みる）

☐ refuse to discuss the issue（その問題について話し合うのを拒む）

☐ resolve to marry him（彼と結婚しようと決心する）

☐ tend to be late（遅れがちである）
☐ tend to overheat（[車などが]よくオーバーヒートする）

☐ I regret to say [inform you, tell you] that ~．（残念ながら~ということを報告します）

☐ strive to improve one's English（英語がうまくなろうと努力する）

Check 3　Sentence

☐ Please don't hesitate to ask me if you have any other questions.（何かほかに質問がありましたら、ご遠慮なく私にお聞きください）

☐ I don't bother to cook when I'm alone.（私は1人のときは、わざわざ料理はしない）

☐ The refugees attempted to cross the border.（難民たちは国境を越えようと試みた）

☐ He refused to answer my question.（彼は私の質問に答えるのを拒んだ）

☐ She resolved to dedicate the rest of her life to charity work.（彼女は残りの人生を慈善活動にささげることを決意した）

☐ People tend to forget the past easily.（人々は過去のことを簡単に忘れる傾向がある）

☐ We regret to tell you that the product you ordered is temporarily out of stock.（残念ながら、ご注文いただいた製品は一時的に在庫切れになっています）

☐ The company has been striving to expand its business activities.（その会社は事業活動を拡大しようと努力を続けている）

continued
▼

Day 60

Check 1　Listen 》CD-B25

0953
threaten to do
Part 5, 6
▶ ❶**～するぞと脅す**、脅迫する　❷**～する恐れがある**
➕これらの意味では(×)threaten doingとは言えない
名threat：❶脅迫、脅し、脅威　❷(悪いことの)兆し、前兆、恐れ(of ～)

0954
choose to do
Part 5, 6
▶ ❶**～することを決める**(≒decide to do)　❷**～するほうを選ぶ**(≒prefer to do)　➕これらの意味では(×)choose doingとは言えない
名choice：❶(～の／…の間の)選択の自由[権利](of ～/between . . .)　❷選択

0955
claim to do
Part 5, 6
▶ **～すると主張する**　➕この意味では(×)claim doingとは言えない
名claim：❶主張　❷要求

0956
decline to do
Part 5, 6
▶ **～することを断る**(≒refuse to do)　➕この意味では(×)decline doingとは言えない
名decline：減少、低下

0957
go on to do
Part 5, 6
▶ **続けて[次に]～する**　➕go on doingは「～し続ける」

0958
pledge to do
Part 7
▶ **～することを誓う**、堅く約束する(≒promise to do, swear to do, vow to do)　➕この意味では(×)pledge doingとは言えない
名pledge：(～するという)誓約、堅い約束(to do)

0959
serve to do
Part 7
▶ **～するのに役立つ**、～する役目をする　➕この意味では(×)serve doingとは言えない
名service：❶(～への)貢献、奉仕(to ～)　❷接客、サービス
名servant：召し使い、使用人

0960
scramble to do
Part 5, 6
▶ **～しようと先を争う**　➕この意味では(×)scramble doingとは言えない
名scramble：(～しようと)先を争うこと(to do)

Day 59 》CD-B24
Quick Review
答えは右ページ下

☐ AをBと交換する　☐ AをBと関係づける　☐ AからBを取り除く　☐ AをBに向ける
☐ AのBを助ける　☐ AのBを許す　☐ AのBを許す　☐ AをBから守る
☐ AをBに制限する　☐ AをBのことで非難する　☐ AをBから救助する　☐ AをBに委託する
☐ AをBの理由でしかる　☐ AをBの責任にする　☐ AをBにつなぐ　☐ AをBだとして退ける

Check 2 Phrase

- threaten to file suit（訴訟を起こすと脅す）
- threaten to rain（[itを主語にして]雨が降る恐れがある）

- choose to resign（辞職することを決める）
- choose to stay home rather than go out（外出するより家にいるほうがいい）

- claim to know nothing（何も知らないと主張する）

- decline to comment on the plan（その計画についてコメントするのを断る）

- go on to say that ~（続けて~と言う）

- pledge to abandon one's nuclear weapons（核兵器を放棄することを約束する）

- serve to promote health and prevent disease（健康の促進と病気の予防に役立つ）

- scramble to get good seats（いい席を取ろうと先を争う）

Check 3 Sentence

- The abductors threatened to kill the hostages unless the ransom was paid.（身代金が支払われなければ人質を殺すと誘拐犯たちは脅迫した）

- She chose to run for election.（彼女は選挙に立候補することを決めた）

- The suspect claims to have no recollection of the incident.（容疑者はその事件の記憶がないと主張している）

- The US declined to join the Kyoto Protocol in 2001.（アメリカは2001年に京都議定書に参加することを断った）

- After leaving the Navy he went on to become a police officer.（海軍を退役後、次に彼は警察官になった）

- Both countries pledged to resolve their problems through bilateral negotiations.（両国は2国間交渉を通じて諸問題を解決することを誓った）

- Some economists say that economic development and growth will serve to reduce poverty.（経済の発展と成長が貧困の減少に役立つと言う経済学者もいる）

- Shoppers were scrambling to buy gifts.（買い物客たちは贈り物を買おうと先を争っていた）

Day 59))) CD-B24
Quick Review
答えは左ページ下

- trade A for B
- assist A with B
- confine A to B
- scold A for B
- connect A with B
- forgive A for B
- reproach A for B
- blame A on B
- relieve A of B
- excuse A for B
- rescue A from B
- couple A to B
- aim A at B
- guard A against B
- commit A to B
- dismiss A as B

Day 61 動詞句10
「動詞＋to do [doing]」型2

Check 1　Listen ») CD-B26

0961
bear to do [doing]
Part 5, 6

(通例canを伴い、否定・疑問文で) **〜するのを我慢する**、耐える、辛抱する(≒ stand to do [doing])

0962
deserve to do
Part 5, 6

〜する価値がある、〜するのに値する　⊕deserve doingは「〜される価値がある」

0963
mean to do
Part 2, 3

〜するつもりである、〜しようと思う(≒ intend to do)　⊕この意味では(×)mean doingとは言えない
名 meaning：❶意味　❷意義
形 meaningful：意味のある；意義のある
形 meaningless：意味のない；無益な

0964
collaborate to do
Part 5, 6

共同で〜する　⊕この意味では(×)collaborate doingとは言えない
名 collaboration：(〜との／…の間の)協力；共同制作[研究] (with 〜/between [among] ...)
名 collaborator：協力者；共同制作[研究]者

0965
determine to do
Part 5, 6

〜することを決心[決意]する(≒ decide to do, resolve to do)
名 determination：❶(〜しようという)決心(to do)　❷(物事の)決定

0966
vow to do
Part 5, 6

〜することを誓う(≒ promise to do, swear to do, pledge to do)　⊕この意味では(×)vow doingとは言えない
名 vow：(〜の／…する)誓い、誓約(of 〜/to do)

0967
endeavor to do
Part 5, 6

〜しようと努力する(≒ try to do, attempt to do)
⊕この意味では(×)endeavor doingとは言えない
名 endeavor：(〜しようとする)努力、試み(to do)

0968
pretend to do
Part 5, 6

〜するふりをする　⊕この意味では(×)pretend doingとは言えない
名 pretense：(〜という)見せかけ、ふり(that節 〜)
名 pretension：てらい、気取り

continued
▼

本書もとうとう残り10日！ マラソンに例えるなら、35キロを過ぎた辺り。ここからラストスパートをかけて、ライバルを振り切ろう！

- ☐ 聞くだけモード　Check 1
- ☐ しっかりモード　Check 1 ▶ 2
- ☐ かんぺきモード　Check 1 ▶ 2 ▶ 3

Check 2　Phrase

☐ can't bear to lose her（彼女を失うのを我慢できない）

☐ deserve to win（勝つのは当然である）

☐ mean to resign（辞職するつもりである）

☐ collaborate to write a book（共同で本を書く）

☐ determine to become a teacher（教師になることを決意する）

☐ vow to fight terror（テロと戦うことを誓う）

☐ endeavor to improve the quality of products（製品の質を向上させようと努力する）

☐ pretend not to know the truth（事実を知らないふりをする）

Check 3　Sentence

☐ I can't bear to see people suffer.（私は人々が苦しんでいるのを見るのが耐えられない）

☐ He is a man who deserves to lead this company.（彼はこの会社を率いるのにふさわしい人物だ）

☐ Sorry, I didn't mean to say that.（すみません、そんなことを言うつもりではなかったんです）

☐ The two automakers are collaborating to develop electric cars.（その2つの自動車メーカーは共同で電気自動車の開発を進めている）

☐ After long consideration, she determined to accept the job offer.（長い間考えた末、彼女はその仕事の申し出を受けることを決心した）

☐ Though John had vowed to marry Hanna, he didn't keep his promise.（ジョンはハンナと結婚することを誓ったが、彼は約束を守らなかった）

☐ The government is endeavoring to foster the IT industry.（政府はIT産業を育成しようと努力している）

☐ He pretended to be interested in her stories.（彼は彼女の話に関心があるふりをした）

continued
▼

Day 61

Check 1　Listen)) CD-B26

□ 0969
propose doing [to do]
Part 5, 6

〜しようと提案する、〜することを提案する
名proposal：❶(〜しようという)提案(to do)；(〜の)計画(for 〜)　❷結婚の申し込み、プロポーズ
名proposition：❶(〜という)説(that節 〜)；陳述　❷提案、発議

□ 0970
recall doing
Part 5, 6

〜したことを思い出す(≒ remember doing, recollect doing)　➕この意味では(×)recall to doとは言えない

□ 0971
consider doing
Part 5, 6

〜することを検討[熟慮、熟考]**する**　➕この意味では(×)consider to doとは言えない
名consideration：❶考慮、考察　❷思いやり
形considerable：(数量などが)かなりの、相当な
形considerate：思いやりがある、理解がある

□ 0972
admit doing
Part 5, 6

〜したことを認める　➕この意味では(×)admit to doとは言えない
名admission：❶(〜への)入場[入学、入社]許可(to [into] 〜)　❷入場料　❸(罪などの)自白、告白(of 〜)

□ 0973
mind doing
Part 2, 3

〜するのを嫌だと思う　➕この意味では(×)mind to doとは言えない
名mind：❶心、精神　❷知力、知性

□ 0974
quit doing
Part 2, 3

〜することをやめる(≒ stop doing)　➕この意味では(×)quit to doとは言えない

□ 0975
recommend doing
Part 4

〜することを勧める　➕この意味では(×)recommend to doとは言えない
名recommendation：❶推薦　❷推薦状　❸忠告、勧告

□ 0976
regret doing
Part 4

〜したことを後悔する、残念に思う　➕regret to doは「残念ながら〜する」
名regret：後悔
形regrettable：残念[遺憾]な
副regrettably：遺憾ながら、残念なことには

Day 60)) CD-B25
Quick Review
答えは右ページ下

- □ 〜するのをためらう
- □ わざわざ〜する
- □ 〜しようと試みる
- □ 〜することを拒む
- □ 〜しようと決心する
- □ 〜しがちである
- □ 残念ながら〜する
- □ 〜しようと努力する
- □ 〜するぞと脅す
- □ 〜することを決める
- □ 〜すると主張する
- □ 〜することを断る
- □ 続けて〜する
- □ 〜することを誓う
- □ 〜するのに役立つ
- □ 〜しようと先を争う

Check 2　Phrase

- propose going out for dinner(夕食を食べに外出しようと提案する)
- recall seeing him once(彼に1度会ったことを思い出す)
- consider buying a new laptop(新しいラップトップコンピューターを買うことを検討する)
- admit committing a crime(罪を犯したことを認める)
- Would [Do] you mind doing ~?(~していただけませんか?) ➕「~するのを嫌だと思いますか?」という原意から転じた依頼の表現
- quit talking(話すのをやめる)
- recommend consulting an expert(専門家に意見を求めることを勧める)
- regret lying to her(彼女にうそをついたことを後悔する)

Check 3　Sentence

- The chairman proposed postponing the decision until next week.(議長は決定を来週まで延期することを提案した)
- I recalled visiting the place when I was younger.(小さいころにその場所に行ったことを私は思い出した)
- The company is considering selling its mobile phone division.(その会社は携帯電話部門を売却することを検討している)
- The politician admitted taking bribes from contractors.(その政治家は建設業者からわいろを受け取ったことを認めた)
- I don't mind doing the laundry.(私は洗濯をするのは嫌いではない)
- Why don't you quit playing video games?(テレビゲームをするのをやめたらどうですか?)
- Most manufacturers recommend changing brake fluid every two years.(ほとんどのメーカーは2年おきにブレーキ液を換えることを勧めている)
- I regret not telling her I loved her.(私は彼女に愛していると言わなかったことを後悔している)

Day 60))) CD-B25
Quick Review
答えは左ページ下

- hesitate to do
- bother to do
- attempt to do
- refuse to do
- resolve to do
- tend to do
- regret to do
- strive to do
- threaten to do
- choose to do
- claim to do
- decline to do
- go on to do
- pledge to do
- serve to do
- scramble to do

Day 62　動詞句11
「動詞＋A＋to do [from doing]」型

Check 1　Listen)) CD-B27

□ 0977
authorize A **to** do
Part 2, 3

Aに〜する権限[許可]を与える
名authority：❶(〜に対する)権威、権力(over 〜)　❷(〜する)権限(to do)　❸(the 〜ies)当局
名author：❶著者　❷立案者

□ 0978
motivate A **to** do
Part 7

Aに〜する動機[刺激]を与える
名motivation：(〜に対する／…する)動機づけ、刺激(for 〜/to do)
名motive：❶(〜の)動機(for [of] 〜)　❷(芸術作品の)主題、モチーフ

□ 0979
plead with A **to** do
Part 5, 6

Aに〜してくれと訴える、Aに〜してくれるよう懇願する
名plea：❶嘆願、請願　❷(訴訟での事実の)申し立て、主張　❸弁解、口実

□ 0980
assign A **to** do
ビジネス問題

Aを〜する任務[仕事]に就かせる、Aを〜するように選任する
名assignment：❶任務；(仕事などの)割り当て　❷宿題、研究課題

□ 0981
cause A **to** do
Part 5, 6

Aに〜させる(原因となる)
名cause：❶原因　❷根拠

□ 0982
inspire A **to** do
Part 7

Aを〜する気にさせる、Aを奮起させて〜させる
名inspiration：❶(〜に対して)鼓舞[刺激]する物[人](for 〜)　❷霊感、インスピレーション

□ 0983
advise A **to** do
Part 5, 6

Aに〜するように助言[勧告]する
名advice：(〜についての)助言(on [about] 〜)
名adviser：助言者、相談役、顧問
名advisory：勧告；報告；(気象などの)注意報
形advisory：忠告[勧告]の

□ 0984
appoint A **to** do
ビジネス問題

Aに〜するよう任命する、Aを任命して〜させる
名appointment：❶(面会の)約束、(医師などの)予約　❷任命

continued
▼

今日は「動詞＋A＋to do [from doing]」型の熟語を中心にチェック！ Aを主語にした受け身の文の語順にも注意しよう。

- ☐ 聞くだけモード　Check 1
- ☐ しっかりモード　Check 1 ▶ 2
- ☐ かんぺきモード　Check 1 ▶ 2 ▶ 3

Check 2　Phrase

☐ authorize him to sign the contract（彼にその契約に署名する権限を与える）

☐ motivate employees to work harder（従業員がより熱心に働く動機を与える）

☐ plead with the kidnappers to release the hostages（誘拐犯たちに人質たちを解放するよう訴える）

☐ assign him to lead the project（彼をそのプロジェクトを指揮する任務に就かせる）

☐ cause the economy to recover from a recession（[対策などが]経済を景気後退から回復させる）

☐ inspire children to write poetry（子どもたちを詩を書く気にさせる）

☐ advise patients to exercise regularly（定期的に運動するよう患者に助言する）

☐ appoint her to do the work（彼女にその仕事をするよう任命する）

Check 3　Sentence

☐ Public schools are not authorized to provide religious instruction.（公立学校は宗教教育をする許可を与えられていない）

☐ Teachers need to motivate students to keep studying.（教師は生徒たちに勉強を続ける動機を与える必要がある）

☐ He pleaded with his wife to come back.（彼は妻に戻ってくるよう懇願した）

☐ Mr. Foster was assigned to investigate the corruption case.（フォスター氏はその汚職事件を調査する任務に就いた）

☐ The earthquake caused many buildings to collapse.（その地震が原因で多くのビルが倒壊した）

☐ The movie "Amadeus" inspired him to become a musician.（映画『アマデウス』は彼を音楽家になる気にさせた）

☐ Passengers are advised to arrive at the airport three hours before the flight departure.（乗客たちは離陸の3時間前に空港に到着するよう求められている）

☐ She was appointed to be a high school principal.（彼女は高校の校長になるよう任命された）

continued
▼

Day 62

Check 1 Listen))) CD-B27

0985 command A to do
Part 5, 6

Aに〜するよう命令する (≒ order A to do, direct A to do, instruct A to do)
图command: ❶(言語の)運用力 ❷命令 ❸指揮、統率
图commander: 指揮者、指導者、司令官

0986 direct A to do
Part 7

Aに〜するよう指示[命令、指図]する (≒ order A to do, command A to do, instruct A to do)
图direction: ❶(〜s)道案内 ❷使用法 ❸方角
图director: ❶取締役、重役 ❷(映画などの)監督
形direct: ❶真っすぐな ❷直接の

0987 require A to do
Part 5, 6

Aに〜するよう要求する、命ずる
图requirement: (〜の)必要条件、資格 (for 〜)

0988 compel A to do
Part 5, 6

Aに無理やり[強いて]〜させる (≒ force A to do)
形compulsory: 義務的な、強制的な

0989 expect A to do
Part 5, 6

Aが〜するだろうと思う、期待する
图expectation: 期待、予想
图expectancy: ❶期待、予想 ❷(寿命などの)予測[期待]値
形expectant: ❶(女性が)妊娠中の ❷期待に満ちた

0990 forbid A to do [from doing]
Part 5, 6

Aに〜することを禁じる (≒ ban A from doing, prohibit A from doing)
形forbidden: 禁じられた、禁制の

0991 deter A from doing
Part 5, 6

Aに〜するのをやめさせる、思いとどまらせる
图deterrence: 制止[抑止](物); 戦争抑止力

0992 preclude A from doing
Part 5, 6

Aが〜するのを妨げる (≒ prevent A from doing)

Day 61))) CD-B26 Quick Review 答えは右ページ下

- □ 〜するのを我慢する
- □ 〜する価値がある
- □ 〜するつもりである
- □ 共同で〜する
- □ 〜することを決心する
- □ 〜することを誓う
- □ 〜しようと努力する
- □ 〜するふりをする
- □ 〜しようと提案する
- □ 〜したことを思い出す
- □ 〜することを検討する
- □ 〜したことを認める
- □ 〜するのを嫌だと思う
- □ 〜するのをやめる
- □ 〜することを勧める
- □ 〜したことを後悔する

Check 2　Phrase

- command subordinates to achieve objectives（部下たちに目標を達成するよう命令する）

- direct him to attend the meeting（彼にその会議に出席するよう指示する）

- require guests to wear formal dress（来賓に正装するよう求める）

- compel a suspect to confess（容疑者に自白を強要する）
- feel compelled to do ～（～せざるを得ないように感じる）

- expect him to pass the exam（彼がその試験に合格するだろうと思う）

- forbid students to bring cellphones to school（生徒たちに学校へ携帯電話を持ってくることを禁じる）

- deter him from becoming an actor（彼に俳優になるのをやめさせる）

- preclude negotiations from proceeding（[諸事情などが]交渉が進むのを妨げる）

Check 3　Sentence

- The general commanded his men to surrender.（その将官は部下に降伏するよう命じた）

- The judge directed the jury to give their verdict.（その裁判官は陪審員団に評決を出すよう指示した）

- All applicants are required to send a résumé.（応募者は全員、履歴書を送付するよう求められている）

- The law compels parents to send their children to school between the ages of six and twelve.（法律により、親は子どもを6歳から12歳までの間、学校に通わせる義務がある）

- Few people expect the global economy to recover soon.（世界経済がすぐに回復するだろうと考えている人はほとんどいない）

- Her parents forbade her to see her boyfriend.（彼女の両親は彼女がボーイフレンドに会うことを禁じた）

- The global economic crisis has deterred people from spending money.（世界的な経済危機が人々にお金を使うのを思いとどまらせている）

- Bad weather precluded a welcoming ceremony from taking place.（悪天候が歓迎式典の開催の妨げとなった）

Day 61))) CD-B26
Quick Review
答えは左ページ下

- □ bear to do
- □ deserve to do
- □ mean to do
- □ collaborate to do
- □ determine to do
- □ vow to do
- □ endeavor to do
- □ pretend to do
- □ propose doing
- □ recall doing
- □ consider doing
- □ admit doing
- □ mind doing
- □ quit doing
- □ recommend doing
- □ regret doing

Day 63　動詞句12
「be動詞＋形容詞＋前置詞」型1

Check 1　Listen 》CD-B28

0993
be located in [at]
ビジネス問題

（建物などが）**〜に位置する**、ある（≒be sited in）
图location：場所、位置

0994
be parallel to [with]
Part 1

〜と並行している
图parallel：❶（〜の間の／…との）類似点（between 〜／with...）❷平行線

0995
be associated with
Part 5, 6

〜と関連[関係]している（≒be related with）
图associate：同僚、仲間
图association：❶（共通の目的のための）協会、団体　❷（〜との）提携、つき合い（with 〜）

0996
be equivalent to
Part 7

〜に相当する；〜と同等である（≒be equal to）
图equivalent：相当するもの；同等[同量]のもの

0997
be consistent with
Part 5, 6

（言行などが）**〜と一致[調和、両立]している**（⇔be inconsistent with）
图consistency：❶一貫性　❷（液体などの）濃度

0998
be entitled to
Part 5, 6

〜の資格[権利]がある

0999
be appropriate for
Part 7

〜に適している、ふさわしい（≒be suitable for, be fit for, be proper for）（⇔be inappropriate for）
動appropriate：（appropriate A for Bで）A（金など）をBのために充てる、使用する

1000
be cautious about [of]
Part 5, 6

〜に注意[用心]深い、慎重である
图caution：❶用心、注意、警戒　❷警告
動caution：❶（caution A about [against] Bで）AにBを警告する　❷（caution A to doで）Aに〜するよう忠告する
副cautiously：用心深く、慎重に

continued
▼

今日から2日間は、「be動詞＋形容詞＋前置詞」型の表現をチェック！ まずはCDでチャンツを聞いて、表現を「耳」からインプット！

- ☐ 聞くだけモード　Check 1
- ☐ しっかりモード　Check 1 ▶ 2
- ☐ かんぺきモード　Check 1 ▶ 2 ▶ 3

Check 2　Phrase

☐ be located in a suburb of Tokyo（東京の郊外にある）

☐ be parallel to the railroad（鉄道と並行している）

☐ practices associated with Christmas（クリスマスに関連した習慣）

☐ be equivalent to approximately 90 yen as of December 2008（[1ドルは]2008年12月現在、約90円に相当する）

☐ be consistent with the facts（事実と一致している）

☐ be entitled to the promotion（昇格の資格がある）

☐ be appropriate for cultivation（[土地などが]耕作に適している）

☐ be cautious about using words（言葉遣いが慎重である）

Check 3　Sentence

☐ Our headquarters is located in Chicago.（私たちの本社はシカゴにある）

☐ The road is parallel to the river.（その道は川と並行している）

☐ In many cases, lung cancer is associated with smoking.（多くの場合、肺がんは喫煙と関係している）

☐ One kilometer is equivalent to 1,000 meters or 0.62 miles.（1キロメートルは1000メートルまたは0.62マイルに相当する）

☐ Her deeds are consistent with her words.（彼女の行動は彼女の言葉と一致している）

☐ Every child is entitled to public education.（すべての子どもは公教育を受ける権利がある）

☐ This film is appropriate for children aged 12 and up.（この映画は12歳以上の子ども向けだ）

☐ You should be cautious about opening e-mail attachments from unknown senders.（不明な送信者からの電子メールの添付ファイルを開くのは注意するべきだ）

continued ▼

Day 63

Check 1　Listen))) CD-B28

1001 be **composed of**
Part 5, 6

〜から成り立っている、できている(≒consist of, be comprised of, be made up of)
名composer：作曲家
名composition：❶組み立て；構成　❷(音楽などの)作品

1002 be **concerned about** [for]
Part 5, 6

〜を心配している　⊕be concerned with [in]は「〜に関係している」
名concern：懸念；関心事

1003 be **instrumental in**
Part 7

〜に役立っている、〜の助けになっている
名instrument：❶楽器　❷器具、道具

1004 be **keen on**
Part 5, 6

〜に熱中している、〜したがっている
副keenly：激しく、鋭く

1005 be **worthy of**
Part 5, 6

〜に値する、〜を受ける価値がある
名worthy：名士、立派な人
名worth：価値、重要性
前worth：〜の価値がある
形worthless：価値のない；役立たずの

1006 be **bored with**
Part 5, 6

〜にうんざり[退屈]している
動bore：〜を(…で)退屈させる(with …)
形boring：退屈な、うんざりさせる

1007 be **concerned with** [in]
Part 5, 6

〜に関係している　⊕be concerned about [for]は「〜を心配している」
名concern：懸念；関心事

1008 be **dedicated to**
Part 5, 6

〜に専念[熱中]している
名dedication：(〜への)献身(to 〜)
形dedicated：❶熱心な、ひたむきな、献身的な　❷(装置などが)ある特定の目的用の、専用の

Day 62))) CD-B27
Quick Review
答えは右ページ下

□ Aに〜する権限を与える　□ Aに〜させる　□ Aに〜するよう命令する　□ Aが〜するだろうと思う
□ Aに〜する動機を与える　□ Aを〜する気にさせる　□ Aに〜するよう指示する　□ Aに〜することを禁じる
□ Aに〜してくれと訴える　□ Aに〜するように助言する　□ Aに〜するよう要求する　□ Aに〜するのをやめさせる
□ Aを〜する任務に就かせる　□ Aに〜するよう任命する　□ Aに無理やり〜させる　□ Aが〜するのを妨げる

Check 2 Phrase

- be composed of two hydrogen atoms and one oxygen atom（[水は]水素原子2つと酸素原子1つから成り立っている）

- be concerned about the future of the economy（景気の先行きを心配している）

- be instrumental in improving economic conditions（[政策などが]経済情勢の改善に役立っている）

- be keen on studying abroad（留学したがっている）

- a person worthy of praise（称賛に値する人物）

- be bored with school life（学校生活に退屈している）

- a book concerned with education（教育に関する本）

- be dedicated to one's work（仕事に専念している）

Check 3 Sentence

- The United States of America is composed of 50 states.（アメリカ合衆国は50の州から成り立っている）

- Many people are concerned about global warming.（多くの人が地球温暖化を心配している）

- The new traffic laws have been instrumental in reducing the number of traffic accidents.（新しい道路交通法は交通事故数の減少に役立っている）

- My father is keen on golf.（私の父はゴルフに熱中している）

- His achievements are worthy of attention.（彼の業績は注目に値する）

- She is getting bored with her job.（彼女は仕事にうんざりしてきている）

- The lecture was concerned with the phases of child growth.（その講義は子どもの成長段階に関するものだった）

- For over 20 years, he has been dedicated to improving working conditions.（20年以上にわたって彼は職場環境の改善に打ち込んでいる）

Day 62))CD-B27
Quick Review
答えは左ページ下

- authorize A to do
- motivate A to do
- plead with A to do
- assign A to do
- cause A to do
- inspire A to do
- advise A to do
- appoint A to do
- command A to do
- direct A to do
- require A to do
- compel A to do
- expect A to do
- forbid A to do
- deter A from doing
- preclude A from doing

Day 64 動詞句13
「be動詞＋形容詞＋前置詞」型2

Check 1　Listen 》CD-B29

□ 1009
be embarrassed about
Part 5, 6

〜で恥ずかしい(思いをする)
图 embarrassment: ❶当惑、困惑　❷当惑の種
動 embarrass: 〜に恥ずかしい思いをさせる
形 embarrassing: 厄介な；まごつかせるような

□ 1010
be fluent in
Part 5, 6

(言葉)を流ちょうに話せる、(言葉)に堪能である
图 fluency: (言葉の)流ちょうさ
副 fluently: 流ちょうに、すらすらと

□ 1011
be indispensable to [for]
Part 7

〜に不可欠である、絶対必要である(≒ be necessary for [to], be essential for [to], be requisite for [to])

□ 1012
be intended for
Part 5, 6

〜向けである、〜に用いられる予定である
图 intent: (〜する)意図、意志(to do)
图 intention: (〜する)意図、つもり(of doing [to do])

□ 1013
be open to
Part 7

❶(行事などが)**〜に開放されている**、〜の参加を認めている　❷(人が)(提案など)を受け入れる用意がある
图 opening: ❶(職などの)欠員、空き(for 〜)；就職口　❷開始　❸すき間、穴

□ 1014
be optimistic about
Part 5, 6

〜について楽観[楽天]的である(⇔ be pessimistic about)
图 optimism: 楽観[楽天]主義；楽観論
图 optimist: 楽天家；楽天主義者

□ 1015
be short of [on]
Part 5, 6

〜が不足している(≒ be lacking in)
图 shortage: (〜の)不足(of 〜)

□ 1016
be sited in
Part 5, 6

(建物などが)**〜に位置する**(≒ be located in)
图 site: ❶(建物などの)場所、位置；(〜の)用地(for 〜)　❷(事件などの)現場　❸(インターネットの)サイト

continued
▼

この型の表現は、be動詞を抜いた「固まり」で名詞を後ろから修飾する場合も多い。1011、1012、1024のCheck 2で確認しよう。

☐ 聞くだけモード Check 1
☐ しっかりモード Check 1 ▶ 2
☐ かんぺきモード Check 1 ▶ 2 ▶ 3

Check 2　Phrase

☐ feel embarrassed about speaking English(英語を話すのを恥ずかしく感じる)

☐ be fluent in German(ドイツ語を流ちょうに話せる)

☐ elements indispensable to success(成功に不可欠な要素)

☐ books intended for children(子ども向けの本)

☐ be open to the public(一般の人々に開放されている)
☐ be open to suggestions(提案を受け入れる用意がある)

☐ be optimistic about the future(将来について楽観的である)

☐ be short of funds(資金が不足している)

☐ be sited in the middle of the city(街の中心部にある)

Check 3　Sentence

☐ She was embarrassed about her child's behavior.(彼女は子どもの振る舞いで恥ずかしい思いをした)

☐ He is fluent in four languages.(彼は4カ国語に堪能だ)

☐ Water is indispensable to life.(水は生命に不可欠だ)

☐ This software is intended for personal use only.(このソフトウエアは個人使用のみである)

☐ The competition is open to anyone over the age of 18.(その競技会には18歳以上なら誰でも参加できる)

☐ The market was too optimistic about the prospects of the global economy.(市場は世界経済の見通しについて楽観的過ぎた)

☐ The candidate is short of political experience.(その候補者は政治経験が不足している)

☐ The company's head office is sited in Paris.(その会社の本社はパリにある)

continued
▼

Day 64

Check 1　Listen)) CD-B29

□ 1017
be unfamiliar with
Part 2, 3

〜をよく知らない、〜に精通していない(⇔ be familiar with) ⊕be unfamiliar toは「〜によく知られていない」
名familiarity：❶(〜に)精通していること(with 〜)　❷気安さ

□ 1018
be committed to
Part 5, 6

〜に専心[傾倒]している
名commitment：❶(〜の／…するという)約束、誓約(to 〜/to do)　❷(〜への)献身(to 〜)

□ 1019
be made up of
Part 5, 6

〜から成り立っている(≒ consist of, be composed of, be comprised of)
名makeup：❶化粧　❷構造、構成

□ 1020
be incapable of
Part 5, 6

〜する能力[適性、資格]がない、〜することができない(⇔ be capable of)

□ 1021
be true of
Part 4

〜についても当てはまる
名truth：真実、事実、真相
副truly：全く、本当に

□ 1022
be unaware of
Part 5, 6

〜に気づかないでいる、〜を知らない(⇔ be aware of)

□ 1023
be alarmed by [at, over]
Part 5, 6

〜に驚いている、不安を感じている
名alarm：❶心配、不安　❷警報器[装置]　❸目覚まし時計

□ 1024
be typical of
Part 5, 6

〜に特有である(≒ be unique to, be characteristic of, be peculiar to, be proper to)
名type：❶型　❷典型　❸(集合的に)活字
副typically：❶概して　❷典型的に

Day 63)) CD-B28
Quick Review
答えは右ページ下

- □ 〜に位置する
- □ 〜と並行している
- □ 〜と関連している
- □ 〜に相当する
- □ 〜と一致している
- □ 〜の資格がある
- □ 〜に適している
- □ 〜に注意深い
- □ 〜から成り立っている
- □ 〜を心配している
- □ 〜に役立っている
- □ 〜に熱中している
- □ 〜に値する
- □ 〜にうんざりしている
- □ 〜に関係している
- □ 〜に専念している

Check 2 Phrase

- ☐ be **unfamiliar with** the area (その地域をよく知らない)

- ☐ be **committed to** volunteer work (ボランティア活動に専心している)

- ☐ be **made up of** 12 months ([1年は]12カ月から成る)

- ☐ be **incapable of** the job (その仕事をする能力がない)

- ☐ The same is **true of** 〜. (同じことは〜についても当てはまる)

- ☐ be **unaware of** the danger (危険に気づいていない)

- ☐ be **alarmed by** rising unemployment (増加する失業者数に不安を感じている)

- ☐ customs **typical of** the region (その地域に特有の習慣)

Check 3 Sentence

- ☐ This course is intended for those **unfamiliar with** the use of computers. (このコースはコンピューターの使い方に慣れていない人向けだ)

- ☐ The organization is **committed to** solving environmental problems. (その組織は環境問題の解決に打ち込んでいる)

- ☐ The EU is **made up of** 27 countries. (EUは27カ国で構成されている)

- ☐ The current government seems **incapable of** handling the economic crisis. (現在の政府は経済危機に対処できないように思われる)

- ☐ Japan is aging rapidly and this is **true of** many other industrialized countries. (日本は急速に高齢化しているが、このことはほかの多くの工業国についても当てはまる)

- ☐ Most shareholders were **unaware of** the company's financial difficulties. (ほとんどの株主はその会社の財政難に気がついていなかった)

- ☐ He was **alarmed by** the sound of a bomb exploding nearby. (彼は近くで爆弾が爆発する音に驚いた)

- ☐ The painting is **typical of** Picasso's later work. (その絵はピカソの晩年の作品の特徴を示している)

Day 63))) CD-B28
Quick Review
答えは左ページ下

- ☐ be located in
- ☐ be parallel to
- ☐ be associated with
- ☐ be equivalent to
- ☐ be consistent with
- ☐ be entitled to
- ☐ be appropriate for
- ☐ be cautious about
- ☐ be composed of
- ☐ be concerned about
- ☐ be instrumental in
- ☐ be keen on
- ☐ be worthy of
- ☐ be bored with
- ☐ be concerned with
- ☐ be dedicated to

Day 65　動詞句14
「be動詞＋形容詞＋to do」型

Check 1　Listen)) CD-B30

□ 1025
be eligible to do
Part 7

〜する資格がある
名 eligibility：適格、適任

□ 1026
be reluctant to do
Part 5, 6

〜したくない、〜することに気が進まない（≒ be unwilling to do）
副 reluctantly：嫌々ながら、渋々

□ 1027
be liable to do
Part 5, 6

❶**〜しがちである**、〜しやすい（≒ be likely to do, be apt to do, be inclined to do, tend to do）　❷〜すべき法的責任がある
名 liability：❶（〜に対する）法的責任（for 〜）　❷（〜ies）負債、債務

□ 1028
be inclined to do
Part 5, 6

❶**〜したいと思っている**（≒ want to do）　❷〜しがちである（≒ be likely to do, be apt to do, be liable to do, tend to do）
名 incline：傾斜（面）

□ 1029
be apt to do
Part 5, 6

〜しがちである、〜する傾向がある（≒ be likely to do, be liable to do, be inclined to do, tend to do）

□ 1030
be determined to do
Part 5, 6

〜することを決意[決心]している
名 determination：❶（〜しようという）決心（to do）　❷（物事の）決定

□ 1031
be entitled to do
Part 5, 6

〜する資格[権利]がある
名 entitlement：（受給）資格[権利]

□ 1032
be unwilling to do
Part 5, 6

〜する気がしない（≒ be reluctant to do）（⇔ be willing to do）
副 unwillingly：嫌々ながら、渋々

continued
▼

Quick Reviewは使ってる？ 昨日覚えた表現でも、記憶に残っているとは限らない。学習の合間に軽くチェックするだけでも効果は抜群！

- □ 聞くだけモード　Check 1
- □ しっかりモード　Check 1 ▶ 2
- □ かんぺきモード　Check 1 ▶ 2 ▶ 3

Check 2　Phrase

- □ be eligible to teach mathematics（数学を教える資格がある）

- □ be reluctant to go to work（仕事に行きたくない）

- □ be liable to get angry（怒りっぽい）
- □ be liable to pay the debt（その借金を支払う法的責任がある）

- □ be inclined to go to college（大学へ行きたいと思っている）
- □ be inclined to be lazy（怠けがちである）

- □ be apt to forget（忘れっぽい）

- □ be determined to resign（辞職することを決意している）

- □ be entitled to vote（投票する資格がある）

- □ be unwilling to study（勉強する気がしない）

Check 3　Sentence

- □ In Japan, people 20 years and older are eligible to vote.（日本では、20歳以上の人に選挙権がある）

- □ Lately foreign investors have been reluctant to invest in the US.（最近では、海外投資家はアメリカに投資するのを渋っている）

- □ People are liable to repeat the same mistakes.（人々は同じ間違いを繰り返しがちだ）

- □ I'm not inclined to agree with him on this point.（この点に関しては、私は彼に賛成する気になれない）

- □ Children are apt to imitate the attitudes of their parents.（子どもは親の態度をまねる傾向がある）

- □ He is determined to become a lawyer.（彼は弁護士になることを決意している）

- □ Employees are entitled to receive at least the minimum wage.（従業員は少なくとも最低賃金をもらう権利がある）

- □ The government seems unwilling to address the issue of pensions.（政府は年金問題に取り組む気がないようだ）

continued
▼

Day 65

Check 1　Listen))) CD-B30

□ 1033
be **unlikely** to do
Part 2, 3

～しそうもない（⇔ be likely to do）
前 unlike：❶～と違って　❷～らしくない

□ 1034
be **honored** to do
Part 4

～することを光栄に思う
名 honor：❶光栄　❷名誉　❸尊敬
形 honorable：❶立派な、尊敬すべき　❷名誉ある　❸(the H～)閣下

□ 1035
be **obliged** to do
Part 5, 6

～せざるを得ない、～しなければならない
名 obligation：(～に対する／…する)義務、責任(to ～/to do)
形 obligatory：(～にとって)義務[強制]的な(for [on] ～)；必須の

□ 1036
be **projected** to do
Part 7

～すると予測されている
名 project：❶(～する)計画(to do)　❷(大規模な)事業、プロジェクト
名 projection：(将来の)予測、見積もり

□ 1037
be **set** to do
Part 4

～する準備[用意]ができている（≒ be ready to do）

□ 1038
be **welcome** to do
Part 4

自由に～してよい
名 welcome：歓迎、歓待
動 welcome：～を歓迎する
間 welcome：ようこそ、いらっしゃい

□ 1039
be **licensed** to do
ビジネス問題

～する認可[許可]を与えられている
名 license：免許証、認可証

□ 1040
be **poised** to do
Part 5, 6

～する覚悟[用意]ができている（≒ be ready to do, be prepared to do, be willing to do）
名 poise：❶落ち着き、冷静　❷身のこなし、姿勢

Day 64))) CD-B29
Quick Review
答えは右ページ下

- □ ～で恥ずかしい
- □ ～を流ちょうに話せる
- □ ～に不可欠である
- □ ～向けである
- □ ～に解放されている
- □ ～について楽観的である
- □ ～が不足している
- □ ～に位置する
- □ ～をよく知らない
- □ ～に専心している
- □ ～から成り立っている
- □ ～する能力がない
- □ ～についても当てはまる
- □ ～に気づかないでいる
- □ ～に驚いている
- □ ～に特有である

Check 2　Phrase

- be unlikely to rain（[itを主語にして]雨は降りそうもない）

- be honored to meet the president（大統領に会えることを光栄に思う）

- be obliged to apologize（謝罪せざるを得ない）

- be projected to rise [drop] 10 percent next year（[収益などが]来年10パーセント上がる[下がる]と予測されている）

- be set to take off（離陸する準備ができている）

- be welcome to express one's opinion（自由に意見を言ってよい）

- be licensed to carry a gun（銃を携行する認可を与えられている）

- be poised to start（出発する用意ができている）

Check 3　Sentence

- The current economic environment is unlikely to improve soon.（現在の経済環境はすぐには改善しそうもない）

- I'm honored to have all of you here today.（皆さんに今日、ここにお集まりいただいたことを光栄に思います）❶スピーチなどの冒頭での決まり文句

- The candidate was obliged to admit defeat in the election.（その候補者は選挙での敗北を認めざるを得なかった）

- The country's economy is projected to grow about 5 percent this year.（その国の経済は今年、5パーセントほど成長すると予測されている）

- The plant is set to start production next month.（その工場は来月から生産を開始する準備ができている）

- If you have any questions, you are welcome to ask me.（何か質問がありましたら、自由に私に質問してください）

- The shop is licensed to sell alcohol.（その店はアルコール飲料を売る認可を与えられている）

- He is poised to take over the family business.（彼は家業を継ぐ覚悟ができている）

Day 64 》CD-B29
Quick Review
答えは左ページ下

- be embarrassed about
- be fluent in
- be indispensable to
- be intended for
- be open to
- be optimistic about
- be short of
- be sited in
- be unfamiliar with
- be committed to
- be made up of
- be incapable of
- be true of
- be unaware of
- be alarmed by
- be typical of

Day 66　動詞句15
その他

Check 1　Listen 》CD-B31

1041 take effect
Part 4

❶(法律などが)**実施される**、発効する　❷効果を生じる、(薬などが)効く
- 名 effect：❶影響；(原因に対する)結果　❷(〜に対する)効果(on [upon] 〜)　❸(〜s)個人資産、身の回り品

1042 make it
Part 2, 3

❶(〜に)**到着する**、間に合う(to 〜)　❷(〜に)成功する(in 〜)(≒ succeed)

1043 get [go] nowhere
Part 5, 6

成功しない、何にもならない、徒労に終わる(⇔ get somewhere：成功[進展]する)

1044 take steps [measures]
Part 5, 6

(〜するための)**処置**[措置、対策]**を取る**(to do)
- 名 step/measure：処置

1045 make one's way
Part 5, 6

❶(苦労して)**進む**　❷出世[昇進]する、繁盛する

1046 make sure
Part 2, 3

必ず[確実に]**〜する**(to do [that節 〜])；〜を確かめる(that節 〜)

1047 have trouble doing
Part 5, 6

〜するのに苦労する
- 名 trouble：困難

1048 have yet to do
Part 5, 6

まだ〜していない、これから〜しなければならない

continued
▼

今日でChapter 8は最後！ 時間に余裕があったら、章末のReviewにも挑戦しておこう。忘れてしまった表現も結構あるのでは?!

- □ 聞くだけモード　Check 1
- □ しっかりモード　Check 1 ▶ 2
- □ かんぺきモード　Check 1 ▶ 2 ▶ 3

Check 2　　Phrase

- □ take effect immediately（すぐに実施される）
- □ wait a few minutes for the drug to take effect（薬が効くのを数分待つ）

- □ make it to the meeting（会議に間に合う）
- □ make it in business（事業に成功する）

- □ get nowhere fast（何の進展もない）
- □ get nowhere with this case（この事件に関して何の進展もない）

- □ take appropriate steps（適切な処置を取る）

- □ make one's way through the dark（暗がりの中を進む）
- □ make one's way in the world（立身出世する）

- □ make sure to lock the door（必ずドアに鍵をかける）

- □ have no [little] trouble doing ~（~するのに苦労しない[ほとんど苦労しない]）

- □ have yet to finish one's homework（まだ宿題を終えていない）

Check 3　　Sentence

- □ The new law will take effect next year.（その新法は来年実施される予定だ）

- □ I couldn't make it to class in time for the exam.（私は試験に遅れずに教室に到着できなかった）

- □ A few years of peace talks got nowhere.（数年間にわたる和平交渉は失敗に終わった）

- □ The government should take additional steps to prevent terrorism.（政府はテロを防止するためにさらなる対策を取るべきだ）

- □ She made her way through the crowd to the store entrance.（彼女は人込みをぬって店の入り口へ進んだ）

- □ Please make sure that your seat belts are securely fastened.（シートベルトがしっかりと締まっているかお確かめください）❶機内のアナウンス

- □ I often have trouble making myself understood in English.（私は自分の考えを英語で人に理解してもらうのによく苦労する）

- □ The city council has yet to make a decision on the issue.（市議会はその問題についてまだ決定を下していない）

continued ▼

Day 66

Check 1　Listen))) CD-B31

□ 1049
put A to use
Part 2, 3

Aを使う、利用する
名use：使うこと、使用

□ 1050
think [speak] highly of
Part 2, 3

〜を高く評価する
副highly：非常に、大いに

□ 1051
acquaint oneself with
Part 7

〜に精通する、慣れる
名acquaintance：知人、知り合い

□ 1052
distance oneself from
Part 5, 6

〜から距離を置く：〜にかかわらない
動distance：〜を遠ざける

□ 1053
have access to
Part 2, 3

〜を入手[利用]できる、〜に接近[面会]できる
名access：入手[利用]する権利[機会]

□ 1054
make the most of
Part 2, 3

〜を最大限に利用する　●通例「(有利な条件)を最大限に利用する」を表す。「(不利な条件)を最大限に利用する」はmake the best of

□ 1055
set one's heart on
Part 5, 6

〜を熱望[切望]する：(〜すること)に心を決める(doing)

□ 1056
take credit for
Part 4

〜の功績を認められる、〜を自分の手柄にする
名credit：功績

Day 65))) CD-B30
Quick Review
答えは右ページ下

- □ 〜する資格がある
- □ 〜したくない
- □ 〜しがちである
- □ 〜したいと思っている
- □ 〜しがちである
- □ 〜することを決意している
- □ 〜する資格がある
- □ 〜する気がしない
- □ 〜しそうもない
- □ 〜することを光栄に思う
- □ 〜せざるを得ない
- □ 〜すると予測されている
- □ 〜する準備ができている
- □ 自由に〜してよい
- □ 〜する認可を与えられている
- □ 〜する覚悟ができている

Check 2　Phrase

- [ ] put one's knowledge to good use（自分の知識を十分に利用する）

- [ ] think highly of her abilities（彼女の能力を高く評価する）

- [ ] acquaint oneself with ancient history（古代史に精通する）

- [ ] distance oneself from the controversy（その論争にかかわらない）

- [ ] have access to classified documents（機密文書を入手できる）

- [ ] make the most of one's talent（才能を最大限に利用する）

- [ ] set one's heart on a new car（新車を欲しがる）

- [ ] take credit for the success of the project（そのプロジェクトの成功の功績を認められる）

Check 3　Sentence

- [ ] I think I can put some of your ideas to use.（あなたのアイデアのいくつかは使えると思う）

- [ ] Many critics think highly of the movie.（多くの評論家がその映画を高く評価している）

- [ ] You need to acquaint yourself with your new place of work.（あなたは新しい職場に慣れる必要がある）

- [ ] The politician has distanced himself from the party's conservatives.（その政治家は党の保守派たちから距離を置いている）

- [ ] We have access to huge amounts of information on the Internet.（私たちはインターネット上で膨大な量の情報を入手できる）

- [ ] You must make the most of your time to achieve results.（成果を上げるために、あなたは時間を最大限に利用しなければならない）

- [ ] He has set his heart on going to medical school.（彼は医学部に行くことを決心している）

- [ ] If the economy improves, the president will take credit for it.（経済が改善したら、それは大統領の功績になるだろう）

Day 65))) CD-B30
Quick Review
答えは左ページ下

- [ ] be eligible to do
- [ ] be reluctant to do
- [ ] be liable to do
- [ ] be inclined to do
- [ ] be apt to do
- [ ] be determined to do
- [ ] be entitled to do
- [ ] be unwilling to do
- [ ] be unlikely to do
- [ ] be honored to do
- [ ] be obliged to do
- [ ] be projected to do
- [ ] be set to do
- [ ] be welcome to do
- [ ] be licensed to do
- [ ] be poised to do

Chapter 8 Review

左ページの(1)～(20)の熟語の同意熟語・類義熟語（または同意語・類義語）（≒）、反意熟語・反対熟語（または反意語・反対語）（⇔）を右ページのA～Tから選び、カッコの中に答えを書き込もう。意味が分からないときは、見出し番号を参照して復習しておこう（答えは右ページ下）。

- □ (1) comply with (0817) ≒は？（　　）
- □ (2) compensate for (0840) ≒は？（　　）
- □ (3) turn down (0859) ≒は？（　　）
- □ (4) fail in (0860) ⇔は？（　　）
- □ (5) add to (0869) ≒は？（　　）
- □ (6) look to (0877) ≒は？（　　）
- □ (7) hold on (0881) ⇔は？（　　）
- □ (8) assign A to B (0897) ≒は？（　　）
- □ (9) charge A with B (0905) ≒は？（　　）
- □ (10) confuse A with B (0924) ≒は？（　　）
- □ (11) forgive A for B (0934) ≒は？（　　）
- □ (12) refuse to do (0948) ≒は？（　　）
- □ (13) pledge to do (0958) ≒は？（　　）
- □ (14) mean to do (0963) ≒は？（　　）
- □ (15) command A to do (0985) ≒は？（　　）
- □ (16) be appropriate for (0999) ≒は？（　　）
- □ (17) be made up of (1019) ≒は？（　　）
- □ (18) be reluctant to do (1026) ≒は？（　　）
- □ (19) be inclined to do (1028) ≒は？（　　）
- □ (20) be poised to do (1040) ≒は？（　　）

A. succeed in
B. be unwilling to do
C. reject
D. promise to do
E. mistake A for B
F. increase
G. be suitable for
H. appoint A as B
I. excuse A for B
J. obey
K. intend to do
L. depend on
M. be ready to do
N. accuse A of B
O. order A to do
P. make up for
Q. decline to do
R. want to do
S. hang up
T. consist of

【解答】 (1) J (2) P (3) C (4) A (5) F (6) L (7) S (8) H (9) N (10) E
(11) I (12) Q (13) D (14) K (15) O (16) G (17) T (18) B (19) R (20) M

CHAPTER 9
形容詞句・副詞句

Chapter 9では、数語で1つの形容詞・副詞の働きをする熟語をチェック。どれも「固まり」で覚えるのがポイントです。本書も残りわずか4日。ゴールを目指してラストスパートをかけましょう！

Day 67【形容詞句・副詞句1】
▶ 310
Day 68【形容詞句・副詞句2】
▶ 314
Day 69【形容詞句・副詞句3】
▶ 318
Chapter 9 Review
▶ 322

TOEIC的格言

Heaven helps those who help themselves.

天は自ら助くる者を助く。

Day 67　形容詞句・副詞句1

Check 1　Listen))) CD-B32

☐ 1057
in bulk
ビジネス問題

大量に、大口で
名 bulk：大きいこと

☐ 1058
in one's opinion
Part 2, 3

(人)**の考え**[意見]**では**
名 opinion：考え、意見

☐ 1059
in order
Part 2, 3

❶**順番に**　❷整然と　❸調子よく(⇔out of order)　❹適切な、ふさわしい
名 order：順番；整頓；調子

☐ 1060
in person
Part 4

(代理でなく)**自分で**、自ら(≒personally)

☐ 1061
in return
Part 5, 6

(〜の)**お返しに**、返事[返礼]として、代わりに(for 〜)
名 return：返すこと

☐ 1062
in stock
ビジネス問題

在庫があって、仕入れて(⇔out of stock：品切れで)
名 stock：在庫品

☐ 1063
in vain
Part 5, 6

無駄に、空しく(≒vainly)
形 vain：無駄な

☐ 1064
in force
Part 4

❶(法律などが)**有効で**、効力のある、実施中で　❷大挙して
名 force：(法律などの)効力

continued
▼

Chapter 9では、3日をかけて形容詞句・副詞句48をチェック。まずはCDでチャンツを聞いて、表現を「耳」からインプットしよう。

- □ 聞くだけモード　Check 1
- □ しっかりモード　Check 1 ▶ 2
- □ かんぺきモード　Check 1 ▶ 2 ▶ 3

Check 2　Phrase

□ order [buy] in bulk（大量に注文する[買う]）

□ in my poor opinion（卑見では）

□ in chronological order（年代順に）
□ put one's thoughts in order（考えをまとめる）

□ apply in person（自分で申し込む）

□ demand nothing in return（お返しに何も要求しない）

□ goods in stock（在庫品）

□ end up in vain（無駄に終わる）

□ be no longer in force（［法律などが］もはや効力を失っている）
□ show up in force（大挙して現れる）

Check 3　Sentence

□ The company buys products in bulk from manufacturers and distributes them to retailers.（その会社はメーカーから製品を大量に買い、小売業者に配給している）

□ In his opinion, the project could not be completed by the end of the year.（彼の考えでは、そのプロジェクトは年末までに終わらないかもしれない）

□ The names of students are listed in alphabetical order.（生徒たちの名前はアルファベット順に記載されている）

□ You have to go to the bank in person to open the account.（口座を開くには自分で銀行に行かなければならない）

□ The defendant is asking for a lighter sentence in return for his cooperation with the investigation.（その被告は調査に協力した見返りとして軽い刑を求めている）

□ The product you ordered is no longer in stock.（あなたが注文した製品はもう在庫がない）

□ I tried to persuade him to change his mind, but in vain.（私は彼に考えを変えるよう説得したが無駄だった）

□ A curfew will be in force between 7 p.m. and 5 a.m.（午後7時から午前5時の間、夜間外出禁止令が実施される予定だ）

continued
▼

Check 1　Listen))) CD-B32

1065
in full
ビジネス問題

全額、全部

1066
in no time
Part 4

すぐに、直ちに

1067
in an attempt to do
Part 5, 6

～しようとして、～するために
名attempt：試み、企て

1068
at all times
Part 5, 6

いつも、常に(≒always)

1069
at one's convenience
Part 5, 6

都合のよい時に
名convenience：好都合な時

1070
at a time
Part 7

一度に；同時に

1071
at any price [cost]
Part 7

どんな犠牲[代償]を払っても、ぜひとも　⊕at a priceは「かなりの値段で」
名price/cost：犠牲

1072
at risk
Part 5, 6

(～の)危険にさらされて(of [from] ～)
名risk：危険

Day 66))) CD-B31
Quick Review
答えは右ページ下

□ 実施される　□ 進む　□ Aを使う　□ ～を入手できる
□ 到着する　□ 必ず～する　□ ～を高く評価する　□ ～を最大限に利用する
□ 成功しない　□ ～するのに苦労する　□ ～に精通する　□ ～を熱望する
□ 処置を取る　□ まだ～していない　□ ～から距離を置く　□ ～の功績を認められる

Check 2 Phrase

- ☐ pay the mortgage in full（住宅ローンを全額支払う）

- ☐ will be back in no time（すぐに帰ってくる）

- ☐ in an attempt to increase productivity（生産性を上げようとして）

- ☐ carry photo identification at all times（写真つきの身分証明書をいつも携帯する）

- ☐ at your earliest convenience（ご都合のつき次第）

- ☐ deal with things one at a time（一度に1つずつ事を処理する）

- ☐ achieve victory at any price（どんな犠牲を払っても勝利を収める）

- ☐ be at risk of bankruptcy（倒産の危険にさらされている）

Check 3 Sentence

- ☐ The bill must be paid in full by the due date.（請求金額は支払期日までに全額支払われなければならない）

- ☐ He solved the math problem in no time.（彼はその数学の問題をすぐに解いた）

- ☐ The company has announced that it will cut 1,000 jobs in an attempt to reduce costs.（その会社は経費を削減するため1000人を解雇する予定だと発表した）

- ☐ Dogs must be kept on a lead at all times in public places.（公共の場所ではイヌは常にひもにつながれていなければならない）

- ☐ Please fill out the survey at your convenience and mail it to the address below.（ご都合のいい時に調査書にご記入いただき、下記の住所まで郵送してください）

- ☐ We will interview applicants two at a time.（私たちは一度に2人ずつ応募者と面接する予定だ）

- ☐ We must maintain the peace at any price.（私たちはどんな犠牲を払っても平和を維持しなければならない）

- ☐ One in four mammal species is at risk of extinction.（哺乳類の4分の1は絶滅の危機にさらされている）

Day 66 》CD-B31
Quick Review
答えは左ページ下

- ☐ take effect
- ☐ make it
- ☐ get nowhere
- ☐ take steps
- ☐ make one's way
- ☐ make sure
- ☐ have trouble doing
- ☐ have yet to do
- ☐ put A to use
- ☐ think highly of
- ☐ acquaint oneself with
- ☐ distance oneself from
- ☐ have access to
- ☐ make the most of
- ☐ set one's heart on
- ☐ take credit for

CHAPTER 1
CHAPTER 2
CHAPTER 3
CHAPTER 4
CHAPTER 5
CHAPTER 6
CHAPTER 7
CHAPTER 8
CHAPTER 9
CHAPTER 10

Day 68　形容詞句・副詞句2

Check 1　Listen)) CD-B33

1073 at the moment　Part 4
(ちょうど)**今**、今のところ(≒ now)
名 moment：現在

1074 at times　Part 2, 3
時々(≒ occasionally, sometimes, now and then, from time to time)

1075 for a change　Part 2, 3
たまには、いつもと違って；気分転換に

1076 for free　Part 5, 6
無料[無償]で(≒ for nothing, free of charge, free)

1077 for now　Part 4
今のところ、当分は、差し当たり(≒ for the present, for the time being)

1078 for the most part　Part 5, 6
大抵は、大部分は(≒ mostly)

1079 with caution　Part 5, 6
用心[注意]して、慎重に(≒ cautiously)
名 caution：用心、注意

1080 with care　Part 5, 6
注意して(≒ carefully)
名 care：注意

continued ▼

形容詞句・副詞句は「固まり」で覚えよう。そのためには、読むだけでなく、「声に出す＝音読する」ことが必要不可欠！

☐ 聞くだけモード　Check 1
☐ しっかりモード　Check 1 ▶ 2
☐ かんぺきモード　Check 1 ▶ 2 ▶ 3

Check 2　Phrase

☐ **be very busy at the moment**（今はとても忙しい）

☐ **go to the gym at times**（時々ジムへ行く）

☐ **wear jeans for a change**（たまにはジーンズをはく）

☐ **replace defective parts for free**（欠陥部品を無料で交換する）

☐ **be under construction for now**（現在、工事中である）

☐ **work at home for the most part**（大抵は家で働いている）

☐ **with extreme caution**（細心の注意を払って）

☐ **handle the vase with care**（注意してその花瓶を扱う）

Check 3　Sentence

☐ **I'm not available at the moment. Please leave a message after the beep.**（ただ今電話に出ることができません。発信音の後に伝言を残してください）

☐ **At times she feels a little isolated from her colleagues.**（彼女は時々、同僚たちから少し孤立していると感じることがある）

☐ **It's nice to read an optimistic article for a change.**（たまに楽観的な記事を読むのはいいものだ）

☐ **My car was repaired under warranty for free.**（私の車は保証期間中で無料で修理された）

☐ **The shop is closed for now and will reopen sometime in the near future.**（その店は今は閉まっているが、近い将来に営業を再開する予定だ）

☐ **The movie is boring for the most part.**（その映画の大部分は退屈だ）

☐ **If you have a stomach ulcer, you must use aspirin with caution.**（胃潰瘍がある場合は、慎重にアスピリンを使わなければならない）

☐ **The roads are wet, so drive with care.**（道路がぬれているので、注意して運転してください）

continued ▼

Day 68

Check 1　Listen)) CD-B33

1081 with confidence　Part 5, 6
自信[確信]を持って　⊕in confidenceは「秘密に、内緒で」
图confidence：自信

1082 with ease　Part 2, 3
容易[簡単]に、たやすく(≒easily)
图ease：容易さ

1083 without notice　Part 7
予告なしに、無断で
图notice：予告

1084 under [in] no circumstances　Part 7
どんなことがあっても～ない、決して～ない
图circumstance：状況

1085 under way　Part 7
進行中で、始まって(≒in progress)　⊕underwayと1語でつづる場合もある

1086 under consideration　Part 5, 6
(事が)検討[考慮]中で[の]
图consideration：考慮

1087 by any chance　Part 2, 3
ひょっとして、もしかして
图chance：偶然

1088 by leaps and bounds　Part 7
飛躍的に、急速に、とんとん拍子に
图leap/bound：跳躍

Day 67)) CD-B32
Quick Review
答えは右ページ下

- □ 大量に
- □ ～の考えでは
- □ 順番に
- □ 自分で
- □ お返しに
- □ 在庫があって
- □ 無駄に
- □ 有効で
- □ 全額
- □ すぐに
- □ ～しようとして
- □ いつも
- □ 都合のよい時に
- □ 一度に
- □ どんな犠牲を払っても
- □ 危険にさらされて

Check 2　Phrase

- [ ] act with confidence(自信を持って行動する)

- [ ] with relative ease(比較的容易に)

- [ ] dismiss employees without notice(予告なしに従業員を解雇する)

- [ ] Under no circumstances should you do ~.(どんなことがあっても~すべきではない) ➕under no circumstancesが文頭に来ると、疑問文の語順に倒置される

- [ ] get under way(始まる)

- [ ] issues under consideration(検討中の課題)

- [ ] Do you know ~ by any chance? (ひょっとして~を知っていますか?)

- [ ] advance by leaps and bounds(飛躍的に進歩する)

Check 3　Sentence

- [ ] The candidate said with confidence that he would win the election.(その候補者は自分が選挙に勝つだろうと自信を持って言った)

- [ ] Usain Bolt won the men's 100m race with ease.(ウサイン・ボルトは男子100メートル走に楽勝した)

- [ ] Prices are subject to change without notice.(価格は予告なしに変更されることがある) ➕カタログなどの表現

- [ ] Under no circumstances is war justified.(いかなることがあっても戦争は正当化されない)

- [ ] Informal peace talks are under way in Libya.(非公式の和平会談がリビアで進行している)

- [ ] The bill was under consideration in the Senate.(その法案は上院で検討された)

- [ ] Are you from Canada by any chance? (もしかしてあなたはカナダの出身ですか?)

- [ ] The population of Internet users has grown by leaps and bounds.(インターネットの使用者人口は飛躍的に増加している)

Day 67 》CD-B32
Quick Review
答えは左ページ下

- [ ] in bulk
- [ ] in one's opinion
- [ ] in order
- [ ] in person
- [ ] in return
- [ ] in stock
- [ ] in vain
- [ ] in force
- [ ] in full
- [ ] in no time
- [ ] in an attempt to do
- [ ] at all times
- [ ] at one's convenience
- [ ] at a time
- [ ] at any price
- [ ] at risk

CHAPTER 1
CHAPTER 2
CHAPTER 3
CHAPTER 4
CHAPTER 5
CHAPTER 6
CHAPTER 7
CHAPTER 8
CHAPTER 9
CHAPTER 10

Day 69　形容詞句・副詞句3

Check 1　Listen 》CD-B34

□ 1089
by no means
Part 7

決して〜でない[しない]（≒ far from）

□ 1090
on end
Part 2, 3

続けて、継続的に

□ 1091
(all) on one's own
Part 4

❶**1人で**、単独で（≒ alone）　❷独力で

□ 1092
on the books
Part 7

名簿に載って、記録されて
名 book：(the 〜s)名簿

□ 1093
above all (things, else)
Part 5, 6

何よりも（まず）、とりわけ、中でも

□ 1094
after all
Part 2, 3

結局（のところ）

□ 1095
as a whole
Part 5, 6

全体として（の）
名 whole：全体

□ 1096
before long
Part 5, 6

間もなく、やがて（≒ soon）

continued
▼

今日でChapter 9は最後！ 時間に余裕があったら、章末のReviewにも挑戦しておこう。忘れてしまった表現も結構あるのでは?!

- ☐ 聞くだけモード　Check 1
- ☐ しっかりモード　Check 1 ▶ 2
- ☐ かんぺきモード　Check 1 ▶ 2 ▶ 3

Check 2　Phrase

☐ **be by no means satisfactory**
（[結果などが]決して満足のいくものではない）

☐ **talk for hours on end**（何時間も立て続けに話す）

☐ **leave her on her own**（彼女を1人にしておく）
☐ **finish the job on one's own**（自分だけでその仕事を終える）

☐ **keep one's name on the books**（名簿に名前を載せておく、在籍している）

☐ **value honesty above all**（何よりも誠実さを尊重する）

☐ **decide to marry him after all**（[いろいろあったが]結局、彼と結婚することにする）

☐ **the world as a whole**（世界全体）

☐ **will be back before long**（間もなく戻ってくるだろう）

Check 3　Sentence

☐ **The fight against terrorism is by no means over.**（テロとの戦いは決して終わってはいない）

☐ **It's been raining for days on end.**（何日間も雨が降り続いている）

☐ **He likes living on his own.**（彼は1人暮らしが気に入っている）

☐ **She claims to have graduated from Yale, but her name is not on the books.**（彼女はエール大学を卒業したと主張しているが、彼女の名前は名簿に載っていない）

☐ **Above all, I want my family to be happy.**（何よりも、私は家族に幸せでいてほしい）

☐ **The economy will naturally stabilize with time after all.**（結局、経済は時がたつにつれて自然に安定するだろう）

☐ **The report is well written as a whole.**（その報告書は全体としてはよく書かれている）

☐ **The construction of the facility will be completed before long.**（その施設の建設は間もなく終わる予定だ）

continued ▼

Day 69

Check 1 Listen))) CD-B34

1097 **free of charge** Part 4	無料で (≒ for nothing, for free, free) 名 charge：料金
1098 **much less** Part 4	(否定文に続けて) まして [いわんや] 〜ではない (≒ let alone)
1099 **all in all** Part 5, 6	全般的に見て、概して
1100 **all the way** Part 2, 3	はるばる、わざわざ、途中ずっと
1101 **hardly [scarcely] ever** Part 5, 6	めったに [ほとんど] 〜しない (≒ seldom, rarely)
1102 **once and for all** Part 4	これを最後に、きっぱりと
1103 **second to none** Part 2, 3	何 [誰] にも劣らない [負けない]
1104 **no doubt** Part 5, 6	恐らく、多分、きっと、疑いなく (≒ probably) 名 doubt：疑い

Day 68))) CD-B33
Quick Review
答えは右ページ下

- □ 今
- □ 時々
- □ たまには
- □ 無料で
- □ 今のところ
- □ 大抵は
- □ 用心して
- □ 注意して
- □ 自信を持って
- □ 容易に
- □ 予告なしに
- □ どんなことがあっても〜ない
- □ 進行中で
- □ 検討中で
- □ ひょっとして
- □ 飛躍的に

Check 2 Phrase & Sentence

- deliver orders free of charge (注文品を無料で配達する)

- can't read French, much less write it (フランス語を読めないし、まして書くこともできない)

- All in all, his health is improving. (全般的に見て、彼の健康は回復している)

- run all the way to the post office (郵便局までずっと走る)

- hardly ever read books (めったに本を読まない)

- quit smoking once and for all (きっぱりと禁煙する)

- be second to none in quality (品質の点でどれにも劣らない)

- will no doubt come (多分来るだろう)

Check 3 Sentence

- My camera was fixed free of charge. (私のカメラは無料で修理された)

- She can't make a sandwich, much less cook a meal. (彼女はサンドイッチを作れないし、まして料理を作ることもできない)

- All in all, the project was a success. (全般的に見て、そのプロジェクトは成功だった)

- Thank you for coming all the way from Australia. (オーストラリアからはるばるお越しくださいまして、ありがとうございます)

- My wife and I hardly ever go to the movies. (私の妻と私はめったに映画を見に行かない)

- She decided to leave him once and for all. (彼女はこれを最後に彼と別れることを決心した)

- The cuisine at the restaurant is second to none. (そのレストランの料理はどこにも劣らない)

- The slowing US economy will no doubt have a negative impact on the world economy. (減速するアメリカ経済は世界経済に間違いなく悪影響を及ぼすだろう)

Day 68 » CD-B33
Quick Review
答えは左ページ下

- at the moment
- at times
- for a change
- for free
- for now
- for the most part
- with caution
- with care
- with confidence
- with ease
- without notice
- under no circumstances
- under way
- under consideration
- by any chance
- by leaps and bounds

Chapter 9 Review

左ページの(1)〜(16)の熟語の同意熟語・類義熟語（または同意語・類義語）（≒）を右ページのA〜Pから選び、カッコの中に答えを書き込もう。意味が分からないときは、見出し番号を参照して復習しておこう（答えは右ページ下）。

- (1) in person (1060) ≒は？（　）
- (2) in vain (1063) ≒は？（　）
- (3) at all times (1068) ≒は？（　）
- (4) at the moment (1073) ≒は？（　）
- (5) at times (1074) ≒は？（　）
- (6) for free (1076) ≒は？（　）
- (7) for the most part (1078) ≒は？（　）
- (8) with caution (1079) ≒は？（　）
- (9) with ease (1082) ≒は？（　）
- (10) under way (1085) ≒は？（　）
- (11) by no means (1089) ≒は？（　）
- (12) on one's own (1091) ≒は？（　）
- (13) before long (1096) ≒は？（　）
- (14) much less (1098) ≒は？（　）
- (15) hardly ever (1101) ≒は？（　）
- (16) no doubt (1104) ≒は？（　）

A. vainly
B. cautiously
C. now
D. personally
E. in progress
F. always
G. occasionally
H. alone
I. for nothing
J. mostly
K. soon
L. easily
M. far from
N. seldom
O. probably
P. let alone

【解答】 (1) D (2) A (3) F (4) C (5) G (6) I (7) J (8) B (9) L (10) E (11) M (12) H (13) K (14) P (15) N (16) O

CHAPTER 10
群前置詞

Chapter 10では群前置詞をマスター。ここでも、「数語で1つの前置詞」といった具合に「固まり」で覚えることが重要です。このChapterで本書も終了！ 800点を突破して「最後に笑う」のはあなたです！

Day 70【群前置詞】
▶ 326
Chapter 10 Review
▶ 330

TOEIC的格言

He laughs best who laughs last.

最後に笑う者が一番よく笑う。

Day 70　群前置詞

Check 1　　Listen)) CD-B35

□ 1105
in addition to
Part 5, 6

〜に加えて (≒ besides, as well as)
名 addition：追加

□ 1106
in need of
Part 5, 6

〜を必要として
名 need：必要(性)

□ 1107
in pursuit of
Part 5, 6

〜を追求[追跡]して、〜を求めて、〜を得ようとして
名 pursuit：追求；追跡

□ 1108
in the process of
Part 5, 6

〜の過程で、〜が進行中で
名 process：過程、進行

□ 1109
in exchange for
Part 4

〜と引き換え[交換]に、〜の代わりに
名 exchange：交換

□ 1110
in opposition to
Part 5, 6

〜に反対[反抗]して
名 opposition：反対

□ 1111
in response to
Part 5, 6

〜に応えて、〜に応じて
名 response：応答

□ 1112
in the mood for
Part 2, 3

〜したい気分で、〜する気持ちになって
名 mood：気分

continued
▼

今日で『キクタンTOEIC Test Score 800』も最後。ここまで続けてくれて本当にありがとう！ We're proud of you!!

- ☐ 聞くだけモード　Check 1
- ☐ しっかりモード　Check 1 ▶ 2
- ☐ かんぺきモード　Check 1 ▶ 2 ▶ 3

Check 2　Phrase

☐ in addition to regular salary（基本給に加えて）

☐ a house in need of repair（修理が必要な家）

☐ in hot pursuit of ~（~を激しく追跡して）

☐ in the process of investigation（調査の過程で）
☐ in the process of construction（建設中で）

☐ in exchange for the information（その情報と引き換えに）

☐ be in opposition to the plan（その計画に反対している）

☐ in response to her request（彼女の依頼に応えて）

☐ be in the mood for studying（勉強したい気分である）
☐ be in no mood for doing ~（~する気がしない）

Check 3　Sentence

☐ Employees receive up to nine paid holidays each year in addition to a day off for birthdays.（従業員は誕生日休暇に加えて9日まで有給休暇を毎年与えられる）

☐ The country is in need of food and medical aid.（その国は食糧と医療の援助を必要としている）

☐ The union has gone on strike in pursuit of a 15-percent pay raise.（その労働組合は15パーセントの賃上げを求めてストに突入した）

☐ The company is in the process of restructuring.（その会社はリストラの過程にある）

☐ The terrorists have demanded $1 million in exchange for the hostages.（テロリストたちは人質と引き換えに100万ドルを要求している）

☐ The NGO has organized demonstrations in opposition to nuclear weapons.（そのNGOは核兵器に反対するデモを計画している）

☐ The management granted a 5-percent pay raise in response to the union's demand.（経営陣は労働組合の要求に応じて5パーセントの賃上げを受け入れた）

☐ I'm not in the mood for joking now.（今は冗談を言う気分になれない）

continued
▼

Day 70

Check 1   Listen)) CD-B35

☐ 1113
in anticipation of
Part 5, 6

　～を見越して、当てにして、期待して
　名 anticipation：期待

☐ 1114
in excess of
Part 7

　～よりも多く、～を超過して(≒ more than)
　名 excess：超過

☐ 1115
in recognition of
Part 4

　～を評価して[評価されて]、～を認めて[認められて]
　名 recognition：評価、認識

☐ 1116
as for
Part 2, 3

　(通例、文頭で用いて)**～に関しては**、～について言えば(≒ as to, with regard to)

☐ 1117
for want of
Part 5, 6

　～不足のために、～がないので(≒ for lack of)
　名 want：不足

☐ 1118
on the verge of
Part 7

　～の寸前[間際]**で**
　名 verge：寸前、間際

☐ 1119
at the expense of
Part 5, 6

　❶ **～を犠牲にして**　❷ ～の費用[負担]で
　名 expense：犠牲；費用

☐ 1120
to the advantage of
Part 5, 6

　～に有利に[な]
　名 advantage：有利な点

| Day 69)) CD-B34
Quick Review
答えは右ページ下 | ☐ 決して～でない
☐ 続けて
☐ 1人で
☐ 名簿に載って | ☐ 何よりも
☐ 結局
☐ 全体として
☐ 間もなく | ☐ 無料で
☐ まして～ではない
☐ 全般的に見て
☐ はるばる | ☐ めったに～しない
☐ これを最後に
☐ 何にも劣らない
☐ 恐らく |

Check 2 Phrase

- ☐ **in anticipation of** one's bonus(ボーナスを当てにして)

- ☐ work **in excess of** standard weekly hours(標準週間労働時間よりも多く働く)

- ☐ **in recognition of** outstanding achievements(顕著な業績を評価して)

- ☐ **as for** today's weather(今日の天気について言えば)

- ☐ **for want of** evidence(証拠不足のために)

- ☐ an animal **on the verge of** extinction(絶滅寸前の動物)

- ☐ **at the expense of** one's health(健康を犠牲にして)
- ☐ **at the expense of** the government(国費で)

- ☐ **to the advantage of** the defendant(被告に有利に)

Check 3 Sentence

- ☐ Investors buy assets **in anticipation of** future price increases.(投資家は将来の価格上昇を見越して資産を買う)

- ☐ The CEO's annual salary is **in excess of** $2 million.(そのCEOの年収は200万ドルを超えている)

- ☐ He was presented with an award **in recognition of** his 40 years of service.(彼は勤続40年を評価されて賞を贈られた)

- ☐ **As for** unemployment, it was up 0.2 percent in November, compared to October.(失業率に関しては、10月と比較して11月は0.2パーセント上昇した)

- ☐ The building of the mall has been stopped **for want of** funds.(そのショッピングセンターの建設は資金不足のために中止されている)

- ☐ The company is **on the verge of** bankruptcy.(その会社は倒産寸前だ)

- ☐ He pursued his career **at the expense of** his family.(彼は家族を犠牲にしてまで仕事を続けた)

- ☐ Free market forces rarely work **to the advantage of** consumers.(自由市場の原理が消費者に有利に働くことはめったにない)

Day 69))) CD-B34
Quick Review
答えは左ページ下

☐ by no means	☐ above all	☐ free of charge	☐ hardly ever
☐ on end	☐ after all	☐ much less	☐ once and for all
☐ on one's own	☐ as a whole	☐ all in all	☐ second to none
☐ on the books	☐ before long	☐ all the way	☐ no doubt

CHAPTER 1
CHAPTER 2
CHAPTER 3
CHAPTER 4
CHAPTER 5
CHAPTER 6
CHAPTER 7
CHAPTER 8
CHAPTER 9
CHAPTER 10

Chapter 10 Review

左ページの(1)～(4)の熟語の同意熟語・類義熟語（または同意語・類義語）（≒）を右ページのA～Dから選び、カッコの中に答えを書き込もう。意味が分からないときは、見出し番号を参照して復習しておこう（答えは右ページ下）。

- ☐ (1) in addition to (1105) ≒は?（　）
- ☐ (2) in excess of (1114) ≒は?（　）
- ☐ (3) as for (1116) ≒は?（　）
- ☐ (4) for want of (1117) ≒は?（　）

Day 70)) CD-B35
Quick Review
答えは右ページ下

- ☐ ～に加えて
- ☐ ～を必要として
- ☐ ～を追求して
- ☐ ～の過程で
- ☐ ～と引き換えに
- ☐ ～に反対して
- ☐ ～に応えて
- ☐ ～したい気分で
- ☐ ～を見越して
- ☐ ～よりも多く
- ☐ ～を評価して
- ☐ ～に関しては
- ☐ ～不足のために
- ☐ ～の寸前で
- ☐ ～を犠牲にして
- ☐ ～に有利に

A. more than
B. with regard to
C. besides
D. for lack of

【解答】(1) C (2) A (3) B (4) D

Day 70)) CD-B35
Quick Review
答えは左ページ下

- [ ] in addition to
- [ ] in need of
- [ ] in pursuit of
- [ ] in the process of
- [ ] in exchange for
- [ ] in opposition to
- [ ] in response to
- [ ] in the mood for
- [ ] in anticipation of
- [ ] in excess of
- [ ] in recognition of
- [ ] as for
- [ ] for want of
- [ ] on the verge of
- [ ] at the expense of
- [ ] to the advantage of

> ねぇねぇ、どれくらい覚えてる？
> Hey, how many do you remember?

Index

*見出しとして掲載されている単語・熟語は赤字、それ以外のものは黒字で示されています。それぞれの語の右側にある数字は、見出し番号を表しています。赤字の番号は、見出しとなっている番号を示します。

Index

A

- [ ] a lot 0812
- [ ] a mass of 0706
- [ ] A rather than B 0783
- [ ] a stack of 0238
- [ ] a trace of 0925
- [ ] **abandon** 0260
- [ ] abandon oneself to 0260
- [ ] **abide by** 0845, 0817
- [ ] ability 0517
- [ ] able 0376
- [ ] about 0769
- [ ] **above all** 1093
- [ ] above all else 1093
- [ ] above all things 1093
- [ ] abroad 0675
- [ ] absence 0423
- [ ] absolute 0789
- [ ] **absolutely** 0789
- [ ] **absorb** 0587
- [ ] absorbing 0587
- [ ] absorption 0587
- [ ] abstain from 0821
- [ ] **abstract** 0348
- [ ] abstraction 0348
- [ ] abundance 0326
- [ ] **abundant** 0326, 0763
- [ ] accept 0197, 0237, 0274, 0440, 0689
- [ ] **acceptable** 0689, 0440
- [ ] **acceptance** 0440, 0689
- [ ] access 0752, 1053
- [ ] **accessible** 0752
- [ ] accident 0457
- [ ] **accommodate** 0237, 0121
- [ ] **accommodation** 0121, 0237
- [ ] **accomplish** 0588, 0220, 0558
- [ ] **accomplishment** 0558, 0102, 0588
- [ ] account 0040, 0129, 0818
- [ ] **account for** 0818, 0040, 0129
- [ ] **accountant** 0040, 0129, 0818
- [ ] **accounting** 0129, 0040, 0818
- [ ] **accumulate** 0648
- [ ] accumulation 0648
- [ ] accuracy 0295, 0805
- [ ] **accurate** 0295, 0299, 0805
- [ ] **accurately** 0805, 0295
- [ ] accuse A of B 0905
- [ ] accused 0487
- [ ] **ache** 0287
- [ ] achieve 0102, 0220, 0588
- [ ] **achievement** 0102, 0558
- [ ] **acknowledge** 0274
- [ ] acknowledgement 0274
- [ ] acquaint 0157
- [ ] acquaint A with B 0157
- [ ] **acquaint oneself with** 1051, 0157
- [ ] **acquaintance** 0157, 1051
- [ ] **acquire** 0253, 0188, 0214
- [ ] **acquisition** 0188, 0253
- [ ] **acute** 0327
- [ ] ad 0107
- [ ] adaptable 0323
- [ ] add A and B 0636, 0922
- [ ] **add to** 0869
- [ ] addition 0869, 1105
- [ ] additional 0869
- [ ] **adequate** 0303, 0333, 0759, 0794
- [ ] **adequately** 0794, 0303
- [ ] **adjust** 0247, 0443
- [ ] adjust to 0247, 0443
- [ ] adjustable 0247, 0443
- [ ] **adjustment** 0443, 0247
- [ ] administer 0072, 0718
- [ ] **administration** 0072, 0718
- [ ] **administrative** 0718, 0072
- [ ] **admirable** 0738
- [ ] admiration 0738
- [ ] admire 0738
- [ ] admire A for B 0738
- [ ] **admission** 0012, 0972
- [ ] admit 0012, 0274
- [ ] admit A into B 0012
- [ ] admit A to B 0012
- [ ] **admit doing** 0972, 0012
- [ ] adopt 0604
- [ ] adorn 0574
- [ ] advance 0728
- [ ] **advanced** 0728
- [ ] advantage 1120
- [ ] advertise 0596, 0107, 0479
- [ ] **advertisement** 0107, 0479, 0596
- [ ] **advertising** 0479, 0107, 0596
- [ ] advice 0983
- [ ] **advise A to do** 0983
- [ ] adviser 0983
- [ ] advisory 0983
- [ ] **affect** 0201, 0174
- [ ] **affection** 0174, 0201
- [ ] affirm 0279
- [ ] affluent 0326, 0763
- [ ] **after all** 1094
- [ ] afterward 0776
- [ ] age 0143
- [ ] aged 0453
- [ ] aggression 0709
- [ ] **aggressive** 0709
- [ ] aggressively 0709
- [ ] agreement 0005, 0190, 0458
- [ ] aid A with B 0930
- [ ] aim 0424, 0833, 0941
- [ ] **aim A at B** 0941
- [ ] **aim at** 0833

☐ air	0644	
☐ aisle	0019	
☐ alarm	0544, 1023	
☐ alert	0175	
☐ alike	0382	
☐ all in all	1099	
☐ all on one's own	1091	
☐ all the way	1100	
☐ allege	0279	
☐ allow	0117	
☐ allow A to do	0117	
☐ allowance	0117	
☐ almost	0774, 0781	
☐ alone	1091	
☐ alter	0581	
☐ alteration	0581	
☐ alternate	0298	
☐ alternative	0298	
☐ always	1068	
☐ amaze	0681	
☐ amazing	0681	
☐ amazingly	0681	
☐ ambition	0700	
☐ ambitious	0700	
☐ ample	0333, 0303, 0326, 0763	
☐ amply	0333	
☐ analysis	0584	
☐ analyst	0584	
☐ analytical	0584	
☐ analyze	0584	
☐ and yet	0791	
☐ anger	0454	
☐ anniversary	0091	
☐ annoy	0229	
☐ annoyance	0229	
☐ annoying	0229	
☐ annual	0290, 0795	
☐ annually	0795, 0290	
☐ answer	0635	
☐ anticipate	0221	
☐ anticipation	0221, 0439, 1113	
☐ apologize	0416	
☐ apologize to A for B	0416	
☐ apology	0416
☐ apparatus	0385
☐ apparel	0474
☐ apparent	0685, 0775
☐ apparently	0775
☐ appear	0244, 0775, 0866
☐ appear to do	0775
☐ appearance	0775
☐ appetite	0161
☐ applaud	0626, 0609
☐ applause	0626
☐ applicant	0820
☐ application	0820
☐ apply for	0820
☐ apply to	0820
☐ appoint	0233
☐ appoint A as B	0897
☐ appoint A to B	0897
☐ appoint A to do	0984
☐ appointment	0152, 0984
☐ appraisal	0192, 0511
☐ appraise	0592, 0646
☐ appreciate	0212, 0397
☐ appreciation	0397, 0212
☐ approach	0622
☐ appropriate	0293, 0303, 0915, 0999
☐ appropriate A for B	0915, 0293, 0999
☐ approval	0016, 0835
☐ approve	0016, 0271
☐ approve of	0835, 0016
☐ approximate	0769
☐ approximately	0769
☐ architect	0389
☐ architectural	0389
☐ architecture	0389
☐ area	0105
☐ argument	0017, 0023
☐ aroma	0414
☐ arrest	0591
☐ arrival	0032
☐ arrive	0250, 0866
☐ arrive at	0278
☐ artificial	0353
☐ as a result	0777, 0786
☐ as a whole	1095
☐ as for	1116
☐ as to	1116
☐ as well as	1105
☐ aspect	0110
☐ assemble	0256, 0572
☐ assembly	0572, 0256
☐ assert	0279
☐ assertion	0279
☐ assertive	0279
☐ assess	0646, 0511, 0592
☐ assessment	0511, 0192, 0646
☐ asset	0062, 0100
☐ assign	0015
☐ assign A to B	0897, 0015
☐ assign A to do	0980, 0015
☐ assignment	0015, 0897, 0980
☐ assist A in B	0930
☐ assist A with B	0930
☐ assistance	0930
☐ assistant	0930
☐ associate	0084, 0031, 0145, 0917, 0995
☐ associate A with B	0917, 0084, 0145, 0933
☐ association	0145, 0084, 0917, 0995
☐ assume	0206
☐ assumption	0206
☐ astonishing	0681
☐ at a price	1071
☐ at a time	1070
☐ at all times	1068
☐ at any cost	1071
☐ at any price	1071
☐ at first	0803
☐ at once	0780
☐ at one's convenience	1069

☐ at risk 1072	☐ be alarmed at 0544, 1023	☐ be destined to do 0045
☐ at the expense of 1119	☐ be alarmed by	☐ be determined to do
☐ at the moment 1073	1023, 0544	1030
☐ at times 1074, 0806	☐ be alarmed over	☐ be disappointed about
☐ athlete 0153	0544, 1023	0741
☐ athletic 0153	☐ be amazed at 0681	☐ be disappointed at 0741
☐ athletics 0153	☐ be amazed to do 0681	☐ be disappointed with 0741
☐ atmosphere 0067	☐ be annoyed at 0229	☐ be eligible to do 1025
☐ atmospheric 0067	☐ be annoyed with 0229	☐ be embarrassed
☐ attachment 0174	☐ be appropriate for	about 1009
☐ attain 0220	0999, 0293, 0915	☐ be engaged in 0152
☐ attainment 0220	☐ be apt to do	☐ be engaged to 0152
☐ attempt 0125, 0947, 1067	1029, 0950, 1027, 1028	☐ be enthusiastic about
☐ attempt to do	☐ be associated with	0050
0947, 0125, 0967	0995	☐ be entitled to 0998
☐ attend 0124, 0509	☐ be aware of 0185, 1022	☐ be entitled to do 1031
☐ attend to	☐ be bored with 1006	☐ be equal to 0996
0848, 0124, 0509	☐ be capable of 0441, 1020	☐ be equivalent to
☐ attendance 0509, 0124	☐ be cautious about	0996, 0046
☐ attendant 0124, 0509	1000, 0169	☐ be essential for 1011
☐ attention 0848	☐ be cautious of 0169, 1000	☐ be essential to 1011
☐ audience 0114	☐ be characteristic of	☐ be familiar to 0900
☐ author 0271, 0977	0166, 1024	☐ be familiar with
☐ authority 0271, 0977	☐ be committed to 1018	0900, 1017
☐ authorize 0271	☐ be composed of	☐ be fascinated by
☐ authorize A to do	1001, 0843, 1019	0607, 0731
0977, 0271	☐ be comprised of	☐ be fascinated with
☐ award 0002	0843, 1001, 1019	0607, 0731
☐ aware 0185	☐ be concerned about	☐ be fit for 0293, 0999
☐ awareness 0185	1002, 0674, 1007	☐ be fluent in 1010
☐ awful 0703	☐ be concerned for	☐ be grateful to A for B 0488
	0674, 1002, 1007	☐ be gratified by 0488
	☐ be concerned in	☐ be honored by 0711
B	0674, 1002, 1007	☐ be honored for 0711
	☐ be concerned with	☐ be honored to do 1034
☐ back up 0895	1007, 0674, 1002	☐ be impressed by 0684
☐ backup 0895	☐ be confused with 0471	☐ be impressed with 0684
☐ ban 0209, 0266	☐ be consistent with	☐ be inappropriate for 0999
☐ ban A from doing	0997, 0322, 0843	☐ be incapable of 1020
0209, 0266, 0990	☐ be dedicated to	☐ be inclined to do
☐ bankrupt 0308	1008, 0715	1028, 0950, 1027, 1029
☐ bankruptcy 0308	☐ be dependent on 0088	☐ be inconsistent with 0997
☐ banquet 0043	☐ be depressed about 0176	☐ be independent of 0088
☐ barn 0392	☐ be depressed over 0176	☐ be indispensable for 1011
☐ barrel 0426	☐ be destined for 0045	☐ be indispensable to
☐ be absorbed in 0587		
☐ be absorbed into 0587		

どれだけチェックできた？ 1 ☐ 2 ☐

		1011
☐ be infected with		0177
☐ be inferior to		0714
☐ **be instrumental in**		
		1003
☐ **be intended for**		1012
☐ be intent on		0424
☐ be intent upon		0424
☐ be involved in		0245, 0531
☐ be involved with		0531
☐ be irritated about		0756
☐ be irritated at		0756
☐ be irritated by		0756
☐ be irritated with		0756
☐ **be keen on**		1004
☐ be lacking in		1015
☐ **be liable to do**		
	1027, 0950, 1028, 1029	
☐ **be licensed to do**		1039
☐ be likely to do		
	0950, 1027, 1028,	
	1029, 1033	
☐ be located at		0210, 0993
☐ **be located in**		
	0993, 0054, 0210, 1016	
☐ **be made up of**		
	1019, 0843, 1001	
☐ be necessary for		1011
☐ be necessary to		1011
☐ **be obliged to do**		
	1035, 0469	
☐ be occupied with		0104
☐ **be open to**		1013
☐ **be optimistic about**		
		1014
☐ **be parallel to**		0994
☐ be parallel with		0994
☐ be particular about		0528
☐ be peculiar to		
	0166, 0341, 1024	
☐ be pessimistic about		1014
☐ **be poised to do**		1040
☐ be prepared to do		1040
☐ **be projected to do**		
		1036

☐ be proper for	0293, 0999
☐ be proper to	
	0166, 0341, 1024
☐ be qualified for	0037
☐ be ready to do	
	0801, 1037, 1040
☐ be related with	0995
☐ be relieved to do	0937
☐ **be reluctant to do**	
	1026, 1032
☐ be requisite for	1011
☐ be requisite to	1011
☐ be satisfied with	
	0150, 0727
☐ **be set to do**	1037
☐ **be short of**	
	1015, 0423, 0671,
	0816, 0873
☐ be short on	
	0423, 0671, 0816,
	0873, 1015
☐ **be sited in**	
	1016, 0054, 0993
☐ be sorry to do	0951
☐ be suitable for	0293, 0999
☐ be superior to	0714
☐ be surprised at	0811
☐ be surprised by	0811
☐ be surprised to do	0811
☐ **be true of**	1021
☐ **be typical of**	1024, 0166
☐ **be unaware of**	1022
☐ be uncertain about	0472
☐ be uncertain of	0472
☐ be unfamiliar to	1017
☐ **be unfamiliar with**	
	1017
☐ be unique to	0166, 1024
☐ **be unlikely to do**	1033
☐ **be unwilling to do**	
	1032, 1026
☐ **be welcome to do**	1038
☐ be willing to do	
	1032, 1040
☐ **be worthy of**	1005

☐ bear doing	0961
☐ **bear to do**	0961
☐ **before long**	1096
☐ **beforehand**	0776
☐ begin	0270, 0624
☐ beginning	0086
☐ belong	0180
☐ belong to	0180
☐ **belonging**	0180
☐ **beneficial**	0331, 0839
☐ benefit	0331, 0839
☐ benefit by	0331, 0839
☐ **benefit from**	0839, 0331
☐ besides	0815, 1105
☐ bias	0464
☐ **bite**	0554
☐ blame	0936
☐ blame A for B	
	0905, 0932, 0935
☐ **blame A on B**	0936
☐ blame B for A	0936
☐ blot	0041
☐ **blueprint**	0568
☐ **bond**	0170
☐ bondage	0170
☐ book	1092
☐ booking	0118
☐ **booklet**	0523
☐ **boom**	0501
☐ **boost**	0241
☐ bore	1006
☐ boring	1006
☐ bother	0946
☐ bother doing	0946
☐ **bother to do**	0946
☐ bound	1088
☐ branch	0119
☐ **break out**	0861, 0412
☐ **breed**	0547
☐ breeder	0547
☐ breeding	0547
☐ **brief**	0345
☐ brief A on B	0345
☐ **briefing**	0345
☐ briefly	0345

☐ **bring in** 0891	☐ **cathedral** 0575	☐ clapping 0609
☐ **bring together** 0867	☐ cause 0099, 0981	☐ classification 0736, 0901
☐ broadcast 0644	☐ **cause A to do** 0981	☐ **classified** 0736, 0901
☐ brochure 0523	☐ **caution**	☐ classify 0736
☐ broke 0308	0169, 1000, 1079	☐ **classify A as B**
☐ **budget** 0058	☐ caution A about B	0901, 0736
☐ build 0579, 0656	0169, 1000	☐ classify A into B
☐ bulk 1057	☐ caution A against B	0736, 0901
☐ bulletin 0571	0169, 1000	☐ clear
☐ **burden** 0097	☐ caution A to do	0685, 0788, 0893, 0921
☐ burden A with B 0097	0169, 1000	☐ **clear A of B** 0921, 0788
☐ but yet 0791	☐ cautious 0169	☐ clear B from A 0921
☐ buy 0219	☐ cautiously 1000, 1079	☐ **clear up** 0893, 0788
☐ **by any chance** 1087	☐ **cellphone** 0519	☐ **clearly** 0788, 0893, 0921
☐ **by leaps and bounds**	☐ cellular phone 0519	☐ clerk 0124
1088	☐ ceremony 0569	☐ clothes 0474
☐ **by no means** 1089	☐ **certificate** 0070	☐ clothing 0474
	☐ certify 0070	☐ **clue** 0116
C	☐ chance 1087	☐ coarse 0720
☐ calamity 0420	☐ change	☐ **code** 0055
☐ **calculate** 0288	0036, 0227, 0564, 0581	☐ coherent 0322
☐ calculation 0288	☐ change A into B 0903	☐ **coincide with** 0876
☐ calculator 0288	☐ chaos 0445	☐ coincidence 0876
☐ **call in** 0842	☐ character 0166	☐ **collaborate to do** 0964
☐ candidacy 0003	☐ **characteristic** 0166	☐ collaboration 0964
☐ **candidate** 0003	☐ charge 0905, 1097	☐ collaborator 0964
☐ **cap** 0639	☐ **charge A with B** 0905	☐ **collapse** 0158
☐ capability 0441	☐ charitable 0449	☐ **collar** 0542
☐ capable 0376, 0441	☐ **charity** 0449	☐ **colleague** 0031, 0084
☐ **capacity** 0441	☐ chase 0215	☐ collective 0796
☐ captive 0591	☐ **checkup** 0489	☐ **collectively** 0796
☐ **capture** 0591	☐ chief 0677	☐ color 0542
☐ care 1080	☐ choice 0954	☐ combination 0926
☐ careful 0371	☐ **choose to do** 0954	☐ combine 0926
☐ carefully 1080	☐ **chop** 0281	☐ **combine A with B** 0926
☐ **cargo** 0407	☐ chronic 0327	☐ **come by** 0890
☐ **carrier** 0502	☐ circulate 0504	☐ **come down with** 0855
☐ carry 0502, 0598	☐ **circulation** 0504	☐ **come out** 0883, 0244
☐ carry out	☐ **circumstance**	☐ comfortable 0334, 0381
0255, 0265, 0601	0063, 1084	☐ **command** 0436, 0985
☐ cash 0498	☐ citation 0603	☐ **command A to do**
☐ **cashier** 0498	☐ **cite** 0603	0985, 0436, 0986
☐ catastrophe 0420	☐ claim 0279, 0955	☐ commander 0436, 0985
☐ catch 0591	☐ **claim to do** 0955	☐ **commence** 0624
☐ catch up with 0658, 0854	☐ **clap** 0609, 0626	☐ commencement 0624

☐ comment	0874	☐ compliment 0009
☐ **comment on**	0874	☐ complimentary 0009
☐ **commission**		☐ **comply with** 0817, 0845
0096, 0396, 0943		☐ **component** 0094
☐ commit	0096, 0396	☐ composer 1001
☐ **commit A to B**		☐ composition 1001
0943, 0096, 0396		☐ **comprehend** 0668, 0189
☐ **commitment**		☐ **comprehension**
0396, 0096, 0943, 1018		0189, 0668
☐ **commodity** 0018		☐ comprehensive
☐ common 0755		0189, 0668
☐ communicate 0598		☐ **compromise** 0111
☐ comparable 0077		☐ **compulsory**
☐ compare 0077		0338, 0717, 0719, 0988
☐ compare A to B 0077		☐ conceal 0203, 0275, 0640
☐ compare A with B 0077		☐ concern 0674, 1002, 1007
☐ **comparison** 0077		☐ **concerned** 0674
☐ compel 0338		☐ concise 0299
☐ **compel A to do**		☐ **conclude**
0988, 0338		0243, 0086, 0634
☐ compensate 0033		☐ **conclusion** 0086, 0243
☐ compensate A for B 0033		☐ conclusive 0086, 0243
☐ **compensate for**		☐ concrete 0348
0840, 0033		☐ condition 0109, 0764
☐ **compensation**		☐ **conditional** 0764
0033, 0840		☐ confer 0071
☐ **compete**		☐ **conference** 0071, 0080
0282, 0103, 0301		☐ confidence 1081
☐ competence 0376		☐ confine 0597
☐ **competent** 0376		☐ **confine A to B** 0931
☐ competition		☐ confined 0931
0103, 0282, 0301		☐ confinement 0931
☐ **competitive**		☐ **conflict** 0146, 0864
0301, 0103, 0282		☐ **conflict with** 0864
☐ **competitor**		☐ conform to 0817, 0845
0103, 0282, 0301		☐ conform with 0817, 0845
☐ complement 0009		☐ **confront** 0262
☐ complete 0499, 0634		☐ confrontation 0262
☐ completely		☐ confuse 0471
0499, 0778, 0789		☐ **confuse A with B**
☐ **completion** 0499		0924, 0471
☐ compliance 0817		☐ confusing 0471
☐ **complicate** 0627		☐ **confusion**
☐ complicated 0627		0471, 0445, 0924
☐ complication 0627		☐ **congress** 0431

☐ congressional 0431
☐ congressman 0431
☐ connect A to B
0902, 0940
☐ **connect A with B**
0933, 0902, 0917
☐ connection 0933
☐ **conquer** 0585
☐ conqueror 0585
☐ conquest 0585
☐ consecutive 0754
☐ consensus 0190, 0831
☐ **consent** 0190, 0831
☐ **consent to** 0831, 0190
☐ **consequence**
0139, 0434, 0777
☐ consequent 0139, 0777
☐ **consequently**
0777, 0139, 0786
☐ **conservation**
0462, 0330, 0563
☐ **conservative**
0330, 0462, 0682
☐ conserve
0277, 0330, 0462
☐ consider 0165, 0371
☐ **consider doing**
0971, 0165
☐ considerable
0165, 0328, 0701, 0971
☐ considerate 0165, 0971
☐ **consideration**
0165, 0971, 1086
☐ **consist of**
0843, 1001, 1019
☐ consistency
0322, 0843, 0997
☐ **consistent** 0322, 0843
☐ conspiracy 0455, 0526
☐ **construct** 0579, 0004
☐ **construction** 0004, 0579
☐ constructive
0004, 0579, 0751
☐ **consult** 0594, 0483
☐ **consult with**

どれだけチェックできた？ 1 ☐ 2 ☐

	0853, 0483, 0594	☐ cooperative 0663
☐ consultant		☐ **cope with** 0826
	0483, 0594, 0853	☐ **corporate** 0350, 0663
☐ **consultation**		☐ corporation 0350
	0483, 0594, 0853	☐ correct 0295, 0299
☐ **consume**		☐ correspond 0538
	0264, 0181, 0391	☐ **correspond to**
☐ **consumer**		0846, 0538
	0181, 0264, 0391	☐ correspond with
☐ **consumption**		0538, 0846
	0391, 0181, 0264	☐ correspondence
☐ contact 0278		0538, 0846
☐ contagion 0177		☐ **correspondent**
☐ contain 0527		0538, 0846
☐ **container** 0527		☐ cost 1071
☐ contamination 0148		☐ count 0288, 0740, 0827
☐ **contemporary** 0360		☐ **count on**
☐ continue 0824		0827, 0740, 0877, 0887
☐ contract 0630		☐ **counterpart** 0413, 0046
☐ contribute 0101		☐ **countless** 0740, 0827
☐ contribute A to B 0101		☐ couple 0940
☐ contribute A toward B		☐ **couple A to B** 0940
	0101	☐ couple A with B 0940
☐ **contribute to**		☐ courteous 0053
	0832, 0101	☐ **courtesy** 0053
☐ **contribution**		☐ cover 0066
	0101, 0514, 0832	☐ **coverage** 0066
☐ control 0436		☐ coworker 0031, 0084
☐ **controversial**		☐ **cozy** 0334
	0337, 0023	☐ credit 1056
☐ **controversy**		☐ criminal 0500
	0023, 0017, 0337	☐ **crisis** 0452, 0317
☐ convenience 1069		☐ **critic** 0122
☐ **convention**		☐ **critical** 0317, 0122, 0452
	0080, 0071, 0732	☐ criticism 0122, 0317
☐ **conventional**		☐ criticize 0122, 0317
	0732, 0080	☐ crossing 0556
☐ **convey** 0598		☐ **crosswalk** 0556
☐ conveyance 0598		☐ **crucial**
☐ oonviction 0927		0364, 0289, 0317, 0365
☐ **convince A of B** 0927		☐ crucially 0364
☐ convincing 0927		☐ crude 0720
☐ **cooperate** 0663, 0350		☐ cruel 0381
☐ cooperate to do 0663		☐ cure 0123
☐ cooperation 0663		☐ **currency**

0068, 0297, 0779
☐ **current**
0297, 0068, 0779
☐ **currently**
0779, 0068, 0297
☐ curriculum vitae 0008

D

☐ damage	0464
☐ **deadline**	0112
☐ deadly	0316
☐ deal with	0625, 0848
☐ dearth	0423
☐ debatable	0337
☐ debate	0023
☐ **debt**	0007
☐ debtor	0007
☐ **decade**	0156
☐ decency	0378
☐ **decent**	0378
☐ decently	0378
☐ decide to do	
	0211, 0949, 0954, 0965
☐ decision	0154
☐ declaration	0254
☐ **declare**	0254
☐ **decline**	0197, 0956
☐ **decline to do**	
	0956, 0197, 0948
☐ decorate	0574
☐ decrease	0098, 0197
☐ dedicate	0715
☐ **dedicate A to B**	
	0906, 0715
☐ **dedicated**	
	0715, 0735, 0906, 1008
☐ dedication	
	0715, 0906, 1008
☐ deep	0662
☐ **deepen**	0662
☐ deeply	0662
☐ defeat	0252
☐ **defect**	0049
☐ defective	0049
☐ **defendant**	0487

☐ defensive 0709	☐ deserve doing 0962	☐ **disappointing** 0741
☐ defer 0199	☐ **deserve to do** 0962	☐ disappointment 0741
☐ **deficit** 0131	☐ **desirable** 0688	☐ disapproval 0016
☐ **define** 0617, 0785	☐ desire 0161, 0688	☐ **disaster** 0420
☐ definite 0617, 0785	☐ desire to do 0688	☐ disastrous 0420
☐ **definitely** 0785, 0617	☐ **destination** 0045	☐ **discipline** 0149
☐ definition 0617, 0785	☐ destined 0045	☐ **disclose**
☐ **defy** 0666	☐ destroy 0579, 0751	0275, 0203, 0640, 0652
☐ delay 0199	☐ destruction 0004, 0751	☐ disclosure 0275
☐ **deliberate** 0371	☐ **destructive** 0751	☐ **discrimination**
☐ deliberate about 0371	☐ detail 0384	0409, 0464
☐ deliberate on 0371	☐ **detailed** 0384	☐ **dismiss A as B** 0944
☐ deliberate over 0371	☐ **detect** 0234	☐ dismissal 0944
☐ deliberately 0371	☐ detection 0234	☐ disperse 0246
☐ delicacy 0342	☐ detective 0234	☐ **dispute** 0017, 0023
☐ **delicate** 0342	☐ **deter A from doing**	☐ dissatisfaction 0150
☐ delicately 0342	0991	☐ distance 1052
☐ deliver 0075	☐ determination	☐ **distance oneself from**
☐ **delivery** 0075	0154, 0965, 1030	1052
☐ **demonstrate** 0286	☐ determine 0285	☐ distinct 0325
☐ demonstration 0286	☐ **determine to do**	☐ distinction 0325
☐ demonstrator 0286	0965, 0211, 0949	☐ distinguish 0325
☐ demote 0202	☐ deterrence 0991	☐ distinguish A from B 0325
☐ demotion 0034	☐ development 0186	☐ **distinguished** 0325
☐ deny 0274	☐ devote 0735	☐ **distribute** 0218
☐ **depart** 0250, 0032, 0878	☐ devote A to B 0735	☐ distribution 0218
☐ **departure** 0032, 0250	☐ devote oneself to 0735	☐ distributor 0218
☐ depend on	☐ **devoted** 0735, 0715	☐ district 0105
0827, 0877, 0887	☐ devotion 0396, 0735	☐ **disturb** 0268
☐ dependable 0307	☐ **diagram** 0562	☐ disturbance 0268
☐ dependence 0088	☐ Diet 0431	☐ **disturbing** 0268
☐ **dependent** 0088	☐ difference 0465, 0533	☐ **diverse** 0305, 0533
☐ depict 0623	☐ diligence 0321, 0792	☐ diversify 0305, 0533
☐ **deposit** 0042, 0232	☐ **diligent**	☐ **diversity** 0533, 0305
☐ depreciate 0212	0321, 0713, 0792	☐ divide 0039
☐ depreciation 0397	☐ **diligently** 0792, 0321	☐ **divide A by B**
☐ depress 0176	☐ direct 0986	0922, 0039, 0636
☐ depressing 0370	☐ **direct A to do**	☐ **division** 0039, 0922
☐ **depression** 0176, 0069	0986, 0985	☐ **dizzy** 0737
☐ **deregulate** 0632, 0521	☐ direction 0986	☐ **dock** 0559
☐ **deregulation**	☐ director 0986	☐ doctor 0095
0521, 0632	☐ disagree 0146	☐ domestic 0339
☐ describe 0623	☐ disagree with 0864	☐ donate 0514
☐ desert 0374	☐ disagreement 0005, 0146	☐ donate A to B 0514
☐ **deserted** 0374	☐ disappoint 0741	☐ **donation** 0514, 0101

どれだけチェックできた？ 1 ☐ 2 ☐

☐ **double** 0608	☐ electric 0555	☐ epidemic 0534
☐ **doubt** 0583, 0635, 1104	☐ electrical 0555	☐ epoch 0143
☐ doubtful 0583	☐ **electrician** 0555	☐ equally 0382
☐ doubtless 0583	☐ electricity 0555	☐ equipment 0385
☐ downward 0352	☐ elementary 0347, 0728	☐ **equivalent**
☐ **draft** 0155	☐ eligibility 1025	0046, 0413, 0996
☐ **drain** 0259	☐ **eliminate** 0272	☐ **era** 0143
☐ drainage 0259	☐ elimination 0272	☐ **erect** 0656
☐ draw 0549	☐ **embark on** 0829	☐ erection 0656
☐ drawer 0549	☐ embark upon 0829	☐ **errand** 0460
☐ **drawing** 0549	☐ embarkation 0829	☐ essential 0089
☐ **drop** 0614	☐ embarrass 1009	☐ establish 0447
☐ duty 0469	☐ embarrassing 1009	☐ **establishment** 0447
☐ dwell in 0621	☐ embarrassment 1009	☐ **estate** 0100, 0062
	☐ **emerge** 0244, 0074	☐ **estimate** 0060, 0235
E	☐ **emergency** 0074, 0244	☐ estimated 0060
☐ earn 0387	☐ emigrant 0463	☐ estimation 0060
☐ **earning** 0387	☐ emotion 0184, 0690	☐ **ethnic** 0704, 0742
☐ ease 1082	☐ **emotional** 0690	☐ ethnicity 0704
☐ easily 0801, 1082	☐ **emphasis** 0171	☐ **evaluate**
☐ eccentric 0341	☐ emphasize 0171, 0660	0592, 0192, 0646
☐ edit 0552	☐ employment 0104, 0393	☐ **evaluation**
☐ **edition** 0552	☐ empty 0336	0192, 0511, 0592
☐ editor 0552	☐ **enclose** 0198	☐ event 0770
☐ editorial 0552	☐ enclosure 0198	☐ eventual 0770
☐ effect	☐ encode 0055	☐ **eventually** 0770
0139, 0201, 0434, 1041	☐ encourage 0604	☐ evidence 0685
☐ effective 0306	☐ end 0086, 0243	☐ **evident** 0685
☐ **efficiency**	☐ **endeavor** 0125, 0967	☐ evidently 0685
0430, 0315, 0797	☐ **endeavor to do**	☐ **evolution** 0186, 0629
☐ **efficient**	0967, 0125	☐ **evolve** 0629, 0186
0315, 0430, 0797	☐ engage 0152	☐ exact 0295, 0299
☐ **efficiently**	☐ **engagement** 0152	☐ exactly 0800
0797, 0315, 0430	☐ **enormous**	☐ examination 0130
☐ effort 0125	0312, 0706, 0730	☐ examine 0230
☐ **elaborate** 0722	☐ enormously 0312	☐ **exceed** 0226, 0163
☐ elaborately 0722	☐ enough 0303, 0333, 0748	☐ excellent 0375
☐ elaboration 0722	☐ **ensure** 0257, 0600	☐ except 0725
☐ **elderly** 0453	☐ **enthusiasm** 0050	☐ exception 0725
☐ elect 0656	☐ enthusiastic 0050	☐ **exceptional** 0725
☐ **elect A to B** 0908	☐ entitlement 1031	☐ exceptionally 0725
☐ election 0908	☐ environment 0363, 0545	☐ **excess** 0163, 0226, 1114
☐ elector 0908	☐ **environmental** 0363	☐ excessive
☐ electoral 0908	☐ environmentalist 0363	0163, 0226, 0300
☐ electorate 0908	☐ environmentally 0363	☐ exchange 1109

どれだけチェックできた？ 1 ☐ 2 ☐

☐ exchange A for B 0929	0640, 0178, 0203, 0275, 0652	☐ fatigue 0399
☐ exclude 0272, 0335, 0810	☐ expose A to B 0178, 0640	☐ faucet 0647
☐ exclude A from B 0335, 0810	☐ **exposure** 0178, 0640	☐ fault 0049
☐ exclusion 0335, 0810	☐ **extend** 0251, 0142, 0369, 0798	☐ favor 0695, 0799
☐ **exclusive** 0335, 0368, 0810	☐ **extension** 0142, 0251, 0369, 0798	☐ **favorable** 0695, 0799
☐ **exclusively** 0810, 0335	☐ **extensive** 0369, 0142, 0251, 0798	☐ **favorably** 0799, 0695
☐ **excursion** 0135	☐ **extensively** 0798, 0142, 0251, 0369	☐ favorite 0695, 0799
☐ excuse 0938	☐ external 0339	☐ feast 0043
☐ **excuse A for B** 0938, 0934	☐ extra 0163	☐ **federal** 0366
☐ **execute** 0601, 0051	☐ **extract** 0628	☐ federalism 0366
☐ execution 0051, 0601	☐ extraction 0628	☐ federalist 0366
☐ **executive** 0051, 0601	☐ **extraordinary** 0698	☐ federation 0366
☐ **exercise** 0650, 0522	☐ extreme 0300	☐ feeling 0184
☐ **exhaust** 0267, 0570, 0734, 0849		☐ fiasco 0420
☐ **exhausted** 0734, 0267, 0570	**F**	☐ **file** 0586
☐ **exhaustion** 0570, 0267, 0734	☐ face 0262	☐ **file for** 0838, 0586
☐ **exhibit** 0065, 0106	☐ facilitate 0061	☐ fill in 0825
☐ **exhibition** 0106, 0065	☐ **facility** 0061, 0517	☐ **fill out** 0825
☐ **expand** 0204, 0115	☐ **faculty** 0517	☐ final 0634
☐ **expansion** 0115, 0204	☐ **fail in** 0860	☐ **finalize** 0634
☐ expect 0221, 0439, 0683	☐ failure 0860	☐ finally 0634
☐ **expect A to do** 0989, 0439	☐ faint 0332	☐ **fine** 0356, 0720, 0809
☐ expect to do 0439	☐ fair 0772	☐ **finely** 0809
☐ expectancy 0989	☐ **fairly** 0772	☐ finish 0243
☐ expectant 0989	☐ fake 0359	☐ firm 0372
☐ **expectation** 0439, 0989	☐ **fame** 0438, 0076	☐ first 0294
☐ expected 0683	☐ familiar 0900	☐ fit 0303
☐ **expedition** 0529	☐ familiarity 0900, 1017	☐ **fix** 0285, 0208
☐ expenditure 0001	☐ **familiarize A with B** 0900	☐ **flexibility** 0506, 0323
☐ expense 1119	☐ famous 0325, 0367, 0438	☐ **flexible** 0323, 0372, 0506
☐ experience 0224, 0729	☐ **fancy** 0687	☐ **flu** 0120
☐ **experienced** 0729	☐ far away 0311	☐ fluency 1010
☐ explain 0655	☐ far from 1089	☐ fluently 1010
☐ **exploration** 0466	☐ **fascinate** 0607, 0731	☐ **fluid** 0406
☐ exploratory 0466	☐ **fascinating** 0731, 0607	☐ focal 0913
☐ explore 0466	☐ fascination 0607, 0731	☐ focus 0913
☐ explorer 0466	☐ **fasten** 0207	☐ **focus A on B** 0913
☐ **expose**	☐ **fatal** 0316	☐ **fold** 0195
	☐ fate 0316	☐ follow 0817, 0845
		☐ foolish 0708
		☐ **for a change** 1075
		☐ **for free** 1076, 1097
		☐ for lack of 1117
		☐ for nothing 1076, 1097

どれだけチェックできた？ 1 ☐ 2 ☐

Term	Page
for now	1077
for the most part	1078
for the present	1077
for the time being	1077
for want of	1117
forbid	0209, 0266
forbid A from doing	0990
forbid A to do	0990, 0209, 0266
forbidden	0990
force	1064
force A to do	0988
forecast	0020
foreign	0339
foretell	0020, 0222
forgive A for B	0934, 0938
forgiveness	0934
formula	0492
formulae	0492
formulate	0492
fortunate	0686
fortunately	0686, 0782
fortune	0686
foster	0604
fraction	0536
fragile	0342
fragrance	0414
free	1076, 1097
free of charge	1097, 1076
freight	0407
frequency	0696, 0812
frequent	0696, 0702, 0812
frequently	0812, 0696
friend	0157
friendly	0721
from time to time	1074
fuel	0631
fulfill	0255
fulfillment	0255
full	0778
fully	0778
fundamental	
	0749, 0682
fundamentally	0749
furnish A with B	0899
furniture	0899
furthermore	0815
fury	0454

G

Term	Page
gain	0214, 0253
garbage	0390, 0403
garment	0474
garnish	0574
gather	0256
gaze	0182
gaze at	0182
gaze into	0182
generate	0240
generation	0240
generator	0240
generosity	0507, 0292
generous	0292, 0507
generously	0292, 0507
genuine	0359
genuinely	0359
get	0214, 0253
get along with	0888
get better from	0851
get nowhere	1043
get rid of	0880
get somewhere	1043
get together	0872
get-together	0872
gift	0517
give up	0260
gloomy	0370
go into	0879
go nowhere	1043
go on doing	0957
go on to do	0957
good-looking	0701
grab	0231
grand	0380
grant	0442
grasp	0589
grateful	0488
gratify	0488
gratitude	0488
graze	0664
green	0716
grim	0768
grocery	0029
guarantee	0193
guard	0942
guard A against B	0942
guess	0513
gulf	0422

H

Term	Page
hail	0602
halt	0261
handsome	0701
hang on	0881
hang up	0822, 0881
hardly ever	1101
hardworking	0321, 0713
harm	0680
harmful	0680
harmless	0680
harsh	0381, 0679
harshly	0381
harvest	0217
have access to	1053
have trouble doing	1047
have yet to do	1048
head office	0119
headquarters	0119
hear from	0885
hear of	0885
help A with B	0930
heritage	0486
hesitate to do	0945
hesitation	0945
highlight	0660
highly	1050
hold	0573
hold on	0881, 0822
holding	0573
home	0437
honor	0711, 1034

☐ **honorable** 0711, 1034	☐ important 0289, 0317, 0749	☐ inconsistent 0322
☐ **horn** 0541	☐ **impose A on B** 0898	☐ increase 0613, 0636, 0802, 0869
☐ **horrible** 0703	☐ imposing 0898	☐ **increasingly** 0802
☐ horror 0703	☐ imposition 0898	☐ indecent 0378
☐ hospitable 0497	☐ impress 0684	☐ **indicate** 0194, 0496
☐ hospital 0497	☐ impression 0684	☐ **indication** 0496, 0194
☐ **hospitality** 0497	☐ **impressive** 0684	☐ industrial 0713
☐ **hostile** 0721	☐ in addition 0815	☐ **industrious** 0713, 0321
☐ hostility 0721	☐ **in addition to** 1105	☐ industriousness 0713
☐ **house** 0593, 0437	☐ in advance 0776	☐ industry 0713
☐ **household** 0081	☐ **in an attempt to do** 1067	☐ **inevitable** 0349
☐ **housing** 0425, 0593	☐ **in anticipation of** 1113	☐ inevitably 0349
☐ however 0808	☐ **in bulk** 1057	☐ inexperienced 0729
☐ HQ 0119	☐ in confidence 1081	☐ infancy 0432
☐ huge 0312, 0706, 0730	☐ **in excess of** 1114	☐ **infant** 0432
☐ human resources 0014	☐ **in exchange for** 1109	☐ **infect** 0177
☐ **humble** 0343, 0319	☐ **in force** 1064	☐ **infection** 0177
☐ humility 0343	☐ **in full** 1065	☐ infectious 0177
	☐ **in need of** 1106	☐ infer 0258
I	☐ in no circumstances 1084	☐ inflexible 0323
☐ ID 0126	☐ **in no time** 1066	☐ influence 0201, 0743
☐ **identification** 0126, 0147, 0909	☐ **in one's opinion** 1058	☐ **influential** 0743
☐ identify 0126, 0147	☐ **in opposition to** 1110	☐ influenza 0120
☐ **identify A as B** 0909, 0126, 0147	☐ **in order** 1059	☐ ingratitude 0488
☐ **identity** 0147, 0126, 0909	☐ **in person** 1060	☐ **ingredient** 0137
☐ idle 0321	☐ in progress 1085	☐ **inhabit** 0621
☐ ignore 0242	☐ **in pursuit of** 1107	☐ inhabitant 0087, 0621
☐ **illegal** 0358	☐ **in recognition of** 1115	☐ **inherit** 0248, 0486
☐ illegally 0358	☐ **in response to** 1111	☐ **inheritance** 0486, 0248
☐ **illustrate** 0655	☐ **in return** 1061	☐ inhibit 0621
☐ illustrate A with B 0655	☐ **in stock** 1062	☐ **initial** 0294, 0028, 0270
☐ illustration 0655	☐ **in the mood for** 1112	☐ **initiate** 0270, 0028, 0294
☐ **immense** 0730, 0312, 0706	☐ **in the process of** 1108	☐ initiation 0028, 0270, 0294
☐ immensely 0730	☐ **in vain** 1063	☐ **initiative** 0028, 0270, 0294
☐ **immigrant** 0463	☐ inaccessible 0752	☐ inner 0339
☐ immigrate 0463	☐ inaccurate 0295	☐ **innovate** 0133, 0676
☐ immigration 0463	☐ **inadequate** 0759, 0303	☐ **innovation** 0133, 0676
☐ **implement** 0265, 0601	☐ inadequately 0759	☐ **innovative** 0676, 0133
☐ implication 0258	☐ incidence 0457	☐ inorganic 0705
☐ **imply** 0258	☐ **incident** 0457	☐ input 0162
☐ importance 0481	☐ incidental 0457	☐ inquire 0128
	☐ incline 1028	☐ **inquire about** 0828, 0128
	☐ income 0001, 0387	

どれだけチェックできた？ 1 ☐ 2 ☐

☐ inquiry 0128, 0828	☐ invent 0456	☐ lack 0423, 0435
☐ insert 0907	☐ invention 0456	☐ landscape 0092
☐ insert A in B 0907	☐ invest 0172, 0478	☐ last 0766
☐ insert A into B 0907	☐ invest A in B	☐ lasting 0766
☐ insertion 0907	0911, 0172, 0478	☐ launch 0205
☐ insight 0516	☐ investigate 0580, 0159	☐ laundry 0417
☐ insist on 0852	☐ investigation	☐ law 0025
☐ insistence 0852	0159, 0128, 0466, 0580	☐ lay off 0850
☐ insistent 0852	☐ investigator 0159, 0580	☐ layoff 0850
☐ inspect 0230, 0130	☐ investment	☐ lazy 0321
☐ inspection 0130, 0230	0172, 0478, 0911	☐ leak 0606
☐ inspector 0130, 0230	☐ investor	☐ leakage 0606
☐ inspiration 0982	0478, 0172, 0911	☐ lean 0823
☐ inspire A to do 0982	☐ invisible 0692	☐ lean against 0823
☐ install 0233	☐ involve 0245, 0531	☐ lean on 0823
☐ installation 0233	☐ involvement 0531, 0245	☐ leap 1088
☐ instinct 0421	☐ iron 0269	☐ leave 0250
☐ instinctive 0421	☐ irrelevant 0304	☐ leave out 0653
☐ instinctively 0421	☐ irritate 0756	☐ legal 0358
☐ institute 0446	☐ irritating 0756	☐ legislation 0025
☐ institution 0446	☐ irritation 0756	☐ legislative 0025
☐ instruct A to do	☐ issue 0635	☐ legislator 0025
0985, 0986	**J**	☐ legislature 0025
☐ instrument 0265, 1003	☐ job 0104	☐ lengthen 0612, 0671
☐ insufficient 0748	☐ join A to B 0940	☐ let alone 1098
☐ insurance 0600	☐ jointly 0796	☐ liability 0062, 1027
☐ insure 0600, 0257	☐ juror 0510	☐ license 1039
☐ intend 0424	☐ jury 0510, 0553	☐ likely 0761
☐ intend to do 0424, 0963	☐ justification 0560, 0590	☐ likeness 0465
☐ intense 0310	☐ justify 0590, 0560	☐ limit 0597
☐ intensify 0310	**K**	☐ limit A to B 0931
☐ intensity 0310	☐ keen 0327	☐ link 0904
☐ intensive 0369	☐ keenly 1004	☐ link A to B 0904, 0940
☐ intent 0424, 1012	☐ keep A away from B	☐ link A with B 0904
☐ intention 0424, 1012	0918	☐ linkage 0904
☐ intentional 0371	☐ keep A from doing 0266	☐ liquid 0406
☐ intermediate 0744	☐ keep up with 0854	☐ litter 0390, 0403
☐ internal 0339	☐ knee 0894	☐ live in 0621
☐ interrupt 0268, 0515	☐ kneel down 0894	☐ live up to 0870
☐ interruption 0515	**L**	☐ load 0097, 0919
☐ intervene 0482	☐ lab 0191	☐ load A into B 0919
☐ intervene in 0482	☐ laboratory 0191	☐ load A onto B 0919
☐ intervention 0482		☐ load A with B 0919
☐ intuition 0421		☐ locate 0210
☐ invalid 0306		☐ location 0210, 0993

☐ lodge	0567	
☐ **lodging**	**0567**	
☐ **look through**	**0862**	
☐ **look to** 0877, 0827, 0887		
☐ **look up**	**0857**	
☐ loose	0678	
☐ loosen	0657	
☐ love	0174	
☐ lucky	0686	
☐ lucrative	0313	
☐ luxurious	0089	
☐ **luxury**	**0089**	

M

☐ machine	0073
☐ **machinery**	**0073**
☐ magnificent	0380
☐ main	0677
☐ mainly	0807
☐ maintain	0044, 0279, 0641
☐ **maintenance**	**0044**
☐ major in	0819
☐ **make it**	**1042**
☐ **make one's way**	**1045**
☐ **make out**	**0836**
☐ **make sure**	**1046**
☐ make the best of	1054
☐ **make the most of**	**1054**
☐ make up for	0840
☐ makeup	1019
☐ **mall**	**0520**
☐ mandatory	0338
☐ **manufacture**	**0196, 0183**
☐ **manufacturer**	**0183, 0196**
☐ **manuscript**	**0505**
☐ many	0302
☐ **margin**	**0475**
☐ marginal	0475
☐ marvelous	0362
☐ mass	0706
☐ **massive**	**0706, 0312, 0730**
☐ **masterpiece**	**0565**

☐ masterwork	0565
☐ material	0611
☐ **matter**	**0611**, 0635
☐ maximize	0383
☐ **maximum**	**0383**, 0354
☐ **mean to do**	**0963**
☐ meaning	0481, 0963
☐ meaningful	0963
☐ meaningless	0963
☐ measure	1044
☐ meet	0255
☐ **memorize**	**0672**
☐ memory	0672
☐ menace	0551
☐ mend	0208, 0285
☐ mention	0141, 0603
☐ **mere**	**0745**
☐ merely	0745
☐ **mess**	**0445**
☐ mess up	0445
☐ messy	0445, 0693
☐ **microscope**	**0494**
☐ microscopic	0494
☐ mild	0381
☐ mind	0611, 0973
☐ **mind doing**	**0973**
☐ minimize	0354
☐ **minimum**	**0354**, 0383
☐ minutes	0495
☐ miss	0242, 0691
☐ **missing**	**0691**
☐ mistake A for B	0924
☐ mobile	0519
☐ mobile phone	0519
☐ **moderate**	**0300**
☐ moderately	0300
☐ modern	0360
☐ **modest**	**0319**, 0343
☐ modestly	0319
☐ modesty	0319
☐ modification	0227
☐ **modify**	**0227**
☐ moment	1073
☐ **monetary**	**0673**
☐ **monitor**	**0280**

☐ monopolize	0508
☐ **monopoly**	**0508**
☐ mood	1112
☐ more and more	0802
☐ more significantly	0289, 0793
☐ more than	1114
☐ moreover	0815
☐ mortal	0316
☐ most significantly	0289, 0793
☐ mostly	1078
☐ **motivate A to do**	**0978**
☐ motivation	0978
☐ motive	0978
☐ **mount**	**0613**
☐ **much less**	**1098**
☐ multiplication	0636
☐ **multiply**	**0636**
☐ multiply A by B	0636, 0922

N

☐ name	0916
☐ **name A after B**	**0916**
☐ natural	0353
☐ **near**	**0622**, 0781
☐ **nearly**	**0781**, 0622
☐ **neat**	**0693**
☐ neatly	0693
☐ necessary	0749
☐ need	1106
☐ negotiable	0011, 0637
☐ **negotiate**	**0637**, 0011
☐ **negotiation**	**0011, 0637**
☐ neighbor	0546
☐ **neighborhood**	**0546**
☐ neighboring	0546
☐ **nevertheless**	**0808**
☐ **newsletter**	**0571**
☐ **no doubt**	**1104**
☐ nonetheless	0808
☐ notice	0578, 1083
☐ now	0779, 1073
☐ now and then	0806, 1074

どれだけチェックできた？ 1 ☐ 2 ☐

Word	Number
☐ **nuclear**	0699
☐ **nuisance**	0402
☐ **numerous**	0302

O

Word	Number
☐ obey	0817, 0845
☐ object	0005, 0059, 0830
☐ **object to**	0830, 0005, 0059
☐ **objection**	0005, 0059, 0830
☐ **objective**	0059, 0830
☐ **obligation**	0469, 1035
☐ obligatory	0338, 0469, 0717, 0719, 1035
☐ oblige	0469
☐ **obtain**	0214, 0253, 0890
☐ obverse	0318
☐ obvious	0127, 0685
☐ occasion	0702, 0806
☐ **occasional**	0702, 0696, 0806
☐ **occasionally**	0806, 0702, 1074
☐ **occupation**	0104
☐ occupied	0336
☐ occupy	0104
☐ odd	0341
☐ **odor**	0414
☐ offend	0500
☐ **offender**	0500
☐ offense	0500
☐ offensive	0500
☐ offer	0440
☐ often	0787, 0812
☐ old	0453
☐ omission	0653
☐ **omit**	0653
☐ **on end**	1090
☐ **on one's own**	1091
☐ **on the books**	1092
☐ **on the verge of**	1118
☐ on time	0771
☐ **once and for all**	1102
☐ opaque	0739
☐ opening	1013
☐ operation	0476
☐ opinion	0184, 1058
☐ oppose	0615
☐ opposite	0318
☐ opposition	1110
☐ optimism	1014
☐ optimist	1014
☐ option	0717
☐ **optional**	0717
☐ **oral**	0747
☐ order	0436, 1059
☐ order A to do	0436, 0985, 0986
☐ ordinary	0698
☐ **organic**	0705
☐ organism	0705
☐ organization	0145, 0200
☐ **organize**	0200
☐ **origin**	0525, 0803
☐ original	0525, 0803
☐ **originally**	0803
☐ originate	0525
☐ **ornament**	0574
☐ out of order	1059
☐ out of stock	1062
☐ **outbreak**	0412, 0861
☐ **outcome**	0434, 0139
☐ **outlook**	0477, 0092
☐ **output**	0162
☐ **outskirt**	0576
☐ **outstanding**	0291
☐ **overall**	0351
☐ **overcome**	0252
☐ **overflow**	0619
☐ **overhead**	0113
☐ overhead costs	0113
☐ overhead expenses	0113
☐ **overlook**	0242
☐ **overseas**	0675
☐ **overtake**	0658
☐ **overtime**	0813

P

Word	Number
☐ **pact**	0458
☐ **pamphlet**	0523
☐ **panel**	0553, 0510
☐ panelist	0553
☐ parallel	0994
☐ Parliament	0431
☐ part	0108, 0757
☐ **partial**	0757
☐ partially	0757
☐ **participant**	0136, 0540
☐ participate	0136, 0540
☐ participate in	0136, 0540
☐ **participation**	0540, 0136, 0531
☐ **particle**	0528
☐ particular	0528
☐ particularly	0528
☐ partner	0557
☐ **partnership**	0557
☐ **patent**	0127
☐ pave	0524
☐ paved	0524
☐ **pavement**	0524
☐ pay	0543
☐ pay attention to	0848
☐ **pay off**	0868
☐ **peculiar**	0341
☐ peculiarity	0341
☐ peculiarly	0341
☐ pedestrian crossing	0556
☐ penetrate	0537
☐ **penetration**	0537
☐ **pension**	0138
☐ pensioner	0138
☐ **perish**	0518
☐ **perishable**	0518
☐ permission	0190
☐ personal	0014
☐ personally	1060
☐ **personnel**	0014
☐ **perspective**	0485
☐ persuade A of B	0927
☐ phase	0610

☐ phenomena	0468	
☐ **phenomenon**	0468	
☐ physical	0095	
☐ **physician**	0095, 0388	
☐ pier	0559	
☐ pile	0238	
☐ **plague**	0534	
☐ plain	0687	
☐ plaintiff	0487	
☐ plan	0455	
☐ plea	0979	
☐ **plead with A to do**	0979	
☐ pledge	0958	
☐ **pledge to do**	0958, 0966	
☐ **plentiful**	0763, 0326	
☐ plenty	0763	
☐ pliable	0323	
☐ **plot**	0526, 0455	
☐ plot to do	0526	
☐ **plow**	0659	
☐ **plunge**	0530	
☐ poise	1040	
☐ **poll**	0386	
☐ pollute	0148	
☐ **pollution**	0148	
☐ poor	0435	
☐ poorly	0435	
☐ popular	0450	
☐ **popularity**	0450	
☐ **portion**	0108	
☐ portrait	0623	
☐ **portray**	0623	
☐ portrayal	0623	
☐ position	0109	
☐ possess	0428	
☐ **possession**	0428	
☐ possessive	0428	
☐ possible	0355	
☐ post	0491	
☐ **postage**	0491	
☐ **postpone**	0199	
☐ postpone doing	0199	
☐ **potential**	0355	
☐ **poverty**	0435	
☐ practical	0774	
☐ **practically**	0774
☐ practice	0774
☐ praise	0626
☐ **precaution**	0057
☐ **precise** 0299, 0295, 0800
☐ **precisely**	0800, 0299
☐ precision	0299, 0800
☐ **preclude A from doing**	0992
☐ **predict** 0222, 0020, 0512
☐ **prediction**	0512, 0222
☐ prefer	0394
☐ **prefer A to B**	0912
☐ prefer to do	0394, 0954
☐ preferable	0394, 0912
☐ preferably	0394, 0912
☐ **preference**	0394, 0912
☐ **prejudice**	0464, 0409
☐ prejudice A against B	0464
☐ **preliminary**	0379
☐ **premise**	0532
☐ preparatory	0379
☐ prescribe	0006
☐ prescribe A for B	0006
☐ **prescription**	0006
☐ present	0297
☐ **preservation** 0563, 0277
☐ preservative	0277, 0563
☐ **preserve**	0277, 0563
☐ press	0269
☐ **pretend to do**	0968
☐ pretense	0968
☐ pretension	0968
☐ prevail against	0865
☐ prevail among	0865
☐ prevail in	0865
☐ **prevail over**	0865
☐ prevailing	0865
☐ prevalent	0865
☐ prevent A from doing 0266, 0992
☐ previous	0790
☐ **previously**	0790
☐ price	1071
☐ **primarily**	0807, 0347
☐ **primary**	0347, 0807
☐ prime	0347, 0807
☐ **principal**	0677
☐ principally	0677
☐ principle	0677
☐ prior	0444
☐ prior to	0444
☐ **priority**	0444
☐ **privilege**	0168
☐ privileged	0168
☐ prize	0002
☐ probably	1104
☐ problem	0635
☐ **procedure** 0026, 0035, 0824, 0875
☐ **proceed** 0035, 0026, 0495, 0824, 0875
☐ **proceed to** 0875, 0026, 0035, 0495
☐ **proceed with** 0824, 0026, 0035, 0495, 0875
☐ **proceeding** 0495, 0035, 0824, 0875
☐ process	1108
☐ produce 0187, 0196, 0240, 0329
☐ producer	0181
☐ product 0018, 0187, 0329
☐ production 0162, 0187, 0329, 0391
☐ **productive**	0329, 0187
☐ **productivity**	0187, 0329
☐ profession	0104
☐ **profile**	0461
☐ profit	0140, 0313
☐ profitability	0313
☐ **profitable**	0313
☐ **prohibit**	0266, 0209
☐ prohibit A from doing 0209, 0266, 0990

☐ prohibition 0266	☐ put in 0233	☐ recede 0069
☐ project 1036	☐ put off 0199	☐ receive 0151, 0401
☐ projection 1036	☐ put together 0256	☐ receptacle 0527
☐ **prolong** 0612		☐ **reception** 0151, 0401
☐ prominence 0367	**Q**	☐ **receptionist** 0401, 0151
☐ **prominent** 0367	☐ **qualification** 0037, 0841	☐ recess 0069
☐ promise to do 0958, 0966	☐ qualify 0037	☐ **recession** 0069, 0176
☐ **promote**	☐ **qualify as** 0841, 0037	☐ recipe 0395
0202, 0034, 0604	☐ qualify for 0037, 0841	☐ **recognition** 0079, 1115
☐ **promotion** 0034, 0202	☐ quality 0082	☐ recognize 0079
☐ promotional 0034, 0202	☐ quantitative 0082	☐ recognize A as B 0079
☐ **prompt** 0361, 0771	☐ **quantity** 0082	☐ recollect 0582
☐ prompt A to do	☐ queer 0341	☐ recollect doing 0970
0361, 0771	☐ query 0635	☐ **recommend doing**
☐ **promptly** 0771, 0361	☐ **question** 0635, 0128	0975
☐ proper 0293, 0303	☐ quick 0361	☐ recommendation 0975
☐ property 0062, 0100, 0573	☐ quickly 0771, 0801	☐ record 0228
☐ proposal 0969	☐ **quit** 0213	☐ **recover from** 0851
☐ **propose doing** 0969	☐ **quit doing** 0974, 0213	☐ recovery 0851
☐ propose to do 0969	☐ quotation 0235	☐ **recruit** 0263
☐ proposition 0969	☐ **quote** 0235, 0603	☐ reduce 0098
☐ **prospect** 0022	**R**	☐ **reduction** 0098
☐ prospective 0022	☐ race 0742	☐ refer 0141
☐ prosper 0427, 0753	☐ **racial** 0742, 0704	☐ refer to 0141, 0603
☐ **prosperity** 0427, 0753	☐ racism 0742	☐ refer to A as B 0141
☐ **prosperous** 0753, 0427	☐ racist 0742	☐ **reference** 0141
☐ protect A against B 0942	☐ **radical** 0682	☐ **refrain from** 0821
☐ proud 0319, 0343	☐ **rage** 0454	☐ refresh 0048
☐ prove 0286	☐ **rally** 0539	☐ **refreshment** 0048
☐ provide 0459	☐ rare 0755	☐ **refuel** 0631
☐ provide A with B	☐ rarely 1101	☐ refusal 0948
0459, 0899	☐ **rather** 0783	☐ refuse
☐ provide for 0459	☐ rational 0690	0197, 0390, 0403, 0859
☐ provided 0459	☐ **reach** 0278	☐ **refuse to do** 0948, 0956
☐ **provision** 0459	☐ reach for 0278	☐ **region** 0105, 0324
☐ punctual 0361	☐ react to 0837	☐ **regional** 0324, 0105
☐ punctually 0771	☐ **readily** 0801	☐ **register**
☐ punish 0149	☐ ready 0801	0228, 0404, 0694, 0834
☐ **purchase** 0219	☐ real 0359	☐ **register for**
☐ purpose 0424	☐ reasonable 0306, 0746	0834, 0228, 0404, 0694
☐ **pursue** 0215	☐ **rebuild** 0670	☐ **registered** 0694, 0834
☐ pursuit 0215, 1107	☐ rebuke A for B 0932, 0935	☐ **registration**
☐ **put A through to B**	☐ **recall** 0582	0404, 0228, 0694, 0834
0902	☐ **recall doing** 0970	☐ regret 0951, 0976
☐ put A to use 1049		☐ **regret doing** 0976, 0951

どれだけチェックできた？ 1 ☐ 2 ☐

- ☐ **regret to do** 0951, 0976
- ☐ regrettable 0951, 0976
- ☐ regrettably 0951, 0976
- ☐ regular 0787
- ☐ **regularly** 0787
- ☐ regulate 0632, 0787
- ☐ regulation 0787
- ☐ reject 0859
- ☐ relative 0784
- ☐ **relatively** 0784
- ☐ **relevant** 0304
- ☐ reliability 0307
- ☐ **reliable** 0307
- ☐ reliance 0307
- ☐ relief 0937
- ☐ **relieve A of B** 0937
- ☐ relieved 0937
- ☐ **relocate A to B** 0928
- ☐ relocation 0928
- ☐ reluctantly 1026
- ☐ rely 0307
- ☐ rely on 0307, 0827, 0877, 0887
- ☐ remain 0503
- ☐ **remainder** 0503
- ☐ **remark** 0085, 0344
- ☐ **remarkable** 0344, 0085
- ☐ **remedy** 0123
- ☐ remember 0582
- ☐ remember doing 0970
- ☐ **remodel** 0633
- ☐ **remote** 0311
- ☐ **renew** 0223
- ☐ renewal 0223
- ☐ renown 0438
- ☐ repair 0208, 0285
- ☐ **repay** 0649
- ☐ replace 0083
- ☐ **replace A as B** 0923
- ☐ **replacement** 0083, 0923
- ☐ report 0847
- ☐ **report to** 0847
- ☐ represent 0010, 0623
- ☐ representation 0010

- ☐ **representative** 0010
- ☐ reproach 0935
- ☐ **reproach A for B** 0935, 0932
- ☐ **reproduce** 0665
- ☐ reproduction 0665
- ☐ reputable 0076
- ☐ **reputation** 0076, 0438
- ☐ require 0173
- ☐ **require A to do** 0987, 0173
- ☐ **requirement** 0173, 0987
- ☐ rescue 0939
- ☐ **rescue A from B** 0939
- ☐ resemblance 0465, 0577
- ☐ **resemble** 0577
- ☐ **reservation** 0118, 0563
- ☐ reserve 0118, 0277
- ☐ reserve A for B 0118
- ☐ **residence** 0437, 0087, 0724
- ☐ **resident** 0087, 0437, 0724
- ☐ **residential** 0724, 0087, 0437
- ☐ **resign** 0249, 0213
- ☐ resignation 0249
- ☐ **resist** 0615, 0419
- ☐ **resistance** 0419, 0615
- ☐ resistant 0419, 0615
- ☐ **resolution** 0154, 0211, 0949
- ☐ **resolve** 0211, 0154, 0949
- ☐ **resolve to do** 0949, 0154, 0211, 0965
- ☐ **resource** 0038
- ☐ resourceful 0038
- ☐ respect 0760
- ☐ **respectful** 0760
- ☐ respective 0760
- ☐ **respond to** 0837
- ☐ respondent 0837
- ☐ response 0837, 1111

- ☐ **rest with** 0889
- ☐ **restoration** 0535, 0208
- ☐ **restore** 0208, 0535
- ☐ **restrict** 0597, 0480
- ☐ restrict A to B 0931
- ☐ restricted 0480, 0597
- ☐ **restriction** 0480, 0597
- ☐ result 0139, 0434, 0856
- ☐ result from 0856
- ☐ **result in** 0856
- ☐ **resume** 0236, 0008, 0223
- ☐ **résumé** 0008
- ☐ resumption 0236
- ☐ **retail** 0405
- ☐ retailer 0405
- ☐ **retain** 0284
- ☐ retention 0284
- ☐ retire 0024, 0213, 0249, 0765
- ☐ **retired** 0765, 0024
- ☐ retiree 0024, 0765
- ☐ **retirement** 0024
- ☐ return 0535, 1061
- ☐ **reveal** 0203, 0275, 0640, 0652
- ☐ revelation 0203
- ☐ **revenue** 0001
- ☐ **reverse** 0318
- ☐ reviewer 0122
- ☐ **revise** 0239
- ☐ revision 0239
- ☐ revolution 0186
- ☐ revolve 0629
- ☐ ridicule 0708
- ☐ **ridiculous** 0708
- ☐ right 0295, 0299
- ☐ **rigid** 0372, 0323
- ☐ rigidly 0372
- ☐ rigorous 0372, 0377
- ☐ **rinse** 0654
- ☐ risk 1072
- ☐ rite 0569
- ☐ **ritual** 0569
- ☐ **rosy** 0762

どれだけチェックできた？ 1 ☐ 2 ☐

- routine 0473
- routinely 0473
- rubbish 0390, 0403
- ruin 0445
- run out of 0873
- **run short of** 0873
- **rural** 0314, 0320
- rustic 0314, 0320

S

- **sacrifice** 0093
- safe 0357
- salary 0543
- **salute** 0661
- **satisfaction** 0150, 0727
- **satisfactory** 0727, 0150, 0376
- satisfy 0150, 0255, 0727
- save A from B 0939
- scarce 0763
- scarcely ever 1101
- **scatter** 0246
- **scenery** 0418, 0092
- scent 0414
- **scheme** 0455, 0526
- **scholar** 0451, 0442
- scholarly 0442, 0451
- **scholarship** 0442, 0451
- scientist 0451
- **scold A for B** 0932, 0935
- scramble 0960
- **scramble to do** 0960
- **screen** 0618
- screening 0618
- scrutiny 0130
- sculptor 0179
- **sculpture** 0179, 0548
- seal 0892
- **seal off** 0892
- **second to none** 1103
- **sector** 0167
- **secure** 0357
- security 0357
- seldom 1101
- select 0550, 0914
- **select A as B** 0914, 0550
- **selection** 0550, 0914
- senator 0010, 0431
- senior citizens 0453
- sensitive 0342
- **sentiment** 0184
- sentimental 0184
- serious 0327, 0679
- servant 0959
- **serve to do** 0959
- service 0959
- **session** 0078
- set 0285
- **set off** 0878
- **set one's heart on** 1055
- set out 0878
- **setting** 0545
- settle 0211
- **severe** 0679, 0327
- severely 0679
- severity 0679
- share 0108
- sharp 0327, 0669
- **sharpen** 0669
- sharply 0669
- ship 0467
- shipment 0467
- **shipping** 0467
- shopping center 0520
- short 0345, 0423, 0671, 0816, 0873
- **shortage** 0423, 0671, 0816, 0873, 1015
- **shorten** 0671, 0816
- **shortly** 0816, 0423, 0671
- show 0866, 0920
- **show A around B** 0920
- **show up** 0866
- **shut down** 0858
- **sidewalk** 0448
- sight 0092
- sign 0064
- **significance** 0481, 0289, 0793
- **significant** 0289, 0481, 0793
- **significantly** 0793, 0289, 0481
- silly 0708
- similar 0382, 0465
- **similarity** 0465
- simultaneous 0780
- **simultaneously** 0780
- sincere 0359
- **site** 0054, 1016
- situation 0109
- skill 0710
- **skilled** 0710, 0376
- skillful 0710
- **skip** 0651
- **skyscraper** 0134
- slide 0616
- **slip** 0616
- slippery 0616
- slump 0501
- smell 0414
- social security 0090
- **sole** 0368
- solely 0368
- solid 0406
- **solution** 0047
- solve 0047, 0211
- sometimes 1074
- soon 0816, 1096
- sophisticate 0373
- **sophisticated** 0373
- sophistication 0373
- **sound** 0697
- **source** 0099
- **spark** 0645
- speak highly of 1050
- special 0819
- **specialize in** 0819
- **species** 0164
- specific 0276
- specification 0276

☐ **specify** 0276	☐ stiff 0372	0896, 0056
☐ spectacle 0723	☐ **stimulate** 0225, 0490	☐ substitution 0056, 0896
☐ **spectacular** 0723	☐ stimulation 0225, 0490	☐ **subtle** 0332
☐ **spectator** 0114	☐ stimuli 0490	☐ subtlety 0332
☐ speculate 0513	☐ **stimulus** 0490, 0225	☐ subtly 0332
☐ **speculation** 0513	☐ stingy 0292	☐ subtract A from B
☐ **spell** 0642	☐ stock 1062	0636, 0922
☐ spelling 0642	☐ stop 0261	☐ **suburb** 0160, 0576
☐ spirit 0611	☐ stop A from doing 0266	☐ suburban 0160
☐ **splendid** 0356	☐ stop doing 0213, 0974	☐ succeed 0754, 0868, 1042
☐ splendor 0356	☐ **storage** 0415	☐ succeed in
☐ spoil 0445	☐ store 0415	0754, 0844, 0860
☐ **spot** 0578	☐ **strain** 0144	☐ **succeed to** 0844, 0754
☐ spread 0707	☐ strange 0341	☐ successful 0753
☐ **squeeze** 0643	☐ strategic 0021	☐ **succession** 0754, 0844
☐ stability 0340	☐ strategically 0021	☐ **successive** 0754, 0844
☐ stabilize 0340	☐ strategist 0021	☐ successor 0754, 0844
☐ **stable** 0340	☐ **strategy** 0021	☐ **sue A for B** 0910
☐ **stack** 0238	☐ strength 0620	☐ suffer 0641
☐ staff 0014	☐ **strengthen** 0620	☐ sufficient
☐ **stage** 0610	☐ stress 0660	0303, 0333, 0748
☐ **stain** 0041	☐ strict 0372, 0814	☐ suit 0910
☐ stainless 0041	☐ **strictly** 0814	☐ suitable 0293, 0303
☐ **staircase** 0561	☐ strife 0952	☐ **sum up** 0863
☐ stairs 0561	☐ strike 0726	☐ summarize 0400, 0863
☐ stairway 0561	☐ **striking** 0726	☐ **summary** 0400
☐ **stall** 0283	☐ stringent 0372	☐ **superior** 0714
☐ stand doing 0961	☐ **strive to do** 0952	☐ superiority 0714
☐ stand to do 0961	☐ strong 0620	☐ supply A with B 0899
☐ **standpoint** 0566	☐ **structural** 0767	☐ **surgeon**
☐ start 0270, 0446, 0624	☐ structure 0767	0388, 0095, 0476
☐ state 0109	☐ stuff 0611	☐ **surgery** 0476, 0388
☐ statistical 0132	☐ stupid 0708	☐ surplus 0131
☐ statistician 0132	☐ **subcontract** 0630	☐ surprise 0811
☐ **statistics** 0132	☐ subject 0470	☐ surprising 0811
☐ **statue** 0548, 0179	☐ subjective 0059	☐ **surprisingly** 0811
☐ **status** 0109	☐ submission 0216	☐ surveillance 0030
☐ **steadily** 0773	☐ **submit** 0216	☐ **survey** 0030
☐ steady 0322, 0340, 0773	☐ submit to 0216	☐ suspect 0487
☐ stealing 0410	☐ substance 0328, 0611	☐ **suspend** 0599
☐ **steep** 0346	☐ **substantial** 0328	☐ suspense 0599
☐ steeple 0346	☐ substantially 0328	☐ suspension 0599
☐ steeply 0346	☐ **substitute** 0056, 0896	☐ suspicion 0733
☐ step 1044	☐ substitute A for B 0056	☐ **suspicious** 0733
☐ stern 0679	☐ **substitute for**	☐ suspiciously 0733

どれだけチェックできた？ 1 ☐ 2 ☐

☐ **sustain** 0641	☐ throw out 0880	☐ trouble 1047
☐ sustainable 0641	☐ thus 0777, 0786	☐ truly 1021
☐ swear to do 0958, 0966	☐ tidy 0693	☐ truth 1021
☐ **symptom** 0064	☐ **tight** 0678, 0657	☐ try to do
☐ synthesize 0584	☐ **tighten** 0657, 0678	0125, 0947, 0952, 0967
	☐ tire 0758	☐ **turn down** 0859, 0197
T	☐ tired 0734, 0758	☐ **turn out** 0882
	☐ tiredness 0399	☐ **turn to** 0887, 0827, 0877
☐ **tackle** 0625	☐ tiresome 0758	☐ turn up 0859
☐ take back 0232	☐ **tiring** 0758	☐ turnout 0882
☐ take care of 0848	☐ **to the advantage of**	☐ type 1024
☐ **take credit for** 1056	1120	☐ typical 0166
☐ **take effect** 1041	☐ tool 0265	☐ typically 1024
☐ take measures 1044	☐ total 0757	
☐ **take on** 0886	☐ trace 0925	**U**
☐ **take out** 0884	☐ trace A back to B 0925	
☐ **take steps** 1044	☐ **trace A to B** 0925	☐ unavoidable 0349
☐ talent 0517	☐ trade 0929	☐ uncertain 0472
☐ **tap** 0647	☐ **trade A for B** 0929	☐ uncertainly 0472
☐ telescope 0494	☐ trade A with B 0929	☐ **uncertainty** 0472
☐ **tend to do**	☐ trader 0929	☐ **uncommon** 0755
0950, 1027, 1028, 1029	☐ train 0149	☐ unconditional 0764
☐ tendency 0950	☐ transact 0027	☐ unconventional 0732
☐ tense 0433	☐ **transaction** 0027	☐ **uncover**
☐ **tension** 0433	☐ transform 0564	0652, 0203, 0275, 0640
☐ term 0078	☐ **transform A into B**	☐ **under consideration**
☐ **terminal** 0398	0903, 0564	1086
☐ terminate 0398	☐ **transformation**	☐ **under no circum-**
☐ termination 0398	0564, 0903	**stances** 1084
☐ terrible 0362, 0703	☐ transit 0036	☐ **under way** 1085
☐ **terrific** 0362	☐ **transition** 0036	☐ **undergo** 0224
☐ **theft** 0410	☐ transitional 0036	☐ understand
☐ **theme** 0470	☐ **translucent** 0739	0589, 0668, 0836
☐ **therefore** 0786, 0777	☐ **transmission**	☐ understanding
☐ thief 0410	0411, 0273	0189, 0397, 0589
☐ **think highly of** 1050	☐ **transmit** 0273, 0411	☐ undertake 0206
☐ **thorough**	☐ transparency 0739	☐ underway 1085
0296, 0682, 0804	☐ **transparent** 0739	☐ undesirable 0688
☐ **thoroughly** 0804, 0296	☐ transport 0052	☐ unemployed 0393
☐ **threat** 0551, 0953	☐ **transportation** 0052	☐ **unemployment** 0393
☐ threaten 0551	☐ **trash** 0403, 0390	☐ **unexpected** 0683
☐ **threaten to do**	☐ **treaty** 0458	☐ unexpectedly 0683
0953, 0551	☐ **tremendous** 0375	☐ unfasten 0207
☐ thriving 0753	☐ trip 0135	☐ unfold 0195
☐ through 0296	☐ **triple** 0638	☐ unfortunate 0686, 0782
☐ **throw away** 0880		☐ **unfortunately** 0782

どれだけチェックできた？ 1 ☐ 2 ☐

☐ unlawful	0358	
☐ unlike	0761, 1033	
☐ **unlikely**	0761	
☐ unproductive	0329	
☐ **unreasonable**	0746	
☐ unreliable	0307	
☐ unskilled	0710	
☐ unstable	0340	
☐ unusual	0755	
☐ unwillingly	1032	
☐ **upward**	0352	
☐ **urban**	0320, 0314	
☐ urbanize	0320	
☐ urge	0309	
☐ urge A to do	0309	
☐ urgency	0309	
☐ **urgent**	0309	
☐ use	0667, 1049	
☐ usefulness	0484	
☐ utensil	0265	
☐ **utility**	0484, 0667	
☐ utilization	0484, 0667	
☐ **utilize**	0667, 0484	
☐ **utmost**	0750	

V

☐ vacancy	0336	
☐ **vacant**	0336	
☐ **vacuum**	0595	
☐ vacuum cleaner	0595	
☐ vain	1063	
☐ vainly	1063	
☐ **valid**	0306	
☐ validate	0306	
☐ validation	0306	
☐ variety	0533	
☐ various	0305	
☐ verbal	0747	
☐ verge	1118	
☐ view	0092	
☐ viewpoint	0485, 0566	
☐ vigor	0377	
☐ **vigorous**	0377	
☐ vigorously	0377	
☐ violate	0493	

☐ **violation**	0493	
☐ visibility	0692	
☐ **visible**	0692	
☐ vision	0692	
☐ visitor	0087	
☐ **vital**	0365, 0289, 0364	
☐ vitality	0365	
☐ vitally	0365	
☐ **vivid**	0712	
☐ vividly	0712	
☐ void	0306	
☐ **voluntary**	0719, 0338	
☐ volunteer	0719	
☐ volunteer to do	0719	
☐ vow	0966	
☐ **vow to do**	0966, 0958	

W

☐ **wage**	0543	
☐ want	0423, 1117	
☐ want to do	1028	
☐ warning	0169, 0175	
☐ warranty	0193	
☐ **water**	0605	
☐ weaken	0620	
☐ wear	0474	
☐ **wear out**	0849	
☐ weariness	0399	
☐ welcome	1038	
☐ **welfare**	0090	
☐ well-being	0090	
☐ wharf	0559	
☐ whole	1095	
☐ wholesale	0405	
☐ **widespread**	0707	
☐ **wildlife**	0429	
☐ willful	0371	
☐ willingly	0801	
☐ win	0865	
☐ **with care**	1080	
☐ **with caution**	1079	
☐ **with confidence**	1081	
☐ **with ease**	1082	
☐ with regard to	1116	
☐ **withdraw**	0232, 0042, 0408	
☐ **withdraw from**	0871	
☐ **withdrawal**	0408, 0232, 0871	
☐ **without notice**	1083	
☐ work out	0522	
☐ **workout**	0522	
☐ **workshop**	0013	
☐ worsen	0616	
☐ worth	1005	
☐ worthless	1005	
☐ worthy	1005	
☐ written	0747	

Y

☐ **yet**	0791	
☐ **yield**	0140	
☐ yield to	0140	

聞いて覚える英単語 キクタン TOEIC® Test Score 800

発行日	2009年2月27日(初版) 2014年2月10日(第13刷)
編著	一杉武史
編集	英語出版編集部
英文校正	Peter Branscombe、Joel Weinberg、Owen Schaefer
アートディレクション	細山田 光宣
デザイン	若井夏澄(細山田デザイン事務所)
イラスト	shimizu masashi (gaimgraphics)
ナレーション	Greg Dale、Julia Yermakov、紗川じゅん
音楽制作	東海林 敏行
録音・編集	千野幸男(有限会社ログスタジオ)
CDプレス	株式会社 学研教育出版
DTP	株式会社 秀文社
印刷・製本	図書印刷株式会社
発行者	平本照麿
発行所	株式会社 アルク 〒168-8611　東京都杉並区永福2-54-12 TEL：03-3327-1101　FAX：03-3327-1300 Email：csss@alc.co.jp Website：http://www.alc.co.jp/

・落丁本、乱丁本は弊社にてお取り替えいたしております。アルクお客様センター(電話：03-3327-1101　受付時間：平日9時〜17時)までご相談ください。
・本書の全部または一部の無断転載を禁じます。
・著作権法上で認められた場合を除いて、本書からのコピーを禁じます。
・定価はカバーに表示してあります。

©2009 Takeshi Hitosugi/ALC PRESS INC.
shimizu masashi (gaimgraphics)/Toshiyuki Shoji (onetrap)
Printed in Japan.
PC：7009038
ISBN：978-4-7574-1548-5

地球人ネットワークを創る
アルクのシンボル「地球人マーク」です。